Jay E Holet

John F. Norman

ONE THOUSAND
NEW ILLUSTRATIONS

REV. AQUILLA WEBB, D.D., LL.D.

ONE THOUSAND NEW ILLUSTRATIONS

BY

REV. AQUILLA WEBB, D.D., LL.D.

WITH INTRODUCTION BY

JAMES A. BARKLEY

ASSOCIATE PROFESSOR OF HISTORY AND POLITICAL SCIENCE,
UNIVERSITY OF DELAWARE

RICHARD R. SMITH, Inc.
NEW YORK
1931

PRINTED IN THE UNITED STATES OF AMERICA
BY THE CORNWALL PRESS, CORNWALL, N. Y.

THIS BOOK IS AFFECTIONATELY DEDICATED

To
JANE AND BETTY
TWO LITTLE GIRLS IN KENTUCKY

"Of such is the Kingdom of Heaven."

FOREWORD

Every minister of our Lord Jesus Christ is concerned about seeking and saving the lost, and then building them up in the most holy faith.

We are concerned in this book not with Methods but with the Message. We have been forced in these times to realize that success in the ministry depends upon getting down intelligently and lovingly to fundamentals and not in working up occasional spasms over accidentals.

A Jewish Rabbi, Abba Hillel Silver, says in his splendid book, "Religion in a Changing World," "Religion is, in a sense, a summary of the basic spiritual interests and needs of all ages. It is concerned with what is timeless and fundamental."

The man in the pew wants the truth and the truth so presented that he can grasp it and carry it away with him through the week. He looks upon the minister as an ambassador from the High Court of Heaven. As he settles down in his pew he practically says, as Cornelius said to Peter, "Now therefore are we all here present before God, to hear all things that are commanded thee of God."

And most ministers realize this. What an opportunity! Burdened with a message they endeavor to present the truth that the Holy Spirit has given to them. The effectiveness of the message depends largely upon simplicity. No matter how profound the truth it must be presented so the people may comprehend it fully. Often a wisely selected illustration is the window through which the whole subject is illuminated and made beautiful.

The Rev. Dr. E. P. Hood says, "There can be no doubt, that, for the purpose of teaching, one illustration is worth a thousand abstractions. They are windows of speech: through them truth shines; and the ordinary minds fail to perceive truth clearly, unless it is presented to them through this medium."

The Rev. Dr. Theodore L. Cuyler, a great Presbyterian preacher in Brooklyn, said, "I have generally found that the most intellectual auditors prefer to hear simple scriptural and spiritual preaching. The late Judge McLean of the U. S. Supreme Court (a good Methodist too) once said to me, "I was glad to hear you give that solemn personal incident in your discourse last night. Ministers now-a-days are getting above telling a story in a sermon; but I like it."

But there must be a very careful use of illustrations. In preparing my sermons I have often searched out many, many illustrations, good illustrations in themselves, before I found one that exactly illustrated the particular truth being presented. The illustrations in my book have accumulated through a period of years after this fashion.

With a sincere desire to help all workers in the teaching ministry these illustrations are given to the public.

—AQUILLA WEBB.

INTRODUCTION

We are living in an age of doubt and questioning. The World War seems to have left humanity stunned. Mankind is groping in spiritual darkness. The opponents of orthodox Christianity are confident that they are about to undermine and destroy for all time the fundamentals that have been the guide and stay of our people for a century and a half. To the mind that takes only a casual view of the times the religious and moral structure so carefully built by our ancestors is about to collapse. Agnostics and atheists are raising their shouts of triumph. The noise and tumult seems to have paralyzed many devout souls. Organized crime is hurling into the face of law-abiding citizens one of the greatest challenges they have ever faced. The sanctity of the marriage vow, the only safeguard of the Christian home, is often looked upon with no more respect than the most trivial engagement.

Times like these demand strong men and women. Our pulpits and platforms need men grounded in the faith and who know the scripture. The hope of the future rests with the youth of to-day. In all my experience as a teacher I have never taught a finer group of young men and women than those I find in our schools and colleges. They are seeking for absolute facts and will be satisfied with nothing less. The clergy of the present day have the greatest opportunity and the greatest task of all time. These young people are going to accept Christ as revealed in the scripture or atheism. There will be no middle ground. Here is the opportunity for strong men who know the scripture and who are filled with the spirit of the Master. Such a man is Dr. Webb. I have studied him in his pulpit and on the platform. He knows the Bible and can reveal its truths in a more clear and convincing manner than any clergyman I have ever known. His sermons are strong and convincing because they reveal so clearly the great truths of the Bible. He preaches Christ the Saviour, and, like his Master drives his lessons home by the skillful use of illustrations. Some sermons are dull and entirely fail because they contain no illustrations to tie them to the everyday life of the people. Others are so full of common-place illustrations that what scripture they contain is entirely lost. Both types are fatal, especially in dealing with our young people. Teachers of history know how necessary it is to tie the great facts of the past to the present by illustrations.

Dr. Webb has learned the art of bringing the great truths of the Spirit into the actual facts of life as it is. His sermons are not of the highly emotional type, nor are they dryly scholastic. Every sermon bespeaks the spirit of a man who has mastered his subject and knows how to make it real. This volume shows the same scholarly, painstaking care that one finds reflected in his sermons. It is a treasure-house of illustrations that are of priceless value, not alone to the preacher who is trying to reveal spiritual and moral truth, but to all who are working with human problems. The index is so full and the topics so definitely arranged that a person who is overburdened with work can quickly turn to the illustration he most needs. This book will be a great source of power to the clergyman who is endeavoring to interpret the life and teaching of Christ to the present generation.

University of Delaware.

JAMES A. BARKLEY,
ASSOCIATE PROFESSOR OF HISTORY AND
POLITICAL SCIENCE

SUBJECT INDEX

PAGE

ASSURANCE 1
    Ark—Safe in the.
    Assurance.
    Assurance Brings Rest.
    Assurance—Ground of.
    Assurance—Lost and Found.
    Assurance—Perfect.
    Assurance—Reception of.
    Protection from God.
    Security.
    Security—The Believer.
    Witness—Intimidated.
    A Solitary Way.

ATONEMENT 5
    Atonement in the Two Testaments.
    Atonement—Evading the.
    Atonement—Extent of.
    Atonement—Necessity of.
    Atonement—Realizing the.
    Atonement—Sheltered Under.
    Atonement—Sign of.
    Atonement—Need of.
    Love—Atoning.
    Mediator—The.
    One Mediator.
    Real Cleansing.
    Redemption—Price of.
    Substitute.
    Sinner's Substitute.
    Twice Bought.
    Vicarious Suffering.

BACKSLIDING 10
    Backsliders—Afflictions of.
    Backsliding—Gradual.
    Backsliding—Guard Against.
    Backslider—Punishment of.
    Difficulties—Overcoming.
    Heroism—Faulty.
    Joy Bells.
    Moral Bankruptcy.
    Retreat—Difficulties of.

PAGE

BERLIEVER'S SECURITY 13
    Crisis Hour.
    Environment and Character.
    Blessings—Unrealized.
    Believer's Strength.
    Refuge—Seeking.
    Security—The Christian's.

BIBLE 15
    Bible—A Personal.
    Bible—A Useless.
    Bible and the Holy Spirit.
    Bible—Best Recommendation.
    Bible—Constant Reading.
    Bible—Freedom in.
    Bible—Half Read.
    Bible—Illustrations in the.
    Bible—Inspiration of.
    Bible—Joy in.
    Bible—Life Giving.
    Bible—Misused.
    Bible—Moody's.
    Bible—Prejudiced Against.
    Bible Reading.
    Bible—The Newspaper.
    Bible—The Open.
    Bible—Wisely Using the.
    God's Bread and Man's Theories.
    Gospel—Incarnate.
    God's Word—Obscuring.
    Gospel Mirror.
    Gospel—Substitutes for the.
    Gospel the Power of God.
    Perverting the Gospel.
    Scriptures, Foolish Handling of.
    Simplifying Safety.
    The Foolish Apothecary.
    Truth—Seekers.
    Unknown—Perils of the.

BROTHERHOOD 23
    Brother—A Real.
    Brother—Self-Denying.
    Brotherly Spirit.
    Burden—Bearing Another's.
    Enemies—Forgiving.
    Co-Laborers.
    Co-Laborers.
    Friend—A Protecting.
    Friend—A Real.

PAGE

Friend at Court.
Friend—Fighting Our.
Friend in Need.
Friendship—Marks of.
Friends—Unknown.
God's Watch-Care.
Idle Hands.
Influence—Secret of.
Laborers Together.
Magnanimous Conduct.
Praise—Bishop and Choir.
Patience—Perfect.
Servant—Sympathetic.
Silence—Golden.
Sympathy.
Sympathy—Brotherly.
The Changed Partnership.
The Staff Method.
"Victory, O Lord."
Whosoever.
Companion—A Constant.
Man's Ingratitude.
"Pass It On."
What to Forget.

CHRIST 32
Christ's Love an Individual Love.
Author—Loving the.
Authority—Keys of.
Christ—Ashamed of.
Christ—A Vision of.
Christ—Birth of.
Christ's Disciple.
Christ—Fellowship With.
Christ—Hid in.
Christ—Holding Up.
Christ—Knowing.
Christ—Making Way for.
Christ—Memorial of.
Christ—Mercy of.
Christ our Advocate.
Christ our Refuge.
Christ's Sacrifice.
Christ—Patience of.
Christ—Popular with.
Christ—Putting on.
Christ—Renunciation by.
Christ the Door.
Christ—The Image of.
Christ—The Needed One.
Christ—The Real.

PAGE

Christ: The Rock of Ages.
Christ the Way.
Christ—Touch of.
Christ—Triumph in.
Christ—Union with.   *3 9*
Christ—Witnessing for.
Clock of Time.
Conversion—Gen. Lew Wallace's.
Cross—Protection of.
Deliverer—The Great.
"Eager Heart."
Everybody Somebody to Jesus.
Guide—Following our.
Heart—Christ in the.
If Jesus Had Not Come.
In His Steps.
Inspiration—Wesley's Argument.
Jesus—Looking to.
Jesus—Standing Up For.
Jesus—Tenderness of.
Jesus—The Great Pilot.
Lives—Reflected.
Lord Forever.
Master—Following the.
Mediator.
Messian—The True.
Pilot—A New.
Pilot—A Safe.
Pleasing Men or Serving Christ.
Revelation—Progressive.
Saviour—Linked to the.
Saviour—No Room for.
Sowing Good Seed.
Spirit—The Master's.
"Suffered in all Points."
Teacher—The Great.
The Great Physician.
The Powerful and Powerless Grave.
Tomb—The Unique.
Wings—Our.
Word of Life.
Christus Consolator.
Comfort in Christ.
The Christ Ideal.

CHURCH 51
Church—A Cold.
Church—A Defective.
Church—A Live.
Church—A Strong.
Church Attendance.

PAGE

Church Atmosphere.
Church—False Efforts in.
Church Members—Fussy.
Church Members Marking Time.
Church On Fire.
Church Union.
Church—Protection of.
Church—The True.
Church—Trouble in.
Church—Joining.
Church—Judging the.
Christian Unity.
Dissensions—Trivial.
Example—A Good.
Manned by Dead Men.
Spiritual Strength.
Unity—Strength in.
Voice of Another World.
Washington and Worship.
Worship or Natural Emotion.

CHRISTIANS 58
Blessings—Count Your.
Christian Comfort.
Christian—A Banished.
Christian—A Humble.
Christian—A Sleepy.
Christian—A Useful.
Christian—Be Watchful.
Christians—Bigoted.
Christians—Criticizing.
Christians—Detached.
Christians—Differences in.
Christians—Dwarfed.
Christians—False.
Christians—Faulty.
Christian—Half Way.
Christian—Honoring a.
Christians—Selfish.
Christian Influence.
Christians—Loafing.
Christian—Misjudging.
Christians—Plain.
Christian Power.
Christian Service.
Christian—The Marks of.
Christianity—Effect of.
Christianity—Hermetically Sealed.
Christianity Not on Trial.
Empty Sacks.

PAGE

Fair-Weather Christians.
Fatal Sleep.
Holiness—Beauty of.
Jewels—God's.
Life—The Real.
Listening to the Will.
Laborers Together.
Prison of Worldliness.
Saints—Communion of
Sonship.
Spirit—A Christian.
Unfaithful Leaders.

CONFESSION 67
Choice—An Impossible.
Confession—Christian.
Confession—Difficult.
Decision—Instant.
Decision—Prompt.
Testimony—A Joyful.

CONSCIENCE 69
Conscience—A Faulty.
Conscience—A Good.
Conscience—A Quiescent.
Conscience and Immortality.
Conscience—Arousing.
Conscience Like a Clock.
Conscience—Stifling the.
Conscience—The Awakened.
Conscience—The Guide.
Conscience—Indestructibility of.
Conscience—The Voice of.
Conscience—Unenlightened.
Signal Lights.

CONSECRATION 73
A Good Soldier.
Character—Unrecognized.
Consecrated Art.
Consecration Complete.
Surrender—A Complete.
Consecration—Complete.
Consecration—Grateful.
Consecration—Lack of Complete.
Conquering our Habits.
Good—Unconscious.
If Consecrated.
Life—The Higher.
Man—The Whole.
Sanctification—Complete.

PAGE

Self-Sacrifice—The Daughters.
Self-Surrender.
Work—Artistic.
Workers—God's Fellow.
Will—A Determined.

DEATH 80
Death—A Universal Preacher.
Death—Companion in.
Death—Prepared for.
Death—Trying to Bribe.
Death—Uncertainty of.
Death—Sudden Call of.
Death—Great.
Prepared for Death.

DECISION 83
Begin Again.
Beginnings—Resist.
Blessings—Receiving.
Bury it.
Choosing.
Courage—Moral.
Conviction.
Decision of Character.
Decision—Early.
Decision—Immediate.
Decision—Immediate.
Decision Inevitable.
Decision—Inevitable.
Doubt—How to Use.
Guide—An Unfailing.
Impressions Fixed.
Liberty—Personal.
Signals.
Life's Slacker.
Line of Least Resistance.
Marching Orders.
Obedience—Instant.
Opportunity—Ready for.
Right of Way.
Season—The Critical.
The Down Road.
Trouble—Ignoring.
Warnings—Unheeded.
Why He Gave Up.

ETERNITY 91
Danger—Hidden.
Door—The Open.
Punishment—Endless.

PAGE

    Immortality—Belief in.
    Life—End of.

EXAMPLES 93
    A Hard Lesson.
    Burdens—Laying Down.
    Courtesy.
    Destitute of Moral Principle.
    Enemies—Patience with.
    Example—Careful of.
    Fear of Man.
    Meditation—Influence of.
    Name—Value of.
    Perfection in Trifles.
    Plays—Incomplete.
    Pouter Pigeons.
    Small Hinges.
    Value of a Good Name.

EXCUSES 97
    Duty—Forgotten.
    Duty—Shirking.
    Excuse to Rest.
    Staff-Method.

FAITH 98
    Belief Possible.
    Cast Iron Faith.
    Faith and Action.
    Faith and Character.
    Faith and Works.
    Faith and Works.
    Faith in Progress.
    Faith's Progress.
    Faith—Christian.
    Faith—Definition of.
    Faith—Expressing.
    Faith—Foundation of.
    Faith—Influence of.
    Faith—Necessity of.
    Faith—Saving.
    Faith—Trial of.
    Faith—Triumph of.
    Faith—Upward Look of.
    Faith—Wings of.
    Faith—Won by.
    Trust—Absolute.

FORGIVENESS 104
    Forgiveness—A Definition of.
    Forgiveness—Absolute.

PAGE

    Forgiveness—Brotherly.
    Forgiveness—Complete.
    Forgiveness—Effects of.
    Forgiveness—Power of.
    Forgiveness—Seeking.
    Hard to Forgive Self.
    Mercy—Plea for.
    Sins Blotted Out.

FEELINGS 107
    Alarmists.
    Emotions—Evanescent.
    Emotion—Discipline of.
    Feeling and Fact.

GRACE 109
    Christian Nurture.
    Door of God's Grace.
    Grace.
    Grace—Beginnings of.
    Grace—God's.
    Grace—Growing in.
    Grace—Growth in.
    Grace—Persistent.
    Grace—Power of God's.
    Grace—Silent.
    Grace Sufficient for Trials.
    Grace—Unmerited.
    Life—Gift of.

GOD 112
    A Sleeping Deity.
    Agents—God's.
    Faith in God.
    God's Goodness.
    God's Goodness Proved.
    God's Great Gift.
    God's Image.
    God Makes No Mistakes.
    God Our Refuge.
    God Our Shield.
    God's Kingdom Stands.
    God's Map—No Edge to.
    God's Watch-Care.
    God—A Bearer of.
    God—A False.
    God—A Friend of.
    God—A Helper.
    God—Acknowledging.
    God—Approach to.
    God—Confidence in.

PAGE

God's Existence—Certainty of.
God—Fear and Fascination of.
God's Honor—Guarding.
God's Voice.
God—Knowing.
God—Likeness.
God—Moved.
God—Neglecting.
God—Praise of.
God—Robbing.
God the Only Giver.
God—Trust in.
Jewels—God's.
Life—Mysterious Origin of.
Will—Accepting God's.
God—Waiting Upon.
God—Strangers to.

GRATITUDE 122
Gifts—Reason for.
Gratitude.

HEART 123
Heart Argument.
Heart—A Careless.
Heart—A Changed.
Heart—A Clean.
Heart—A Generous.
Heart—Ice-Bound.
Heart Ignorance.
Heart of Stone.
Heart—A Sympathetic.
Heart—Guarding the.
Heart—Hardened.
Heart—Protecting the.
Heart-Service.
Life—Fountain of.
Penitent Tears.
Heart—A Warm.

HOLY SPIRIT 128
Comforter—The.
Holy Spirit as a Dove.
Holy Spirit Our Guide.
Holy Spirit—Breath of the.
Holy Spirit—Coming of.
Holy Spirit—Misunderstanding.
Holy Spirit—Necessity of the.
Spirit—Quenching the.
Holy Spirit—Receiving the.

PAGE

Holy Ghost—Sin Against.
Temple—A Spiritual.

HUMILITY 131
Humility.
Humility.
Humility—Beauty of.
Humility—Knowledge of.
Humility—Knowledge Through.
Humility—Ministerial.
Humility—Necessity of.
Humility—The Angel of.
Revival—Beginning of.
Stooping to Conquer.
Strength in Weakness.
Unity—Pleasantness of.
Weakness—Strength in.
Humble Paths.

HYPOCRISY 135
Appearance—Deceitful.
False Teaching.
Hypocrisy.

JUDGMENT 136
Ambition—Worldly.
Censure—Habit of.
Character Building.
Character—Incomplete.
Fears—False.
Glory—Forfeited.
Judgment Day.
Judgment—Charitable.
Judgment—Dread of.
Judgment—False and True.
Judgment—Intelligent.
Judgment—Personal.
Judgment—Self.
Judgment—The Lord's.
Lost by Disobedience.
Owe No Man Anything.
Punishment—Eternal.
Retribution—Physical.
The Desert of Traitors.
The Master—Judgment of.
Judgment—Throne.

LOVE 141
Enemy—Loving Our.
Guidance—Love's.
Heart—A Loving.

PAGE

Love Without Arms.
Love—Influence of.
Love Never Faileth.
Love Wrought This.
Love—Incomplete Knowledge of.
Love—Memory of.
Love—Proof of.
Love—Sacrificial.
Love—Sacrificial.
Love—Touch of.
Love—Unfailing.
Love—Union of.
Love—Value of.
Love—Winsome.
Serving in Love.
Throne—Love on the.
Truth in Love.
Love—Remembering.
Love—The Call of.
Love—Touch of.

NEUTRALITY 148
Character—A Negative.
Live-Service.

MINISTERS 149
A Minister's Fears.
Dead—Arousing.
Doctrine and Deed.
Duty—Path of.
Engine Trouble.
Evangelical Simplicities.
Good Fruit.
Gospel Ministers.
Guides—Ignorant.
Life—A Fruitful.
Marching Orders.
Messenger—The Needed.
Minister—Helping the.
Neglecting Christ's Work.
Preacher's Foundation.
Preacher—A Patient.
Preacher—A Persistent.
Preacher an Obstacle.
Preacher—A Tireless.
Preacher—An Unusual.
Preaching—Constant.
Preaching—Effective.
Preaching—Interesting.
Preaching—Pleasing.
Preaching—Real.

PAGE

Preaching—Red-Hot.
Scoffer Turned Preacher.
Sermons Controversial.
Sermons—Likes in.
Sermons—Purpose of.
Sermons—Repeating.
Sermon—The First.
Statistics and Service.
Unconverted Minister.
Unconverted Minister.
What Ministers Must Preach.
Words and Deeds.

PARDON 158
Conviction and Pardon.
Foundation—Defective.
Offenses—Forgiving.
Pardon and Praise.
Pardon—A Surprising.
Pardon—Christ's.
Pardon Needed.
Pardon—The Forgotten.
Pardon—Witholding a.
The Great Purifier.

PEACE 161
Trust in the Lord.
Trust—A Fixed.
Peace in Quietness.
Rest—Pictures of.
Peace—Plural.
Quiet Places.
Trust—Lack of.

PERSONAL WORK 163
Be-Attitudes.
Disciples—Making.
Effort—Aggressive.
Joy in Unselfishness.
Leadership—Personal.
Opportunities—Missed.
Patience—Perfect Mark of.
Personal Work Difficult.
Personal Work—Hesitancy in.
Service—True.
Soul-Winning—Patience in.
Success of Personal Work.
Without a Goal.
Word in Season.
Workers, Not Observers.

PAGE

Praise 168
    Joy—Reason for.
    Light and Noise.
    Music in the Storm.
    No Music in Unbelief.
    Praise—Deserved.
    Praise—Unrestrained.
    Servant—A Faithful.
    Singing His Song.
    Singing the New Song.
    The Persistent Note.
    The Old Hymns.

Prayer 172
    Angels—The Two.
    Childish Prayer.
    Enemy—Prevailing Against the.
    Prayer and Revivals.
    Prayer Answered.
    Prayer Changes Things.
    Prayer in Jesus' Name.
    Prayer-Book—The Lost.
    Prayer—Alone in.
    Prayer—Answer to.
    Prayer—Delayed Answer to.
    Prayer—Delayed Answers to.
    Prayer—Deliverance in.
    Prayer—Faith in.
    Prayer—Foolish.
    Prayer—Humility in.
    Prayer—Information of.
    Prayer—Instant in.
    Prayer—Listening to.
    Praying Warriors.
    Prayer, A Constant Privilege.
    Prayers—Recorded.
    Prayer—Relying on.
    Prayer—Safety in.
    Prayer—Secret.
    Prayer—Strength in.
    Prayer—True.
    Prayers—Unanswered.
    Prayer—Value of United.
    Prayer-Meeting.
    The Shut Door.
    Prayer for Peace.
    Prayer—Answered.

Procrastination 181
    Delay—Danger of.
    Delay—Danger of.

PAGE

Delay—Danger of.
Delay—Dangers of.
Delay—Dangerous.
Delay—Fatal.
Delay—No Time for.
Danger—Playing with.
"First" Means First.
Indecision—Terrace of.
Invitations—Delayed.
Life—Renewed.
Lingering—Folly of.
Opportunities—Laziness and.
Opportunity—Lost.
Procrastinate.
Procrastination—Cause of.
Procrastination—Origin of.
The Danger of Delay.
The Folly of Lingering.
Time—None to Lose.

REPENTANCE 186
Conviction and Repentance.
Penitence and Pardon.
Repentance—Continual.
Repentance—Death-Bed.
Repentance—Death-Bed.

REGENERATION 187
Born Again.
Cleansing—Divine.
Converts—Man's.
Cure—Internal.
Immediate Obedience.
Life—Aim of.
Man—Reform of.
New Birth.
New Birth—Necessity of.
New Birth—Necessity of.
Punishment—Failure of.
Regeneration—Necessity of.

RELIGION 190
Foundations of Sand.
Godliness—Genius for.
Kingdom—Unable to Stop the.
No Religion.
Religious Problems.
Religion—Attractive.
Religion—Constancy of.
Religion—Half Way.
Religion, No Time for.

PAGE

Religion—Testing.
Religion—Understanding.
Voice of Common Sense.
Wheelbarrow Religion.

REWARD 193
Crown—Obtaining a.
Encouragement—Example of.
Instant in Season.
Memory—The Best.
Old Age—Fruit of.
Reward—Royal.
Work—The End Crowns.
Serving by Waiting.
Waiting.

SABBATH 196
Good Deeds Exempt.
Sabbath Day Holy.
Sabbath, Appointed of God.
Sabbath—Blessing of the.
Sabbath—Gain of.
Sabbath—Need of.
Sabbath—Seeing on the.
The Pilgrim's Sabbath.

SACRIFICE 199
Amputation Needed.
Deliverance Through Sacrifice.
Healing—Permanent.
Life in Renunciation.
Power of the Cross.
Sacrifice—Fragrant.
Sacrifice—Progress by.
Self-Sacrifice—The Daughters.
"Shadow of the Cross."
Hero of the Race.

SALVATION 202
Feeling in Salvation.
Lacking One Thing.
No Safety in Our Works.
Salvation All of Grace.
Salvation is for All.
Salvation Provided.
Salvation Rejected.
Salvation—Assurance of.
Salvation—Selling.
Salvation—The Most Wonderful.
Salvation—Uttermost.

PAGE

    Saved, By Destruction of Works.
    Saved—Almost.

SATAN 206
    Antichrist—Teaching of.
    Devil—Fighting the.
    Devil—Resisting.
    Judas Honored.
    Satan's Commentary.
    Satan's Language.
    Satan's Servants.
    Satan—Evil Influences of.
    Satan—Exposed.
    The Devil in Print.
    The Devil's Inheritance.
    The Devil's Business.

SECOND COMING 209
    Hidden Treasure.
    Lord—Watching for the.
    Ticket—Round Trip.

SIN 210
    Sins—Attractive.
    Faults—Hidden.
    Guilt—Indirect.
    Original Sin.
    Sinners Called.
    Sinner Needs God.
    Sin's Burden.
    Sin in the Heart.
    Sins Forgotten.
    Sins of Neighbors.
    Sin—A Habitual State of.
    Sin—Bondage of.
    Sin—Clinging to.
    Sin—Covered.
    Sins—Danger of Small.
    Sin—Deceitfulness of.
    Sin—Detracting Power of.
    Sin—Disguised.
    Sin—Gradual Growth of.
    Sin—Grip of.
    Sin—Growth of.
    Sins—Little.
    Sin—Physician for.
    Sin—Punishment of.
    Sin—Redeeming from.
    Sin—"Palace of Art" and.
    Sins—Perils of Secret.
    Sin of Presumption.

PAGE

Sins—Presumptuous.
Sin—Seeing Our.
Sin—Senseless.
Sin—Sorrow Over.
Sin—Wreck of.
Sinner—Hopeful for.
Sinner—Only Hope for.
Sin—Root of.
Sin—Unrecognized.
Sin—Mark of.

SOUL 220

Body—Care of.
Lost Souls.
Martyr Souls.
Soul—A Dead.
Soul—A Generous.
Soul—A Restored.
Soul—Bankruptcy.
Soul—Battling for the.
Soul—Cramping the.
Soul—Cleansing the.
Souls—Foolish.
Souls—Kingly.
Souls—Repairing.
Soul—Restoration of.
Souls—Seeking.
Souls—Trusted with.
Souls—Value of.
Soul—Value of.
Souls—Sleepy.

SELF 226

Character—A Sterling.
Destroying Self.
Destruction—Personal.
Divided Allegiance.
Duty—Call of.
Enemy—Our Worst.
Looking-Glasses.
Punishment of Self.
Self—Ashamed of.
Self-Control.
Self-Control and Tact.
Self-Conquering.
Self-Discovery.
Self-Effacement.
Self-Effacing.
Self-Righteousness.
Self—Giving of.
Self—Love of.

PAGE

STEWARDSHIP 230
> Avarice—Danger of.
> Benevolence.
> Bled to Death.
> Charity—Beauty of.
> Charity—Parade of.
> Checks—Worthless.
> Destruction—Escape from.
> Evil—Prolific Root of.
> Gift—The Best.
> Giving and Receiving.
> Giving Our Best.
> Giving—Growth in.
> Giving—Ways of.
> God—Robbing.
> Gold and the Grave.
> Greed of Gold.
> Inheritance Withheld.
> Key of Loyalty.
> Offering—Unprepared for.
> Poor—Friends of the.
> Prosperity—Shadow of.
> Purse and Piety.
> Riches—Fleeting.
> Riches—Wishing for.
> Stewardship—Fritz Kreisler's.
> Tithing or Tipping.
> Treasures—Seeking.
> Giving—Unselfish.
> Giving—Greatness in.
> God the Only Giver.

TEMPTATION 237
> Character—Testing.
> Made Strong by Trials.
> Temptation—Courting.
> Temptation—Fighting.
> Temptation—Little.
> Temptation—Resisting.
> Testings—Severe.
> Trials—Blessing in.

TESTING 239
> Adversity—Blessing in.
> Beauty—Secret of.
> Blessings Hidden.
> Blessings—Trampling on.
> Burdens and Blessings.
> Duty and Pleasure.
> Guidance—Providential.
> Guide—Pasts Recalled.

PAGE

Life—Love of.
Music in the Storm.
Pain—Blessing Through.
Providence and Inheritance.
Sorrow—Blessing in.
Sorrow—Ministry of.
Sorrow—Sanctified.
Sorrow—Transformed.
Spirits—Ministering.
Spiritual Beauty.
Stepping-Stones.
Suffering—Perfected in.
Testing Times.
Testing to Reveal.
Thorn in the Flesh.
Trouble—Mission of.

VISION 245

Blindness—Blessing in.
Eyes Opened.
Eyes—Blinded.
Eyes That See Not.
"Expectation Corners."
Light for Others.
Light Not Shining.
Light—A Useful.
Light—Going Against.
Light—Hiding the.
Light—Life Giving.
Light—Missing the.
Light—Plenty of.
Light—Progressive.
Light—Protection of.
Light—Receiving.
Light—Sufficient.
Light—The World's.
Look—The Backward.
Seeing Into the Depths.
Spiritual Vision Blurred.
Vision—A Clear.
Vision—A Glorious.
Vision—Blurred.
Vision—Defective.
Vision—The Unerring.
Vision—Value of.
Vision—A Full.

WITNESSES 252

Angel—A Ministering.
Confessing Christ—Duty of.
Confession—Reason for.

PAGE

 Example—A Holy.
 Fidelity to Duty.
 Life—Abundant or Anemic.
 Loyalty—Power of.
 Providence—Guidance of.
 Redemption—Discovering.
 Saints—Transparent.
 Testimony—Bearing.
 Testimony—Cheerful.
 Tongue—A Loose.
 Water of Life.
 Water of Life.
 Witnessing for Christ.
 Witness—A Fearless.
 Witness—An Honorable.
 Witness—Most Efficient.
 Workers—Unknown.
 Workers—Unknown.

FATHER 258
 Example—A Father's.
 Father—Acknowledging His.
 Father's Example.
 Father-Hearted.
 Father—Joy of.
 Father—Love of.
 Guide—Father as.
 Memorials—Intimate.

MOTHER 260
 Face—A Beautiful.
 God's Good Woman.
 Like Mother.
 Love for Mother.
 Love—Mother's.
 Melody in the Soul.
 Mother an Impartial.
 Mother's Covenant.
 Mother's Devotion.
 Mother's Face.
 Mother's Faithfulness.
 Mothers Help God.
 Mother—Honoring.
 Mother's Letter.
 Mother's Prayer.
 Mother's Prayers.
 Mother's Strong Boy.
 Mother's Traits.
 Mother Waiting.
 Mothers—Influence of.
 Mother—Memory of.

PAGE

Mother—Memories of.
Woman—A Great.
A Cradle Rocking.

CHILDREN 268

Acts—Good.
Ambition—Worldly.
Both Knees.
Boy Foreshadows the Man.
Boys—Kindness to.
Child—Generosity of.
Child Sower.
Children—Care of.
Children and Christ.
Children—Conversion of.
Children—Early Conversion.
Children—Faith in.
Children in the Fold.
Children—Influence Over.
Children—Obedient.
Children—Value of.
Early Conversion—Importance of.
Early Piety—Importance of.
Early Repentance.
Envy—Wicked.
Faith as a Child.
Girl—A Good Shepherd.
Lamb's Book of Life.
Love—Voice of.
Memory of Youth.
Sanctification—Test of.
Seed—Planting.
Seed-Planting.
Son—A True Son.
Will—A Surrendered.
Word in Season.
Youth—Blessing of.
Youth—Promising.
Youth—Perpetual.
The Bridge Builder.

HOME 277

Home Influence.
Home Makes the Man.
Home—A Christian.
Home—A Defective.
Home—An Ideal.
Home—Christ in the.
Memory—Grateful.
Home—Jesus in the.
Home—Love in.

PAGE

Home—Sight of.
Modern Marriage.
No Home.
Spiritual Orphans.
The House of Quiet.
The Revival Needed.

HEAVEN 281
Heaven a Prepared Place.
Heaven Always Light.
Heaven in the Heart.
Heaven—Homesick for.
Heaven—Hope of.
Heaven—Material.
Heaven—Road to.
Heaven—Traveling.
Heaven—Waiting for.
Riches in Glory.

ONE THOUSAND NEW ILLUSTRATIONS

ASSURANCE

Ark—Safe in the.

When I was in Manchester, I went into the gallery one Sunday night to have a talk with a few inquirers, and while I was talking a business man came in and took his seat on the outskirts of the audience. I think at first he had come merely to criticize, and that he was a little skeptical. At last I saw he was in tears. I turned to him and said: "My friend, what is your difficulty?" "Well," he said: "Mr. Moody, the fact is, I cannot tell." I said: "Do you believe you are a sinner?" He said: "Yes, I know that." I said: "Christ is able to save you"; and I used one illustration after another, but he did not see it. At last I used the ark, and I said: "Was it Noah's feelings that saved him? Was it Noah's righteousness that saved him, or was it the ark?" "Mr. Moody," said he, "I see it." He got up and shook hands with me, and said: "Good-night. I have to go. I see it now."

A few days after, he came and touched me on the shoulder, and said: "Do you know me?" I said: "I know your face, but do not remember where I have seen you." He said: "Do you not remember the illustration of the ark?" I said: "Yes." He said: "It has been all light ever since. I understand it now. Christ is the ark; He saves me, and I must get inside Him."—D. L. MOODY.

Assurance.

Arthur Clough, whose early death prevented him from becoming the foremost poet of the age, and who passed through many spiritual vicissitudes, felt and expressed this in his noble lines:

It fortifies my soul to know
That, though I perish, Truth is so:
That, howsoe'er I stray and range,
Whate'er I do, Thou dost not
    change.
I steadier step when I recall
That, if I slip, Thou does not fall.
—W. GARRETT HORDER.

Assurance Brings Rest.

It is said that the way the natives in the East take honey without being stung by the bees is very wonderful. They are protected by their dress in the very least degree, and yet, although surrounded by clouds of angry bees, they rarely suffer. The explanation given is that these natives are quite passive, deliberate in their movements, making no effort to protect themselves, making no attempt to drive the swarm away, and if a bee settles upon them, it stings them no more than in would attempt to sting a log of wood. The Westerner, on the other hand, is nervous, restless, combative; he attempts to frighten the bees, is manifestly scared himself, makes a noise, gesticulates, runs away, and ends by being badly pun-

1

ished. Our troubles in life compass
us about like bees. Let us fret and
fume, and we shall feel the sting
and miss the honey; let us live in
quietness and confidence, and we
shall taste the sweetness and escape
the sting.—*The Epworth Herald*.

Assurance—Ground of.

When Antigonus was ready to
engage in a sea-fight with Ptolemy's
armada, the pilot cried out, "How
many they are more than we!" "'Tis
true," said the courageous king, "if
you count their numbers, they surpass us; but for how many do you
value me?" And so the ground of
our assurance rests not in ourselves,
or anything that is ours,—if it did
it would be presumption—it rests in
Christ and what He has done.

Assurance—Lost and Found.

The Bishop of Exeter in the
course of a conversation mentioned
that, many years since, while walking by a river he lost his watch
and chain, which he supposed had
been pulled from his pocket by
the bough of a tree. Some time
afterwards, when staying in the
same neighborhood, he took a
stroll by the side of the river and
came to a secluded spot where he
had lost his valuables, and there, to
his surprise and delight, he found
them. So with Christians who have
only to retrace their steps like Bunyan's pilgrim when he had slept in
the bowers of ease. Assurance comes
again, as it came at first by prayer,
and penitence, by diligent and con-
scientious search for it Godward and
Christward.—BAXENDALE.

Assurance—Perfect.

As one contemplates Mr. Gladstone's triumphs, one finds oneself
recurring in memory to the beautiful background of domestic quiet
and stately dignity in which he was
as much or more at home than in
the public gaze. I can see him now
in an old wideawake and cloak—
trudging off in the drizzle of an
October morning to an early service. I remember how, at Hawarden
in 1896, on one of the sad evenings
after my father's death, I dined
alone with him and one other guest,
and with what beautiful consideration he talked quietly on about
things in which he thought we
should be interested—things that
needed neither comment nor response, and all so naturally and
easily, that one hardly realized the
tender thoughtfulness of it all. And
last of all, I remember how I came
one evening at a later date to dine
at Hawarden, and was shown into
a little half-lit ante-room next the
dining-room. He was just at the
beginning of his last illness, and he
was suffering from discomfort and
weakness. There on a sofa he sat,
side by side with Mrs. Gladstone;
they were sitting in silence, hand in
hand, like two children, the old warrior and his devoted wife. It
seemed almost too sacred a thing to
have seen; but it is not too sacred
to record, for it seemed the one last
perfect transfiguring touch of love
and home.—A. C. BENSON.

Assurance—Reception of.

Mr. Wesley records, that when he
was enabled to believe in Christ
as his Saviour, under the reading
of Luther's Preface to the Epistle
of St. Paul to the Romans, at about
a quarter before nine, in Aldersgate
Street, that he felt his heart
strangely warmed within him; that
he felt he did trust in Christ alone
for salvation; and that there and
then assurance was given him that
Jesus had taken away all his sins,

even his, and saved him from the law of sin and death.—DR. JOBSON.

the loop kept him from sinking.—W. R. BRADLAUGH.

Protection From God.

A friend of mine has a very powerful microscope. One day he showed me some curious specimens through it. Among these were some tiny little sea animals. They were so small that they could not be seen with the naked eye. They are made to live on the rocks under the water; and, to protect themselves from being swept away by the force of the waves, they are furnished with the tiniest little limbs you ever saw. Each of these is made exactly in the shape of an anchor. This they fasten in the rock; and as I looked at them with wonder through the microscope, I thought: Why, even among these very little creatures we see Jehova-jireh, too! The Lord provides for their protection.—C. H. SPURGEON.

Security.

As one of our American liners was crossing the Atlantic, during a terrific gale, the cry was raised—"Man overboard!" It was impossible to put up the helm of the ship on account of the violence of the hurricane, but one of the crew instantly seized a rope having a loop as the end, and threw it over the stern, crying out, "Lay hold for your life!" Passengers and crew had crowded together at the stern, but the rolling waves and blinding spray prevented them from seeing the drowning sailor. The captain cried out, "Have you got hold of the rope?" and the reply came, "No, but the rope has got hold of me." The sailor when he caught the rope had passed the loop over his shoulders and under his arms, and though too fatigued to hold on to the rope,

Security—The Believer.

A traveler relates that, when passing through an Austrian town, his attention was directed to a forest on a slope near the road, and he was told that death was the penalty of cutting down one of those trees. He was incredulous until he was further informed that they were the protection of the city, breaking the force of the descending avalanche which, without this natural barrier, would sweep over the homes of thousands. When a Russian army was there and began to cut away the fence for fuel, the inhabitants besought them to take their dwellings instead, which was done. Such are the sanctions of God's moral law. On the integrity and support of that law depends the safety of the universe. "The soul that sinneth, it shall die" is a merciful proclamation. "He that offends in one point is guilty of all," is equally just and benevolent. To transgress once is to lay the axe at the foot of the tree which represents the security and peace of every loyal soul in the wide dominions of the Almighty.

Witness—Intimidated.

"I was one day in the Old Bailey, watching a criminal trial, and a witness who had evidently been intimidated by the friends of the prisoner was giving evidence. The examining counsel drew it from her that she did not like to say all she knew in view of the threatened consequences to herself. I remember the words of the judge to that woman right to this day. He said, 'Tell all that you know, and remember that the whole power of England is behind you to protect you. So you need not be afraid.'

To those of us who are His witnesses, all the power of God is about
us to protect us."—J. STUART HOLDEN.

A Solitary Way.

There is a mystery in human hearts,
And though we be encircled by a
host
Of those who love us well, and are
beloved,
To every one of us, from time to
time,
There comes a sense of utter lone-
liness.
Our dearest friend is "stranger" to
our joy,
And cannot realize our bitterness.
"There is not one who really under-
stands,
Not one to enter into all I feel";
Such is the cry of each of us in turn,
We wander in a "solitary way"
No matter what or where our lot
may be;
Each heart, mysterious even to it-
self,
Must live its inner life in solitude.

And would you know the reason
why this is?
It is because the Lord desires our
love.
In every heart He wishes to be
first.
He therefore keeps the secret key
Himself,
To open all its chambers and to
bless
With perfect sympathy and holy
peace,

Each solitary soul which comes to
Him.
So when we feel this loneliness, it is
The voice of Jesus saying, "Come to
Me";
And every time we are "not under-
stood,"
It is a call to us to come again;
For Christ alone can satisfy the
soul,
And those who walk with Him from
day to day
Can never have a "solitary way."

And when beneath some heavy
cross you faint,
And say, "I cannot bear this load
alone,"
You say the truth. Christ made it
purposely
So heavy that you must return to
Him.
The bitter grief, which "no one un-
derstands,"
Conveys a secret message from the
King,
Entreating you to come to Him
again.
The Man of Sorrows understands it
well,
In all points tempted He can feel
with you.
You cannot come too often, or too
near,
The Son of God is infinite in grace,
His presence satisfies the longing
soul,
And those who walk with Him from
day to day
Can never have a solitary way.

ATONEMENT

Atonement in the Two Testaments.

"The difference between the atonement, as set forth in the Old Testament and as presented in the New," says Dr. C. I. Scofield, "is that in the former case the sheep died for the shepherd, in the latter the Shepherd died for the sheep."—*Christian Workers Magazine.*

Atonement—Evading The.

The Rev. Basil Mowll told the story of a train accident. The engine-driver was afterward asked at the inquiry why he did not pull up his train at a certain point. Did he not see the flag? Yes, he had seen the flag, but it was a white one. "No," said the man from the signal box, "it was a red one." It was decided that they had better see the flag. When it was produced they found that it had been red, but the color had gone out of it. The reason so many souls are perishing today is because the Blood is not being preached.—*Christian Herald.*

Atonement—Extent of.

The apostles understood their commissions to be general and indiscriminate for "every creature"; so they received it from Him who laid the foundation of such an extensive ministration by tasting death for every man. Accordingly, they went forth on their commission, to preach the gospel to "all the world." They did not square their message by any human system of theology, nor measure their language to the lines of Procrustean creeds. They employed a dialect that traverses the length and breadth of the world. They did not tremble for such an unreserved exhibition of the ark and the mercy-seat. They could not bring themselves to stint the remedy which was prepared and intended to restore a dying world; nor would they cramp the bow which God had lighted up in the storm that threatened all mankind. —T. W. JENKYN.

Atonement—Necessity of.

The first sermon which he (Robert Hall) delivered at Cambridge, after he had assumed the office of pastor, was on the doctrine of the Atonement, and its practical tendencies. Immediately after the conclusion of the service one of the congregation, who had followed poor Mr. Robinson (his predecessor) through all his changes of sentiment, went into the vestry and said, "Mr. Hall, this preaching won't do for us; it will only suit a congregation of old women." "Do you mean my sermon, sir, or the doctrine?" "Your doctrine." "Why is it that the doctrine is fit only for old women?" "Because it may suit the musings of people tottering upon the brink of the grave, and who are eagerly seeking comfort." "Thank you, sir, for your concession. The doctrine will not suit people of any age, unless it be true, it is not fitted for old women alone, but is equally important at every age."—OLINTHUS GREGORY.

Atonement—Realizing The.

I once heard John McNeill say that of all the people in Jerusalem he thought Barabbas had the best idea of the atonement of Jesus Christ. "You will remember that he should have been crucified and Jesus released, but the order was exactly reversed. The door of the prison swings open and Barabbas is free, and as he comes out into the light of day all the people seem to be hurrying in one direction. He hears that Jesus of Nazareth is to be crucified. He stops a moment to think, and then he exclaims, 'Why, that is the man who is dying in my stead; I will go and see him.' He pushes his way out through the gate of the city and up the hillside until he reaches the surging mob about the cross. He stands in the outer circle a moment, and then pushes his way to the very inner circle, and stands so near that he can reach out his hand and touch the dying Saviour, and I can hear him say, 'I do not know who you are, but I know you are there in my stead.'" "And," said John Mc-Neill, "until you can give a better theory of the atonement, take that of Barabbas—Christ, your substitute dying in your place."—J. WILBUR CHAPMAN.

Atonement—Sheltered Under.

There is a legend that on that night of the Exodus a young Jewish maiden—the first-born of the family—was so troubled on her sick-bed that she could not sleep. "Father," she anxiously inquired, "are you sure that the blood is there?" He replied that he had ordered it to be sprinkled on the lintel. The restless girl will not be satisfied until her father has taken her up and carried her to the door to see for herself; and lo! the blood is not there! The father makes haste to put on his door the sacred token of protection, because the order has been neglected. The legend may be false; but it teaches a very weighty and solemn admonition to every sinful soul who may be near eternity and is not yet sheltered under the Atonement of Jesus Christ.—CUYLER.

Atonement—Sign of.

There is a day coming when the shed blood of the Lamb of God will be the only badge of honor. You may wear the square and compass, you may wear the triple link,

you may wear the woodman's ax, you may know every grip from the thumb and finger to the whole two hands, but none of these will answer in that day. God says: "When I see the blood, I will pass over you."— *Bible Messages.*

Atonement—Need of.

When I was a pastor in Chicago, a father had sent for a great physician from Australia. The papers said that his fee was twenty thousand dollars, besides all his expenses. He came to do something for the little daughter of the rich man. I do not know what was the matter with the child, but it was something serious because of what the father did about it. What is sin? I do not know, but I know it is very serious from what the Father did about it.—C. B. McAFEE.

Love—Atoning.

What is the atonement? That Christ gave God the right to be compassionate? That he came down to this world, and made a bargain, and agreed that he would suffer so much if God afterwards would exercise compassion and leniency towards men? Away with your shop logic! Away with your commercial theories! Go down among the moles and bats, and grope with such detestable notions of truth as that by agreement Christ came among men to suffer and give God a chance to be gracious! Over all these heresies of hell I lift up the glorious words, "God so loved the world that he gave his Son." Love before Christ came was the bow which sent that silver arrow into the world.— H. W. BEECHER.

Mediator, The.

During one of the journeys of Queen Victoria a little boy was desirous of seeing her. He determined to go direct to the castle where she was residing, and ask to see her. He was stopped at the gate by the sentry, who demanded what he wanted. "I want to see the Queen," he replied. The soldier laughed at the boy, and with the butt-end of his musket pushed him away, and told him to be off immediately, or he would shoot him. The boy turned to go away, and gave vent to his tears. He had not gone far when he was met by the Prince of Wales, who inquired why he was crying. "I want to see the Queen," replied the boy, "and that soldier won't let me." "Won't he?" said the Prince; "then come along with me, and I'll take you to the Queen." He accordingly took him by the hand and led him towards the castle. On passing the sentinel he, as usual, presented arms to the Prince, and the boy was terrified, and ran away, fearing that the soldier was going to shoot him. The Prince soon quieted his fears, and led him past the gates into the presence of Her Majesty. The Queen, with surprise, inquired of her son whom he had there; and upon being informed of what had happened, she laughed heartily, spoke kindly to her little visitor, and, to his great delight, dismissed him with a piece of money. As the Prince presented the boy to the Queen, so Christ presents us to His Father.—*Biblical Treasury.*

One Mediator.

The incident occurred in a city restaurant. The men at one of the tables were conversing on the subject of religion, and the argument grew so lively that it was impossible for those at the nearest tables not to hear. The argument was as to whether salvation was by works or grace. A Roman Catholic in the party insisted that no man can know he is saved until he dies, and as a final argument he exclaimed: "Well, all I can say is this. I have placed myself in the hands of my priest, and he is responsible for my salvation." At this point a gentleman arose from his table, and lifting his hat, said, "Gentlemen, I believe I am well known in the Law Courts and in this room. I could not help hearing the argument, and I feel bound to say that our Roman Catholic friend is quite logical in what he says. I also have placed myself in the hands of my Priest and He is responsible for my salvation. The mistake our friend has made is that he has chosen the wrong priest. My Priest is the Lord Jesus Christ."— *Evangelical Christian.*

Real Cleansing.

An English officer in India awoke one morning to find his body covered with leeches which, during the night, had found their way into his tent and fastened on his body. He was about to tear them off with his fingers when his native servant stopped him, and told him that such action would cause his death, because part of the animal would remain in the wounds and prove fatal through blood-poisoning. The servant prepared a bath, into which the officer plunged, and immediately the foul parasites dropped off and left the man uninjured, because not poisoned. This is the only cure for sins; the poison must come out. "The blood of Jesus Christ his Son cleanseth us from all sin."—*London Sunday School Times.*

Redemption—Price of.

During the holiday season when you were purchasing gifts, how often did you hear some one say, "Be sure to rub off the price mark?" Certainly you did not care to have the price paid for the article left visible. It was proper to erase it.

The believer in Christ is not his own. He was bought with a price. The price paid was the blood of Christ. There is no way to "rub off" or erase the price paid by Christ Jesus for his purchased possession. The blood bought are blood marked. The mark of the purchase price is on you and to remain. You need not be ashamed, O Christian, at the price paid for your redemption.— *Wonderful Word.*

Substitute.

One of our boys had committed an offense so bad that Mr. Gibb, his teacher, though rarely using the rod, felt it necessary to make an example of him. The punishment was to be publicly inflicted, "that others might fear." But when the culprit, who had only been a few days in our school, was stripped, he was such a living skeleton, that the master had not the heart to beat him. At his wit's end what to do—for the crime must be punished—it occurred to him to make such an appeal as, to compare small things to great, reminds us of the mystery of salvation, and the love of Him who "was wounded for our transgressions, and bruised for our iniquities, and by whose stripes we are healed." Turning to the others, "It goes," he said, "against my heart to lay a hand on that miserable creature. Will any one take his place, and he punished in his stead?" The words had hardly left his lips when, with tears of pity brimming in his eyes, a boy stepped bravely out, pulled his jacket off, and pushing the culprit aside, offered his own back and shoulders to the rod. A ragged-school boy, he was a hero in his way, presenting an example of courage and kindness, of sympathy and unselfishness, rare in schools—or anywhere else.—DR. GUTHRIE.

Sinner's Substitute.

Christ is the sinner's substitute. Dr. James M. Gray says: "In Dr. Bainbridge's 'Around the World Tour of Christian Mission,' written now twenty years ago, I suppose, there is this curiously interesting and suggestive incident: When in his journey the traveler had reached Tokio, Japan, intending to remain there some little time, he was waited upon one morning by an official, with this singular inquiry: 'Who stands for you?' Supposing it to be a question of passports, he presented his, but that was not what was wanted. He then offered some letters of introduction which he had, but they also were unsatisfactory, and the question was repeated, 'Who stands for you?' It was then explained that there was an ordinance in that city to the effect that no foreigner could take up his residence there for any length of time, unless he provided himself with a 'substitute.' And as a matter of fact there were natives who hired themselves out to foreigners for this purpose. If the foreigner transgressed any law the substitute suffered the penalty for it. If the penalty were even death, the substitute suffered death. Dr. Bainbridge secured a substitute, and was thereafter permitted to remain in peace and security as long as he chose."—*Our Hope.*

Twice Bought.

A little boy made a boat, sailed it down the stream, and lost it. Some time after he saw it in a shop. The man would not give it to him unless he paid the price, which he did. As he carried it home he said, "Now you are twice mine! First I made you, and then I bought you!"—*Record of Christian Work.*

Vicarious Suffering.

Stanley, in one of his books on African travel, tells of the crime of Uledi, his native coxswain, and what came of it. Uledi was deservedly popular for his ability and courage, but having robbed his master, a jury of his fellows condemned him to receive "a terrible flogging." Then uprose his brother Shumari, who said, "Uledi has done very wrong; but no one can accuse me of wrong-doing. Now, mates, let me take half the whipping. I will cheerfully endure it for the sake of my brother." Scarcely had he finished when another arose, and said, "Uledi has been the father of the boat, boys. He has many times risked his life to save others; and he is my cousin; and yet he ought to be punished. Shumari says he will take half the punishment; and now let me take the other half, and let Uledi go free."—B. J. Gibbon.

BACKSLIDING

Backsliders—Afflictions of.

Like as if a sheep stray from his fellows, the shepherd sets his dog after it, not to devour it, but to bring it back again: even so our heavenly Shepherd, if any of his sheep disobey him, he sets his dog of affliction after us to bring us home to a consideration of our duty towards him. His dogs are poverty, sickness, death, war, loss of goods or friends, etc.—CAWDRAY.

Backsliding—Gradual.

Some time ago, two ministers were walking along the banks of a river, when they came to a tree which had been blown down in a recent gale. It was a mighty, noble tree, tall and substantial, with large outspreading roots and ample foliage. It must have been the growth of the greater part of a century; and any one who had seen it would have said there was no cause why it should not have stood a century longer. Approaching to examine it, they found it had been snapped off just above the roots; and, on looking still closer, found that there was only an outer shell of sound wood, and the heart was rotten. Unnoticed, the decay had been going on for years. "Do you know," said Mr. —— to his companion, "that a tree never breaks off in this way, unless there has been previous decay?"—"A very suggestive lesson," was the answer, "for you and me, and for your people and mine. Is it not so with the falls of many of the members of our churches? Men seldom fall all at once into notorious, flagrant sin."—BOWES.

Backsliding—Guard Against.

Among the prisoners taken captive at Waterloo, there was a Highland piper. Napoleon, struck with his mountain dress and sinewy limbs, asked him to play on his instrument, which is said to sound so delightfully in the mountains and glens in Scotland. "Play a pibroch," said Napoleon; and the Highlander played. "Play a march"; it was done. "Play a retreat."—"Na, na," said the Highlander, "I never learned to play a retreat."

Backsliding—Punishment of.

The old shepherd who offered prayer in a Welsh revival meeting put it exactly right when he lamented his backslidings in these words: "Lord, I got among the thorns and briars, and was scratched and torn and bleeding; but, Lord, it is only fair to say that it was not on thy ground; I had wandered out of thy pasture."—*The Epworth Herald.*

Difficulties—Overcoming.

If you will row down stream the water will not bubble around you a particle: it will make your passage very easy. But now turn about and go up stream, and see how the force of the current heaps the water about you. So long as a man is content to go down stream in life, and does not attempt to go up stream, he goes easily; but let him undertake to go up stream for the sake of a higher life, and see if on every side he does not find difficulties to be overcome and trials to be borne. Yet, if he perseveres, by and by so many of them will be mastered and he will have gained such momentum that his career will be, comparatively speaking, joyous, though it may not be easy.—H. W. BEECHER.

Heroism—Faulty.

There is an old story in the Greek annals, of a soldier under Antigonus who had a disease about him, an extremely painful one, likely to bring him soon to the grave. Always first in the ranks was this soldier, and in the hottest part of the fray; he was always to be seen leading the van, the bravest of the brave, because his pain prompted him to fight that he might forget it; and he feared not death because he knew that in any case he had not long to live. Antigonus, who greatly admired the valour of his soldier, finding out that he suffered from a disease, had him cured by one of the most eminent physicians of the day, but alas! from that moment the warrior was absent from the front of the battle. He now sought his ease, for, as he remarked to his companions, he had something worth living for—health, home, family, and other comforts, and he would not risk his life now as aforetime.—C. H. SPURGEON.

Joy Bells.

There is a very beautiful story told of a king who, when he came to his throne a young man, had a silver bell made and placed in a high tower of his palace. Then the announcement was set forth that whenever the king was happy his subjects would know it by the ringing of this bell. It was never to be rung except when the king was perfectly happy, and then by no hand but his own. Days passed into weeks, and weeks into months, and the months into years; but no sound of the bell rang out either day or night to tell that the king was happy. At last the king, grown old and grey in his palace, lay on his death-bed. His weeping subjects gathered around him, and he learned how through all the years his people had loved him; and then he was happy, and in his joy, with dying hands, he rang out the silver bell. How many years of wasted happiness because the king did not come to know and appreciate the love of his people! The little story may suggest to us a still greater loss in ourselves. Only the consciousness of God's love can make us perfectly happy. Many people go through life from childhood to youth, from youth to manhood, from manhood to age, and the lines of care deepen in their faces, and the silver bell of happiness never rings out, because all the while they are getting further from God, and there is no consciousness of that Divine love which alone can give perfect happiness and peace to the human heart.—L. A. BANKS.

Moral Bankruptcy.

There are two chief reasons why at this time our rich, splendid America is the most criminal country in the world. The first is, our people have not rendered unto Caesar that which is his due—they have not upheld the authority and sanctity of the law of the land, as faithful and obedient citizens. The second is, they have not rendered unto God that which is his due— they have not recognized the importance of religion in our national life. The result has been a sort of moral bankruptcy, an increase of crime and a falling off of spirituality!—*Christian Herald.*

Retreat—Difficulties of.

Disheartened by the extraordinary dangers and difficulties of their enterprise, a Roman army lost courage, and resolved on a retreat. The general reasoned with his soldiers. Expostulating with them, he appealed to their love of country, to their honor, and to their oaths. By all that could revive a fainting heart he sought to animate their courage and shake their resolution. Much they trusted, they admired, they loved him, but his appeals were all in vain. They were not to be moved; and carried away, as by panic, they faced round to retreat. At this juncture they were forcing a mountain pass, and had just cleared a gorge where the road, between two stupendous rocks on one side and the foaming river on the other, was but a foot-path, broad enough for the step of a single man. As a last resort he laid himself down there, saying, "If you will retreat, it is over this body you go, trampling me to death beneath your feet." No foot advanced. The flight was arrested. His soldiers could face the foe, but could not mangle beneath their feet one who loved them, and had often led their ranks to victory—sharing like a common soldier all the hardships of the campaign, and ever foremost in the fight. The sight was one to inspire them with decision. Hesitating no longer to advance, they wheeled round to resume their march, deeming it better to meet sufferings, and endure even death itself, than trample under foot their devoted and patriot leader. Their hearts recoiled from such an outrage. . . . A more touching spectacle bars our return. Jesus, as it were, lays Himself down on our path; nor can any become backsliders, and return to the practice and pleasure of sin, without trampling Him under their feet. These, Paul's very words, call up a spectacle from which every lover of Christ should recoil with horror: "He," says that Apostle, "who despised Moses' law died without mercy; . . . of how much sorer punishment, suppose ye, shall he be thought worthy who hath trodden under foot the Son of God?"—GUTHRIE.

Crisis Hour.

A small vessel was nearing the Steep Holmes, in the Bristol Channel. The captain stood on the deck, his watch in his hand, his eye fixed on it. A terrible tempest had driven them onward. No one dared to ask, "Is there hope?" Every moment they were hurried nearer to the sullen rock which knew no mercy, and on which many ill-fated vessels had foundered. Still the captain stood motionless, speechless, his watch in his hand. "We are lost!" was the conviction of many around him. Suddenly his eye glanced across the sea; he stood erect; another moment and he cried, "Thank God! we are saved—the tide has turned; in one minute more we should have been on the rocks!"

Environment and Character.

You have seen a lily floating in the black sullied waters of a foul bog in the country. All about it are foulness and impurity; but amid all the vileness the lily is pure as the white snowflakes that fall from the winter clouds. It floats on the surface of the stained waters, but never takes a stain. It ever holds its pure face towards God's blue sky, and pours its fragrance all about it, like the incense from the censer of a vestal priestess. So it is possible for a true soul to live in this sinful world, keeping itself unsullied, and breathing out the fragrance of love.—J. R. MILLER.

Blessings—Unrealized.

A yacht was cruising the isles of Scotland, when a gale caught the frail craft off a perilous shore. The skipper made for a harbor, leagues away. At length she swung into smooth water, and they dropped anchor, and, turning into their berths, went peacefully to sleep. In the morning the owner came on deck and surveyed the scene—a little haven, girt about by dark purple mountains. Looking toward the entrance, he saw a narrow channel, with sharp rocks jutting here and there, all awash with boiling surf. To think of passing that way! The least swerving of the tiller, and those jagged teeth would catch the frail bark and grind it to splinters, and every life would perish. Turning to the skipper, he exclaimed: "Did we—did we pass there in the darkness?" This is a parable of life. We know something of the goodness and mercy that have followed us all our days, but we shall never realize fully the debt we owe to our unseen Guide until we are safely within the harbor.—*Christ's Ambassadors.*

Believer's Strength.

A Christian man was traveling on a Continental train, and was the sole occupant of a compartment, save for a young man who was reading an English newspaper. This young Englishman, for so he turned out to be, was also a Christian; but so weak was his faith and so many his temptations, that he said he did not think he would be able to stand a week longer. The man took from his pocket a Bible and penknife, and said, "Sir, I will make this penknife stand up on the cover of this Bible in spite of the rocking of the train." The young man, thinking this was some conjuring trick, watched the proceeding with interest, saying, "I am afraid that it won't be easy to do that, sir." "But," said the man, "I am doing it." "Oh but you are holding it," retorted his fellow-passenger. "Why, of course. Did you ever hear of a penknife standing up on its end without being held up?" "I see," was the young man's comment, "I see. You mean to teach me that I cannot stand unless Christ holds me. Thank you for reminding me of that."—*Christian Herald.*

Refuge,—Seeking.

Some parts of the coast of the Isle of Wight abound in caves. In one of these was found the body of a poor Frenchman. He had been a prisoner, and had escaped from prison, and for a long time concealed himself there, probably in the hope of escaping by some vessel which might pass. Many a weary day passed, however, and he still remained a prisoner, till at last not venturing to leave his retreat, he perished from want. So it is with those who seek refuge in insufficient places. "They make lies their refuge, and under falsehood hide themselves." They find out their mistake when it is too late.—C. S. BOWES.

Security—The Christian's.

Were you ever at sea in a storm, when the ship reeled to and fro like a drunken man, and struggling, as for life in the arms of death, now rose to the top of the billow, and now plunged into the trough of the sea? Partially infected with others terror, did you ever leave shrieking women and pale men below, to seek the deck and look your danger bravely in the face? In such circumstances I know nothing so reassuring as . . . the calm confidence that sits on the brow of that weather-beaten man who with iron strength leans upon the wheel and steers our ship through the roaring billows. Such, only much higher, is the confidence we draw from the confidence of God, as expressed in the words, "I have spoken, and I will do it."—GUTHRIE.

Bible—A Personal.

I was once called to visit a dying lady, in the city of Philadelphia, of an English family. She and her husband were in a boarding house there. I spent much time with her, knelt often in prayer with her, and with great delight. Her husband was an Atheist, an English Atheist —a cold-hearted English Atheist. There is no such being beside him on the face of the globe. That was her husband. On the day in which that sweet Christian woman died she put her hand under the pillow and pulled out a little beautiful well-worn English Bible. She brought out that sweet little Bible, worn and thumbed and moistened with tears. She called her husband, and he came; and she said, "Do you know this little book?" and he answered, "It is your Bible." Replied she, "It is my Bible; it has been everything to me. It has converted, strengthened, cheered, and saved me. Now I am going to Him that gave it to me, and I shall want it no more; open your hands"—and she put it in between his hands and pressed his two hands together. "My dear husband, do you know what I am doing?" "Yes, dear; you are giving me your Bible." "No, darling, I am giving you your Bible, and God has sent me to give you this sweet book before I die. Put it in your hands; now put it in your bosom— will you keep it there? Will you read it for me?" "I will, my dear."
I placed this dear lady, dead, in the tomb behind my church. Perhaps three weeks afterward that big Englishman came to my study weeping profusely. "Oh, my friend," said he, "my friend, I have found what she meant—I have found what she meant! it is my Bible; every word in it was written for me. I read it over day by day; I read it over night by night; I bless God it

is my Bible. Will you take me into your church where she was?" "With all my heart"—and that proud, wordly, hostile man, hating this blessed Bible, came, with no arguments, with no objection, with no difficulties suggested, with no questions to unravel, but binding it upon his heart of memory and love. It was God's message of direct salvation to his soul, as if there were not another Bible in Philadelphia, and an angel from heaven had brought him this.—Tyng.

Bible—A Useless.

Phillips Brooks used to tell the story of some savages, to whom was given a sun-dial. So desirous were they to honor it and keep it sacred that they housed it in, and built a roof over it. Is this the way we treat the Bible? It is not too sacred for daily use. Learn to use it. Let God in on your life.—*The Sunday School Chronicle.*

Bible and the Holy Spirit.

In the diamond-fields of South Africa a diamond was found, celebrated lately under the title of fly-stone; placed under a magnifying-glass, you see enclosed in all its brilliancy a little fly, with body, wings, and eyes, in the most perfect state of preservation. How it came there no one knows, but no human skill can take it out. So in Holy Scripture the Spirit of God is found in a place from which no power of man can remove it.—M'Ewan.

Bible—Best Recommendation.

A youth seeking for a place came to New York City, and, on inquiring at a counting-room if they wished a clerk, was told that they did not. He then spoke of the recommendation he had, one of which was from a highly respectable citizen. In turning over his carpet-bag to find his letters, a book rolled out on the floor. "What book is that?" said the merchant. "It is the Bible, sir," was the reply. "And what are you going to do with that book in New York?" The lad looked seriously into the merchant's face, and replied, "I promised my mother I would read it every day; and I shall do so." The merchant at once took him into his service.

Bible—Constant Reading.

I have for many years made it a practice to read through the Bible once a year. My custom is to read four or five chapters every morning immediately after rising from my bed. It employs about an hour of my time, and seems to me the most suitable manner of beginning the day. In what light soever we regard the Bible, whether with reference to revelation, to history, or to morality, it is an invaluable and inexhaustible mine of knowledge and virtue.—JOHN QUINCY ADAMS.

Bible—Freedom In.

A European who had been seized and imprisoned by an Abyssinian king was allowed to go at large, but a heavy iron fetter on each ankle kept him from making his escape. A European traveler saw and pitied him, but dared not openly help him, as he was watched by the king's officers. He was, however, allowed to give the captive a book. The poor prisoner was disappointed. He did not want books, and would have been much better pleased with a gift of food or clothing. The book was laid aside and forgotten. Three years afterwards, in an idle moment, he examined the book. There was something hard in the back of it. He pulled it out, and, behold, it was

a file! It was the thing of all others he most needed. He made his way to the woods, filed off his fetters, and in a few days had reached the coast and was safe from pursuit. He could not forgive himself for having endured those three years of slavery. If he had only looked in the book before, he might have been free. So men neglect the Bible, which would set them free from the slavery of sin.—*The Christian Herald.*

Bible—Half Read.

A certain wayward young man ran away from home and was not heard of for years. In some way, hearing that his father had just died, he returned home and was kindly received by his mother. The day came for the reading of the will; the family were all gathered together, and the lawyer commenced to read the document. To the great surprise of all present the will told in detail of the wayward career of the runaway son. The boy in anger arose, stamped out of the room, left the house, and was not heard from for three years. When eventually he was found he was informed that the will, after telling of his waywardness, had gone on to bequeath to him $15,000. How much sorrow he would have been saved if he had only heard the reading through! Thus many people only half read the Bible and turn from it dissatisfied. The old Book says: "The wages of sin is death," yea, verily, but it says more, it says, "but the gift of God is eternal life." —*The Expositor.*

Bible—Illustrations in the.

It has pressed into its service the animals of the forest, the flowers of the field, the stars of heaven, all the elements of nature. The lion spurning the sands of the desert, the wild roe leaping over the mountains, the lamb led in silence to the slaughter, the goat speeding to the wilderness, the rose blossoming in Sharon, the lily drooping in the valley, the apple-tree bowing under its fruit, the great rock shadowing a weary land, the river gladdening the dry place, the moon and the morning star, Carmel by the sea, and Tabor among the mountains, the dew from the womb of the morning, the rain upon the mown grass, the rainbow encompassing the landscape; the light, God's shadow; the thunder, his voice; the wind and the earthquake, his footsteps; all such varied objects are made as if naturally designed from their creation to represent him to whom the book and all its emblems point. Thus the quick spirit of the book has ransacked creation to lay its treasures on Jehovah's altar, united the innumerable rays of a far-streaming glory on the little hill Calvary, and woven a garland for the bleeding brow of Immanuel, the flowers of which have been culled from the garden of a universe.— G. GILFILLAN.

Bible—Inspiration of.

Conspicuous in John Randolph's library was a Family Bible. Surrounding it were many books, some for and others against its truthfulness as an inspired revelation. One day Mr. Randolph had a clergyman as his guest, and the Family Bible became a topic of conversation. The eccentric orator said, "I was raised by a pious mother (God bless her memory!), who taught me the Christian religion in all its requirements. But, alas! I grew up an infidel—if not an infidel complete, yet a decided deist. But when I became a man, in this as well as in political and all other matters, I re-solved to examine for myself, and never to pin my faith to any other man's sleeve. So I bought a Bible; I pored over it; I examined it carefully. I sought and procured those books for and against it; and when my labors were ended I came to this irresistible conclusion: The Bible is true. It would have been as easy for a mole to have written Sir Isaac Newton's treatise in Optics as for uninspired men to have written the Bible."—*Christian Age.*

Bible—Joy in.

A lay preacher wrote to his friend. The letter was sealed but he wished to add a word of cheer, so on the address side of the envelope he wrote, "Be of good cheer, brother." When the man received the letter, he found that the post-office authorities had stamped against the word of counsel this intimation, "Contrary to Regulations." How many Christians read this word of Christ as if it were, "Be of good cheer, brother —Contrary to Regulations!" The light of His face is joy, and it is in harmony with every rule of the Christian life to dwell in it.—*Northfield Echoes.*

Bible—Life Giving.

In making excavations in Pompeii a workman came upon an ancient spring, the water of which bubbled up at once, clear and sparkling. For centuries it had been buried beneath the ashes of the volcano. But the moment it was opened it poured forth streams as cool and copious as ever. So it is with the word of God. It may have been hidden, buried away, unread, giving no blessing or refreshing. But the moment it is opened again, and its words come to our hearts, they bring their own refreshing and reviving.

Bible—Misused.

How wretched a spectacle is a garden into which cloven-footed beasts have entered! That which yesterday was fragrant and shone all over with crowded beauty, is to-day rooted, despoiled, trampled, and utterly devoured; and all over the ground you shall find but the rejected cuds of flowers and leaves and forms that have been champed for their juices and then rejected. Such to me is the Bible, when the pragmatic prophecy—monger and the swinish utilitarian have toothed its fruits and craunched its blossoms. —*Beecher.*

Bible—Moody's.

Repentance—A change of mind.
New mind about God.
Conversion—A change of life.
New life for God.
Regeneration—A change of nature.
New heart for God.
Justification—A change of state.
New standing for God.
Adoption—A change of family.
New relationship toward God.
Sanctification—A change of service.
Separation unto God.
Glorification—A change of place.
New condition with God.
—*Found in flyleaf of Moody's Bible.*

Bible—Prejudiced Against.

It is related of Napoleon that when Marshal Duroc, an avowed infidel, was once telling a very improbable story, giving it as his opinion that it was true, the Emperor quietly remarked, "There are some men who are capable of believing everything but the Bible."— *King's Business.*

Bible Reading.

A great many have a superstitious feeling about reading the Bible. Men carry texts as Indians carry amulets, with the superstitious idea that God will bless them to their good. The mere reading of the Bible, or carrying of texts, will not do you any good. A man may own a farm, and yet go to the poorhouse. His land must be cultivated, or it will do him no good. —H. W. BEECHER.

Bible—The Newspaper.

A story is told of a minister who taught an old man in his parish to read. He proved a proficient scholar. After the teaching had come to an end the minister was not able to call at the cottage for some time, and when he did he only found the wife at home. "How's John?" said he. "He's canny, sir," said the wife. "How does he get on with his reading?" "Nicely, sir." "Ah! I suppose he will read his Bible very comfortably now." "Bible, sir! Bless you! he was out of the Bible and into the newspaper long ago." There are many other persons who, like this old man, have long been out of the Bible and into the newspaper. They have forsaken the fountain of Living Waters, and have gone about among muddy pools and stagnant morasses to seek something which might slake their thirst.—*Clerical Library.*

Bible—The Open.

After the battle before Richmond had been over several days a man was found dead with his hand on the open Bible. The summer insects had taken the flesh from the hand, and there was nothing but the skeleton left; but the skeleton fingers lay on the open page, and on this passage—"Yea, though I walk through the valley of the shadow of death, I will fear no evil; Thy rod and Thy staff they comfort me." Well, the time will come when all the fine novels we have on our bedroom shelf will not interest us, and all the good histories and all the exquisite essays will do us no good. There will be one Book, perhaps its cover worn out and its leaf yellow with age, under whose flash we shall behold the opening gates of heaven.—TALMAGE.

Bible—Wisely Using the.

Once the clumsy camel driver of a medical missionary caused a lot of tabloid medicines to be thrown from the camel's back and scattered over the sands. They were all mixed up, could not be separated, and so were left lying on the ground. But one of the quack native doctors gathered them up, and some years later the medical missionary called on him and found on a shelf a large bottle labeled "Assorted Pills." "These," said he, "are more sought than any of my drugs. I give them only to patients whose cases I do not understand." This is a parable of Bible study. Too often we go to our Bibles as that native doctor went to his bottle of "Assorted Pills." What wonder that the Bible, used in that way, has no healing virtue for our souls! The Bible is a complete pharmacopœia. It contains a cure for every ill. But it is not to be treated as a book of necromacy.— *Christian Herald.*

God's Bread and Man's Theories.

An old negro was sent to the hospital, and one of the nurses put a thermometer in his mouth to take his temperature. Presently, when the doctor made his rounds, he said: "Well, Mose, have you had any nourishment?" "A lady done gimme a piece of glass to suck, boss,

but I'se still powerful hungry."— *The Pathfinder.*

Gospel—Incarnate.

One night, just before the late Captain Bickel was retiring to rest, he met at the deckhouse door a ruffian who had been wonderfully converted on one of these voyages. Mr. Bickel was very tired, but he had a little talk with the man. He asked him if he would take a Bible to a certain man on the morrow. He shook his head. "No, no, Captain; he does not need that." "But why not?" "It won't do him any good." "But why?" "Because it is too soon. That is your Bible, and, thank God! it is now mine; but it is not his Bible." "What, do you mean by that?" "Why, simply that he has another Bible; you are his Bible; he is watching you. As you fail, Christ fails. As you live Christ, so Christ is revealed to him." Writing of this incident, Captain Bickel said: "Friends, I did not sleep that night. I had been called a thief, liar, foreign spy, traitor, devil, in public and private, and had not flinched; but to face this! 'As you live, so Christ lives' —in that man's soul, in that house, in that village, in four hundred villages. As you fail to live Christ, Christ is crucified again."—*Men and Missions.*

God's Word—Obscuring.

A man once visited Robert Hall to make exception to some statement which the preacher had made in his sermon. It was evident that the man was in the grip and bondage of the love of money. When Hall had gauged the man's character he took a half-sovereign out of his pocket, and, opening the Bible, pointed to the word "God." "Can you see that?" said Robert Hall.

"Certainly," replied the man. Then the preacher took the half-sovereign and placed it over the word. "Can you see it now?" he asked. The man immediately understood the symbol, and through it was led unto the light. Gold hid God. Money blocked the vision. Love of money shut out the face of the Father.— *The Sunday Circle.*

Gospel Mirror.

There is in the Church of St. Peter's at Rome a very wonderful painting, but it is so far up in the heights of the great dome that the eye is unable to discern its marvelous beauty and significance. To overcome this difficulty, an ingenious arrangement was conceived by the idea of placing a large mirror near the floor, and there reflected in that mirror can be easily seen the great masterpiece. So, in like manner, the glory of God as seen in the heavenly heights by celestial beings we could not as mortals behold; but God has given us a manifestation, the epiphany of Himself, in His beloved Son, who has brought down in the mirror of the gospel the glory of the blessed God; and as we gaze upon His face in the mirror of the Word, the Holy Spirit transforms our lives into the same image from glory to glory.— T. R. COLEMAN.

Gospel—Substitutes for the.

Did you ever hear a man say: "I was an outcast, a wretched inebriate, a disgrace to my race, and a nuisance to the world, until I began to study mathematics, and learned the multiplication table, but since that time I have been happy as the day is long. I feel like saying all the time; my soul is full of triumph and peace?" Did you ever hear a man ascribe his salvation from intemperance and sin and vice to the multiplication table or the science of mathematics or geology? But thousands will tell you: "I was wretched; I was lost; I broke my poor mother's heart; I was ruined, reckless, helpless, homeless, hopeless, until I heard the words of the Bible!"—*Presbyterian Record.*

Gospel the Power of God.

Some years ago a woman delivered a lecture in Lancashire against Christianity, in which she declared that the Gospel narrative of the life of Christ is a "myth." One of the mill-hands who listened to her obtained leave to ask a question. "The question," said he, "I want to ask the lady is this: 'Thirty years ago I was a curse to this town, and everybody shrank from me that had any respect for himself. I often tried to do better, but could not succeed. The teetotalers got hold of me, but I broke the pledge so often that they said it was no use trying me any longer. Then the police got hold of me, and I was taken before the magistrate, and the wardens of the prison all tried me in vain. Then Christ took hold of me, touched my heart, and made me a new man. And now I am an honored and respected fellow-worker in gospel and Sunday-school work with many dear to me. And I ask, if Christ is a myth, how comes it to pass that that myth is stronger than all the others put together?'" The lady was silent. "Nay, miss," said he, "say what you will, the gospel is the power of God unto salvation."—*Anti-infidel.*

Perverting the Gospel.

If, at the tent door, the Arab offers to the thirsty passer-by a cup of water, clear, cool, and sparkling in the cup, but in which he has cleverly concealed a painful and deadly poison, he would deserve and receive the anathema of all honest men. Much more terrible shall be the doom of him who, pretending friendship with the souls of men, and offering them in their need, instead of the pure water of life the deadly poison of false doctrine, shall bring down upon himself the righteous and unerring anathema of God. —R. Brewin.

Scriptures, Foolish Handling of.

The Bible is used as a book of magic. Many open it at random, expecting to be guided by the first passage that they see, as Peter was told to open the mouth of the first fish that came up, and he would find in it a piece of money. A missionary of high standing with whom I am acquainted was cured of this form of superstition by consulting the Bible on an important matter of Christian duty, and the passage that met his gaze was, "Hell from beneath is moved to meet thee at thy coming."—J. M. Buckley.

Simplifying Safety.

No one who is in an automobile even a short time can fail to notice the endless variety of safety signals put up to guide or warn motorists and other users of the highways. They are of all sizes, all colors, all styles of types, and they are stuck up in every imaginable place. Moreover, their phrasing is constantly varied, and the laws back of them have not even the semblance of uniformity or consistency. In an hour a motorist will pass through a dozen towns, each with a different speed limit, from ten miles an hour to go as you please. During the hour he will pass hundreds of safety signals, no two alike, probably, and no two emanating from the same source.

It is no wonder that the average driver, confused and angry, gives to these signals only a small part of the heed that proper signals would receive from him.

Now, however, the Public Safety division of the National Safety Council has decided to attempt the standardizing of all safety signs in all the streets and roads of the nation, this as part of a country-wide effort to lessen the immense number of highway accidents. It is high time that this effort was made.

And while they are unifying the safety signals on the highways, would that they might do the same thing for the signals shown on the spiritual highways of life! Here the multiplicity of signals and their enormous diversity is endlessly confusing. Books, magazines, papers, orators, statesmen and politicians, all are advising us, all are warning us, and the counsels of no two are alike. One only gives unified and consistent advice, and He is the Wonderful Counselor. One book only is an unfailing safety signal, and that book is the Bible. Christ and the Bible! these are the standard warnings and guides for all the roads of time and eternity!—Amos R. Wells.

The Foolish Apothecary.

Once upon a time there was an apothecary, the only drug-seller in a certain country neighborhood. He was a lazy fellow, and, as he had bought the establishment from another druggist, he had actually never looked over his stock to see what it contained. He was acquainted with a few of the bottles, and when the farmers came in for their remedies, if he did not know where to find what was asked for, he would persuade them to take their doses from one of the bottles he knew about. That community, therefore, got pretty well dosed with quinine and camphor and ipecac and a few other drugs, and the doctors grumbled, and the people died.

Well, one day the apothecary's oldest son was taken suddenly and violently ill, and the doctor that was called in declared, with a very sober face, that nothing on earth could save the lad's life except a certain rare medicine. There was some of it in the stock of the late druggist, he was sure, and he had no doubt it had not been used up; but where was it? Almost frantic, the foolish apothecary turned his store upside down, fairly throwing the bottles here and there in his anxiety to hit upon the right one.

And while he was hunting, his boy died.

You think there never was so foolish an apothecary? Probably not. But there are just as foolish men and women by the hundred thousand. For the Bible is our pharmacy, crammed by the Great Physician with whatever is needed for a sick soul going down to death. And how few of us have even read it clear through to find out what is in it, to learn, as it were, the names on the outside of the bottles, so that, for a case of doubt or sorrow or of trouble of any kind, we can put our hands at once upon the right remedy! Alas, how few!—Amos R. Wells.

Truth-Seekers.

"Why did God not make the Bible so plain that every one could understand it?" asked one. "If God made coal as fuel, why did he not put it on the top of the ground instead of burying it deep underneath the surface?" was the reply.—*Sunday at Home*.

Unknown—Perils of the.

The old discoverers who sailed into unknown seas must have felt a peculiar pleasure in their daring undertakings. Spreading the canvas to the wind, they ventured out to the mysterious ocean in search of new countries. But their delight was mingled with anxiety and fear; for, possessing no charts, they knew not what perils awaited them in their bold endeavor—what rocks and sandbanks might be in their way, or what monsters they might meet with in the lands they hoped to discover. The search for new truth also has its delights. It is pleasant to leave the tame, unromantic shores of common belief, and to start on a voyage of discovery over the boundless ocean of intellectual speculation. But there is danger also in this enterprise. The dreary land of skepticism, and chaos of No-faith, and the black regions of despair, are somewhere out in those seas; and many have ventured there who never returned.—Thomas Jones.

BROTHERHOOD

Brother—A Real.

"Behind the (Greek) word which is translated 'lowliness' is our word 'tapestry,' and I think I shall not be far away from the apostle's mind when I say that he counsels us to lay our life down like a soft tapestry carpet—in kindly thoughts and gracious sympathies and helpful services, in order that the weary, bruised feet of other people may find ease and comfort on the road. For some of the ways of life are very rough and flinty, and the sharp, jagged edges of circumstances cut the feet most sorely, and 'going' is for many people a matter of ceaseless pain. It is the blessed privilege of Christians to lay a soft surface on the roads, by spreading over them the graciousness of tender compassion, so stooping, that other pilgrims can 'walk over us,' and so forget the hardships of the way."— J. H. JOWETT.

Brother—Self-Denying.

While Dr. James H. Franklin, a foreign missionary of the Baptist Church, was traveling across the continent, an old Negro-porter on his car asked him, "Say, boss, is you a preachah?" "Yes, how did you guess that?" "Oh, Ah just saw a book in your seat, and Ah thought you must be a preachah. Ah was almost a preachah myself once." "Why did you give it up?" "Well, sah, Ah's got a young brothah, and when Ah told him Ah wanted to be a preachah, why, he'd been converted and preached hisself, boss. Well, sah, we talked it ovah, and decided he'd go ahead to college and be a preachah, and Ah'd come back on the road and work, so Ah did, boss; and every month Ah sent him money and he went to college." "And did he finally become a preacher?" "Yes, sah, in Africy.

They call him Bishop Scott." "Bishop Scott!" Dr. Franklin gazed with amazement at the noble figure before him. Bishop Scott is said to be the first colored preacher whom the Methodist Episcopal Church made a bishop. Dr. Franklin had often read of his heroic life among his people in Africa. Later Dr. Franklin met Bishop Scott in a little town of Georgia. After the service he went up and shook hands with him. "Have you a brother who is a porter on a sleeping car, Bishop?" he asked him. Then he told of the incident on the train. "Yes," said the Bishop, and the tears ran down his cheeks, "he's my brother, and may God bless him. I owe everything to him."— *The Heart and Life.*

Brotherly Spirit.

An Austrian officer arrived one day in a town in Germany celebrated for its baths. He seemed very near his end, and, in consequence, he was refused admission at several hotels, whose proprietors feared he would die on their hands. When he presented himself at the last hotel at which he could hope to get rooms, he received the same answer: there were none vacant.

A gentleman living in the hotel heard the landlord's answer, and noted the condition of the applicant. "This officer is my near relation," he said, stepping forward, "and I shall share my room with him. He may have my bed and I can sleep on the sofa." The landlord felt obliged to consent, and the invalid was carried to the room of his newly-found friend. When he had recovered strength enough to speak, he said: "May I ask your name, my kind friend? How are you related to me?—on what side?"

"I am related to you," was the reply, "through our Lord Jesus

Christ, for I have learned from Him that my neighbor is my brother."

This stranger brother maintained the character he thus claimed. He nursed his guest tenderly, and carried to him with his own hand the first glass of medical water, and sought, while thus ministering to his body, to lead him to Jesus, the physician of the soul.

Burden—Bearing Anothers.

Some years ago a war raged in India between the English and a native monarch, Tippoo Saib. On one occasion several English officers were taken prisoners, among them one named Baird. One day a native officer brought in fetters to be put on each of the prisoners, the wounded not excepted. Baird had been severely wounded, and was suffering from pain and weakness. A gray-haired officer said to the native official, "You do not think of putting chains upon that wounded young man?" "There are just as many pairs of fetters as there are captives," was the answer, "and every pair must be worn." "Then," said the officer, "put two pairs on me; I will wear his as well as my own." Baird lived to regain his freedom, lived to take that very city, but the generous friend died in prison.—GRAY.

Enemies—Forgiving.

Archbishop Cranmer appeared almost alone in the higher classes as the friend of truth in evil times, and a plot was formed to take away his life. The providence of God, however, so ordered it that the papers which would have completed the plan were intercepted and traced to their authors, one of whom lived in the archbishop's family, and the other he had greatly served. He took these men apart in his palace, and told them that some persons in his confidence had disclosed his secrets, and even accused him of heresy. They loudly censured such villainy, and declared the traitors to be worthy of death; one of them adding, that if an executioner was wanted he would perform the office himself. Struck with their perfidy, after lifting up his voice to heaven, lamenting the depravity of man, and thanking God for his preservation, he produced their letters, and inquired if they knew them. They now fell on their knees, confessed their crimes, and implored forgiveness. Cranmer mildly expostulated with them on the evil of their conduct, forgave them, and never again alluded to their treachery. His forgiveness of injuries was so well known, that it became a byword, "Do my lord of Canterbury an ill-turn, and you make him your friend for ever."—*Moral and Religious Anecdotes.*

Co-Laborers.

In the establishment of one of our great goldsmiths is a vast iron safe with many locks, containing immense treasure. But no one person can open that chest; the keys are in the hands of many trustees, and only by their concurrence can the hidden wealth be made manifest. Thus it is in the natural and in the spiritual world, the wealth of divine blessing can be reached only through the brotherhood of saints. —W. L. WATKINSON.

Co-Laborers.

When Martin Luther set out on the work which shook the world his friend Myconius expressed sympathy. "But," he said, "I can best help where I am. I will remain and pray while you toil." Myconius prayed day by day, but as he prayed he began to feel uncomfortable. One night he had a dream. He thought the Saviour himself approached and showed him his hands and feet. He saw the fountain in which he had been cleansed from sin. Then looking earnestly into his eyes the Saviour said, "Follow me." The Lord took him to a lofty mountain and pointed eastward. Looking in that direction Myconius saw a plain stretching away to the horizon. It was dotted with white sheep—thousands and thousands of them. One man was trying to shepherd them all. The man was Luther. The Saviour pointed westward. Myconius saw a great field of standing corn. One reaper was trying to harvest it all. The lonely laborer was spent and exhausted, but still he persisted in his task. Myconius recognized in the solitary reaper his old friend Luther. "It is not enough," said Myconius when he awakened, "that I should pray. The sheep must be shepherded; the fields must be reaped. Here am I; send me." And he went out and shared his old friend's labors.—F. W. Boreham.

Friend—A Protecting.

A blind man tapped the pavement with his stick, in New York, near the Pennsylvania Station. He felt about the curb at the busy crossing, and shouted confidently: "How about it, Charley?" The traffic officer in the middle of the avenue looked up, saw the blind man, held up his hand, and blew his whistle. "All right, Ben," he called, smiling. And the blind man fearlessly crossed the street between the lines of vehicles held up for him. It's a picture of the way God's providence "holds up the traffic" for us. —*The Expositor.*

Friend—A Real.

A recent magazine article on the "Big Brother Movement" of New York tells of a boy sent to the House of Refuge, and therefore attending the school at that institution. One day, in one of the classes, he was asked to spell the word "friend." The letters came slowly, "F-r-i-e-n-d," and then the teacher asked, "What does the word mean?" The little fellow studied for a moment for a way to express his thought. "Oh," he said, "he's a feller that knows all about ye, an' likes ye just the same." It was the highest thing in friendship his brief life had taught him. That is the wonderful tie that binds us to our Friend in heaven. He knows it all, the mistakes, the falls, the disloyalty, the far wanderings, and still He cares. The Elder Brother is the need of all the earth.—*Forward.*

Friend at Court.

Two men who had been friends in their youth met in a police court: the one a magistrate, the other a prisoner. The case was tried, and the prisoner was found guilty. Would the judge in consideration of their friendship forbear to pass judgment? No, he must fulfill his duty. Justice must be done. He gave out the sentence—two weeks of hard labor or a fine of twenty pounds. The condemned man had nothing with which to pay, so the prison cell was before him. But as soon as he had pronounced the sentence the judge threw aside his magistrate's robes, and, stepping down beside the prisoner, paid his fine for him, and then said, "Now, John, you are coming home to supper with me." God has so dealt with the sinner. He cannot overlook sin, but Jesus paid the debt and allows the sinner to go free.—*Scriptural Anecdotes.*

Friend—Fighting Our.

"For your lives!" cried the Portuguese captain of an African slave ship to a band of naked Negroes, as he pointed to an English ship that had been in hot chase of him for some hours. "Fight for your lives!" he cried out, as he gave each man a weapon. And the deluded and terrified Negroes did as they were told, and in so doing they wounded and killed their best friends, who had come to deliver them. So Jesus came to set the captives of sin free; but the chief priests rose against Jesus, and the very men he loved and came to free hied on to kill him.—*Christian Herald.*

Friend in Need.

A story is told of a certain British regiment in India which was called upon to undergo "Kitchener's Test," i.e., to march a certain number of miles along a sandy track in a specified time without one man falling out. After covering a part of the distance a young recruit marching by the side of an "old timer" named Bill, said to him: "Bill, I can't stick it." The heat was terrific and the lad was wellnigh overcome. Bill, seeing it, said: "Here, give me your rifle." After another two miles, Bill noticing again the lad's distress, took over another part of his equipment, and before they had gone all the way he was carrying the remainder of the boy's kit. At the command "Halt" every man was in his place and the honor of the regiment saved. Unload all your burdens upon Him (your friend) for he careth for you.—*Jamaica Wesleyan Record.*

Friendship—Marks of.

Pythias was condemned to death by Dionysius the tyrant. He begged leave to go home to wish his friends good-by and to arrange his affairs. He had a friend named Damon, who said, "Let him go, and I will remain in prison and die for him if he does not return." Dionysius consented, and Pythias went off home, and came back just in time to meet his fate, and save the friend who had risked death for his sake. The tyrant was so struck by the nobility of heart in the two men that he pardoned Pythias, and said: "Let me be a third person in so sacred a friendship."—S. GREGORY.

Friends—Unknown.

"For your lives!" cried the Portuguese captain of an African slaveship to a band of naked negroes as he pointed to an English ship which had been in hot chase of him for some hours. "Fight for your lives!" he cried out, as he gave each man a weapon. And the deluded and terrified negroes did as they were told, and in so doing they wounded and killed their best friend, who had come to deliver them. So Jesus came to set the captives of sin free, but the Pharisees rose against Jesus, and the very men He loved and came to free, they hied on to kill Him.—*The Christian Herald.*

God's Watch—Care.

"Can I go and help grandpa along the walk, mamma?"

"Help him!" laughed Guy, before mamma could answer. "Why, you're a little tot of a girl, Bertha, and grandpa is very tall. He's deaf as a post, too."

"Yes, dearie, you can go," said mamma, as quietly as though Guy had not said a word.

"And I can make him hear with my hand," smiled Bertha.—A. PERCIVAL HODGSON.

Idle Hands.

When I was in the army before Port Hudson I remember that night after night, when our campfires were built, we boys used to sit around them and discuss various matters; and sometimes our discussions became very heated, and sometimes we lost our tempers, and sometimes we said angry words. But one night, right in the midst of a discussion, there broke upon us that awful, startling sound which, once heard, is never forgotten. Away off, on the right of the line, it began; but it rolled in a thundering, awful echo, until it chilled our hearts. It was the long roll, and every man was on his feet, and every man shook hands with his comrade and said, "Forgive me. When we were idle we could afford to discuss; but now there is work to do, it finds us brothers."—REV. G. HEPWORTH.

Influence—Secret of.

General Havelock, when questioned concerning the secret of his unique influence over the brave soldiers of his regiments, answered: "I keep close to them; I come personally into contact with each man, and know the name of every individual." Here is the secret of power. Sinners cannot be influenced for good while they are kept at arm's length.

Laborers Together.

To Sir Christopher Wren belongs the undying honor of having designed the great cathedral of St. Paul, with its world-famous dome, in London. But Sir Christopher Wren could never in a million years have built the dome alone. He was dependent upon the humblest laborers who toiled upon the hidden base, or reared the turrets of the mighty structure, as they were dependent upon him. In so far as they used to the uttermost their talents and opportunities, to them is due a full share of the glory.—C. B. KENNLEYSIDE.

Magnanimous Conduct.

When Conkling precipitated himself from the Senate, it was very much against General Grant's judgment, and that was known, and yet he attempted in every way to befriend Mr. Conkling, and shield him; so much so that everybody thought he had gone over to his side, and a man expostulated with him, saying, "General Grant, how is this? You don't believe that he did right, do you?" "No, sir; I don't." "How is it, then, that you are on his side now?" His reply was worthy to be written in letters of gold. "When is the time to show a man's self friendly, except when his friend has made a mistake? That is not the time to leave a man—when he has made a blunder or a mistake." That is one of those unimpeachable moral principles which appeal to the universal conscience. Stand by a man who is your friend. Stand by him in his adversity, if you don't stand by him at any other time.—H. W. BEECHER.

Praise—Bishop and Choir.

One day at Perth Bishop Wilkinson (late of Truro) noticed a thin-faced boy looking as if he wanted to speak to him, and he went up to him, asking if the boy wished to speak to him. "No, sir," said the boy, "only I sing in the same choir as you are in." The Bishop's friends laughed at the boy's idea of his association with the Bishop in the Church, but the boy was not laughed at by the Bishop.—*Life of Bishop Wilkinson.*

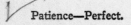

Patience—Perfect.

It is told of a sage that one day, after the fashion of the schools, he was questioned, "Master, what is the test of good manners?" Whereto he answered, "It is being able to put up pleasantly with bad ones." —*Free Churchman.*

Servant—Sympathetic.

Melancthon's friends were astonished at his liberality, and wondered how, with his small means, he could afford to give so much in charity. It is said to have been principally owing to the care and good management of an excellent and faithful servant named John, a native of Sweden. The whole duty of provisioning the family was entrusted to this domestic, whose care, assiduity, and prudence amply justified the unbounded confidence reposed in him. He made the concerns of the family his own, avoiding all needless expenditure, and watching with a jealous eye his master's property. He was also the first instructor of the children during their infancy. John grew old in his master's service, and expired in his house amidst the affectionate regrets of the whole family. Melancthon invited the students of the university to attend the funeral of his faithful servant, delivered an oration over his grave, and composed a Latin epitaph for his tombstone.

Silence—Golden.

Some folks lay themselves out to be as unpleasant as they can, and say disagreeable things. They are the wasps of human intercourse. The candid friends whom Canning so abhorred, the people who "speak their mind," but have a mind that were far better not spoken.—H. O. MACKEY.

Sympathy.

"Weep with them that weep." Just as we should be glad in the gladness of others, so we must grieve in the griefs of others. There are people who find it almost impossible to do this. They can neither feel for nor with others. They are naturally unsympathetic. This exhortation comes to such as a duty. They must learn the art, and so thoroughly that they will sympathize naturally and truly. It is no excuse to say that we cannot. We must. Dr. Dale is a case in point. This is what his son says of his father: "He was not selfish, but he was apt to be self-absorbed, engrossed by his own thoughts, and so absorbed as to be heedless of those whom he met, and of what was going on around him; he often gave offense unwittingly. His nature was not sympathetic. The faculty so bestowed on some, he had to cultivate sedulously and patiently as one of the moral virtues. . . . He was conscious of his defect, and set himself to overcome it, not as a mere infirmity, but as a fault. He became sympathetic by sympathizing." Dr. Dale was not singular in this instinctive lack of sympathy. There are many similarly destitute of the grace of sorrowing.—*Homilist.*

Sympathy—Brotherly.

When Mr. Roosevelt was police commissioner of New York City, he read for the first time Jacob Riis' book, "How the Other Half Lives," and at once desired to meet the writer. Going into lower Manhattan, he climbed the stairs to the modest little room, and knocked on the door. There was no response; Mr. Riis was not at home. Taking out his card, the visitor simply wrote, "Have read your book, and came to help. THEODORE ROOSEVELT." —*The Christian Endeavor World.*

The Changed Partnership.

A Buffalo man had a dishonest partner who almost wrecked the business of the firm by his questionable financial methods. The only way to win seemed to be to buy out the scamp's interest, and get a more reliable partner. But even after this was done the business did not pick up. One day an old business man came along, and the remaining member of the firm complained of the way that fate had used him. "Well, I can explain that," said the visitor. "You haven't let the world know that you changed partners. They still think that Smith is in the firm. The old sign still hangs over the door. You must take down 'Smith and Jones' and put up 'Brown and Jones.'" The old sign came down and the new sign was put up. The notice was also put in the windows and on the doors and in the newspapers. It read about as follows: "John Smith and George Jones have dissolved partnership, John Smith retiring from the business. Charles Brown has been admitted to the firm and Brown and Jones will continue at the old stand." Everybody read it, and trade picked up. Reader, have you let the world know that you have renounced the Devil and all his works? It must be done. Then hang out your sign. Put on the armor of light. You have broken partnership with the Devil, who was running your spiritual interests, have you? Then why not take down the old sign?—*The King's Business.*

The Staff Method.

Social reformers are discovering that they can do little good for people of any sort while they hold them at arm's length. "I have learned," says a worker in one of the University settlements, "that you can get access to the people who need you only by living with them. They will not come to you; but Jew and Gentile will make you welcome if you come to them. Our meetings for their benefit are a failure. Our personal intercourse with them, man to man, has been promising great good. It is of no use to come once or twice to see them; you must live with them if you are to do anything for them."—R. E. THOMPSON.

"Victory, O Lord."

One of Millais' most powerful pictures is that in the Manchester Art Gallery, entitled "Victory, O Lord." It represents the incident related in Ex. xvii. 10-12, of Moses sitting on the top of the hill, while Joshua is leading the Israelites against the Amalekites on the plains below. Moses, the great lawgiver, is represented seated upon a stone, his body bent with age and weariness. Aaron and Hur stand on either side of him supporting his upraised arms, since as long as these were held up Israel prevailed. The faces of the two supporters are ablaze with zeal. They watch the conflict below, and can hardly remain passive through agitation. Yet there they remain holding up the arms of the aged leader. The whole picture is a lesson in the practice of prayer.

Whosoever.

Dr. Greene, pastor of the Calvary Baptist Church in Washington, D. C., on the same morning received into that church the Hon. Charles E. Hughes, a Chinese, and a washerwoman. As he saw the strange group standing before him, he paused and said, "My friends, I will have you to notice that at the cross of Christ the ground is level."—*Front Rank*.

Companion—A Constant.

When He appoints to meet thee, go
  thou forth.
  It matters not
If south or north,
  Bleak waste or sunny plot.
Nor think, if haply He thou seek'st
  be late,
  He does thee wrong;
To stile or gate
  Lean thou thy head, and long!
It may be that to spy thee He is
  mounting
  Upon a tower,
Or in the counting
  Thou hast mista'en the hour.
But, if He come not, neither do thou
  go
  Till Vesper chime;
Belike thou then shalt know
  He hath been with thee all the
    time.
        —T. E. Brown.

Man's Ingratitude.

Blow, blow, thou winter wind,
Thou art not so unkind
  As man's ingratitude;
Thy tooth is not so keen,
Because thou art not seen,
  Although thy breath be rude.

Freeze, freeze, thou bitter sky,
Thou dost not bite so nigh
  As benefits forgot:

Though thou the waters warp,
Thy sting is not so sharp
  As friend remember'd not.
        —Shakespeare.

"Pass It On,"

Have you had a kindness shown?
  Pass it on;
'Twas not given for thee alone,
  Pass it on;
Let it travel down the years,
Let it wipe another's tears,
Till in heav'n the deed appears—
  Pass it on.

Did you hear the loving word?
  Pass it on;
Like the singing of a bird?
  Pass it on;
Let its music live and grow,
Let it cheer another's woe;
You have reaped what others sow,
  Pass it on.

'Twas the sunshine of a smile,
  Pass it on;
Staying but a little while!
  Pass it on;
April beam, the little thing,
Still it makes the flow'rs of spring,
Makes the silent birds to sing—
  Pass it on.

Have you found the heav'nly light?
  Pass it on;
Souls are groping in the night,
  Daylight gone;
Hold thy lighted lamp on high,
Be a star in some one's sky,
He may live who else would die—
  Pass it on.

Be not selfish in thy greed,
  Pass it on;
Look upon thy brother's need,
  Pass it on;
Live for self, you live in vain;
Live for Christ, you live again;
Live for Him, with Him you reign—
  Pass it on.

What to Forget.

"If you see a tall fellow ahead of a
    crowd,
A leader of men marching fearless
    and proud,
And you know of a tale whose
    mere telling aloud
Would mean that his head must in
    anguish be bowed,
It's a pretty good plan to forget it.

"If you know of a skeleton hidden
    away
In a closet, and guarded and kept
    from the day
In the dark; and whose showing,
    whose sudden display,
Would cause grief and sorrow and
    life-long dismay,
It's a pretty good plan to forget it.

"If you know of a thing that will
    darken the joy
Of a man or a woman, a girl or a
    boy,
That will wipe out a smile, or the
    least way annoy
A fellow, or cause any gladness to
    cloy,
It's a pretty good plan to forget it."

—*The Expositor.*

Christ's Love an Individual Love.

The great trouble is that people take everything in general, and do not take it to themselves. Suppose a man should say to me: "Moody, there was a man in Europe who died last week, and left five million dollars to a certain individual." "Well," I say, "I don't doubt that; it's rather a common thing to happen," and I don't think anything more about it. But suppose he says: "But he left the money to you." Then I pay attention; I say: "To me?" "Yes, he left it to you." I become suddenly interested. I want to know all about it. So we are apt to think Christ died for sinners; He died for everybody, and for nobody in particular. But when the truth comes to me that eternal life is mine, and all the glories of heaven are mine, I begin to be interested.—MOODY.

Author—Loving the.

There was a literary woman who stood high among book critics. One day in reviewing a book she said, "Who wrote this book? It is beautifully written, but there is something wrong here and there!" She proceeded to criticize with a good deal of severity. Some months afterwards this lady became acquainted with the author of the book, fell in love, and married him. She took the same book again and said, "What a beautiful book! There are some mistakes here and there, but they ought to be overlooked." The book was just the same as it had been before, but the critic had changed. When she began to love the author it changed her attitude toward the book. So it is with us and the Bible. People do not love the Bible because they do not love Christ.—G. JACKSON.

Authority—Keys of.

Mr. A. J. Cassatt, the late president of the Pennsylvania Railway, was once making a quiet tour over one of the branches of the system, and wandered into an out-of-the-way switchyard, where something one of the yardmen was doing did not meet with his approbation. He made some suggestion to the man, who asked: "Who are you that's trying to teach me my business?" "I am an officer of the road," replied Mr. Cassatt. "Let's see your switchkey then," said the man, suspiciously. Mr. Cassatt pulled from his hip pocket his key ring, to which was attached the switchkey, which no railroad man in service is without. It was sufficient proof for the switchman, who then did as he was told. The story suggests a great spiritual lesson. If you are going to have any real leadership in dealing with the souls of men they must see in your conversation, in the tone of your character, in the spirit of your life, that you possess the "switchkey," the evident presence of Jesus Christ.—*The Epworth Herald.*

Christ—Ashamed of.

A Hindoo of rank was troubled in his conscience on the subject of a future state. He had heard of Christians, and longed to converse with them about their religion, and to know who Christ was. So he visited England, the Christian's land, supplied with introductions to some leading people. Being asked to a great dinner, he turned to his neighbor in the course of conversation, and said: "Can you tell me something about Christ, the founder of your religion?" "Hush," replied his new acquaintance, "we do not speak of such things at dinner-parties." Subsequently, he was invited to a large ball. Dancing with a young and fashionable lady, he took an opportunity of asking her who the founder of her religion, Jesus Christ, was. And again he was warned that a ball was no place to introduce such subjects. Strange, thought the Hindoo, are these Christians in England. They will not speak of their religion, nor inform me about Christ, its founder. —*Sunday School Times.*

Christ—A Vision of.

This is the origin of Longfellow's "Legend Beautiful," as told by Moncure D. Conway in his autobiography: A Father of the Desert daily gave alms to the poor at the convent gate. In his cell Christ appeared to him with face and attitude as he had supposed Christ would look, but indistinct. "Sometimes he doubted if it were there; then it would glow a little." As he gazed with rapture, the bell sounded the hour when the needy would await their alms at the gate. But how could he leave the one heavenly vision of his lifetime? Yet he could not keep out of his thoughts the images of the sufferers, and with tears bade the Christ vision farewell. When he had relieved the haggard men, women, and children, it was night; but as he was about to strike a light, his cell was filled with a celestial brightness, and there stood the form clear as the sun, no longer like the church pictures, but with the tender smile and eyes bent on him, and as he fell before the stupendous vision, the divine One lifted him and said, "Hadst thou not gone, I had gone indeed!"

Christ—Birth of.

An artist drew a picture of a wintry twilight,—the trees heavily laden with snow, and a dreary, dark house, lonely and desolate in the midst of the storm. It was a sad picture. Then, with a quick stroke of yellow crayon, he put a light in one window. The effect was magical. The entire scene was transformed into a vision of comfort and cheer. The birth of Christ was just such a light in a dark world.—*The Sunday School Chronicle.*

Christ's Disciple.

The Emperor Henry, who was a pious prince, wearied with cares of state, proposed to abdicate, and enter a monastery, which was ruled by a good man named Richard. His abdication at that time would have been the cause of many evils to the Empire, which needed all his strength and vigilance. Accordingly, when the Emperor made his application to be received into the monastery, "Will you," said Richard, "practise obedience unto death, following the rule and example of Jesus Christ?" He replied that he would do this with all his heart. "And I," said Richard, "receive you from this moment into the number of my brethren, and take you into my spiritual charge, provided that on your side you promise to follow, as in the sight of God, all that I shall order you." Henry promised, and the abbot proceeded, "I desire, then, and order you to take up again the government of the Empire, which has been confided to your care by Divine Providence, and that you ensure, as far as in you lies, the safety and advantage of your subjects, by your vigilance and firmness in doing justice." The Emperor did not hear without reluctance that unexpected command. He obeyed, nevertheless; but he always from that time regarded himself as the disciple of Abbot Richard.—S. J. Eales.

Christ—Fellowship With.

The president of one of the largest banks of New York City told that after he had served for several years as an office boy in the bank, the then president called him into his office one day and said, "I want you to come into my office and be with me." The young man replied, "But what do you want me to do?" "Never mind that," said the president; "you will learn about that soon. I just want you to be in here with me." "That was the most memorable moment of my life," said the great banker. "Being with that man made me all that I am to-day." What must the disciples have received by being with Jesus?—*The Christian Herald.*

Christ—Hid In.

One day a friend of mine, in passing down a Glasgow street, saw a crowd at a shop door, and had the curiosity to look in. There he saw an auctioneer holding up a grand picture so that all could see it. When he got it in position, he remained behind it and said to the crowd, "Now look at this part of the picture, . . . and now at this other part," and so on, describing each detail of it. "Now," said my friend, "the whole time I was there I never saw the speaker, but only the picture he was showing." That is the way to work for Christ, He must increase, but we must be out of sight.—ANDREW A. BONAR.

Christ—Holding Up.

It is said that one day John Ruskin was entertaining a company of friends in his home. He was chatting with them in his library, pointing out some of the pictures on the walls of his study. He had been describing the well-nigh hidden splendor and wonder of some of Turner's great paintings, whose works he adored. In the midst of this description he was called out of the room for a moment, and when he left his aged father turned to the guests and said, "I think John sees more in Turner than Turner meant to portray." Then one of the guests replied, "Not at all, we never understood Turner until John Ruskin was born." Somehow that is true of that manger beneath the Syrian skies. It brought God out of the reaches of the unknown and useless speculation into the realm of our daily work and life. We never understood God until Jesus came. Bethlehem illumines our way to the love of God.—*The Expositor.*

Christ—Knowing.

When Bishop Beveridge was on his death-bed he did not know any of his relatives or friends. A minister with whom he had been well acquainted visited him; and when conducted into his room he said, "Bishop, do you know me?" "Who are you?" asked the Bishop. Being told who the minister was, he said that he did not know him. Another friend came, who had been equally well known, and accosted him in a similar manner, "Do you know me, Bishop?" "Who are you?" said he. Being told who the minister was, he was unable to recollect him. His wife then came to his bedside, and asked him if he knew her. But the dying man did not recognize even this his nearest relative. "Well," said one, "Bishop, do you know the Lord Jesus Christ?" "Jesus Christ!" said he, reviving, as if the name had produced on him the influence of a charm, "Oh, yes, I have known Him these forty years; precious Saviour, He is my only hope!"—S. J. EALES.

Christ—Making Way For.

Are you willing to be a highway over which Jesus Christ shall come to your town and into the lives of your friends and neighbors? Right of way costs something. When President Garfield was shot, he was taken to a quiet, isolated house where he could have absolute quiet and rest in his fight for life, and a special railway was constructed to facilitate the bringing of doctors, nurses, and loved ones to his bedside. The engineers laid out the line to cross a farmer's front yard, but he refused to grant the right of way until they explained to him that it was for the President, when he exclaimed, "That is different. Why, if that railroad is for the President, you can run it right through my house." Are you willing to give Him right of way across your front yard? It may run right through some of your plans, or social engagements, or business appointments. But will you give him the right of way?—*Michigan Christian Advocate.*

Christ—Memorial of.

In the Highlands of Scotland, in a wild region, there is a spring at which Prince Albert once stopped to quench his thirst. The owner of the spring fenced it in and built a tasteful monument, making the waters flow into a basin of hewn stone, on which he placed an inscription. Every passing stranger stooping to drink at this fountain reads the inscription and recalls the memory of the noble prince whom it honors. Thus the spring is both a memorial and a blessing; it keeps in mind the great man, and it gives drink to the weary and the thirsty. The Lord's Supper is a memorial to Christ, but it is food and drink to every one who rightly receives it.—S. MARRIOTT.

Christ—Mercy of.

After the victory of Areole the indefatigable Bonaparte passed through the camp during the night. He found a sentinel who had fallen asleep; raising his gun gently and without waking the soldier he took the duty, till about the time the watch would be relieved. At last the soldier woke. Imagine his alarm when he saw his general performing his duty. He cried out, "Bonaparte! I am a lost man." Bonaparte answered, "Be at peace: the secret is mine; and it is excusable when a brave soldier like thyself, after so much fatigue, should fall asleep; only another time choose a more fitting moment."—C. LACRETELLE'S *Histoire de la Revolution Francaise.*

Christ Our Advocate.

Some years ago, during the war, there was a judge who felt great interest in the welfare of the suffering soldiers. He had a dear boy of his own in the army, and this made him feel the greatest sympathy for the soldiers. But one time he was very busy in studying out an important law case that was coming before him to be tried. And while he was thus engaged, he made up his mind not to be interrupted by any persons begging for help. One day, during this time, a poor soldier came into his office. His clothes were torn and thin, and his face showed that he was suffering much from sickness. The judge went on with his work, pretending not to notice him. The soldier was fumbling in his pockets for a good while, and then, seeing that he was not welcome, he said in a disappointed tone, "I did have a letter for you, sir." The judge made no answer. Presently the soldier's thin trembling hand pushed a little note along the desk. The judge looked up, and was going to say, "I am too busy now to attend to anything of this kind." But just then his eye fell on the note, and he saw the handwriting of his own son. In a moment he picked it up and read thus:—"Dear Father, The bearer of this note is one of our brave soldier boys. He has been dismissed from the hospital, and is going home to die. Please help him, in any way you can, for Charlie's sake." And so when we ask anything for Jesus' sake, God, our heavenly Father, will surely give it to us, if it be well for us to have it.—RICHARD NEWTON.

Christ Our Refuge.

We once saw an earnest engineer who was praying most importunately for faith in Christ and for peace to his troubled soul. But, while he prayed, a cloud of darkness gathered across his horizon. And against that cloud, which swung like a funeral pall before his vision, played the strange lightnings of the Almighty's wrath. The thunders of God's law roared against him. Instead of peace came only the sword, instead of the calm he sought came the fearful tempest; and under the stress of its terrors the poor baffled soul betakes himself to the "covert" which Christ had raised on Calvary. There he finds the peace he so earnestly prayed for.

Christ's Sacrifice.

When the Birkenhead, with five hundred soldiers on board, was sinking, the soldiers were drawn up in their ranks on the deck of the ship while the women and children were quietly put into one of the boats.

Every one of them did as he was directed, and there was not a murmur or a cry among them till the vessel made her final plunge. Even so, silently and uncomplainingly, did Christ "give Himself up" for our salvation.—R. BREWIN.

Christ—Patience of.

I know a mother who has an idiot child. For it she gave up all society, almost everything, and devoted her whole life to it. "And now," said she, "for fourteen years I have tended it, and loved it, and it does not even know me. Oh! it is breaking my heart!" Oh! how the Lord might say this of hundreds here. Jesus comes here, and goes from seat to seat, asking if there is a place for Him. Oh! will not some of you take Him into your hearts?—MOODY.

Christ—Popular with.

One winter's day I was at the railway station at New York. There was a large crowd of persons desiring to go from New York to Boston, and we all had to pass through a narrow way by the gatekeeper. Everybody had to show his ticket, and, as usual, there were many who could not conveniently find them. They said they had them, but the gatekeeper was inexorable. "You must show your ticket," he said, "if you please." There was both grumbling and swearing on the part of the passengers. After most of them had passed through a gentleman said to the ticket-collector, "You don't seem to be very popular with this crowd." He just cast his eyes upwards to the ceiling on the floor above, where the superintendent's office was, and said, "I don't care anything about being popular with this crowd; all I care for is to be popular with the man up there."—Dr. Pentecost.

Christ—Putting On.

It is told of a Roman youth who, notwithstanding a mother's unwearied prayers, had lived a life of self-seeking and sinful indulgence, that one day, as he sat in the garden, in the cloudless beauty of an autumn day, a great struggle took place in his mind. Throwing himself on his knees he prayed earnestly to God, "O Lord, how long—how long—how long wilt thou be angry with me? Must it be for ever to-morrow, and to-morrow, and to-morrow? Why should it not be to-day?" Suddenly in his agony he seemed to hear the voice as of a little child repeating, "Take up and read"; "Take up and read." And taking up the Epistles of St. Paul which he had happened to be reading, and opening the book at random, his eye caught these words: "Not in rioting and drunkenness, not in chambering and wantonness, not in strife and envying. But put ye on the Lord Jesus Christ, and make not provision for the flesh, to fulfill the lusts thereof" (Rom. xiii. 13, 14.) The words came to him as a direct message from God, and in one instant strong resolve, he determined for ever to break with his old life and in the might of Christ to enter on the new. Augustine put on Christ.—G. Milligan.

Christ—Renunciation By.

I read a wonderful story about Buddha, which is a strange adumbration of this experience of our Lord. It is said that when Buddha, before he was styled the enlightened one, was sitting at the base of the tree of meditation, there passed before him in procession temptations of various sorts. First temptations of the flesh, and Gautama Buddha put these aside. Then temptations of the mind, and Buddha put these aside. Then various temptations of the spirit, and Buddha put these aside. And then came a subtle temptation. A temptress whispered in his ear, "Thou hast now overcome all the temptations; enter into Nirvana now"—Nirvana being the Buddhist heaven. And Buddha very nearly gave way, the legend says. But lo! as he sat at the base of the tree, he heard a rustling in the leaves of the tree above him. And the rustling of the leaves was caused by the agitation of those little creatures of God that crept amongst the leaves, who were looking forward, says the legend, to being saved through Buddha; but if he escaped now into Nirvana by himself they would be left unsaved; and the tree rustled with the agitation of the little creatures; and Buddha was recalled, and he refused the temptation to enter Nirvana then.—G. A. Johnston Ross.

Christ the Door.

There be some who teach us that the earthly Church, composed of human beings, surrounded with human devices, human ordinances, human governments, human systems, is the Door. Never! Never! Christ is the Door. No organization can take his place. None can represent him, even. We may make use of the Church as we make use of a hotel when we are traveling home to see father and mother; but no landlord of any hotel shall tell me that he is my father, or my mother, or that his hotel is my home. Churches are God's hotels, where travelers put up for the night, as it were, and then speed on their way home. Christ is the one Door. All that pass through that Door are of the one church, and belong to him.—H. W. Beecher.

Christ—The Image of.

There is produced in a telescope an image of a star. There is produced in a soul an image of God. When does the image of the star start up in the chamber of the telescope? Only when the lenses are clear and rightly adjusted, and when the axis of vision in the tube is brought into exact coincidence with the line of rays of light from the star. When does the image of God, or the inner sense of peace and pardon, spring up in the human soul? Only when the faculties of the soul are rightly adjusted in relation to each other, and the will brought into coincidence with God's Will. How much is man's work, and how much is the work of the light? Man adjusts the lenses and the tube; the light does all the rest. Man may, in the exercise of his freedom, as upheld by Divine power, adjust his faculties to spiritual light, and when adjusted in a certain way God flashes through them.—Joseph Cook.

Christ—The Needed One.

An infidel woman came to a gospel preacher once after the sermon and said: "You have something I lack—what is it?" He replied, "You have the wrong word, madam. You should not say 'something,' you should say 'some one.'" She saw the point, and was persuaded to trust in Jesus Christ.

Christ—The Real.

A very learned man once said to a little child who believed in the Lord Jesus, "My poor little girl, you don't know whom you believe in. There have been many christs.

In which of them do you believe?" "I know which one I believe in," replied the child. "I believe in the Christ who rose from the dead."— *Pentecostal Evangel.*

Christ: The Rock of Ages.

A sailor in a shipwreck was once thrown upon a small rock, and clung to it, in great danger, until the tide went down. "Say, Jim," asked his friends after he was rescued, "didn't you shake with fear when you were hanging on that rock?" "Yes; but the rock didn't," was the significant reply. Christ is the Rock of Ages.— *Sabbath Reading.*

Christ the Way.

It is a dark, stormy night, and a little child, lost in the streets of the city, is crying in distress. A policeman, gathering from the child's story enough to locate the home, gives directions after this manner: "Just go down this street half a mile, turn to your right and follow the river down a little way, and you'll see then where you are." The poor child only half comprehending, chilled by the wind and bewildered in the storm, is turning about blindly, when another voice speaks and says in a kindly tone, "Just come with me." The little hand is clasped in a stronger one, the corner of a warm cloak is thrown over the shoulders of the shivering child, and the way home is made easy. The first one had told the way; this one condescends to be the way.—D. H. Strong.

Christ—Touch of.

A strange instrument hung on an old castle wall, so the legend runs. No one knew its use. Its strings were broken and covered with dust. Those who saw it wondered what it was and how it had been used. Then one day a stranger came to the castle gate and entered the hall. His eyes saw the dark object on the wall, and taking it down, he reverently brushed the dust from its sides, and tenderly reset its broken strings. Then chords long silent woke beneath his touch, and all hearts were strangely thrilled as he played. It was the master, long absent, who had returned to his own.

It is but a legend, yet the meaning is plain. In every human soul there hangs a marvelous harp, dust-covered, with strings broken, while yet the Master's hand has not found it. Let the Master enter and repair the strings which sin has broken, and sweep them with his skillful fingers.—J. R. MILLER.

Christ—Triumph In.

A godly Church of England vicar was troubled with a violent and apparently u n g o v e r n a b l e temper. Many a time he had prayed about it with tears, and he had struggled much to conquer it, but had been beaten and was almost in despair. One day he had prayed and confessed his sin and believed he had obtained help to keep down the violent temper, and so he had left his study to go about his duties. Alas! not long afterward he re-entered his study beaten and almost broken-hearted, and in his sorrow he fell asleep and dreamed he was in his study and, looking out, saw coming towards him a glorious man who evidently intended to be his guest. He became at once conscious that his study was in much disorder and unfit to receive such a guest who, he knew, was the Lord Jesus Christ. He swept and watered and dusted the room, but the more he worked the worse it became. The stranger knocked. "Oh, what shall I do," he said to himself. "I cannot let him into a room in such disorder as this," and he kept on sweeping, watering, and dusting till the stranger knocked again, and again he said, "Oh, I cannot open while the room is so unfit to receive Him." But all his efforts were in vain, and when the stranger knocked again, overpowered with shame and confusion, he opened the door, saying, "Master, I can do no more; come in if thou wilt into such a room." The Master came in, and, most strange, when He came in the dust was laid, the disorder disappeared, and all was bright and clean and joyful. The Master's presence alone had done all that his utmost efforts had failed to accomplish. He awoke, and it was a dream, but in the dream God had spoken to him, and he now saw where his mistake had been, and wherein lay his strength for an overcoming life.—*Life of Faith.*

Christ,—Union With.

When I was a little child I often stood near a forge and watched the blacksmith at work, admiring the strength and skill of the wonder-working man. He was wont to treat me kindly and bear with me patiently, although I sometimes stood in his way. At one time he would benevolently answer my childish questions, and at another, instead of answering, would continue to handle his tools with his strong, bare arms, throwing glances of tenderness towards me from time to time out of his deep, intelligent eyes, only all in silence. When two pieces of iron, placed in the fire in order to be welded together, became red, I thought and said he should take them out and join them; but he left them lying still in the fire, without saying a word. They grew redder and hotter as they threw out angry sparks; now, thought I, he should certainly lay them together and strike; but the skillful man left them still lying in the fire, and meantime fanned it into a fiercer glow. Not till they were white and bending with their own weight when lifted, like lilies on their stalks—not till they were at the point of becoming liquid did he lay the two pieces alongside of each other, and by a few gentle strokes weld them into one. Had he laid them together sooner, however vigorously he had beaten, they would have fallen asunder in his hands. The Lord knows, as we know not, what preparation we need in order that we may be brought into union with Himself. He refuses, delays, disappoints—all in wise love, that He may bring the seeker's heart up to such a glow of desire as will suffice to unite it permanently with His own.—ARNOT.

Christ—Witnessing For.

A few years ago two young men, who had been like David and Jonathan from their boyhood days to their college days, and from that time until they were lawyers together in a certain city, went down to the dock of the White Star steamer. One of them was to go on a long journey around the world. They were utterly unlike in one thing only; one was devoutly pious, and the other, though not a skeptic, had adjourned this question. All along down on the train the Christian man said: "I will speak to him when we get down to the Fifth Avenue hotel." He did not. When they stood on the dock, "I will speak a word when we are going down the gangplank." He did not. "I will spring up on the rail of the pier, just as the ship is swinging off, and speak then." He did not. The great ship turned her head out into the stream, and the two parted, and

he had not said his word of Christian warning. Only a year and a half ago, half way around the globe that friend lost out the connecting link and September did not come after August for him. And now, in his beautiful library, that living man sits and looks up at his dead friend's picture, and talks to him, and says: "O Jonathan, my friend, I ask you to be a Christian! I pray you to be a Christian!" But the pictured lips upon the wall make no reply. The lamp burned till midnight and went out. If you have a word of warning to say to your friend, you had better say it now.— EMORY J. HAYNES.

Clock of Time.

It is beautiful to observe how the motions of the stars of heaven in their orbits are represented by the flowers of earth in their opening and closing, in their blossoming and fading. The clock of time has two faces: the one above, on which the hours are marked by the rising and setting of the orbs of heaven; the other below, on which the hours are marked by the blossoming and the fading, the opening and closing of the flowers. The one exactly corresponds with the other. The movements of the living creatures depend upon the movements of the lifeless stars. The daisy follows with its golden eye the path of the sun through the sky, opens its blossom when he rises, and closes it when he sets. Thus should it be with our souls. There should be a similar harmony between them and the motions of the heavenly bodies which God has set in the firmament for signs to us. Our spiritual life should progress with their revolutions; should keep time with the music of the spheres; our thoughts should be widened with the process of the suns. This is the true astrology. And as the daisy follows the sun all day to the west with its open eye, and acknowledges no other light that falls upon it—lamplight, moonlight, or starlight—remaining closed under them all, except under the light of the sun; so should we follow the Sun of Righteousness whithersoever He goeth, and say with the Psalmist, "Whom have we in the heavens but Thee; and there is none upon the earth whom we desire besides Thee."—H. MACMILLAN.

Conversion—Gen. Lew Wallace's.

Two infidels once sat in a railway car discussing Christ's wonderful life. One of them said, "I think an interesting romance could be written about Him." The other replied, "And you are just the man to write it. Set forth the correct view of His life and character. Tear down the prevailing sentiment as to His divineness and paint Him as He was—a man among men." The suggestion was acted on and the romance was written. The man who made the suggestion was Colonel Ingersoll; the author was General Lew Wallace; and the book was "Ben-Hur." In the process of constructing it he found himself facing the unaccountable Man. The more he studied His life and character the more profoundly he was convinced that He was more than a man among men; until at length, like the centurion under the cross, he was constrained to cry, "Verily, this was the Son of God."—D. J. BURRELL.

Cross—Protection of.

The prairie fire is a never-to-be-forgotten sight. If the wind is blowing very strongly, the prairie fire will travel faster than a horse can gallop. Those who have settled on the prairies see the devouring flames come, and they know they cannot run away from them. What do they do? They burn a large space in the vicinity of their home; in a short time a very large piece of ground is absolutely cleared and blackened. Then they go and stand on the ground where the fire has already been. When the great devouring prairie fire comes up it stops there—it can go no farther—there is nothing to burn. There is one place of safety for us. It is where the fire has already been. That is the Cross of Calvary, the Cross of the Lord Jesus Christ.—*The Sunday at Home.*

Deliverer—The Great.

If you lay imprisoned in some great fortress, and one who loved you went forth to try to rescue you, and fell and died fighting, you would cherish the memory of your friend's valiant effort on your behalf, but you would *still remain in chains,* undelivered. So would it have been with those whom Christ came to save if he had not risen; those for whom he gave his life would have been undelivered. But Christ has conquered death and holds in his hands the keys of the grave.—J. R. MILLER.

"Eager Heart."

A few days ago there was performed in the hall of Lincoln's Inn, London, a mystery play called "Eager Heart." The story is briefly this. Eager Heart is a poor maiden living in a wayside cottage, who has heard that the king is going to pass that way, and that he will take up his quarters for a night somewhere in the neighborhood. With all diligence she prepares the best room in her cottage for his reception, hoping that she may be the favored one whom he will honor with a visit. Her two sisters, Eager Fame and Eager Sense, deride her expectations, and assure her that the king would never condescend to enter so humble an abode, and that he will, as a matter of course, seek hospitality with some of the great folk in that part of the country. She, however, has a strong premonition that her hopes are not ill-founded, and goes on with her preparations. When all is ready, a knock is heard at the door, and a poor woman with an infant at her breast begs the charity of a night's lodging. Eager Heart, sad and disappointed, yet feeling that she cannot refuse such a request, gives up to the distressed wayfarers the room which she had prepared for the king; and then goes forth into the night in the hopes of meeting him and at least expressing her goodwill to have entertained him had it been possible. On her way she meets a company of shepherds, who tell her they have seen a vision of angels, who have assured them that the king has already come, and is in the village. And as they return, they are joined by another pilgrim band, of eastern princes, who are making their way, guided by a heavenly light, to pay their homage to their sovereign lord. Needless to say, it is to the cottage of Eager Heart herself that they are guided. The infant is Himself the King, and the homeless woman is the Queen Mother.—H. Lucas.

Everybody Somebody to Jesus.

Down the High Street of Edinburgh there came rushing a carriage and some horses, the horses having taken fright. A road was instantly cleared for them. At the bottom of the hill was a little child in the center of the street, who was standing quite unconscious of the certain death rushing down upon it. The people stood aghast; no one rushed to save the child, and still the horses dashed on. A Scotch-woman walking along suddenly saw the dangerous position that the child was in; she sprang like lightning, caught the child in her arms, and rescued it from the imminent danger in which it was placed. Some came instantly to the woman and said, "Ma'am, is that child yours?" "No," she said, "it is not mine, I do not know whose it is, but it is somebody's bairn."—Guthrie.

Guide—Following Our.

Mr. Dallgetty, an Indian missionary, said that many years ago, away out in the northwest of India, he was aroused at three o'clock in the morning to go through a desert and pass a buried city of ancient date. The morning was very dark. His leader and guide was a dark-skinned man who said to him in his own language, "Keep close to me." As they went through the darkness, the guide first and Mr. Dallgetty following, they talked to each other, and by and by as he looked down at his feet, he could see no road. They seemed to be turning this way and that, going on and on, and he feared the way was missed. In his anxiety of heart he cried, "Where is the way?" The guide turned around and said, "I am the way. There is no way to be seen but here with me. Follow step by step with me, and the end of the journey will come." And it came. We need day by day as life goes on to concentrate less and less upon the road, and more and more upon the Guide. —*The King's Business.*

Heart—Christ in the.

A soldier of Napoleon's army was wounded one day by a bullet which

CHRIST

entered his breast above his heart; he was carried to the rear, and the surgeon was probing the wound with his knife, when at length the guardsman exclaimed, "An inch deeper, and you will find the emperor." And the Christian soldier, even when most sorely pressed and pierced by his foes, is conscious that were his heart laid open by their wounds, it would only discover the name of his great Captain deeply engraven there.—*Independent*.

If Jesus Had Not Come.

Bobby had read in his Bible lesson with Daddy just before bedtime the words, "If I had not come." When he (thought he) awoke Christmas morning there was no stocking or holly wreath. He went for a walk and found factories busy at work; he went to the orphanage and found only a vacant lot. Then he went to his church and found a "For Sale" sign with "If I had not come" written at the bottom. Again he found these words over a gate post of an empty lot, where he went to find a hospital. Disconsolate, he ran home and picked up his Bible, but all the last part of the Book had blank pages. He awoke, and lo! it was a dream. Do you wonder he slipped down on his knees and said, "Oh, dear Jesus, I am so glad that you did come. Help me to tell others about you." —*Missionary Monthly*.

In His Steps.

St. Matthew suffered martyrdom by being slain with a sword at a distant city of Ethiopia. St. Mark expired at Alexandria, after having been cruelly dragged through the streets of that city. St. Luke was hanged upon an olive-tree in the classic land of Greece. St. John was put into a caldron of boiling oil, but escaped death in a miraculous manner, and was afterwards banished to Patmos. St. Peter was crucified at Rome with his head downward. St. James the Greater was beheaded at Jerusalem. St. James the Less was thrown from a lofty pinnacle of the temple, and then beaten to death with a fuller's club. St. Philip was hanged up against a pillar at Heiropolis in Phrygia. St. Bartholomew was flayed alive. St. Andrew was bound to a cross, whence he preached to his persecutors until he died. St. Thomas was run through the body with a lance at Coromandel in the East Indies. St. Jude was shot to death with arrows. St. Matthias was first stoned, and then beheaded. St. Barnabas of the Gentiles was stoned to death by the Jews at Salonica. St. Paul, after various tortures and persecutions, was at length beheaded at Rome by the Emperor Nero.— SCHUMACHER.

Inspiration—Wesley's Argument.

John Wesley gave a short argument for the inspiration of the Scriptures that is well worth remembering.

"The Bible must be the invention either of good men or angels, bad men or devils, or of God.

"1. It could not be the invention of good men or angels, for they neither would nor could make a book and tell lies all the time they were writing it, saying, 'Thus saith the Lord,' when it was their own invention.

"2. It could not be the invention of bad men or devils, for they could not make a book that commands all duty, forbids all sin, and condemns their own souls to hell for all eternity.

"3. Therefore, draw the conclusion that the Bible must be given by divine inspiration."

Jesus—Looking to.

A visitor in the home of a wealthy friend was surprised to discover hanging upon the wall of his host's bedroom a somewhat faded, water-discolored life preserver. He asked for an explanation. "That isn't an ordinary life preserver to me," explained the host. "It kept me afloat ten hours after the steamer on which I had embarked had been sent to the bottom of the ocean by a submarine. I keep it where I can see it the last thing at night and the first thing in the morning. It helps to keep me thankful and appreciative." If Christians kept Christ before them more consistently, they would not only be far better Christians, but far more grateful Christians. The thought of pleasing Christ would be with them the first thing in the morning and the last thing at night. Not only this—they would eagerly grasp every opportunity to tell others of the great things Christ has done for them.—*Moody Bible Institute Monthly.*

Jesus—Standing Up For.

Fifty years ago, at a dinner party which was given in the West End of London, the conversation of the gentlemen turned on what (to describe it no more closely) was dishonoring to Christ our Lord. One guest was silent, and presently he asked that the bell might be rung. On the appearance of the servant he ordered his carriage, and with perfect and polished courtesy apologized to the host for his enforced departure, "for he was still a Christian." It was the late Sir Robert Peel.—Canon Liddon.

Jesus—Tenderness of.

Richard III went out at twilight to reconnoiter; he found a sentinel fast asleep at the outposts. The king promptly stabbed him to the heart and left upon his breast a paper with the stern inscription, "I found him asleep and I left him so." What a contrast to the patience and tenderness of the Lord with his sleeping disciples—and with all of us.—William S. Bowden.

Jesus, the Great Pilot.

I remember the first time I came down the St. Lawrence; as the Long Sault Rapids hove in sight, all the passengers were intently looking at the rushing, foaming waters in the distance. Soon the boat was brought to a stand and a man taken on board. He was an Indian, a man about fifty-five, stalwart and strong, and, I believe, the only pilot that had ever attempted to steer a vessel through those raging waters. I watched him with peculiar interest, as he put his hands upon the wheel and pointed the boat towards the rapids. With hands busily plying the wheel at times, and his eyes riveted, as it were, upon some object before him, he held that great vessel steady to its course; and as we were flying, with almost the rapidity of thought, I beheld, little more than an arm's length from the vessel, huge rocks protruding out of the water. I thought: "So He bringeth us." My dear friends, I beseech you to halt this morning, and put out the rope of faith, that Jesus, the great Pilot, may come on board. You may be nearing agitated waters and dangerous rapids, which will wreck you for ever without His guidance.—Thos. Kelly.

Lives—Reflected.

"How do you know that Christ is risen?" some one asked an old fisherman, whose faith in Jesus seemed very simple and sure. "Do you see those cottages near the cliff?" he replied. "Well, sometimes, when I am far out at sea, I know that the sun is risen by the reflection in those windows. How do I know that Christ is risen? Because I see His light reflected from the faces of some of my fellows every day, and because I feel the light of His glory in my own life." A reflector of Jesus! You and I may be that. His glory may shine through us.—*The Sunday Circle.*

Lord Forever.

A Christian worker put the words C-H-R-I-S-T I-S L-O-R-D on the dial of his watch in the place of the numbers, and whenever he looked at his watch he would say, "Well, Christ is Lord, whatever time it is." —*Sunday School Builder.*

Master—Following The.

Mechanics are well aware that the engines on which they spend their powers are far from perfect. But, if some day a machine immensely superior to any that had been produced were devised and constructed by one of themselves, the whole trade would at once undergo a revolution. Employers, designers, draftsmen, molders, finishers, fitters, the whole population of the place, would vie with one another in their efforts to equal or surpass the achievement. If, perhaps, like ignorant Russian peasants, they broke the splendid instrument, or if they put it into a glass case as a mere curiosity, yet, after a while, a wiser counsel would prevail. Our great Fellow-workman produced a matchless work; and although for a time His jealous comrades endeavored to crush it and to suppress the very mention of it, yet, in the end, they began to copy it. The life of Jesus, if it had been an example and nothing more, must certainly have left its mark on the customs of the world.—C. N. MOODY.

Mediator.

In foreign courts we have ministers and ambassadors to intercede for us. They are mediators; they are intercessors. There is an unacquaintance, a strangeness, in foreign courts, of the affairs of another people, either from attending to their own business, or some other cause, and hence the necessity of our sending ambassadors to them. But it cannot be supposed that there is any such ignorance of our affairs in the mind of God. You must drop all such idea of the intercessorship of Christ as that he is one to convey information, to adjust facts, or to make things clearer in the divine mind than they were already. His mediatorship affects us, not God.— H. W. BEECHER.

Messiah—The True.

A Jewish soldier had been attending services where he heard much of the character and teaching of Christ. He went to his Rabbi and said: "Rabbi, the Christians say that the Christ has already come, while we claim that he is yet to come." "Yes," assented the Rabbi. "Well," asked the young soldier, "When our Christ comes, what will he have on Jesus Christ?" What the Rabbi said we do not know. What could he say?—*A Camp Pastor.*

Pilot—A New.

As a great ocean steamer nears a coast, the captain and helmsman need a minuteness of knowledge which they do not possess. Unknown dangers, hidden rocks and shoals, are all around them. So a pilot comes off from shore, climbs on board, and takes his place at the wheel. Instantly the control of the ship is transferred from ignorance to knowledge and incompetency to ability. Just such a transfer takes place in a life that is surrendered to the Infinite Pilot. He knows every sea, to the least shifting bar and the slightest wind that blows. He will bring us to the desired haven.—*Christian Commonwealth.*

Pleasing Men or Serving Christ.

A railway-gate keeper who, one cold night required every passenger to show his ticket before passing through to the train, and was rewarded with considerable grumbling and protesting, was told, "You are a very unpopular man to-night." "I only care to be popular with one man," was the reply, "and that is the superintendent." He might have pleased the passengers, disobeyed orders, and lost his position. He was too wise for that; his business was to please one man—the man who hired him, gave him his orders, and rewarded him for faithfulness, and who would discharge him for disobedience. The servant of Christ has many opportunities to make himself unpopular. There are multitudes who would be glad to have him relax the strictness of his rules. If he is their servant they demand that he should consult their wishes. But if he serves them, he cannot serve the Lord. "No man can serve two masters." He who tries to be popular with the world, will lose his popularity with the Lord. He will make friends, but he will lose the one Friend who is above all others. He will win plaudits, but he will not hear the gracious word, "Well done!"—T. GUTHRIE.

Pilot—A Safe.

A passenger, who had been looking with great interest at the "man at the wheel" as he was directing the course of a steamboat through the windings of an intricate channel, said to him: "I suppose, sir, you are the pilot of this boat?" "Yes," replied the man at the wheel, "I have been a pilot on these waters for over thirty years." "Indeed!" continued the inquirer; "you must, then, by this time, know every, rock and bar and shoal on the whole coast!" "No, I don't; not by a long ways," said the pilot. "You don't!" responded the passenger, in great surprise; "what, then, do you know?" "I know," answered the pilot with strong emphasis, "I know where the deep water is."

Revelation—Progressive.

A friend of mine visited Mr. Prang's chromo establishment in Boston. Mr. Prang showed him a stone on which was laid the color for making the first impression toward producing the portrait of a distinguished public man, but he could see only the faintest possible line of tinting. The next stone that the paper was submitted to deepened the color a little, but still no trace of the man's face was visible. Again and again was the sheet passed over successive stones, until at last the outline of a man's face was dimly discerned. Finally, after some twenty impressions from as many different stones, the portrait of the distinguished man stood forth so perfectly that it seemed to lack only the power of speech to make it living. Thus it is with

Christ in the Scriptures.—G. JACK-SON.

Saviour—Linked to the.

Two travelers, who fancied they were abundantly able to take care of themselves, entered a railway carriage when the train was being made up and found comfortable seats. They had dropped into conversation when a porter looked in and told them to go forward. "What is the matter with this coach?" they asked. "Nothing," he grinned, "only 'taint coupled on to anything that'll take you anywhere." That is the trouble with many beautiful creeds and theories—they sound well, but they do not take you anywhere. The soul that would journey heavenward must make sure of the coupling. This is it: "Whosoever shall call upon the name of the Lord shall be saved."—*The Sunday School Chronicle.*

Saviour—No Room for.

One of Rev. Murray M'Cheyne's elders was in deep darkness and distress for a few weeks, but one Sunday after the pastor's faithful preaching he found his way to the Lord. At the close of the service, he told Mr. M'Cheyne, who knew of his spiritual concern, that he had found the Lord. When he was asked to explain how this happy change had come about, he said, "I have been making a great mistake. I have always been coming to the Lord as something better than I was, and going to the wrong door to ask admittance; but this afternoon I went round to the sinner's door, and for the first time cried, like the publican, 'Lord, be merciful to me a sinner'; and, oh, sir, I received such a welcome from the Saviour!" Are any of our readers like the self-righteous Phar-

isee? Such have no room for the Saviour; for the Lord "came not to call the righteous, but sinners to repentance."

Sowing Good Seed.

It was a Jew who brought the Gospel to Rome; a Roman who took it to France; a Frenchman who took it to Scandinavia; a Scandinavian who took it to Scotland; a Scotchman who evangelized Ireland, and an Irishman in turn made the missionary conquest of Scotland. No people have ever received the Gospel except at the hands of an alien.—*Southern Christian Advocate.*

Spirit—The Master's.

How deeply must those who believed in Jesus for His works' sake have endeared themselves to Him in the midst of so much unbelief and opposition! History tells of a young paint-grinder in the studio of Italy's greatest master, who developed striking evidences of artistic skill. When an enemy of the great teacher came to the boy and urged him to found a school of his own, saying that wealth and honors and invitations to kings' palaces might be his, the youth answered in effect: "I am not ambitious to found a school or dwell in a palace, but I am ambitious to catch Raphael's spirit, and reproduce in myself his ideals."—ORSIN EDSON CROOKER.

"Suffered In All Points."

They tell us, that, in some trackless lands, when one friend passes through the pathless forests, he breaks a twig ever and anon as he goes, that those who come after may see the traces of his having been there, and may know that they are not out of the road. Oh! when we are journeying through the murky night, and the dark woods of affliction and sorrow, it is something to find here and there a spray broken, or a leafy stem bent down with the tread of His foot and the brush of his hand as he passed; and to remember that the path he trod he has hallowed, and that there are lingering fragrances and hidden strengths in the remembrance, "in all points tempted as we are," bearing grief for us, bearing grief with us, bearing grief like us.—J. MAC-LAREN.

Teacher—The Great.

A young pianist was giving concerts in the provinces of Germany, and, to add to her renown, she announced herself as a pupil of the celebrated Liszt. Arriving at a small provincial town, she advertised a concert in the usual way; but what was her astonishment and terror to see in the list of new arrivals at the hotel the name of "M. l'Abbe Liszt!" What was she to do? Her deception would be discovered, and she could never dare to give another concert. In her despair she adopted the wisest course, and went direct to the Abbe himself. Pale, trembling, and deeply agitated, she entered the presence of the great maestro to confess her fraud, and to implore forgiveness. She threw herself at his feet, her face bathed in tears, and related to him the history of her life. Left an orphan when very young, and possessing nothing but her musical gifts, she had ventured to shelter herself under the protection of his great name, and thus to overcome the many obstacles which opposed her. Without that she would have been nothing—nobody. But could he ever forgive her? "Come, come," said the great artist, helping her to rise, "we shall see what we can do. Here is a piano. Let me hear a piece intended for the concert tomorrow." She obeyed, and played, at first timidly then with all the enthusiasm of reviving hope. The maestro stood near her, gave her some advice, suggested some improvements, and when she had finished her piece, said most kindly—"Now, my child, I have given you a music lesson. You are a pupil of Liszt." Before she could recover herself sufficiently to utter a word of acknowledgment, he added, "Are the programmes printed?" "Not yet, sir." "Then let them add to your programme that you will be assisted by your master, and that the last piece will be played by the Abbe Liszt." Could any reproof be keener than such forgiving kindness —such noble generosity as this? The illustrious musician would no doubt have been questioned, and it would have been impossible for him to speak anything but the truth. But charity is ingenious in covering "a multitude of sins."—*Christian Chronicle.*

The Great Physician.

Mary recognized that the Lord could deal direct with the servants without doing it through her. A poor Romanist was contending with a missionary in favor of virgin intercesson. The missionary replied by asking, "When you are sick, whom do you send for?" "Why, a doctor, of course." "Why don't you send for the doctor's mother?"—*The Armor of Light.*

The Powerful and Powerless Grave.

A stanza from an old hymn says that Jesus Christ "burst the bars" of the grave and "tore the bars away." If a man bursts the bars of State's prison all the police force of the commonwealth is after him to bring him back. If, on the contrary, he has served out his full time, all the power in the State cannot retain him a single hour longer. Jesus Christ must remain in the grave three days according to Scripture, but after the three days had expired there was not power enough in Heaven or in hell to retain him another moment.—*Moody Bible Institute.*

Tomb—The Unique.

When the Garden Tomb was discovered in 1885, the godly General Gordon was convinced that this was the place where the body of Jesus had lain. There is a traditional tomb inside the wall of modern Jerusalem but no certainty attaches to the site. The Garden Tomb, hidden for centuries, was covered with rubbish twenty feet high. When they first cleared the spot, with great caution they gathered all the dust and débris from within the tomb and carefully shipped it to the Scientific Association of Great Britain. Every part of it was analyzed, but there were no traces of human remains. If this is the real tomb of Christ, then Jesus was the first to be laid there and he was also the last.—*The Alliance Weekly.*

Wings—Our.

An evangelist was asked, "What is the more necessary, secret prayer or searching the Scripture?" He answered by asking another question, "What is the more necessary for a bird, the right wing or the left wing?"—*Moody Monthly.*

Word of Life.

The other day I was reading a story of a Frenchman who was being entertained by a Christian chief in one of the Pacific Islands.

The chief had a Bible, which the Frenchman sneered at, saying that in Europe they had got past that. The chief led his guest out of the house, showed him where they used to cook and eat their meals in cannibal days, and clinched everything by saying, "My friend, if it had not been for that Book, I should have been dining upon you now."—J. R. WALKER.

Christus Consolator.

"I am the Resurrection and the Life; he that believeth in Me, though he were dead, yet shall he live: and whosoever liveth and believeth in Me shall never die."— JESUS.

Beside the dead I knelt for prayer,
And felt a Presence as I prayed,
Lo! it was Jesus standing there.
He smiled: "Be not afraid!"

"Lord, Thou hast conquered death, we know;
Restore again to life," I said,
"This one who died an hour ago."
He smiled: "He is not dead!"

"Asleep, then, as Thyself didst say,
Yet Thou canst lift the lids that keep
His prisoned eyes from ours away!"
He smiled: "He doth not sleep!"

"Nay, then, tho' haply he do wake,
And look upon some fairer dawn,
Restore him to our hearts that ache!"
He smiled: "He has not gone!"

"Alas! too well we know our loss,
Nor hope again our joy to touch
Until the stream of death we cross."
He smiled: "There is no such!"

"Yet our beloved seem so far,
The while we yearn to feel them near,
Albeit with Thee we trust they are."
He smiled: "And I am here!"

"Dear Lord, how shall we know
  that they
 Still walk unseen with us and
  Thee,
Nor sleep, nor wander far away?"
He smiled: "Abide in Me."

Comfort in Christ.

When the lights of life are gleam-
  ing,
  Where its blossoms bud and
  bloom;
When each brow is bound with
  roses,
  As we bask in their perfume:
Just beyond the smiles and sun-
  shine,
All unseen the Master stands,
Waiting ever, ever waiting,
  Holding out His pierced hands.

When the lights of life are dark-
  ened,
  As its flowers fall and fade,
And we watch our loved ones van-
  ish
  Thro' the silence, and the shade:
Then the Master draweth nearer,
  Thro' the circling shadow lands;
Waiting ever, ever waiting,
  Holding out His pierced hands.

When the shades of night are fall-
  ing,
  Where each heart must stand
  alone,
And the world has left us nothing
  We can call or claim our own:
Then we turn to meet the Master,
  Where a halo lights the past,
Waiting ever, ever waiting,
  Till we clasp His hands at last.

The Christ Ideal.

James Russell Lowell was a
poet, a statesman, a man of the
world. You know his poem, "A
Parable":

Said Christ our Lord, "I will go and
  see
How the men, My Brethren, believe
  in Me.

Great organs surged through arches
  dim
Their jubilant floods in praise of
  Him:
And in church, and palace, and judg-
  ment-hall,
He saw His own image high over
  all.
But still, wherever His steps they
  led,
The Lord in sorrow bent down His
  head:
And from under the heavy founda-
  tion-stones,
The Son of Mary heard bitter
  groans.

"Have ye founded your thrones and
  altars, then,
On the bodies and souls of living
  men?
And think ye that building shall
  endure,
Which shelters the noble and
  crushes the poor?"

Then Christ sought out an artisan,
A low-browed, stunted, haggard
  man,
And a motherless girl, whose fin-
  gers thin
Pushed from her faintly want and
  sin.
These set He in the midst of them,
And as they drew back their gar-
  ment-hem,
For fear of defilement, "Lo, here,"
  said He,
"The images ye have made of Me!"

CHURCH

Church—A Cold.

"One day, when I was serving my apprenticeship in a factory on the banks of the Merrimac River," says the Hon. N. P. Banks, late Governor of Massachusetts, "a party of the hands saw a man a quarter of a mile down the river struggling amongst the broken cakes of ice. We could none of us for the moment determine his political complexion or bodily color, but he proved, in the end, to be a negro in the water. Of course the first care was to rescue him; but twice the victim slipped from the plank that was thrown him. The third time it was evident to our inner hearts that it was the negro's last chance, and so he evidently thought; but as he again slipped from the board, he shouted, 'For the love of God, gentlemen, give me hold of the wooden end of the plank this time.'" We had been holding him the icy end." How often do Christians make the same mistake! We turn the icy end of the plank to our fellows, and then wonder why they do not hold on, and why our efforts do not save them.—*Preacher's Lantern.*

Church—A Defective.

A father took his little child out into the field one Sabbath, and he lay down under a beautiful shady tree, it being a hot day. The little child ran about gathering wild flowers and little blades of grass, and coming to his father and saying: "Pretty! pretty!" At last the father fell asleep, and while he was sleeping the child wandered away. When he awoke, his first thought was "where is my child?" He looked all around, but he could not see him. He shouted at the top of his voice, and all he heard was the echo of his own voice. No response! Running to a little hill, he looked around, but all he heard was his own voice. Then going to a precipice at some distance, he looked down, and there upon the rocks and briers, he saw th mangled form of his loved child. He rushed to the spot, and took up the lifeless corpse, and hugged it to his bosom, and accused himself of being the murderer of his own child. While he was sleeping his child had wandered over the precipice. I thought as I heard that, what a picture of the Church of God! How many fathers and mothers, how many Christian men are sleeping now while their children wander over the terrible precipice a thousand times worse than that precipice, right into the bottomless pit of hell. Father, where is your boy to-night?—Moody.

Church—A Live.

The Bishop of Nelson (New Zealand), at a recent meeting, told of two men who met recently, and one asked the other for a subscription for his church. The reply was that the church was always wanting money. The other friend said, "When my lad was a boy, he was costly; he always wanted boots and shoes, stockings and clothes, and wore them out fast, and the older and stronger he grew the more money had to be spent on him, but he died, and does not now cost me a shilling." "Yes," said the Bishop, "a live church always wants money."—*The Christian Herald.*

Church—A Strong.

"Is it a strong congregation?" asked a man respecting a body of worshipers. "Yes," was the reply. "How many members are there?" "Seventy-six." "Seventy-six! Are they so very wealthy?" "No, they are poor." "How, then, do you say it is a strong church?" "Because," said the gentleman, "they are earnest, devoted, at peace, loving each other, and striving together to do the Master's work. Such a congregation is strong, whether composed of a dozen or five hundred members!" And he spoke the truth.

Church Attendance.

Hoffman, the famous German chemist, once related an experience he had. In 1890 he visited Glasgow, arriving in the town late on Saturday night. The following morning he went to call on Sir William Thompson, after Lord Kelvin. The door-bell was answered by the parlor maid, of whom Hoffman asked if Sir William were at home. "Sir, he most certainly is not." "Could you tell me where I might find him?" "You will find him in church sir," was the reply—"where you ought to be."—*Sunday School Chronicle.*

Church Atmosphere.

Do not some professors cause sinners to loiter by their own loitering? A man taking a seat at the Tabernacle came to the minister and said, "Sir, do I understand that if I become a seat-holder I shall be expected to be converted?" "Yes," was the reply, "I hope you will, and I pray that it may be so. Do you object?" The answer was, "O sir, I desire it above everything." Was not the man hastened by the general feeling of hopefulness which pervaded the Church? Assuredly there is much in the atmosphere which surrounds a man. Among warm-hearted Christians it is hard for the careless to remain indifferent.—C. H. SPURGEON.

Church—False Efforts In.

Horace Greeley once received a letter from a woman stating that her church was in distressing financial straits. They had tried every device they could think of—fairs, strawberry festivals, oyster suppers, a donkey party, turkey banquets, Japanese weddings, poverty sociables, mock marriages, grab-bags, box sociables and necktie sociables. "Would Mr. Greeley be so kind as to suggest some new device to keep the struggling church from disbanding?" The editor replied: "Try religion."—*Presbyterian Record.*

Church Members—Fussy.

When a man enlists in the army he takes on sacred obligations. If in the midst of a battle he were to quit fighting because the drill sergeant did not call him by his right name, he would not be shot. I do not think he would be even hanged. They would simply throw him into a ditch, away from the sight of noble men. But a full-grown man will unite with the Christian Church, assuming the most sacred, binding and exalted obligations in the world. On the slightest pretext he will quit. Perhaps the minister has not recognized him on the street, one of the deacons failed to call him by name in the church, he is asked for money, or he does not like the choir. Any trivial pretext will do. Immediately he disregards every solemn obligation. If you were to tell him that his sin is worse than perjury, he would be insulted. Yet it is. If you were to tell him that his disloyalty in this regard is more despicable than the disloyalty of a traitor to his country, he would not believe you. Yet it is.—C. A. EATON.

Church Members Marking Time.

Two sailors happened to be on a military parade-ground when the soldiers were at drill, going through the evolution of marking time. One sailor, observing the other watching the movement of the company very attentively, with eyes fixed and arms akimbo, asked him what he thought of it. "Well, Jack," replied his comrade, "I am thinking there must be a pretty strong tide running this morning, for these poor fellows have been pulling away this half-hour, and have not got an inch ahead yet."

Church On Fire.

In my boyhood a large frame church building was burned down in my native village. Although it had not been a very active church, it had a large membership, and there was much interest in the catastrophe. The fire occurred at night, and, as the building was large, it made an immense bonfire, and of course people flocked from far and near to see it. A member of the church said somewhat peevishly to a known skeptic who was in the crowd, "I never saw you come near this church before." "No," replied the other, "but then I never saw this church on fire before."—*Sunday School Times.*

Church Union.

When the tide is out you may have noticed, as you rambled among the rocks, little pools with little fishes in them. To the shrimp, in such a pool, his foot depth of salt water is all the ocean for the time being. He has no dealings with his neighbor shrimp in the adjacent pool, though it may be only a few inches of sand that divide them; but when the rising ocean begins to lip over the margin of the lurking-place, one pool joins another, their various tenants meet, and by-and-by, in place of their little patch of standing water, they have the ocean's boundless fields to roam in.

When the tide is out—when religion is low—the faithful are to be found isolated, here a few and there a few, in the little standing pools that stud the beach, having no dealings with their neighbors of the adjoining pools, calling them Samaritans, and fancying that their own little communion includes all that are precious in God's sight. They forget, for a time, that there is a vast and expansive ocean rising —every ripple brings it nearer,—a mightier communion, even the communion of saints, which is to engulf all minor considerations, and to enable the fishes of all pools—the Christians—the Christians of all denominations—to come together. When, like a flood, the Spirit flows into the Churches, Church will join to Church, and saint will join to saint, and all will rejoice to find that if their little pools have perished, it is not by the scorching summer's drought, nor the casting in of earthly rubbish, but by the influx of that boundless sea whose glad waters touch eternity, and in whose ample depths the saints in heaven, as well as the saints on earth, have room enough to range.—DR. HAMILTON.

Church—Protection of.

A story is told of two sailors who were shipwrecked and thrown upon an unknown island. They began to reconnoitre carefully, thinking that the island might be peopled by cannibals. To get a view of the valley, one of them climbed a high tree, and when he looked around, he suddenly sang out a loud "Hurrah!" "What is it?" cried his companion. "The spire of a church in the valley," was the reply. Where Christ is known, enemies are changed to friends, and men are safe as was prophesied at the birth of John the Baptist.—*The Christian Endeavor World.*

Church—The True.

Some churches are like light-houses, built of stone, so strong that the thunder of the sea cannot move them,—with no light at the top. That which is the light of the world in the Church is not its largeness, not its services celebrant with pomp and beauty, not its music, not the influences in it that touch the taste or instruct the understanding: it is the Christlikeness of its individual members.—H. W. BEECHER.

Church—Trouble in.

The statement was made to me by a friend who gave it as a reason for remaining out of the Church. He believed he was saying something which justified his course. He believes in Jesus, but discounts heavily the Church which Jesus founded and commissioned. The faults of the Church are most clearly seen by those who are doing the tasks assigned to the Church and who are responsible for her nurture. Men do not remain aloof from families, yet there never has been an ideal family except in poetry and fiction. The application of the principle would estop all effort in every line of service. The Church is not an abstract body of perfect beings. Her members are people with prejudices and bad tempers and bad judgment and all that, but folks for whom Christ died.

It is an old story. In Paul's church at Philippi, Euodias and Syntyche had rival plans for the Ladies' Aid and they were disrupting the church by their arguments. It must have been very damaging, for Paul wrote and besought them to get together. Prominent men in another church made shipwreck of faith. It was disconcerting, but these leaders on the shoals were no argument against the Church. In Corinth the church was split over whether a Christian might go into the public market and buy meat for his table without disloyalty to Christ. Modernism broke out in another church and spiritualized the resurrection. Paul called attention to the harm the babblers were doing and kept on building churches. He made note of a defection led by Phygellus and Hermogenes. In the important church of Ephesus a man by the name of Diotrephes aspired to leadership without spiritual qualifications. He so longed for preeminence that he ignored the apostle John. So the story runs in the New Testament, not to speak of the Old, and has continued to run ever since.

But I have always had the comforting notion that our Lord foresaw all this. Satan tempts good men to remain aloof from the Church because of human weaknesses; for the same reason Christ urges good men to enlist in the Church for service. Mistakes look worse in the Church than anywhere else. Hypocrisy becomes evident only when it crawls out of the world into the Church. On the background of the high aspirations of men and the moral beauty of Christ it is seen for what it is. People who are looking for a utopian church will never find it on earth. With the sympathy, patience and charity of Christ, let us carry on in His own organization.—WILLIAM M. CURRY.

Church—Joining.

A writer in the *Messenger* tells the following: The best illustration that I ever heard, showing the disadvantages of living a Christian life outside the church, was given by a young convert whom I had recently received into our church. I expressed my pleasure in the step he had taken when he replied: "I had not made up my mind to join when I came to the meeting tonight, but while you were talking, I thought it was just like buying a ticket to Chicago, and then riding on the platform. I thought I might as well go inside."

Church—Judging the.

An American gentleman said to a friend, "I wish you would come down to my garden, and taste my apples." He asked him about a dozen times, but the friend did not come; and at last the fruit-grower said, "I suppose you think my apples are good for nothing, so you won't come and try them."—"Well, to tell the truth," said the friend, "I have tasted them. As I went along the road, I picked one up that fell over the wall, and I never tasted anything so sour in all my life; and I do not particularly wish to have any more of your fruit."—"Oh," said the owner of the garden, "I thought it must be so. Those apples around the outside are for the special benefit of the boys. I went fifty miles to select the sourest sorts to plant all round the orchard, so the boys might give up as not worth stealing; but, if you will come inside, you will find that we grow a very different quality there, sweet as honey." Those who judge the church by its worst members, those most like the world, make the same mistake.—SPURGEON.

Christian Unity.

When General Grant was in front of Richmond, and his army had been repulsed in the Wilderness, he called together his co-commanders and held a council, and asked them what they thought he had better do. They were General Sherman and General Howard, now leading generals, and all thought he had better

retreat. He heard them through, and then broke up the council of war and sent them back to their headquarters; but before morning an orderly came round with a despatch from the General directing an advance in solid column on the enemy at daylight. That was what took Richmond and broke down the rebellion in our country. Christians, let us advance in solid column against the enemy; let us lift high the standard, and in the name of our God let us lift our voice, and let us work together, shoulder to shoulder, and keep our eye single to the honor and glory of Christ.—MOODY.

Dissensions—Trivial.

Dr. Cannon was once appealed to by a certain church where there was a great commotion in regard to the point, whether in newly painting their church edifice the color should be white or yellow. When the committee had stated their case, and with an emphasis, not to say acrimony, which gave sad proof of the existence of a fearful feud upon the unimportant question, the doctor quietly said, "I should advise you, on the whole, to paint the house black. It is cheap, and a good color to wear, and eminently appropriate for a body that ought to go in mourning over such a foolish quarrel among its members."—*Homiletic Encyclopaedia.*

Example—A Good.

George Washington's pastor said of him: "No company ever kept him away from church. I have often been at Mount Vernon on the Sabbath morning when his breakfast table was filled with guests. But to him they furnished no pretext for neglecting his God and losing the satisfaction of setting a good example.

Instead of staying at home out of fancied courtesy to them, he used constantly to invite them to accompany him."—CHARLES W. ANDERSON.

Manned by Dead Men.

Have you ever read "The Ancient Mariner"? I dare say you thought it one of the strangest imaginations ever put together, especially that part where the old mariner represents the corpses of all the dead men rising up to man the ship,—dead men pulling the rope, dead men steering, dead men spreading sails. I thought what a strange idea that was. But do you know, I have lived to see that time. I have gone into churches, and I have seen a dead man in the pulpit, a dead man as deacon, a dead man handling the plate, and dead men sitting to hear.—SPURGEON.

Spiritual Strength.

To stay away from church services because we have so many other engagements and so little strength left is like staying away from the table because we are so weak and hungry, and it takes all our time to sweep and wash dishes. The church is a place to get spiritual strength for other duties, just as the table is a place to get bodily strength.— *Christian Endeavor World.*

Unity—Strength in.

During the siege of the legations in Peking national lines and religious lines were forgotten. In the presence of the infuriated Boxers all felt that they were one and that their salvation depended upon their standing together. Protestant and Catholic and Greek were one for the time. During the siege wherever the line was hard pressed there the defenders rallied, regardless of what nationality held the hard pressed point, because a failure at one point meant a failure at every point. One of the interesting incidents of the siege was connected with the international gun. This was an old English six-pounder. It was mounted on an Austrian carriage; it was loaded with German powder and Russian shells; it was fired by the trained hand and eye of an American gunner. Had it not been for the spirit of unity that prevailed in that most critical period all must have perished.—A. McLEAN.

Voice of Another World.

One of the most popular legends in Brittany is that relating to an imaginary town called Is, which is supposed to have been swallowed up by the sea at some unknown time. There are several places along the coast which are pointed out as the site of this imaginary city, and the fishermen have many strange tales to tell of it. According to them, the tips of the spires of the churches may be seen in the hollow of the waves when the sea is rough, while during a calm the music of the bells, ringing out a hymn appropriate to the day, rises above the waters. I often fancy that I have at the bottom of my heart a city of Is, with its bells calling to prayer a recalcitrant congregation. At times I halt to listen to these gentle vibrations, which seem as if they came from immeasurable depths, like voices from another world.—E. RENAN.

Washington and Worship.

George Washington, at the beginning of the War of the Revolution, issued an order from which I quote:—"That the troops may have an opportunity of attending public worship, as well as to take some rest after the great fatigue they have gone through, the general in future excuses them from fatigue duty on Sundays, except at the shipyards or on special occasions, until further orders. We can have but little hope of the blessing of Heaven on our arms if we insult it by our impiety and folly."—J. H. VINCENT.

Worship or Natural Emotion.

The enjoyment of noble architecture and music is not worship, and may be mistaken for it. The hush which falls on us, walking the aisles of a church of eight hundred years; the thrill of nerves and heart as the glorious praise begins, whose echoes fail amid fretted vaults and clustered shafts; all that feeling, solemn as it is, has no necessary connection with worshiping God in spirit and in truth. And we may delude ourselves with the belief that we are offering spiritual worship when it is all a mere matter of natural emotion, which the most godless man could share.—A. K. H. BOYD.

CHRISTIANS

Blessings—Count Your.

I was walking along one winter's night hurrying towards home, with my little maiden at my side. Said she, "Father, I am going to count the stars." "Very well," I said; "go on." By and by I heard her counting—"Two hundred and twenty-three, two hundred and twenty-four, two hundred and twenty-five. Oh! dear," she said, "I had no idea there were so many." Ah! dear friends, I sometimes say in my soul, "Now, Master, I am going to count Thy benefits." I am like the little maiden. Soon my heart sighs—sighs not with sorrow, but burdened with such goodness, and I say within myself, "Ah! I had no idea that there were so many."—M. G. PEARSE.

Christian Comfort.

A Quaker gentleman, riding in a carriage with a fashionable lady decked with a profusion of jewelry, heard her complain of the cold. Shivering in her lace bonnet and shawl as light as cobweb, she exclaimed,—

"What shall I do to get warm?"

"I really don't know," replied the Quaker solemnly, "unless thee should put on another breast-pin!"

Christian—A Banished.

In the early history of Burmese missions, a young Burman of superior rank became a convert. His sister was a maid of honor to the queen, and being greatly distressed at his change of religion, and thinking if she could separate him from the missionary he would soon forget the foreign ideas, she obtained for him an appointment, which he was obliged to accept, as governor of a distant province. He had not been long at his new post, when some Karens were brought before him

accused of worshiping a strange God. "What God?" he asked. "They call Him the eternal God," was the reply. A few questions satisfied the young governor that he had fellow-Christians before him. To the great surprise of the accusers he ordered the prisoners to be dismissed.—*Fifteen Hundred Illustrations.*

Christian—A Humble.

A farmer went with his son into a wheat-field to see if it was ready for the harvest. "See, father," exclaimed the boy, "how straight these stems hold up their heads! They must be the best ones. Those that hang their heads down I am sure cannot be good for much." The farmer plucked a stalk of each kind, and said, "See here, foolish child! This stalk that stood so straight is light-headed, and almost good for nothing, while this that hung its head so modestly is full of the most beautiful grain."

Christian—A Sleepy.

A church asleep is as useless as a dead church. A Christian asleep is a standing reproach to Christianity. A French dramatist read his latest production to a circle of critics, and while he was reading one of the critics fell asleep. The reader stopped long enough to say, "How can you criticize my production when you are sound asleep?" "I submit," said the critic, rubbing his eyes, "that sleep is a criticism." And so it is. If Christianity means anything, it means everything, and a sleeping Christian is a perpetual argument against Christianity.—A. C. DIXON.

Christian—A Useful.

The legend tells that the visits of a goddess to an ancient city were always known, although no eye sighted her. She paused before a lightning-blasted tree, and lo! the woodbine sprang up and covered the tree's nakedness. She lingered by the stagnant pool—the pool became a flowing stream. She rested upon a decaying log, and lo! it became a fruitful tree. She crossed a brook, and lo! wherever she put down her foot the flowers came to birth. It is even so with the life nourished and cherished by God. It leaves its mark—a gracious mark—wherever it goes. "The wilderness and the solitary places are made glad."—J. PEARCE.

Christian—Be Watchful.

A recent writer describes the strange alluring splendor of the beds of anemones which cover the floors of some Western seas. These gaudy, dainty flowers appear like blossoms from the garden of Paradise, so brilliantly colored are they. Yet, in fact, they are cruel, devouring monsters, for let a poor fish only touch them, and a thousand poisoned threadlets dart out, seize the victim, and in a moment he is consumed by the innocent-looking blossom. So, under the secret attractions of much of our social, commercial and religious life, there are deadly snares and destructions that lie in wait for the unwary. Many a fair-looking friendship, festivity and recreation holds a peril striking at the soul. We need the Divine wisdom to preserve us, for things are not what they seem.—J. WILBUR CHAPMAN.

Christians—Bigoted.

Jenny Lind once went to hear Father Taylor preach in Boston; but the preacher, ignorant of her presence, paid a glowing tribute to her powers of song. As the Swedish nightingale leaned forward with delight, drinking in this unexpected praise, a tall man who sat on the pulpit-stairs rose and wanted to know whether any one who had died at Miss Lind's concerts would go to heaven. Father Taylor said, "Sir, a Christian will go to heaven wherever he dies; but a fool will be a fool, even though he be on the pulpit-stairs."—*Life of Father Taylor.*

Christians—Criticizing.

The tyrant Dionysius, to palliate his (Plato's) enmity, previous to his departure, made pompous entertainments. At one of them, however, he could not help saying, "I suppose, Plato, when you return to your companions in the Academy, my faults will often be the subject of your conversation." "I hope," answered Plato, "we shall never be so much at a loss for subjects in the Academy as to talk of you."—PLUTARCH.

Christians—Detached.

The bulletin of a Southern church quotes from the railroad coupon this expression, "Not good if detached," and applies it to the members of the church who have detached themselves from it. As the coupon receives value by its relation to the whole ticket, so do church members receive value by their relation to the entire body.—*Christian Union Herald.*

Christians—Differences in.

There are differences of character, which, springing from constitutional peculiarities or early education, grace will modify, but never altogether eradicate on this side of the grave. Such are those in Bunyan's pictures, all painted, no doubt, from life; as well Greatheart the giant-killer, a hero of a hundred battles, as Mr. Feeblemind, who started at his own shadow, and trembled at the falling of a leaf. There are also differences among Christians, which imply no defect; just as there are in countenances which are very unlike, and yet, be the complexion dark or fair, the hair of golden color, or like the raven's wing, are very beautiful. We do no expect, or even wish, all good men to be alike, any more than we would have all the members of a family alike, all flowers alike,—none but roses in the garden, or daisies in the field; the Church of Christ, like the meadows below, or the star-spangled heavens above, owing its beauty in part to that variety in unity which marks all the works of God, and mars none of them.—Dr. Guthrie.

Christians—Dwarfed.

One of the strange freaks of Japanese horticulture is the cultivation of dwarf trees. The Japanese grow forest giants in flowerpots. Some of these strange miniature trees are a century old, and are only two or three feet high. The gardener, instead of trying to get them to grow to their best, takes infinite pains to keep them little. His purpose is to grow dwarfs, not giant trees. From the time of their planting they are repressed, starved, crippled, stunted. When buds appear, they are nipped off. So the tree remains only a dwarf all its life.

Some Christian people seem to do the same thing with their lives. They do not allow themselves to grow. They rob themselves of spiritual nourishment, restrain the noble impulses of their nature, shut out of their hearts the power of the Holy Spirit, and are only dwarf Chris-

tians when they might be strong in Christ Jesus, with the abundant life which the Master wants all His followers to have.—J. R. Miller.

Christians—False.

Gipsy Smith tells of a certain woman he once saw in a gipsy camp. She was well disguised, and was telling fortunes to people. Mr. Smith, because he so thoroughly knew his own people, readily saw that she was not what she claimed to be. After talking with her for a time, she laughed and said: "Oh, I can't fool you; I ain't a real gipsy; I just joined." The sweet-spirited evangelist lamented that there are, in the family home of Christ, so many who have "just joined," and are not "real" Christians.—*The Sunday School Times.*

Christians—Faulty.

Scipio Africanus had a son, who had nothing of the father but the name—a coward,—a dissolute, sorry rake,—the son of one of the greatest generals in the world! This son wore a ring upon his finger, wherein was his father's picture. His life and character were so opposite to those of his father, and so unworthy, that, by an act of the senate, he was commanded to forbear wearing that ring. They judged it unfit that he should have the honor to wear the picture of his father, who would not himself bear the resemblance of his father's excellency. The divine command is, "Let every one that nameth the name of Christ depart from iniquity."—Whitecross.

Christian—Half Way.

In South Africa, in looking for diamonds, they often find a substance that is half charcoal and half diamond. It was intended to be a diamond, but it stopped short, and it is only diamondiferous; it is partly a jewel. It stopped short, and will never get into the king's crown. Don't be content to be sprinkled on one part with diamond and the other part with slag.—W. HETHERINGTON.

Christian—Honoring A.

In one of the older States resided an infidel, the owner of a saw-mill, situated by the side of a highway, over which a large portion of a Christian congregation passed every Sabbath to and from the church. This infidel, having no regard for the Sabbath, was as busy, and his mill was as noisy, on that holy day as any other. Before long it was observed, however, that a certain time before service the mill would stop, remain silent, and appear to be deserted for a few minutes; when its noise and clatter would recommence and continue till about the close of the service, when for a short time it again ceased. It was soon noticed that one of the deacons of the church passed the mill to the place of worship during the silent interval; and so punctual was he to the hour, that the infidel knew just when to stop the mill, so that it should be silent while the deacon was passing, although he paid no regard to the passing of the others. On being asked why he paid this mark of respect to the deacon, he replied, "The deacon professes just what the rest of you do; but he lives, also, such a life, that it makes me feel bad here (putting his hand upon his heart) to run my mill while he is passing."—ELON FOSTER.

Christians, Selfish.

You have seen a selfish child go into a secret place to enjoy some delicious morsel undisturbed by his companions. So it is with some Christians. They feed upon Christ and forgiveness; but it is alone, and for themselves. When Christ found you, He said, "Go work in my vineyard." What were you hired for if it was not to spread salvation?—McCHEYNE.

Christian Influence.

In a gun factory a great bar of steel, weighing five hundred pounds, and eight feet in length, was suspended vertically by a very delicate chain. Near by, a common bottle-cork was suspended by a silk thread. The purpose was to show that the cork could set the steel bar in motion. It seemed impossible. The cork was swung gently against the steel bar, and the steel bar remained motionless. But it was done again and again for ten minutes, and, lo, at the end of that time the bar gave evidence of feeling uncomfortable; a sort of nervous chill ran over it. Ten minutes later, and the chill was followed by a vibration. At the end of half an hour the great bar was swinging like the pendulum of a clock. And yet there are people who dare assert that they exert no influence in the world!—*The Presbyterian Standard.*

Christians—Loafing.

If we travel slowly, and loiter on the road, Jesus will go on before us, and sin will overtake us. If we are dilatory and lazy in the vineyard, the Master will not smile on us when he walks through his garden. Be active, and expect Christ to be with thee: be idle, and the thorns and briers will grow so thickly, that he will be shut out of thy door.—SPURGEON.

Christian—Misjudging.

Some time ago, a countryman said to me: "I was extremely alarmed this morning, sir; I was going down to a lonely place, and I thought I saw a strange monster. It seemed in motion, but I could not discern its form. I didn't like to turn back, but my heart beat; and the more I looked, the more I was afraid. But as I approached I saw it was a man; and who do you think it was?" "I know not." "Oh, it was my brother John!" "Ah!" said I to myself, as he added that it was early in the morning, and very foggy, "how often do we thus mistake our Christian brethren."— W. JAY.

Christians—Plain.

Some years since, a party of Americans were leaving Cairo for a journey across the desert, and bought vessels in which to carry water. Each one chose the kind of vessel that pleased him. One found jars of brass whose fine designs attracted him. Another purchased porcelain vessels of rare beauty. A third, however, took some plain earthenware bottles. The way across the desert was long and wearisome. The heat was intense. Every drop of water was of value. The brass vessels heated; the water became impure, unfit to drink. The costly porcelain jars cracked in the heat, and the water was lost. But the plain earthenware bottles kept the water pure and sweet to the journey's end.—J. R. MILLER.

Christian Power.

A Buddhist monk in Ceylon, who was acquainted with both Christianity and Buddhism, was once asked what he thought was the great difference between the two. He replied, "There is much that is good in each of them, and probably in all religions. But what seems to me to be the greatest difference is that you Christians know what is right and have power to do it, while we Buddhists know what is right but have not any such power."—THE EXPOSITOR.

Christian Service.

The Congressional Library in Washington is one of the most beautiful buildings in the world. Each alcove of the reading-room is decorated with a distinct and separate design, the decorations in one alcove being in honor of art, in another of history, science, music, philosophy, etc. Before the motto was chosen for the alcove of religion, the Committee entrusted with the matter sent out a request to prominent clergymen and leading religious teachers asking them to send in such for competition. The motto finally selected was the text from Micah—"And what does the Lord require of thee, but to do justly, and to love mercy, and to walk humbly with thy God."—A. LEWIS.

Christian—The Marks of.

Elder Knapp was once showing, in a sermon, the difference between a mere professor and a genuine Christian. By the way of illustration he said that if you should turn the former out of the church he would act like a hog, that turns round and tries to root the pen down; but that the other would be like a lamb, that looks wistfully towards the fold, and longs to be within it again.—*Christian Age.*

Christianity—Effect of.

The shock that buried Lisbon in 1755 never ceased to vibrate, till it reached the wilds of Scotland and the vineyards of Madeira. It was felt among the islands of the Grecian Archipelago, and it changed the level of the solitary lakes that sleep beneath the shadows of the North Alps. Even so the shock that Satan's kingdom sustained when Christianity was established will not cease to vibrate till it move the whole world.—HARDWICKE.

Christianity—Hermetically Sealed.

Some people seem to think that if they can pack the gospel away into a sound and orthodox creed it is perfectly safe. It is a sort of canned fruit of Christianity, hermetically sealed and correctly labeled which will keep for years without decay. An extravagant reliance has been placed, therefore, on confessions of faith as the preservatives of a pure gospel. But the heart is greater than the creed; and if the heart is wrong it will very soon corrupt the creed and interline it with its own heresies. Hence the wise injunction of the Apostle, "Holding the mystery of the faith in a pure conscience."—A. J. GORDON.

Christianity Not on Trial.

Some tourists were visiting one of the great galleries in Europe, and as they looked at those wonderful, priceless masterpieces on the wall, one of them said somewhat contemptuously to his friends and in the hearing of the curator, "I do not think much of these pictures." The curator said, "Excuse me, sir, but it i- not the pictures here which are on trial. It is the visitors."— J. STUART HOLDEN.

Empty Sacks.

When asked what he (Athanasius) thought about the purifying nature of deathbed baptism, he re-

plied, in allusion to such unprofitable converts, "An angel came to my predecessor, Peter, and said, 'Peter, why do you send me these empty sacks?'"—R. HAWEIS.

Fair-Weather Christians.

Captain Speke tells a good story concerning the habits of some of the nations on the coast of Western Africa. In the course of his explorations the good Captain, commiserating the scanty apparel of his negro attendants, gave each of them a fine goat-skin mantle, thinking thereby to subserve the proprieties as well as to increase their comfort, and afford them a protection from the severe storms incident to that latitude. The simple natives were in ecstacies of delight at the gift, and strutted about in their new finery, greatly to the amusement of the Captain who reflected upon the fact that now these poor people would have some protection from the chilling autumnal rains. Things went on well for several days. The sun shone with tropical power, but the natives sweltered away bravely under their unwonted load of clothing, and seemed rapidly learning the habits and customs of civilized life. At length the expected storm arrived, and what was Captain Speke's chagrin to see every one of his men, as soon as it began to sprinkle, take off their mantles, fold them up carefully, wrong side out, thrust them under their arms, and go about shivering in the rain! Some people wear their religious profession very much in the same way. It is an excellent garment to look at. It does admirably in fair weather.—*Preacher's Lantern.*

Fatal Sleep.

The story is told that Satan once summoned his angels to inquire what they had been doing. One said, "I saw a company of Christians crossing the desert, and I let loose the winds of heaven, and their bones are bleaching in the sun." "What of that?" said Satan; "perhaps their souls are saved." Another said, "I saw a ship with missionaries on board going to a heathen land, and I raised a storm and drowned them all." "What of that?" said Satan; "perhaps their souls are saved." And then came forward a subtle spirit, who said, "For fifteen years I have been trying to lull an old Christian to sleep, and I have just succeeded." Whereupon there arose a shout of triumph, the bells of hell rang for joy, and Satan spoke approvingly.—H. T. CAVELL.

Holiness—Beauty of.

After the death of the saintly Mc-Cheyne, a letter addressed to him was found in his locked desk, a letter he had shown to no one while he lived. It was from one who wrote to tell him that he had been the means of leading him to Christ, and in it were these words, "It was nothing that you *said* that first made me wish to be a Christian, it was the beauty of holiness which I saw in your very face."—G. H. KNIGHT.

Jewels—God's.

When in Amsterdam, Holland, last summer," says a traveler, "I was much interested in a visit we made to a place then famous for polishing diamonds. We saw the men engaged in the work. When a diamond is found it is rough and dark like a common pebble. It takes a long time to polish it, and it is very hard work. It is held by means of a piece of metal close to the surface of a large wheel, which is kept going round. Fine diamond

dust is put on this wheel, nothing else being hard enough to polish the diamond. And this work is kept on for months and sometimes several years before it is finished. And if a diamond is intended for a king, then the greater time and trouble are spent upon it." Jesus calls His people His jewels. To fit them for beautifying His crown, they must be polished like diamonds, and He makes use of the troubles He sends to polish His jewels.—*Old Testament Anecdotes.*

Life—The Real.

Thorwaldsen, the great sculptor, was told that there was a dispute about the place and time of his birth, some saying he was born in Copenhagen in 1770, others in Brussels, and so on. He was asked to settle the question.

"What matters it?" he asked. "I don't know. But I arrived in Rome on March 8, 1797." His meaning was that not until he came to Rome and began his studies there did he really begin to live.

Many a Christian has felt so about his life. It was not real life that he spent before he was born again. His true life began at his conversion. Lord Lyndhurst, who was converted late in life, used to say in a voice broken by emotion. "My soul is saved, but my life is lost."—*The Christian Herald.*

Listening to the Will.

A gentleman once said to the Rev. Roland Hill, "It is sixty-five years since I first heard you preach, but I well remember that you spoke to us in this way: 'Supposing one is hearing a will read, and expects to get a legacy. Will he spend the time in criticizing the lawyer's manner of reading? No, he will see if anything is left him and how much. Let that be the way in which you listen to the Gospel.' "

Laborers Together.

You remember George Eliot's fine poem on the famous violin-maker of Cremona and its lesson:

... Not God Himself can make man's best
Without best men to help Him
 'Tis God gives skill,
But not without men's hands: He could not make
Antonio Stradivari's violins
Without Antonio.

It is a bold saying, but true. We have a work to do in the world which God cannot do, which we must do, or it will be left undone. Only as we co-operate with Him, can His will be done on earth as in heaven.—JOHN HUNTER.

Prison of Worldliness.

In "The Life of Florence Barclay," by her daughter, it is told hold she purchased a lovely treasure from an art dealer in Florence. It was a wonderful little jeweled box, and when a spring was touched the lid opened, and a tiny bird, hardly an inch high, would spring up and pour forth a flute-like song. She took her little bird to preach his eloquent sermon to a great audience in Manchester. She touched the spring, the little bird sprang up, and his clear notes penetrated to the farthest corner of the hall! "One may be sure that the lesson of the little bird stayed in the minds of those present—that there are people very much like him, ready to stand up in the pew on Sunday and sing a hymn right through, but on Monday morning down goes the lid; they are shut in the prison of worldliness, self-seeking, money-making,

and, like the little bird, they lack, without knowing it, life, light, and liberty."—W. R. CLARK.

Saints—Communion of.

A gentleman on his death-bed was told by his friends of the glories of heaven, its golden streets, its river of life, its crowns and harps, and all the delights and joys of that wonderful life. "That is all very well," he said, "and doubtless is perfectly true; but I would rather remain in a world where I am better acquainted." What an argument for keeping intimate communion with Christ and His saints, with the thoughts and principles of heaven! —PROFESSOR PHELPS.

Sonship.

A visitor was once watching a group of slaves, slouching and shuffling off to their work. One tall, broad-shouldered fellow strode on, head erect and with the gait of a man. "How's that?" the visitor asked. "Oh, he's the son of an African king," was the reply. "He never forgets that." Alas! we forget, amid the drudgeries of earth, that we are sons and daughters of the King of kings, and in training for thrones in His empire!—*The Christian Herald.*

Spirit—A Christian.

A traveling salesman was telling a friend the story of the treatment received in a certain business house at the hands of a member of the establishment with whom he had come in contact. The rudeness and injustice recited stirred the listener to protest. "And you did nothing about it afterwards? You let it go too easily. A fellow like that deserves to be taught a lesson." "Yes, but—I'm not here to avenge personal wrongs, you know; I'm on business for the firm," answered the salesman.—*The Christian Age.*

Unfaithful Leaders.

When a number of ships are moored, or anchored, or buoyed in the river, all have an interest in the safety of each. If some of those that lie farther seaward break off from their moorings, and drift up with wind and tide, they will run foul of us as we lie secure in the channel farther up. The drifting ships may sink, but they will drag others down.—D. GUTHRIE.

CONFESSION

Choice—An Impossible.

A Sunday-school teacher, after telling the story of the rich man and (Lazarus to a class of boys, asked this question, "Now, which would you rather be, boys, the rich man or Lazarus?" One boy promptly replied, "I would be the rich man while I live, and Lazarus when I die." This is the choice that thousands to-day think they can make, but nothing could be more impossible. — *Record of Christian Work.*

Confession—Christian.

We owe it to Christ thus to confess Him. . . . In one of his wars Cyrus took captive an Armenian princess. She was condemned to death. Hearing of this, her husband came into the camp of his conqueror and offered his life in her stead. Cyrus was so touched with the devotion of the prince that he resolved to pardon them both, and to restore them to their dominion. Officers and soldiers stood there talking over the magnanimity of their great leader. The princess was near by, her eyes filled with tears. Some one turned to her with the question, "What do you think of Cyrus?" "I was not thinking of Cyrus," was her reply. "Of whom, then, were you thinking?" And, looking up into the face of her husband, her eyes luminous with love, she answered: "I was thinking of the one who would willingly have died for me." Because of all He has done for you, you ought to confess Christ.—H. G. HARWARD.

Confession—Difficult.

Many years ago, a minister put up for the night with a man who was supposed to possess but little of what people call "common sense." Just as he was about to retire for rest, the man said: "Tell me, sir, what three words in the English language it is the most difficult to pronounce?" "I don't know that I can," was the reply. "Well," said the man, "I'll give you till to-morrow morning to answer me." The minister thought no more of the question till it was proposed to him again in the morning, when he carelessly said he had not thought of it. "Then," said the man, "I will tell you. They are—I am wrong."

Decision—Instant.

A teacher in a mission school in Africa had just explained the parable of the king who invited people to his feast. One of the large boys said he wanted to follow Jesus, and a little boy said the same. "Have you felt for some time that Jesus has been calling you?" asked the teacher. "Oh, no; it is only to-day; but I listened right off when he called," was the sincere answer.— *World Wide Missions.*

Decision—Prompt.

There are many like that Indian native who told a missionary that he believed in Jesus Christ, and meant to give Him his love some day. A native helper turned to him, and said, "If you and I were walking through the jungles and came face to face with a tiger, if I placed myself in front, and said, 'Run, brother, for your life!' would you love me?" "Yes, surely." "When, some day?" The native saw the power of his friend's argument, and said, "I will give myself to him now, and you must baptize me to-morrow."—IRENE ALETHEA HETHERINGTON.

67

Testimony—A Joyful.

In the city of Richmond many years ago a significant event took place. A certain elevated part of the city was recognized by a real estate firm as destined to become the most fashionable part of the city. A little church building had been erected here and a mission church established. The members of this church worshiped their Lord with great enthusiasm. As costly residences were erected near the church the owners finally became disturbed by the singing. These ultra-fashionable people said, "It won't do; they disturb the quiet of our homes with their enthusiasm." They appointed a committee to go to the city council with a petition and have the church declared a nuisance. They brought the petition to a Jew, having no doubt he would be the first to sign it. To their surprise he pushed the petition away from him and said, "Gentlemen, I cannot sign it. If I believed as do these Christians, that my Messiah had come, I would shout it from every housetop and on every street of Richmond, and nobody could stop me."—*Sunday School Times.*

CONSCIENCE

Conscience—A Faulty.

A little girl was asked what conscience was, and she gravely replied: "It's something inside of me that tells me when Johnny does wrong." That kind of conscience is very common, but not particularly useful in reforming one's own life. There are many people, however, who base their assurance of their own high moral standards on their swift perception of other people's wrongdoing.—*The Christian Age.*

Conscience—A Good.

Nicholas Biddle, we have been told, once had for a private secretary a Christian young man, whom he wished to keep at work on the Sabbath. The secretary objected to working on the Lord's Day. "I shall discharge you," said his employer, "if you do not conform to my wishes." The secretary was poor, and had, moreover, a widowed mother dependent upon him; but rather than violate his conscience by doing what he considered wrong, he gave up his place. A day or two after, Mr. Biddle was in the company of some gentlemen who proposed to start a new bank, and the question was, where should they find a suitable man to be its cashier? "I know of one," said Mr. Biddle; and he recommended to them his late secretary, saying, "He had too much conscience for my work, but none too much for the more responsible office you have." And through his recommendation the place was given to him.—A. H. Currier.

Conscience—A Quiescent.

In the church pharmacy are at least four bromides that infallibly produce a quiescent conscience, and gently put the patient to sleep. 1. I work so hard all the week that when Sunday comes——. 2. When I was a boy, I was made to go to church three times on Sunday, and so now——. 3. Company came just as we were about ready. 4. I came twice and not a soul spoke to me.—*Christian Herald.*

Conscience and Immortality.

Kant, the great moralist, based his demonstration of the doctrine of immortality on the demands of the conscience. Conscience bids us aim at perfection. But perfection is not reached upon the earth. If the earth be all, if death ends everything, then we are overweighted in our moral nature. Conscience needs an enduring arena for its operation. Conscience demands immortality.

The facts of life confirm the hope
That in a world of larger scope—
What here is faithfully begun
Will be completed, not undone.

—T. E. Ruth.

Conscience—Arousing.

In a railroad wreck on the Wabash road at Missouri City, Mo., in which several people were killed, a still more appalling disaster was narrowly averted. The passenger train had broken through a trestle, and a freight train, which was following only ten minutes, must be flagged, or scores of passengers, unable to escape in time would be crushed to death. Those who were free rushed back, and were able to flag the freight train within a few feet of the deadly gorge; but those few feet meant safety. There is an illustration that ought to quicken the energy of every Christian worker. Multitudes about us are hastening to disaster. Our only possibility of saving them is to catch their attention and arouse their consciences before it is too late. It is now or never with many a man of our acquaintance.—*Anecdotes and Morals.*

Conscience Like a Clock.

Have you ever heard of the great clock of St. Paul's in London? At midday, in the roar of business, when carriages, and carts, and wagons, and omnibuses, go rolling through the streets, how many never hear that great clock strike, unless they live very near it. But when the work of the day is over, and the roar of business has passed away—when men are gone to sleep, and silence reigns in London—then at twelve, at one, at two, at three, at four, the sound of that clock may be heard for miles around. Twelve! —One! — Two! — Three! — Four! How that clock is heard by many a sleepless man! That clock is just like the conscience of the impenitent man. While he has health and strength, and goes on in the whirl of business, he will not hear conscience. He drowns and silences its voice by plunging into the world. . . . The time will come when he must retire from the world, and lie down on the sick bed, and look death in the face. And then the clock of conscience, that solemn clock, will sound in his heart, and, if he has not repented, will bring wretchedness and misery to his soul.—BP. RYLE.

Conscience—Stifling the.

As the old historian says about the Roman armies that marched through a country burning and destroying every living thing, "They make a solitude and they call it peace." And so men do with their consciences. They stifle them, forcibly silence them, somehow or other; and then, when there is a

dead stillness in the heart, broken by no voice of either approbation or blame, but doleful like the unnatural quiet of a deserted city, then they say it is peace.—MACLAREN.

Conscience—The Awakened.

Those who have seen Holman Hunt's picture of the "Awakened Conscience" will not soon forget it. There are only two figures—a man and a woman, sitting in a somewhat gaudily furnished room, beside a piano. His fingers are on the instrument, his face, which is refle ⁺ed in a mirror, is handsome and vacant, evidently that of a man about town, who supposes the brightest part of creation is intended to administer to his amusement. A music-book on the floor is open at the words, "Oft in the stilly night." That tune has struck some chord in his companion's heart. Her face of horror says what no language could say, "That tune has told me of other days when I was not as now." The tune has done what the best rules that ever were devised could not do. It has brought a message from a father's house.—DENTON.

Conscience, the Guide.

A man may cut away every mast on his ship, and yet pursue his voyage. A man may have everything on deck carried overboard, and yet make some headway. A man in the middle of the ocean can afford to lose everything else better than he can afford to lose the compass in the binnacle. When that is gone he has nothing to steer by. And that conscience which God has given you is your compass and guide. You can afford to lose genius, and taste, and reason, and judgment, better than that. Keep that as the apple of your eye. Keep it clear, and strong, and discerning. Be in love with your conscience; and let your conscience be in love with God.—H. W. BEECHER.

Conscience—Indestructibility of.

Conscience, like every other faculty of the soul, is undeveloped in the infant, and very imperfectly developed in the savage; and moreover, after a long habit of inattention to its voice, and violation of its law, the individual sinner is often judicially given up to carnal indifference; his conscience for a time lying latent. Yet it is certain that it is never destroyed. 1. From the fact that it is often aroused to the agonies of remorse. 2. From the fact that this remorse or accusing conscience constitutes the essential torment of lost souls and devils. This is the worm that never dieth. Otherwise, their punishment would lose its moral character.—A. A. HODGE.

Conscience—The Voice of.

That grand old bell in St. Paul's Cathedral, London, is seldom heard by many during the business hours of the day. The roar and din of traffic in the streets have a strange power to deaden its sound and prevent men hearing it. But when the daily work is over, the desks are locked, and doors are closed, and books are put away, and quiet reigns in the great city, the case is altered. As the old bell strikes eleven, and twelve, and one, and two, and three at night, thousands hear it who never heard it during the day. And so I hope it will be with many a one in the matter of his soul. Now, while in health and strength, in the hurry and whirl of business, I fear the voice of your conscience is often stifled and you cannot hear it. But the day may come when the great bell of conscience will make itself heard, whether you like it or not. Laid aisde in quietness, and obliged by illness to sit still, you may be forced to look within and consider your soul's concerns.—BISHOP RYLE.

Conscience—Unenlightened.

Examining the sun-dial, to ascertain if the clocks were right, Gotthold said to himself, "Dials are no doubt most ingenious contrivances; but, however ingenious, they are of no use when the sun does not shine. It is the same with us. Destitute of the grace of God, and of the quickening and enlightening influence of the Holy Spirit, we, too, whatever be our natural gifts and talents, are good for nothing."

Signal Lights.

"It was well you stopped when the red light flashed,"
She said as we drove along.
"For an officer stood at the corner there
In charge of the traffic throng."
And I smiled and said to my daughter fair,
As we waited on the spot,
"I always stop when the red light shows,
Be an officer there or not."

Then she sat in thought as we drove along
And suddenly this she said:
"There ought to be lights for us all through life,
The amber and green and red.
What a help 'twould be if a red light flashed
When danger and shame were near,

And we all might wait till the
    green light came
To show that the road was clear."

"My dear," said I, "we have tried
    to light
Life's road for your feet to fare,
And we pray you'll stop when the
    red light glows,

Though none of us may be there.
We have tried to teach you the
    signs of wrong
And the way to life serene,
So stop when your conscience post
    shows red,
And go when it flashes green."

—*The Public Ledger.*

CONSECRATION

A Good Soldier.

During the Indian Mutiny a small British host was encamped on the ridge outside Delhi. When the news of the Cawnpore massacres reached them, the general ordered his men to attack Delhi. The doctor inspected the invalided soldiers to ascertain how many of them were strong enough to carry arms. He passed by a sickly youth as being too frail, when the lad cried: "For God's sake, sir, don't say I am not fit for duty; it's only a touch of fever, and the sound of the bugle will make me well."

Character—Unrecognized.

George Eliot preaches a needed gospel when she writes of one of her characters, "He whose fortunes I have undertaken to relate was in no respect an ideal or exceptional character . . . a man whose virtues were not heroic, and who had no undetected crime within his heart; who had not the slightest mystery hanging about him, but was palpably and unmistakably commonplace. . . . But, dear madam, it is so very large a majority of your fellow-countrymen that are of this insignificant stamp. Yet these common-place people—many of them—bear a conscience, and have felt the sublime prompting to do the painful right; they have their unspoken sorrows and their sacred joys; their hearts have perhaps gone out towards their first-born, and they have mourned over the irreclaimable dead. Depend upon it you would gain unspeakably if you would learn to see more of the poetry and pathos, the tragedy and comedy, lying in the experience of a human soul that looks through dull gray eyes and that speaks in a voice of quite ordinary tones."— MARK GUY PEARSE.

Consecrated Art.

For eight years Dannecker, the German sculptor, labored upon a marble statue of the Christ. When he had worked upon it for two years it seemed to him that the statue was finished. What more could he do to add to its perfection? To test the matter, however, he one day called a little girl into his studio, and, directing her attention to the statue, said, "Who is that?" She replied promptly, "A great man." He turned away disheartened. He felt that he had failed, and that his two years of labor had been lost. But he began anew. He toiled on for six years more, and then, inviting another little child into his studio, repeated the inquiry, "Who is that?" This time he was not disappointed. After looking in silence awhile, the child's curiosity deepened into awe and reverence, and bursting into tears, she said softly, "Suffer little children to come unto Me." It was enough. The untutored instinct of the child had led her to the right conclusion, and he knew that his work was a success. Dannecker declared afterwards that in his solitary vigils he had seen a vision of Christ, and had but transferred to the marble the image which the lord had shown him. Some time later Napoleon Bonaparte requested him to make a statue of Venus for the gallery of the Louvre. But he refused, saying, "A man who has seen Christ would commit sacrilege if he should employ his art in the carving of a pagan goddess. My art henceforth is a consecrated thing."—R. F. COYLE.

Consecration Complete.

Dr. Judson, the eminent missionary to Burmah, once examined a Karen woman who was a candidate for baptism. She gave intelligent answers to his questions, but Judson was not quite satisfied. There seemed something lacking. His eye caught the glitter of a necklace of a kind much esteemed by Karens. "Can you give up your ornaments for Christ?" the missionary asked. Tears filled the woman's eyes. The struggle would evidently be a severe one. Judson appealed to her own consciousness of pride and vanity, and the woman broke down. She took her necklace off and looked at it admiringly. It was the most precious treasure in her possession. She thought about it for some time, and laid it down on the missionary's table with the declaration, "I love Christ more than that."—CONSERVATIVE.

Surrender,—A Complete.

When Henry VIII, had determined to make himself head of the English Church, he insisted upon it that Convocation should accept his headship without limiting and modifying clauses. He refused to entertain any compromises, and vowed that "He would have no tantrums," as he called them. Thus when a sinner parleys with his Saviour he would fain have a little of the honor of his salvation, he would save alive some favorite sin, he would fain amend the humbling terms of grace; but there is no help for it, Jesus will be all in all, and the sinner must be nothing at all. The surrender must be complete, there must be no tantrums, but the heart must without reserve submit to the sovereignty of the Redeemer. —SPURGEON.

Consecration—Complete.

Faraday, the great chemist, learned a great lesson in boyhood by a very childish experience. As a little lad, humbly earning his bread by selling newspapers in the street, he was waiting outside the office of an Edinburgh paper for the morning issue, and thrust his head and arms through the railings of the iron gate. He was a born metaphysician, and began to speculate on which side of the railing he was. "My head and hands are on one side," he said to himself, "and my heart and body are on the other." The gate was opened hastily before he could disengage himself, and the wrench he received taught him, as he said in later life, that all true work required head and heart and hands to be on the same side.—*Sunday at Home.*

Consecration—Grateful.

Colonel James Gardiner one night, when he was little thinking of Divine things, but on the contrary had made an appointment of the most vicious kind, was waiting for the appointed hour, when he saw, or thought he saw, before him in the room wherein he sat alone, a visible representation of the Lord Jesus Christ upon the cross, and he was impressed, as if a voice had said to him to this effect—"O sinner, I did all this for thee; what hast thou done for me?" The vision and the words he heard were the means of Colonel Gardiner's conversion. The words quoted, it may be added, suggested Frances Ridley Havergal's well-known hymn beginning:—

I gave My life for thee,
My precious blood I shed,
That thou might'st ransom'd be,
And quicken'd from the dead.
I gave My life for thee;
What hast thou given for Me?

Miss Havergal was staying with a German divine, in whose study was a picture of our crucified Saviour, beneath which was placed the motto: "I did this for thee; what hast thou done for Me?" She had come in weary, and sitting down in front of the picture, the Saviour's eyes seemed to rest upon her. She read the motto, and the lines of her hymn flashed upon her, and she at once wrote them in pencil on a scrap of paper. Looking them over she thought them so poor that she tossed them on the fire, but they fell out untouched. Some months afterwards she showed them to her father, who encouraged her to preserve them, and he wrote the tune "Baca" specially for them. The hymn was published in Good Words, and becoming a favorite soon found its way into the hymnbooks of the Christian Church.—CANON J. DUNCAN.

Consecration—Lack of Complete.

It is told of some old Saxon warrior who came to unite with the Church, that when he was immersed he held up his right hand out of the water. When he was expostulated with, and told that his whole body must be buried, he replied that he would keep that hand to himself for battle with his enemies. There are too many people who reserve some part of their life undevoted when they make their consecration to God.—J. R. MILLER.

Conquering Our Habits.

I have seen in the autumn, when the trees had shed their leaves, that two or three leaves have stuck fast on the branches, and have clung to them all the winter through. Storms have beaten them, frosts have bitten them, snow and rain have blackened them, yet they have held fast to the tree. But when the spring has come, and the sap has begun to ascend and push its way through every branch and every twig, the leaves have disappeared—pushed off by the rising tide of new life, for death can never stand before life. So it is with us. Those old inveterate habits that belong to our fallen nature are very hard to get rid of. We battle with them, and try to beat them off, but again and again we are defeated. . . . But when the Spirit of the Lord fills and possesses us, then these habits disappear almost unconsciously, because death cannot stand before life.—A. J. GORDON.

Good—Unconscious.

There is a legend of a saint whose wonderful deeds astonished the angels, and they came to learn the secret of his piety. Everywhere the man went he diffused virtue as the flower gives out perfume, without being aware of it. The angels asked that the saint might be given the gift of miracles, and God consented. They asked the man if he would like by the touch of his hand to heal the sick. "No," he replied, "I would rather God should do that." "Then would you like to convert guilty souls and bring them back to right paths?" "No," said the saint, "It is the Spirit's mission to convert; I only pray." "Would you like to be a model of patience and draw men by your piety?" "No, if men were attracted to me, they might be estranged from God." "What do you desire?" said the angels. "That God would give me His grace; that I might do a great deal of good without knowing it." The angels were perplexed. Finally they resolved that whenever the shadow of the man should fall where he could not see it, the shadow should cure disease and comfort sorrow. So it came to pass, as the saint passed along, the hearts of men were cheered wherever he walked.—*The Hibbert Journal.*

If Consecrated.

Somewhere I have read of an artist falsely accused and thrown into prison. His brushes and paint were allowed him, but he had no canvas. One day he asked a man in the corridor for something upon which he might paint, and the man indifferently picked up an old soiled handkerchief and tossing it up to him said, "There, see what you can do with that," and the artist began to paint upon it the face of Jesus. The picture that he painted afterward became one of the famous paintings of the Master's face. He labored on it faithfully and when it was finished he showed it to the man and when he looked upon its marvelous sweetness it touched his heart and the tears flowed unbidden down. And as I recall the story the thought comes to me, if a poor artist could take an old soiled rag and so make it glow with the loveliness of Jesus that a careless, indifferent man could be touched into tears as he looked upon it, what might not the glorious Christ do with my life if I would but allow Him to have His way with me to reproduce His likeness through me.— REV. WM. E. BIEDERWOLF.

Life—The Higher.

There was a man who once lived in a place where, close to his house, he had a spring of water. At a little distance from him, there was another spring. We shall call the spring close to his house, "the nether spring," and the other, a little way off, "the upper spring." So he had the nether and the upper spring. The nether spring looked very pleasant when the sun was shining; the water sparkled in its rays; yet, when looked at more closely, the water was black and dark, and very often grew muddy, and the flowers on the side of it never lasted long; and people who drank a great deal of the water from the nether spring seemed to grow sick. The other spring, a little way off, come out of the rock; it required a great deal of patience to get it; but if the cup was held long enough, it would always get filled, and you were never sick from it.

Now this man who lived in the cottage near the nether spring always went to it; he did not like the trouble of going to the upper spring. He had not sufficient patience. So it went on for many years. At last he came to the nether spring and it was dry, not a drop of water in it. So he was obliged to go to the upper spring; he had to wait some time, but at last he had a cup of nice, pure water. It was so sweet and he enjoyed it much. He had never before tasted such water. The nether spring flowed on again, but ever after he went to the upper; and when asked why he went so far, he said, "I cannot leave the upper spring; having once tasted it, I cannot go back to the nether spring."—JAMES VAUGHAN.

Man—The Whole.

Thomas H. Huxley was a severe critic and a chronic neglector of religion in his day, but he said one thing that every church member in America ought to remember. "It doesn't take much of a man to be a Christian, but it takes all there is of him."—*Homiletic Review.*

Sanctification—Complete.

There are two great pictures, each of them by a famous artist. One picture represents a woman in a hospital. The woman is a princess, fair and beautiful to look upon, but the hospital is most loathsome, because it is the home of a number of dying lepers, and this fair and beautiful woman is represented as wiping the face of a dying leper. That picture is a symbol of the dignity and the beauty of social service. But there hangs by its side another picture by another great artist. It represents a woman in her oratory. She is in the attitude of prayer. Beside her stands an angel. She is looking over the open pages of the Holy Bible, which are illuminated. And the legend tells us that while she knelt there in that place of prayer, seven times she was interrupted. Seven times there came a call at her door, a demand upon her love, upon her charity—a sevenfold recognition of the needs of her brother man. And seven times, with a patience and with a moral beauty beyond all description, she goes to the door, relieves these cases of necessity, and returns to her knees, to her attitude of prayer. This is a picture of the supreme dignity and the great worth of personal sanctification.— O. W. Whittaker.

Self-Sacrifice—The Daughter's.

A touching legend of filial piety has connected itself with one of the great bells in a temple near Peking. A famous worker in metals, it is said, had received the Emperor's command to cast a bell of unusual size, the tone of which was to surpass in richness and melody all other bells. Severe penalties were threatened if he came short of the wishes of his exacting master. He tried and failed, tried and failed again, and was upon the point of giving up his task in despair. At this crisis in his fortunes, his only daughter, a maiden of great beauty and virtue, went secretly to consult an astrologer. The man of magic told her the work could be brought to a successful accomplishment only if the blood of a chaste virgin were mingled with the molten metal, when it was ready to be poured into the mold. Returning home she asked leave to watch her father's work, and when the ingredients had been fused and were seething in the vast caldron, in an outburst of filial piety she threw herself into the sea of fire. The bell thus cast proved of incomparable quality, and whenever it is struck, the natives of the district think they hear the girl's dying cry, in the sweetness and pathos of its notes. Such filial piety, if achieved at all, could only be achieved through struggle and consummated in dire distress. The legend represents the last cry of the victim as a weired note of pain, a *vox humana* trembling up out of inscrutable abysses of tribulation. The Chinese imagination had scarcely soared into those spiritual realms where Divine love can change pain into contentment and deep joy.—T. G. Selby.

Self—Surrender.

An architect complains that many of his clients come and ask him to design a house for them, only to let him very speedily discover that they have already designed it for themselves. What they really want is his sanction of their own plan, and the satisfaction of seeing him draw on paper what they have fully in mind. It is in very much the same fashion that we often go to the Great Architect with our lives. We ask Him for wisdom and guidance, but we have already planned how we will build our fortunes and shape our course; and it is not His way we are seeking, but His approval of our way.—J. R. Miller.

Work—Artistic.

It was the strange fancy of a little child, writes George Mac-Donald, as he stood on a summer's evening looking intently and thoughtfully at the great banks of clouds piled like mountains of glory about the setting sun: "Mother, I wish I could be a painter." "Why, my child?" "For then I would help God to paint the clouds and the sunsets." It was strange and beautiful aspiration. But our commonest work in this world may be made far nobler than that. We may live to touch hues of loveliness in immortal spirits which shall endure for ever. Clouds dissolve and float away. The most gorgeous sunset splendors vanish in a few moments. The artist's canvas crumples and his wondrous creations fade. But work done for Christ endures for ever. A life of simple consecration leaves a trace of imperishable beauty on everything it touches. Not great deeds alone, but the smallest, the obscurest, the most prosaic, write their record in fadeless lines.—J. R. MILLER.

Workers—God's Fellow.

It is said that when Thorwaldsen, the Danish sculptor, returned to his native land with those wonderful works of art which have made his name immortal, chiseled in Italy with patient toil and glowing inspiration, the servants who unpacked the marbles scattered upon the ground the straw which was wrapped around them. The next summer flowers from the gardens of Rome were blooming in the streets of Copenhagen, from the seeds thus borne and planted by accident. While pursuing his glorious purpose, and leaving magnificent results in breathing marble, the artist was, at the same time, and unconsciously, scattering other beautiful things in his path to give cheer and gladness.

So Christ's lowly workers unconsciously bless the world. They come out every morning from the presence of God and go to their work, intent upon their daily tasks. All day long, as they toil, they drop gentle words from their lips, and scatter little seeds of kindness about them; and to-morrow flowers from the garden of God spring up in the dusty streets of earth and along the hard paths of toil on which their feet tread. The Lord knows them among all others to be His by the beauty and usefulness of their lives. —J. R. MILLER.

Will—A Determined.

Ralph Tompkins, a one-legged youth of 19 years, left New York on July 30 to walk to Chicago and back for a prize of $500.00. He reached Chicago on October 2, and remaining there two days, started on his return trip. Despite the bad weather he had to encounter he was only twenty-four hours behind the time he planned for himself, and reached New York December 5. He earned money for his trip by singing, and whenever he could do so was the guest of the Young Men's Christian Association of the various places through which he passed. He never stopped more than a night at any one place, was never sick an hour and gained thirty pounds on the journey. He says he made as great speed with his crutches as he could have made with two feet. It was a feat of physical endurance, and of purpose. So many make the journey of life on crutches, with physical and mental infirmities. A distinguished lawyer of Indiana who died the other day went to the front of his profession and to a life of singular Christian usefulness with a crippled leg and a crippled arm which he had carried from his youth. Business men on the streets of every city, men of every profession and calling everywhere, achieve enduring success under the greatest physical disabilities. Many of the men on two crutches are setting a rapid pace in the race of life. Many of the best traits of character are produced by the handicaps of life. It is the will, the all-daring purpose, the lofty moral ideals, and the spirit within that overcomes handicaps and gives success.—*Christian Herald.*

DEATH

Death a Universal Preacher.

Archbishop Leighton, returning home one morning, was asked by his sister, "Have you been hearing a sermon?" "I've met a sermon," was the answer. The sermon he had met was a corpse on its way to the grave; the preacher was Death. —*American National Preacher*.

Death—Companion in.

There is nothing the human heart so much dreads as the thought of being utterly alone. I have felt it when walking about amid the surge and roar of London. To think of these dense masses of human beings utterly cut off from you makes you feel as if you were in the midst of perfect solitude. It is the thought of utter loneliness which gives its power and pathos to Hood's Bridge of Sighs. You remember the picture of the poor unfortunate alone on the bridge on that wild March night. The lines are among the most mournful ever penned. I learned them many long years ago from the lips of a Scone weaver, before I had ever heard of such a man as Hood. The sentiment of loneliness gives them their power. It is the same sentiment that gives its awfulness not only to Christ's death but to all death—that we must all leave the world alone; as De Quincey says: "King and priest, warrior and maiden, philosopher and child,—all must walk those mighty galleries alone." We all like to have a human hand in ours and a human heart beating for our own, at least in the great crises and troubles of life. There is One, the Friend that sticketh closer than a brother, who has promised that He will never leave us, never forsake us, not even when heart and flesh do faint and fail. Let us seek a closer interest in Him, the Holy Lamb of God. It will brighten every joy God may give us in life. It will soothe whatever sorrow He may send us to know and feel that in Christ we have a Brother and a Friend.—Dr. MacGregor.

Death—Prepared for.

Mr. Wesley was once asked by a lady: "Suppose that you knew you were to die at twelve o'clock to-morrow night, how would you spend the intervening time?" "How, madam?" he replied. "Why, just as I intend to spend it now. I should preach this night at Gloucester, and again at five to-morrow morning. After that I should ride to Tewkesbury, preach in the afternoon, and meet the societies in the evening. I should then repair to friend Martin's house, who expects to entertain me, converse and pray with the family as usual, retire to my room at ten o'clock, commend myself to my Heavenly Father, lie down to rest, and wake up in glory."—*Zion's Herald*.

Death,—Trying to Bribe.

When Runjeet Singh, "the Lion of Lahore," was dying, with the hope of staying the hand of death, he sent the costliest offerings—offering after offering—to the idol-temples, in order to propitiate the deities. The nearer the dread moment seemed to come, the more eager was his desire for life, and the more boundless his profusion. He would gladly have given all his hoarded wealth for a few additional moments of life. It has been computed that, on the day of his death, the wealth bestowed by Runjeet in pious gifts amounted to more than a million sterling.—Denton.

Death—Uncertainty of.

In the old times, before the settlements in the great northwest, when the fur companies would establish here and there a great trading post and send out their trappers to all parts of the country, trails were made in every direction, but they all ended at the post. North, south, east, west, for hundreds of miles in every direction, along large rivers, following small streams into the mountains, crossing lakes, searching through deep canyons, the trails would wind, but you could begin a hundred miles away, on any one of them, and however devious its course might be, it would end at the trader's camp. The grave is the end of the trail of this world's life. A man may start where he will. He may climb the heights of wealth or traverse the deep canyons of poverty. He may follow up the mountains of hard struggle or paddle his canoe on a stream of idleness. But when you get to the end of the trail, it is all the same. It is an open grave. Whether he brings many pelts there or few, however great or small have been the spoils of his life chase is of no account, for the grave is too narrow to hold any of them. We brought nothing with us into this world, and it is certain we can carry nothing out. God help us that we may learn over again the old, old lesson that we learn so often and forget so soon—that we are with rapid feet following the trail to the grave. As we go over the trail but once, we never know how near the end is. It may be a long way off. It may be just over the hill.—William Channing Gannett.

Death—Sudden Call of.

If, to-day, there should come flying hither a messenger who should say, "One hundred members of this congregation, now assembled, are to die this year," no matter whether any designation of persons was made, no matter in what month, or in what part of the year it should take place, every man would say, "It may be I." There are some of you that will unquestionably go before the end of the year. No man can tell who. . . . To learn suddenly, when we are engaged in a sultry summer day, that some great and honored personage is, without warning, about to come to our dwelling—what haste! what change of garments! what hurried preparation of the household! But when it is no man, however honored, but God, into whose presence we are soon to go, how natural that we should look at ,the habiliments of the soul, and at everything within us and without us, as we never would at any other time—as perhaps we never could at any other time! What new measures and tests should we apply to ourselves! —H. W. Beecher.

Death—Great.

Looked at from beside the Lord of life and death, "great death" dwindles to a very little thing. We need to revise our notions if we would understand how trivial it really is. To us it frowns like a black cliff blocking the upper end of our valley; but there is a path round its base, and though the throat of the pass be narrow, it has room for us to get through, and up to the sunny uplands beyond. From a mountain top the country below seems level plain, and what looked like an impassable precipice has dwindled to be indistinguishable.—Alexander Maclaren.

Prepared for Death.

It is said of the Rev. Mr. Kidd, a Scotch minister of some prominence, that he was very eccentric, and had his own way of doing things. "Just as the year was opening," says one of his parishoners, "I was very busy in my shop, when, right in the midst of my work, in stepped the Doctor, without knocking or a word of announcement. 'Did you expect me?' was his abrupt inquiry, without even waiting for a salutation. 'No, sir,' was my reply, 'I did not.' 'What if I had been Death?' he asked, in a solemn, earnest tone; and out he stepped, as suddenly as he had come, and was gone almost before I knew it!"

DECISION

Begin Again.

"Waste no tears
Upon the blotted record of the lost years,
But turn the leaf, and smile, oh smile to see
The fair white pages that remain for thee."

Thank God it is always possible to begin again.

Beginnings—Resist.

When you stand and look at the sweeping flames of a prairie on an autumnal day, stretching leagues away, or at night, throwing a lurid light into the broad heaven above, you do not suppose that those vast flames were put there. The negligent hunter, after his evening meal, sat smoking his pipe; he knocked a spark out of it, and it kindled, and grew, and he watched it, thinking that he might at any moment subdue it by the stroke of his boot; but it escaped him, and ran, and spread here and there and everywhere, and swung on, and the wind caught it and nourished it, and it laughed and roared and crackled as it sped along, growing wider and more fierce, consuming harvest, fence, hut, and hovel. It took care of itself after it was once kindled. It had in itself multiplying power. Evil always has: put it out early!
—H. W. Beecher.

Blessings—Receiving.

As a lady, well known as an earnest and devoted servant of God, was going home from a meeting, she was asked to take the arm of a young gentleman who was moving in the highest circles of fashion, a man who had led a very gay life. He did not like taking this lady home; however, being a gentleman, he gave her his arm. She did not talk about the meeting, but as they were drawing near home she led the conversation round to subjects bearing on the well-being of her companion. He replied: "It seems to me that you religious people are always trying to strip us of all our little enjoyments. A young man has only once in his life an opportunity to enjoy himself; he will never have another chance. I am one of those who enjoy life thoroughly. I do not see why you should try to take away all I have got." The lady pressed him on the arm, and said to him very emphatically: "My dear sir, I don't want you to give up; I want you to receive." He said, "What do you mean?" She replied, "I won't say any more, I must leave that word for you to think over." "Well," he said, "I will try to turn it over in my mind, and see if I can understand you." And so it fell out that the word went home to his heart, and he never rested until he had got the reality.—Canon W. Hay, M. H. Aitken.

Bury It.

There are men who pride themselves on their candor, and it degenerates into brutality. One such man said to John Wesley once, "Mr. Wesley, I pride myself on speaking my mind; that is my talent." "Well," said John Wesley, "the Lord wouldn't mind if you buried that!"—W. H. Griffith Thomas.

Choosing.

A father that had three sons was desirous to try their discretion, which he did by giving to each of them an apple that had some part of it rotten. The first eats up his apple, rotten and all; the second throws all his away, because some part of it was rotten; but the third picks out the rotten, and eats that which was good, so that he appeared the wisest: thus, some in these days, for want of discretion, swallow down all that is presented, rotten and sound altogether; others throw away all truth, because everything delivered unto them is not truth, but surely they are the wisest and most discreet, that know how to try the spirits whether they be God or not —how to choose the good and refuse the evil.—J. SPENCER.

Courage—Moral.

It is related that in the Duke of Wellington's campaigns two officers were once despatched upon a service of considerable danger. As they were riding together, the one observed the other to be greatly agitated, with blanched cheek and quivering lip, and limbs shaken as with a paralysis of mortal fear. Reining his steed upon its haunches, he haughtily addressed him, "Why, you are afraid." "I am," was the reply; "and if you were half as much afraid as I am, you would relinquish the duty altogether." Without wasting another word upon his ignoble companion, the officer galloped back to headquarters, and complained bitterly that he had been ordered to march in the companionship of a coward. "Off, sir, to your duty," was the commander's sharp reply, "or the coward will have done the business before you get there."—W. M. PUNSHON.

Conviction.

What would you think of a man who should go to his business as men go to church from Sabbath to Sabbath? A man sits down in his office, and it seems to him that it would be a good thing if he should go into a certain operation. He thinks it all over, sees how it might be done, and is satisfied with it. Then he begins and goes all over it again. He thinks about it all day. He goes home, and sleeps on it; and when he gets up the next morning he is convinced that it would be a good thing. But he never does decide to go into it. By and by another man goes into it, and comes out all right; and this man says, "Well, I might have made a very handsome sum if I had gone into that; I was on the point of doing it, but for some reason I didn't."

Such, have their parallel in those who go to the house of God, and listen to clear instruction, and have the way in which they should go pointed out definitely to them, but who, although they have much right feeling, although they are entirely satisfied in their judgment as to what they ought to do and to be, or ought to begin to do or to be, fool with it (that is the plain English). They turn it over in their minds; but it never results in choice.—H. W. BEECHER.

Decision of Character.

Invading armies always endeavor to leave their ships riding in a safe and sheltered anchorage. In the event of their enterprise proving unsuccessful, they thus secure the means of retreat; and to provide for such an emergency is regarded as a good stroke of generalship. Wellington fought Waterloo with the Forest of Soigny at his back; and the fleet which carried our soldiers to fight the Russians before Sebastopol waited the issue in the Bay of Balaclava. The brave old Romans, whom Ceasar led, invaded our country after a different fashion. The first thing they did on disembarking, was to burn their ships; doing so in sight of thousands who were bravely mustering on the heights of England, to defend their homes, their wives and little ones, their freedom and native land. Not leaving the enemy to cut off their retreat, they cut it off themselves. Their own hands put the torch to the fleet which had brought them to Britain, and, in the event of failure, would have carried them back to Italy. With the glare of that brave conflagration on their eagles, banners, and serried ranks, we cannot wonder that, with such sons to fight her battles, Rome rose from a petty town to be mistress of the world. Both her destiny and their determination were to be plainly seen in the blaze of their burning ships. Bringing to the enterprise such an indomitable spirit and such decision of character, unless the heaven fought against them as against Sisera, how could they fail to conquer?—Dr. Guthrie.

Decision—Early.

Griffith John, the celebrated missionary to China, was admitted to church-membership at the exceedingly early age of eight. His testimony is, "Had I not taken that step then, I doubt whether I should ever have been a missionary, if a member of a Christian Church at all."— J. Morley Wright.

Decision—Immediate.

When a young man made an open profession of the gospel, his father, greatly offended, gave him this advice: "James, you should first get yourself established in a good trade, and then think of the matter of religion." "Father," said the son, "Jesus Christ advises me differently; He says, 'Seek ye first the kingdom of God!'"—C. H. Spurgeon.

Decision—Immediate.

When the packet-ship "Stephen Whitney" struck, at midnight, on an Irish cliff, and clung, for a few moments, to the cliff, all the passengers who leaped instantly upon the rock were saved. The positive step landed them on the rock. Those who lingered were swept off by the returning wave, and engulfed for ever. Your first duty is to flee out of the sinking ship of sin to the everlasting Rock. When in Christ you are safe.—*Christian Age*.

Decision Inevitable.

There is a solemn choice in life. Life and death, light and darkness, truth and lies are set before us. At every instant the cry comes for us to choose one or the other, and the choice of one involves the putting away of the other. And we must choose. That is one of the certainties of life. There is no such thing as offering one hand to God and another to evil; one hand to the self-sacrifice of Christ, and the other to the coveteousness of the world. You cannot serve God and Mammon. You cannot follow Jesus at home, and your own pleasure in your outward life. Your life, whether you like it or not, becomes of one piece.—S. A. Brooke.

Decision—Inevitable.

The river Amazon and the chief tributary of the river Plate rise within a few hundred yards of each other, and the Indians often drag their canoes from one stream to the other over the intervening strip of land. For many miles the little rivers run in parallel channels, and it often seems as though they might unite into one. At last a little knoll or ridge is reached, and the waterways diverge. It is difficult to judge what issues are involved in this turning-point, for it gives complexion to the entire map of South America, and it has put the stamp of destiny upon some great empires. These two rivers never come within sight of each other again, and empty themselves into the sea more than a thousand miles apart.

Doubt—How to Use.

The story is told of a man who spent a considerable time one morning debating with himself as to whether or not his collar was too soiled to be worn another day. Economy was not to be entirely overlooked in his affairs, yet he did not wish to wear an untidy neckpiece. His wife settled the question for him finally by remarking, "If it's doubtful, it's dirty." As a rule avoid the thing that is doubtful, and you will be on the safe side.—*Onward.*

Guide—An Unfailing.

Years ago a Pacific steamship went down off the coast of Alaska by striking an uncharted rock. Four hundred lives were lost. A man who was able to swim ashore through the numbing slush-ice, saving himself and another, told later of the criticism that was expressed, after the accident, because there were any uncharted rocks in that course. There are no uncharted rocks in our life course. God has made the chart; it is our Bible. Better still, we may have on board and in undisputed control all the time a Pilot who has been this way before and who knows all the rocks and perils. God has done all that he can to keep every human life from ever knowing the meaning of the word "wreck." It is for us to decide whether we will accept his guidance and safety. —*The Sunday School Times.*

Impressions Fixed.

The photographer at the first has no security of the picture which he has taken. He cannot be said, in any true sense, to possess it. It is true, the impression is made upon the sensitive plate, but in its first condition, for all practical purposes, it is useless. The slightest exposure to the light would mar it hopelessly. It must be taken into the darkened room, and there, by being immersed in chemical solutions, it becomes fixed and assumes a permanent form. Just so is it with the thoughts which enter the mind. They are volatile and fugitive unless permanently fixed in the chambers of the mind by steadfast meditation.—CHARLES DEAL.

Liberty—Personal.

In a lecture given at Woolwich, Ruskin recalled an incident of his early childhood which his mother was fond of telling him. "One evening when I was yet in my nurse's arms, I wanted to touch the tea-urn, which was boiling merrily. It was an early taste for bronzes, I suppose; but I was resolute about it. My mother bade me keep my fingers back; I insisted on putting them forward. My nurse would have taken me away from the urn, but my mother said—"Let him touch it, Nurse." So I touched it,—and that was my first lesson in the meaning of the word Liberty. It was the first piece of Liberty I got, and the last which for some time I asked for.—E. T. COOK.

Signals.

The late Warren E. Stone, head of the Brotherhood of Locomotive Engineers, said to William H. Ridgway once, "When you hear a 'wet' prating of personal liberty give him this: An engineer in taking his train from Philadelphia to Washington has to pick up over six hundred signals to insure the passenger train's safety. How would Mr. Wet on board with his family like that engineer to exercise the personal liberty Mr. Wet talks about?"—*The Sunday School Times.*

Life's Slacker.

The saddest sort of death to die
  Would be to quit the game called life
And know, beneath the gentle sky,
  You'd lived a slacker in the strife.
That nothing men on earth would find
  To mark the spot that you had filled;
That you must go and leave behind
  No patch of soil your hands had tilled.

I know no greater shame than this:
  To feel that yours were empty years;
That after death no man would miss
  Your presence in this vale of tears;
That you had breathed the fragrant air
  And sat by kindly fires that burn,
And in earth's riches had a share
  But gave no labor in return.

Yet some men die this way, nor care:
  They enter and they leave life's door
And at the end, their record's bare—
  The world's no better than before.
A few false tears are shed, and then,
  In busy service, they're forgot.
We have no time to mourn for men
  Who lived on earth but served it not.

Line of Least Resistance.

Did you ever see a river that was as straight as an arrow? Probably not. They generally wind back and forth from the time they gush out of a mountain spring or seep out of a lake until they find repose in the bosom of the great deep. And why is it that the river is never straight? Let a master of epigram answer and at the same time drive home a wholesome truth: "A river becomes crooked by following the line of least resistance! So does man!"—*King Words.*

Marching Orders.

Once when I was working in Poona, India, I conversed with a naval officer and some army men and their wives. The naval officer said: "Why don't these missionaries stay at home and mind their business? Why do they come here and worry these people? You can get all the converts you want at one rupee a head." It was at the time of the Armenian massacres, and there were rumors that the British fleet might be ordered to Constantinople. I said to the officer: "Suppose you were ordered to Constantinople to-morrow, and I were to say, 'Why don't you stay here and mind your business?'" The man's eyes flashed fire. "I would tell you to mind your business; if we are ordered to go, we must go." I said, "Quite right, but I have marching orders from the divine government. My command was to preach the Gospel to every creature. The primary question is not whether converts in India can be made at so many rupees, or whether I get any converts at all, but whether I am going to obey the last wish of my Lord and Saviour."
—Robert P. Wilder.

Obedience—Instant.

One day during the Boer war, just as the train was starting from Waterloo Station, London, a fine man, hot and weary, entered the carriage where I was sitting, and hastily seating himself, as if more exertion were impossible, exclaimed, "I'm called." He soon fell asleep, and we noticed that he was a stoker, and was black with the soot and oil of his engine. He awoke and again exclaimed, "I'm called." Then he told us he was a reservist, and was to join his regiment at Aldershot immediately. He did not wait to wash or put on his best clothes, but at once obeyed the call of his king. God has called us. Have we answered as readily?—*The Sunday School Chronicle.*

Opportunity—Ready for.

He was a cabin-boy on board an English man-of-war. He had a pious mother, and was trying to be a Christian; and the story shows how the sense he had of Gods presence strengthened him for duty under very trying circumstances, and made him eminently useful to his shipmates and to his country. The sailors called this boy "Cloudy." The incident, to which I refer, took place in the midst of a terrible naval battle between the English and the Dutch. The flagship of the English fleet was commanded by the brave Admiral Narborough. His vessel had got separated somehow from the rest of his fleet, and was drawn in the thickest of the fight. Two of its masts had just been shot away, and had fallen with a fearful crash upon the deck. The Admiral saw that all would soon be lost unless he could bring up the rest of the ships to help him. He summoned a lot of his men upon the quarter-deck. He could not send a boat, but he asked if any of them would volunteer to swim through the fight, and take an order for the rest of the fleet to come at once to his help. A dozen men offered to go; and little Cloudy made the same offer. The Admiral smiled, when he looked at him, and said: "Why, Cloudy, what can you do?" "I can swim sir, as well as any of them. You can't spare these men from the guns, sir. It won't make much matter if I am killed. But I'm sure that God will take care of me. Please, sir, let me go." "Go, my brave lad," said the Admiral, "and may God bless you!" He thanked the Admiral, and running to the side of the ship, sprang over into the sea, and struck out bravely towards the ships, which he was to order up. The men cheered him, and then went back to their guns. The fight went on; but the Dutch were getting the best of it. The Admiral was feeling very sadly. He did not see how he could hold out much longer. He said to himself— "I have never hauled down the flag of old England yet. I'd rather die than do it now. But how can I help it?" Just then he heard a firing to the right. Looking through the clouds of smoke that surrounded him, he saw that the brave boy had got through his long and dangerous swim. He had delivered the order entrusted to him; and the expected ships were coming, crowding down upon the enemy. This turned the tide of battle. The Dutch were soon beaten, and the flag of old England was not hauled down that day. In the evening the Admiral called his men on deck to thank them for their brave conduct. And then, turning to Cloudy, who was also present, he said: "And I want especially to thank you, my brave lad, for your noble conduct. We owe this victory to you. I hope to live to see you have a flagship of your own, some day." And it turned out just so. That cabin-boy went on realizing God's presence; and this gave him strength for duty, till he was knighted by the king, and known in the English navy as—Admiral Sir Cloudesley Shovel.

Right of Way.

Are you willing to be a highway over which Jesus Christ shall come to your town and into the lives of your friends and neighbors? Right of way costs something. When President Garfield was shot, he was taken to an isolated house where he could have absolute quiet and rest in his fight for life, and a special railway was constructed to facilitate the bringing of doctors, nurses, and loved ones to his bedside. The engineers laid out the line to cross a farmer's front yard, but he refused to grant the right of way until they explained to him that it was for the President, when he exclaimed, "That is different. Why, if that railroad is for the President, you can run it right through my house." Are you willing to give Him right of way across your front yard? It may run right through some of your plans, or social engagements, or business appointments. But will you give Him the right of way?—*Michigan Christian Advocate*.

Season—The Critical.

Long before the Amazon reaches the ocean, it has grown so wide that from the channel no shore can be seen on either side. It is still a river, but with all the signs and symptoms of becoming an ocean. There is a period, beginning not far from fourteen, in young lives, when childhood is widened suddenly, and carries its banks so far out that manhood seems begun, though as yet it is far off. The stream is ocean deep. Upon this estuary of youth the currents are shifting—the eddies are many. Here are united the strength of the sea and the hindrances of the land.—H. W. Beecher.

The Down Road.

Jonah not only paid the fare of the ship in which he tried to run away from God, but he also paid the full price of his disobedience. Notice that in his whole career he was going "down." He went "down to Joppa." From the sweet, free highlands, where he walked and talked with God, to the miasma of the lowlands, he went down. He went "down into the ship," and then down into the sea, and then down into the whale, and then, in the whale, down to the very bottom of the great deep! Disobedience to God means always that we go down. "Down" is the key word to every life that flees from God and duty.— *The Faith*.

Trouble—Ignoring.

"Why didn't you tell her she was taking more than her share of room and encroaching upon your rights?" some one asked of a young girl who was merrily describing an old woman who had taken a seat beside her in a crowded railway car, and crammed into the small space a bird-cage, a basket of apples, and bundles numerous and varied. "It wasn't worth while to trouble about it; we had such a little way to go together," was the reply. What a motto that would be for a life-journey! So many little annoyances are not worth noticing, so many small unkindnesses even may be passed by silently, because we have only "such a little way to go together."—J. R. Miller.

Warnings—Unheeded.

A man would not go into a plague hospital and inoculate himself with the plague when he knew that ninety-nine of every hundred that took it would die; but you do! No man seeing twenty or thirty men attempting to walk along the face of a cliff, and all falling over and perishing, would follow them; but you do! No man seeing the flame and the furnace heat of the building, and one fireman falling through, and another, hearing the word, "Stand off!" would go in; but you rush in, even though the others perished before you. Here are men that think they can go down into the house of death, amid the lures of corruption there, and come out unscathed; you are rotten already! Men think they can play the part of a rascal and be prosperous in life; the halter is around their neck! They think that they can drink, and cast off the danger; they are on the broad road, and not far from infamy!

O, slow of heart to believe the testimony of mankind, the testimony of your own experience, and the solemn word of God!—H. W. BEECHER.

Why He Gave Up.

Not long ago a man frankly told me how it came about that he had stopped believing. When he was twenty-six years old he went hunting with his brother. When night came they stopped in the forest to sleep. Just before they lay down he had knelt to pray as he had done from infancy. When he arose his brother said, "So you are still doing those things, are you?" That was all that was said, but from that night he stopped praying. Thirty years had passed, and in that thirty years he had never prayed or attended church. Now it was not the sneer of his brother that had changed him. His religious life had become so hollow and worthless that the pressure of a finger was sufficient to overthrow it.—*Presbyterian.*

ETERNITY

Danger—Hidden.

There is an account of the defeat, forty years ago, of the troops of a distinguished general in Italy. Having taken their stand near Terni, where the waters of the river Velino rush down an almost perpendicular precipice of three hundred feet, and thence toss and foam along through groves of orange and olive trees toward the Tiber, into which it soon empties, they attempted, when pressed by the Austrians, to make their escape over a bridge which spanned the stream just above the falls. In the hurry of the moment, and all unconscious of the insufficient strength of the structure, they rushed upon it in such numbers that it suddenly gave way, and precipitated hundreds of the shrieking and now despairing men into the rapid current below. There was no resisting such a tide when once on its bosom. With frightful velocity they were borne along toward the roaring cataract and the terrific gulf whence clouds of impenetrable mist never ceased to rise. A moment more, and they made the awful plunge into the fathomless abyss, from which, amid the roar of the water, no cry of horror could be heard, no bodies, or even fragments of bodies, could ever be rescued. The peril was wholly unsuspected, but none the less real, and ending in a "destruction" none the less "swift."

May we not see in this the picture of a great throng of immortal men in respect to their moral end? It seems generally to be assumed that, in our relations to eternity, there is no danger except that of which we are distinctly conscious,—which we see, or hear, or feel. But there cannot be a greater delusion. It would be equally rational for the blind man, who wanders among pitfalls, or on the trembling brink of some frightful precipice, to infer that there is no danger because he sees none. Insensibility to danger is, in fact, one of the most startling characteristics of the sinner's condition by nature, just as insensibility in a mortal disease is one of the most alarming symptoms of the disease itself.

Door—The Open.

Over the triple doorways of the Cathedral of Milan there are three inscriptions spanning the splendid arches. Over one is carved a beautiful wreath of roses, and underneath is the legend, "All that which pleases is but for a moment." Over the other is sculptured a cross, and there are the words, "All that which troubles us is but for a moment." But underneath the great central entrance to the main aisle is the inscription, "That only is important which is eternal." If we realize always these three truths, we will not let trifles trouble us, nor be interested so much in the passing pageants of the hour. We would live, as we do not now, for the permanent and the eternal.—*Christian Age.*

Punishment, Endless.

A venerable minister preached a sermon on the subject of eternal punishment. On the next day it was agreed among some thoughtless young men, that one of them should endeavor to draw him into a dispute, with the design of making a jest of him and of his doctrine. The wag accordingly went, and commenced by saying, "I believe there is a small dispute between you and me, sir, and I thought I would call this morning and try to settle it." "Ah," said the clergyman, "what is it?" "Why," replied the wag, "you say that the wicked will go into everlasting punishment, and I do not think that they will." "Oh, if that is all," answered the minister, "there is no dispute between you and me. If you turn to Matt. XXV. 46 you will find that the dispute is between you and the Lord Jesus Christ, and I advise you to go immediately and settle it with Him."

Immortality—Belief in.

The great Roman orator, Cicero, said, "Yes, oh yes! But if I err in believing that the soul of man is immortal I willingly err, nor while I live would I have the delightful error extorted from me; and if after death I shall feel nothing, as some philosophers think, I am not afraid that some dead philosopher shall laugh at me for my mistake." Socrates declared, "I believe a future life is needed to avenge the wrongs of this present life. In the future life justice shall be administered to us, and those who have done their duty here in that future life shall find their chief delight in seeking after wisdom." Yes, the soul is in exile. Like the homing-pigeon released, it hurries back to the bosom of the Father. Man is not satisfied with his humanity! As one writer has put it, our race is homesick.— *Homiletic Review.*

Life—End of.

A certain traveler who had a distance to go, one part of the road leading through green fields, and the other through a tangled road of brambles and thorns, made great preparations for the first part of his journey. He dressed himself in light and gay clothes, and put a nosegay in his bosom, and taking a light, slender cane in his hand, nimbly proceeded on his way along the beaten path across the green meadows. The sun shone in the skies, and on went the traveler, comfortably, pleasantly, and delightfully. After a while the road became rugged, and by the time night drew on the traveler was in a pitiable plight. His provisions were exhausted, his clothes wet through and partly torn from his back by the briars, his flowers were faded, and, weary as he was, his slender cane could not bear his weight; a stream of water was before him, and darkness was around him. "Alas!" said he, smiting his breast, "I am hungry, and have no food; wet to the skin, and have no dry clothes; weary, and have no staff to rest on; I have a stream to cross, and there is no boat; I am bewildered, and have no guide; it is dark, and I have no lantern. Fool that I am! why did I not provide for the end of my journey as well as the beginning?" Time is hastening away. We are all travelers. Life is the beginning, death the end of our journey.— *Biblical Museum.*

EXAMPLES

A Hard Lesson.

I read some time ago of a German captain who was drilling a company of volunteers. The parade ground was a field by the seaside. The men were going through their exercises very nicely, but the captain thought he would give them a lesson about obeying orders. They were marching up and down in the line of the water at some distance from it. He concluded to give them an order to march directly towards the water and see how far they would go. The men are marching along. "Halt, company," says the captain. In a moment they halt. "Right face" is the next word, and instantly they wheel round. "Forwart martch," is then the order. At once they begin to march directly towards the water: on they go, nearer and nearer to it. Soon they reach the edge of the water. Then there is a sudden halt. "Vat for you stop? I no say, Halt," cried the captain. "Why, captain, here is the water," said one of the men. "Vell, vot of it," cried he, greatly excited, "Vater is nothing; fire is nothing; everything is nothing. Ven I say, Forwart Martch, then you must forwart martch." The captain was right; the first duty of a soldier is to learn to obey.—DR. RICHARD NEWTON.

Burdens—Laying Down.

An aged, weary woman, carrying a heavy basket, got into the train with me the other day, and when she was seated she still kept the heavy burden upon her arm. "Lay your burden down, mum," said the kindly voice of a working man. "Lay your burden down, mum; the train will carry both it and you."—J. H. JOWETT.

Courtesy.

It is related of Pope Clement XIV (Ganganelli), that when he ascended the papal chair, the ambassadors of the several states represented at his court waited on him with their congratulations. When they were introduced, and bowed, he returned the compliment by bowing also; on which the master of the ceremonies told His Highness that he should not have returned their salute. "Oh, I beg your pardon," said the good pontiff, "I have not been pope long enough to forget good manners."

Destitute of Moral Principle.

Among the reminiscences of a political leader published by a Boston journal, is one of a national convention of the party to which he belonged. He says that the first day's proceedings developed the fact that the balance of power in the nomination of a candidate for the Presidency would rest with the delegation from a certain State. The delegates met in caucus at night with closed doors. In the discussion that ensued, the name of a prominent man was urged, and was received with favor. Only one of the delegates, a judge of some eminence in the State, knew him personally, and he not intimately. He was asked for his opinion. In reply, he said that he was at college with the prospective candidate, and he would relate one incident of college life. He did so, and it showed that the young man was in those days destitute of moral principle. The delegates were satisfied that, although brilliant, he was a man they could not trust, and they unanimously resolved to cast the votes of the State for his rival. The next day the vote was given, as decided, and the man to whom it was given was nominated and elected. Little did the young college man think, when he committed that escapade, that a score of years later it would be the sole cause of his missing one of the great prizes of earth—that of being the ruler of millions of people. But sin is always loss, and unless it is blotted out by the blood of Christ, it will cause the sinner to lose the greatest prize attainable to a human being in the world beyond the grave—eternal life.

Enemies—Patience with.

Father Graham was an old-fashioned gentleman beloved by every one, and his influence in the little town was great, so good and active was he.

A young man of the village had been badly insulted and came to Father Graham full of angry indignation declaring that he was going at once to demand an apology.

"My dear boy," Father Graham said, "take a word of advice from an old man who loves peace. An insult is like mud; it will brush off much better when it is dry. Wait a little, till he and you are both cool, and the thing is easily mended. If you go now it will only be to quarrel."

It is pleasant to be able to add that the young man took his advice, and before the next day was done the insulting person came to beg forgiveness.

Example—Careful of.

Gray, the poet, once made it a particular request to a friend of his, who was going to the Continent, that he would not pay a visit to Voltaire; and when his friend replied, "What can a visit from a person like me to him signify?" he rejoined with peculiar earnestness,

"Sir, every tribute to such a man signifies."—*Life of Gray.*

Fear of Man.

Burgomeister Guericke constructed a gigantic barometer with a tube thirty feet in height, part of which projected above the roof of his house at Magdeburg. The index was the figure of a man, who, in fair weather, was seen standing full size above the roof; but, when a storm was brewing, he cautiously withdrew for security and shelter. Antitype of religionists and politicians! When the sun shines brightly, and the breezes scarcely breathe across the landscape, how erect and bold they look! But let the clouds gather, and the thunders mutter, and what a drawing-in of diminished heads! O rare, satirical Burgomeister! you must have had an alderman's experience.—W. F. WARREN.

Meditation—Influence of.

Whoever has pondered long over a plan which he is anxious to accomplish, without distinctly seeing at first the way, knows what meditation is. It was in this way that one of the greatest of English engineers, a man uncouth, and unaccustomed to regular discipline of mind, is said to have accomplished his most marvelous triumphs. He threw bridges over almost impracticable torrents, and pierced the eternal mountains for his viaducts. Sometimes a difficulty brought all the work to a pause; then he would shut himself up in his room, eat nothing, speak to no one, abandon himself intensely to the contemplation of that on which his heart was set, and at the end of two or three days would come forth serene and calm, walk to the spot, and quietly give orders which seemed the result of superhuman intuition.

Name—Value of.

I once bore a package of letters to Abraham Lincoln at Washington in the interest of a friend. There were letters from judges, from lawyers, and from merchants, a score of them, most handsomely prepared. As I gave them to the President, he asked, "Whom are they from? What are the names?" I told him. He said, "Hand me that one" (indicating the one he wished). I handed it to him, and he took it and read it, and said, "I do not care for the rest—that is enough."—H. W. Beecher.

Perfection in Trifles.

A friend once saw Michael Angelo at work on one of his statues. Some time afterwards he saw him again, and said, seeing so little done, "Have you been idle since I saw you last?"

"By no means," replied the sculptor. "I have retouched this part and polished that; I have softened this feature and brought out that muscle; I have given more expression to this lip, and more energy to this limb."

"Well, well," said the friend, "all these are trifles."

"It may be so," replied Angelo; "but recollect that trifles make perfection, and that perfection is no trifle."—F. B. Cowl.

Plays—Incomplete.

On the coast of Wales is a small village. It is a most dangerous part of the coast. Many lives have been sacrificed there. The villagers conceived the idea of a life-boat. A house was built, but by the time that was completed the funds ran

out, and the life-boat was never secured. There the house stands—well-built, painted, finished, but there is no life-boat. How true that is of many a young fellow! He has glorious visions, splendid ideas and good intentions, but there is no grand out-reaching purpose, no forthcoming energy, and never a bit of life-boat work is he doing in the angry seas of time.—*The United Methodist.*

Pouter Pigeons.

Speaking of the writer of the "Eikon Basilike," Carlyle said that he was the most portentously self-righteous mortal ever extant in this planet; that seemed to say to the Almighty, in place of asking for His grace and mercy, "Oh, Lord, I have attained to such a pitch of heavenly perfection that I fear it is not even in Thy power to make me any better than I am; but if at the time Thou shouldst find an opportunity for adding a little finish and perfectness to my many excellences I should feel obliged to Thee."—*Mrs. Brookfield and Her Circle.*

Small Hinges.

Great events turn on small hinges. The gospel was first introduced into Japan through a portion of the Scripture that floated ashore, was picked up by a Japanese gentleman who afterwards sent for a whole Bible, and was instructed by the missionaries. When the Queen of Korea lost her little child by death, a slave girl in the palace told her of heaven to which it had gone, and the Saviour who would take her to it, and thus the gospel was first introduced into Korea by a little captive maid. The success of the mission in Telugu depended on the fact that John Clough had studied engineering when he was at college, and was able, therefore, to take the contract for the building of the canal during the famine, and the employment of thousands of laborers to whom he preached every day on the text: "God so loved the world, that he gave his only begotten Son, that whosoever believeth on him should not perish, but have everlasting life." The result of this work was the baptism of ten thousand converts in one year.

The battle of Bennington was gained, it is said, because a little lame boy in Vermont set a shoe on Colonel Warren's tenderfooted horse, and enabled the Colonel to lead up his regiment just in time to save the day, and the victory at Bennington decided the battle of Saratoga, which decided the Revolutionary War. The hunger of the little son of Columbus led him to stop at the monastery in Andalusia and ask for bread. The Prior of the Monastery who had been the confessor of Queen Isabella, on hearing the story of the adventurous navigator, brought about an interview with the Queen, which resulted in the sailing of Columbus for the discovery of America. It all hinged upon the hunger of the boy at the gate of the monastery. Robert Bruce took refuge in a cave from the pursuer who was seeking his life. A spider at once wove a web across the mouth of the cave, and when the pursuer came up, seeing the web he took it for granted that no one had entered, and so he passed on. The destiny of millions of people hinged upon that little spider's web.

We cannot really tell what are the little or the great events of life. God may be in the still small voice while he is not so much in the earthquake, the storm, and the fire. And it is a comfort to remember that he will use insignificant people, small gifts, and feeble efforts for his glory. And when we think that each one of us may be a sort of pivot on which turns the destiny of a nation or an age, how faithful to God we should strive to be.

EXCUSES

Duty—Forgotten.

It is said that a soldier who enlisted in the Civil War took along his kit of watchmaker's tools, and while they were in camp he did considerable business. But one day when the order came to strike tents and prepare for battle, he looked around his tent in dismay and exclaimed, "Why I can't possibly go, for I have twelve watches to repair which I have promised by Saturday night." That man had forgotten what he enlisted for.—*The Dolgeville Republican.*

Duty—Shirking.

A farmer, being short of horses, hitched a mule and an ox together to help with the hauling. After a little while the ox stopped, lay down and refused to move. The farmer said nothing, but quietly unhitched the animal, returned it to the stable, and made the mule pull the wagon the rest of the journey. At night the ox spoke confidentially to the mule. "What did the master say to-day?" he asked. "Nothing that I heard," replied the mule. The next day exactly the same thing happened. "What did the master say this time?" asked the ox that night. "I didn't hear him say anything," replied the mule; "but he's leaning over the fence out there talking to a butcher!"—*Christian Endeavor World.*

Excuse to Rest.

The Christian Commonwealth tells an anecdote and draws a lesson. A dog, hitched to a lawnmower, stopped pulling to bark at a passer-by. The boy who was guiding the mower said: "Don't mind the dog, he is just barking for an excuse to rest." It is easier to be critical than correct. Easier to bark than work. Easier to burn a house than build one. Easier to hinder than to help. Easier to destroy reputation than construct character. Fault finding is as dangerous as it is easy. Anybody can grumble, criticize, or censure, like the Pharisees, but it takes a great soul to go on working faithfully and lovingly, and rise superior to it all as Jesus did.—*The Expositor.*

Staff—Method.

An old legionary asked Augustus to assist him in a cause which was about to be tried. Augustus deputed one of his friends to speak for the veteran, who, however, repudiated the vicarious patron, saying, "It was not by proxy that I fought for you at Actium." Augustus acknowledged the obligation, and pleaded the cause in person.—*Little's Historical Lights.*

Belief Possible.

God has put the matter of salvation in such a way that the whole world can lay hold of it. All men can *believe.* A lame man might not perhaps be able to visit the sick; but he can believe. A blind man, by reason of his infirmity, cannot do many things; but he can believe. A deaf man can believe. A dying man can believe. God has put salvation so simply that young and old, wise and foolish, rich and poor, can all believe if they will.—D. L. MOODY.

Cast-Iron Faith.

"If you believe in God," wrote Robert Louis Stevenson, "where is there any more room for terror? If you are sure that God, in the long-run, means kindness by you, you should be happy." Fighting a losing battle with death, he wrote: "The tragedy of things works itself out blacker and blacker. Does it shake my cast-iron faith? I cannot say that it does. I believe in an ultimate decency of things; aye, and if I woke in hell, should still believe it." Let us thank God for the faith of that high and brave soldier of suffering, going up and down the earth in quest of health, and singing as he went:

If to feel in the ink of the slough,
And sink of the mire,
Veins of glory and fire
Run through and transpierce and
    transpire,
And a secret purpose of glory in
    every part,
And the answering glory of battle
    fill my heart;
To thrill with the joy of girded men,
To go on forever and fail and go on
    again,
And be mauled to the earth and
    arise,

And contend for the shade of a word
    and a thing not seen with the
    eyes:
With the half of a broken hope for
    a pillow at night;
That somehow the right is the
    right
And the smooth shall bloom from
    the rough:
Lord, if that were enough?

Faith and Action.

One of the passengers on board the *Atlantic,* which was wrecked off Fisher's Island, was Principal J. R. Andrews, of New London. He could not swim, but he determined to make a desperate effort to save his life. Binding a life preserver about him, he stood on the edge of the deck, waiting his opportunity, and when he saw a wave moving shoreward, he jumped into the rough breakers, and was borne safely to land. In one sense he saved himself, while in another he depended on God. If he had not used the life preserver, he would have perished; if he had not cast himself into the sea, he would have perished.—CHARLES W. ANDERSON.

Faith and Character.

A. J. Gordon while traveling on a train fell into debate with a fellow passenger on the subject of justification by faith. Said the man to Dr. Gordon: "I tell you, God deals with men, not with a little bit of theological scrip called faith; and when the Almighty admits one to Heaven he makes rigid inquiry about his character, and not about his faith." Presently the conductor came along and examined the tickets. When he had passed, Dr. Gordon said, "Did you ever notice how the conductor always looks at the ticket, and takes no pains at all to inspect the passenger? A railway ticket, if genuine, shows that the person presenting it has complied with the company's conditions and is entitled to transportation. Faith alone entitles a man to that saving grace that is alone able to produce a character well pleasing to God. God cares about character; but 'without faith it is impossible to please God.'"—*Sunday Circle*.

Faith and Works.

"I suppose that John Atkins is one of your best weavers," said a clergyman who was being shown by the foreman through a great mill. "Not much he isn't," replied the foreman. "The trouble with John is that he stands around talking about his religion when he ought to be attending to his loom. He is a good enough fellow, and has the making of a fine weaver in him, but he has not yet learned that while he is in his weaving-shed his religion ought to come out of his fingers, and not out of his mouth." A great deal of religion must accompany a very little talking.—*Record of Christian Work*.

Faith and Works.

"I handled a queer five-dollar bill the other day. It had done a heap of good,—paid the widow's rent, bought food for the hungry, squared up three or four accounts, made a church treasurer happy when he found it on the plate, and made the sexton happier when his back salary was paid by it; but in due course of time it came back to the bank whose name it bore, and lo! the teller threw it out. 'What's wrong?' asked the depositor. 'Counterfeit,' said the teller. All its good deeds had not made it pass the bank where its real character was discovered."—*The Baptist Record*.

Faith in Progress.

I once heard of two men who, under the influence of liquor, came down one night to where their boat was tied. They wanted to return home, so they got in and began to row. They pulled away hard all night, wondering why they never got to the other side of the bay. When the gray dawn of morning broke, behold, they had never loosed the mooring-line or raised the anchor! And that's just the way with many who are striving to enter the kingdom of heaven. They cannot believe, because they are tied to this world. Cut the cord! cut the cord! Set yourself free from the clogging weight of earthly things, and you will soon go on towards heaven.—MOODY.

Faith's Progress.

Dr. Arthur Pink has called attention to some of the first steps in the Christian life that most readers might miss. "The beginning of faith is faith in the beginning," he said. For we read, as the first step, that "by faith we understand that the worlds have been framed by the word of God, so that what is seen hath not been made out of things which appear." There is no true Christian faith that does not begin in recognition of God as the Creator. We must believe that before we can believe anything else. The next step is the worship of God through the blood sacrifice of his Son: "By faith Abel offered unto God a more excellent sacrifice than Cain"; for Cain rejected the atonement and Abel accepted it. The next step is walking with God by faith; Enoch now comes into the record as one who, "before his translation . . . had been well-pleasing unto God"; and Genesis has told us that "he walked with

God." Then comes Noah's work for God in that he "prepared an ark to the saving of his house." There is the necessary and invariable order, after accepting God as Creator: worship, walk, and work. We cannot walk with God until we worship him through the sacrifice of his Son. We cannot work for God until we are walking with him. Are we in step?—*The Sunday School Times.*

Faith—Christian.

You have seen, it may be, an antique, Italian painted window, with the bright Italian sunshine glowing through it. It is the special excellence of pictured glass that the light which falls merely on the outside of other pictures is here interfused throughout the work, illuminating the design, and investing it with a living radiance. . . . Christian faith is a grand cathedral, with divinely pictured windows. Standing without, you see no glory, nor can possibly imagine any. Nothing is visible but the merest outline of dusky shapes. Standing within, all is clear and defined; every ray of light reveals an army of unspeakable splendors.—RUSKIN

Faith—Definition of.

It was a good answer that was once given by a poor woman to a minister who asked her, "What is faith?" She replied: "I am ignorant, and I cannot answer well, but I think it is taking God at his word."—*Home Messenger.*

Faith,—Expressing.

One of his sailor-boys, warming up in an exhortation, speaking of faith, said, "It's like tinder in an old-fashioned tinder-box. Shut it up, and it will go out; give it vent, and it will burn." Slapping him on the back, Father Taylor exclaimed, "Well done, Peter! the Bishop couldn't better that."—*Life of Father Taylor.*

Faith—Foundation of.

When in 1896 the engineers were planning the foundations for the Williamsburg Bridge, New York, the deepest of their twenty-two borings was a hundred and twelve feet below high water. Steel drills had indicated bed-rock from twelve to twenty feet higher than was the actual case; the diamond drill, however, showed the supposed bed-rock to be merely a deposit of boulders. So the diamond drill of God pierces our self-delusions, detects the fallacy of our assumptions, proves what we thought sterling to be only stones of emptiness, discloses the very truth of things far down the secret places of the soul.—W. L. WALKINSON.

Faith—Influence of.

If you have read a little story for children called Little Lord Fauntleroy you have read a magnificent account of the influence of hope on others. You remember how the little lad goes to stay with his grandfather, and that grandfather is one of the most selfish, one of the meanest and most unkind of old men that have ever lived. But the boy believes in him. The boy, only about fourteen, keeps saying to his grandfather, "Oh, grandfather, how they must love you; you are so generous, you are so kind, you are so considerate to every one you meet." And the lesson of that beautiful story is the influence of hope on character. The old gentleman cannot withstand the belief of his boy; and he grows to be the un-

25215

selfish generous man that the boy thought him.

Faith—Necessity of.

I have known a timid traveler whose route lay across the Higher Alps, along a path, no broader than a mule's foothold, that skirted a dreadful precipice, whence could be discerned the river far down below, diminished to a silver thread; and on that dizzy precipice I have known a timid traveler, who fancied it safest to shut her eyes and not attempt to guide the course nor touch the bridle—a fatal touch that would throw steed and rider over, till, bounding from shelf to shelf, they lay a mangled mass in the valley below. And there are times and circumstances in the believer's life when, if he would keep himself from sinful doubts, if he would keep himself from falling into despair, he must, as it were, shut his eyes, lay the bridle on the neck of Providence, commit his way to God, and, however things may look, make this his comfort, "He will never leave me, nor forsake me." In such circumstances the only thing is to trust in God; "Walk by faith, not by sight."—GUTHRIE.

Faith—Saving.

"Mark you," said a pious sailor, when explaining to a shipmate at the wheel, "mark you, it isn't breaking off swearing and the like; it isn't reading the Bible, nor praying, nor being good; it is none of these; for even if they would answer for the time to come, there's still the old score; and how are you to get over that? It isn't anything that you have done or can do; it's taking hold of what Jesus did for you; it's forsaking your sins, and expecting the pardon and salvation of your

soul, because Christ let the waves and billows go over Him on Calvary. This is believing, and believing is nothing else."—*New Cyclopedia of Anecdote.*

Faith—Trial of.

One incident of the voyage to America served as a sharp test to Wesley of his own spiritual condition. Amongst the passengers he found a little group of Moravian exiles, who, by the simplicity and seriousness of their piety, strangely interested him. A storm broke over the ship one evening just as these simple-minded Germans had begun a religious service; Wesley describes what follows: "In the midst of the Psalm wherewith their service began, the sea broke over, split the mainsail in pieces, covered the ship, and poured in between the decks as if the great deep had already swallowed us up. A terrible screaming began amongst the English. The Germans calmly sang on. I asked one of them afterwards, 'Were you not afraid?' He answered, 'I thank God, no.' I asked, 'But were not your women and children afraid?' He replied mildly, 'No; our women and children are not afraid to die.' From them I went to their crying, trembling neighbors, and pointed out to them the difference in the hour of trial between him that feareth God and him that feareth Him not."—W. H. FITCHETT.

Faith,—Triumph of.

In the Life of Robert and Mary Moffat, edited by their son, we are reminded that for ten years the early mission in Bechuanaland was carried on without one ray of encouragement for the faithful workers. No convert was made. The directors at home, to the great grief of the devoted missionaries, began to question the wisdom of continuing the mission. A year or two longer the darkness reigned. A friend from England sent word to Mrs. Moffat asking what gift she should send out to her. And the brave woman wrote back, "Send a communion service; it will be sure to be needed." At last the breath of the Lord moved on the hearts of the Bechuanas. A little group of six were united into the first Christian church, and that communion service from England, singularly delayed, reached Kuruman just one day before the appointed time for the first administration of the Lord's Supper.—*Chronicle of L. M. Society.*

Faith—Upward Look of.

Wesley was walking one day with a troubled man who expressed his doubt of God's goodness. "I don't know what I shall do with all this worry and trouble," he said. At that moment Wesley noticed a cow looking over a stone wall. "Do you know," asked Wesley, "why that cow is looking over that wall?" "No," replied his troubled companion. "I will tell you," said Wesley—"because she cannot see through it. That is what you must do with your wall of trouble—look over it and above it." Faith enables us to look over and above every trouble, to God, who is our help.—*The Sunday Circle.*

Faith—Wings of.

If you will go to the banks of a little stream and watch the flies that come to bathe in it, you will notice that, while they plunge their bodies in the water, they keep their wings high out of the water; and after swimming about a little while they fly away with their wings unwet through the sunny air. Now that is a lesson for us. Here we are immersed in the cares and business of the world; but let us keep the wings of our soul, our faith, and our love out of the world, that with these unclogged we may be ready to take our flight to heaven. —JAMES INGLIS.

Faith—Won by.

The providence of God sent across my path some years ago a thief who had been in prison above twenty times, and who had been twice in penal servitude. I could find no work for him here, because he was well known, and therefore I sent him across the ocean to America, but his character followed him, and he was returned to England. At length we obtained work for him out of Manchester; and he turned out to be a faithful servant. One day the manager of the works was removing his goods to a new house, and the mistress—who did not know what the man had been— called him, saying, "John, this basket contains all our silver; will you please be very careful about it, and carry it to the new house." I said to the man, "And what did you do?" He said, "When I got outside, I looked into the basket and saw the silver shining. I lifted it up, and it felt very heavy." "Well, what did you do then?" He replied, "I cried, because I was trusted." Of course, he carried it safely.—W. BIRCH.

Trust—Absolute.

Dr. J. R. Miller says: It is often given as a wonderful proof of confidence in a friend that once when the great Grecian emperor, Alexander, was ill, it was told to him in a letter that his physician intended to give him poison under the form of medicine. The emperor put the note under his pillow. The physician came, poured out the potion, and gave it to him. The emperor looked his friend full in the face, drank the contents of the goblet, then handed him the letter. It was a beautiful trust. Like confidence we are to have in the will of Christ for us. We are never to doubt His love nor His wisdom.

FORGIVENESS

Forgiveness—A Definition of.

A little boy being asked what forgiveness is, gave the beautiful answer: "It is the odor that flowers breathe when they are trampled upon." Philip the Good, when some of his courtiers would have persuaded him to punish a prelate who had used him ill, he declined, saying, "It is a fine thing to have revenge in one's power; but it is a finer thing not to use it."

Forgiveness—Absolute.

Paul, in describing the forgiveness of God wrought through Jesus Christ, uses this remarkable figure: "Blotting out the handwriting of ordinances that was against us." It is like taking an indictment in court, and tearing it up and throwing it away. It is like taking a title-deed of a man's possession, a paper on which is written evidence that is fatal to his claim, and blotting it, or burning it. It is like taking away proof against a man which may lead to his injury.—H. W. BEECHER.

Forgiveness—Brotherly.

There was once upon a time a bishop of Alexandria, in Egypt, named John the Almsgiver. A nobleman came to see him one day, and the conversation turned on grievance. So-and-so had wronged him cruelly, and never to his dying day could he forgive him. He spoke with warmth and anger, his face darkened with passion, and his eye sparkled. Just at that moment the bell tinkled for prayers in the bishop's private chapel, and he rose and bade the nobleman follow him. St. John the Almsgiver knelt at the altar, and the nobleman knelt immediately behind him. Presently the bishop began in a loud voice the Lord's Prayer, and the nobleman repeated each part with him. "Thy will be done on earth as it is in heaven. Give us this day our daily bread." The bishop stopped abruptly. The nobleman, not thinking, went on alone: "And forgive us our trespasses as we forgive them that trespass against us"; then, finding he was alone, stopped short also. The bishop did not go on, but remained silently kneeling. Then suddenly the sense of the words of the petition he had made rushed on the nobleman's mind. The grace of God worked. He silently rose from his knees, went forth, and finding the man who offended him, frankly forgave him. . . . One day the governor of Alexandria was in high wrath with the bishop, who had remonstrated with him at levying a tax which was peculiarly oppressive to the poor. Backbiters had managed to widen the breach, and the governor, after an interview with the bishop, in which he had given vent to his angry, excited feeling, left for his palace. Towards evening the good old bishop got very troubled at the quarrel. He could not bear that any should be at enmity with him, so he wrote on a slip of parchment the words, "The sun is setting," and sent it to the governor, who at once remembered the words of St. Paul: "Let not the sun go down upon your wrath," and rising from the table where he had been sitting, he hastened to the old prelate to be reconciled to him before the day was done.

Forgiveness—Complete.

I call to mind an occasion when the son of a Christian man was guilty of an act of disobedience in the home. Hearing of it, the father quietly but firmly said, "Son, I am pained beyond measure at your conduct." "How well," said that father, "I remember his return from school at mid-day, his quiet knock at the study-door, his clear tremulous utterance, 'Father, I am so ashamed of myself by reason of my conduct this morning.'" "Refuse to restore him!" said the father. "Unhesitatingly I confess that I never loved my boy more than at that moment, nor did I ever more readily implant the kiss of forgiveness than at that instant. Refuse to restore him; disown him, have him leave the house, take another name, say that he had no place in the family—not my child!" And shall we dare to attribute such conduct to the Holy Father in heaven, "who spared not His own Son, but freely delivered Him up for us all?"—HENRY VARLEY.

Forgiveness, Effects of.

President Lincoln having pardoned a young man under sentence of death or imprisonment, his mother's gratitude was such that she was unable to speak for a while after leaving him. Then she broke out in an excited manner with the words, "I knew it was a lie!" "What do you refer to?" said Mr. Thaddeus Stevens, who accompanied her. "Why, they told me he was an ugly-looking man," she replied with vehemence. "He is the handsomest man I ever saw in my life!" —*Little's Historical Lights.*

Forgiveness—Power of.

There is a story of an incorrigible soldier who had been punished so often for so many offenses, without avail, that his commanding officer despaired of the man's amendment. Again he was under arrest, and the officer spoke hopelessly of him, asking what more could be done to save him from his own undoing. A fellow-officer suggested, "Try forgiving him." The man was brought in and asked what

he had to say for himself. He replied: "Nothing, except that I'm very sorry." "Well," said the officer, "we have decided to forgive you." The man stood dazed for a moment and then burst into tears, saluted, and went out to become the best and bravest soldier in the command.—J. R. MILLER.

Forgiveness—Seeking.

Benhadad, King of Assyria, being overcome by the King of Israel, was told that the kings of Israel were merciful men, and therefore sent his servants, clothed with sackcloth, and ropes about their necks, to entreat pardon and peace. When the king saw their submission, he made a covenant of peace with them. God is merciful; and condemned sinners should hasten to make their submission to him, that they may be forgiven.

Hard to Forgive Self.

There are some sins which, even if forgiven by others, cannot easily be pardoned by the penitent mind. Dr. Bates tells us that the excellent Richard Baxter cherished such self-condemnation on account of his own sinfulness, that he was in the habit of saying, "I can more easily believe that God will forgive me, than that I can forgive myself."—*The Evangelist.*

Mercy—Plea for.

A woodchuck once helped himself to what vegetables he wanted in Mr. Webster's garden. Ezekiel Webster, his son, set a trap and caught him, and said, "Now we'll kill the thief: you've done mischief enough to die, Mr. Woodchuck, and you shall die." His brother Daniel pleaded for his release. The case was brought before the father, who acted as judge. Ezekiel presented the vicious habits of the prisoner, the damage already done to the garden, and the value of his skin, as reasons why he ought to die. Daniel pleaded that the woodchuck was one of the creatures of God, not particularly vicious, having a right to food, life, and liberty. He urged the cruelty of taking the life of the helpless creature. The plea so moved the father that he cried, "Zeke, Zeke, let the woodchuck go!" This was Daniel Webster's first case, won when he was only ten years old.

Sins Blotted Out.

John Maynard was in an old-time country school-house. Most of the year he had drifted carelessly along, but in midwinter some kind words from his teacher roused him to take a new start, and he became distinctly a different boy, and made up for the earlier faults. At the closing examination he passed well, to the great joy of his father and mother, who were present. But the copybooks used through the year were all laid on a table for the visitors to look at; and John remembered that his copybook, fair enough in its latter pages, had been a dreary mass of blots and bad work before. He watched his mother looking over those books, and his heart was sick. But she seemed, to his surprise, quite pleased with what she saw, and called his father to look with her; and afterward John found that his kind teacher had thoughtfully torn out all those bad, blotted leaves, and made his copybook begin where he started to do better. To all who would forsake sin God offers a new chance, and promises to blot out all old sin and make the record begin with the new start.—FRANKLIN NOBLE.

Alarmists.

On a certain December day some villain pulled a fire-alarm box in Boston. There was no fire, but the department did not know that, of course. The engines turned out promptly and went tearing down the icy streets.

The abominable fellow went on a little further and rang another false alarm. Then further, and rang another. Yet further, and sounded a fourth.

By this time the fire chief had guessed what was the matter. He stationed men at the downtown boxes to try to catch the rascal, but they were not successful. He had had enough fun for one evening.

His fun cost the city $300. The condition of the streets was such that it might easily have cost the lives of horses and of men. And all because of an insane craving for excitement.

That exploit, which is by no means unknown in other cities than the Modern Athens, reminds me of the performances of the Alarmist.

Unable or unwilling to do anything himself to make a stir in the world, he goes around sounding alarms.

Society is in danger, he asserts, at this point, at that point, at the other point. He sets the engines tearing down the streets.

If a horse slips on the pavement, if an engine capsizes, if serious loss or injury results, the Alarmist does not care a whit. He has made a stir in the world—by proxy.

And our easy-going civilization does not put detectives on his track, hunt him down, and punish him. No; we run our engines back, take off our coats, and wait for the next alarm.—Amos R. Wells.

Emotions—Evanescent.

Dr. Wayland Hoyt tells the story of a captain whom he met in the pilot-house of a Missouri River steamboat, and who asked his judgment concerning his conduct. He said that when he was a young man, and was first married, his wife was a Christian, and to please her he began to go to church; he never could hear singing and not be moved; the songs they sang in the church touched him strongly. They brought up forgotten memories and unloosed the springs of feeling; he was overcome. Because he wept, they thought he had become a Christian. His wife, the minister, and many friends pressed him to join the church, "But," said the captain, "I could not. I told them I had simply been stirred by the songs as I always am. I knew I had not given up my evil ways."

Emotion—Discipline of.

Froude, in his Erasmus, relates a curious incident in the life of Ignatius Loyola. Loyola, one day, met with a copy of the New Testament. He took it up, opened it, and began to read it. But after a short time he threw it down, because, he said, "it checked his devotional emotions." Froude thinks it very likely did. He found here a religion taught the supreme expression of which was in absolute righteousness, truth, and charity. "If any man deemeth himself to be religious, and bridleth not his tongue, is not just, fair, honorable, open, merciful, that man's religion is vain." Loyola said this sort of thing checked his devotional emotions! Well, if so, it was high time they were checked. For they were running to seed, and not growing, under due discipline, to flower and fruit. In the religion of Jesus, the ethical, the practical, is the ultimate. To keep the Golden Rule is to fulfill the Law and the prophets. —C. S. HORNE.

Feeling and Fact.

Christian workers often hear a man or woman say, "But I don't feel any different." General McClellan, when he had been appointed Major-General of the Union Army, wrote to his wife: "I do not feel any different from what I did yesterday. Indeed, I have not yet donned my new uniform. I am sure that I am in command of the army, however, for the President's order to that effect now lies before me." It is exactly the same with us who are "justified by faith." It is not a question of feeling, but of fact.—The Life of Faith.

GRACE

Christian Nurture.

A nurseryman about to plant a number of young saplings, some straight and some crooked, thus reasoned with himself—"These straight saplings will no doubt grow up to be fine trees without much attention on my part; but I will see if, by proper training, I cannot make something of the crooked ones also. There will be more trouble with them, no doubt, than with the others; but for that very reason I shall be the better satisfied should I succeed."—*New Cyclopedia of Anecdotes.*

Door of God's Grace.

One warm summer afternoon, a bird flew through the open door into a chapel where divine service was being conducted. Full of fear it flew backward and forward near the ceiling and against the windows, vainly seeking a way out into the sunshine. In one of the pews sat a lady who observed the bird, thinking how foolish it was not to fly out through the open door into liberty. At last the bird's strength being gone, it rested a moment on one of the rafters. Then, seeing the open door, it flew out into the sunshine, venting its joy in a song. The lady who had been watching the little bird thought to herself: "Am I not acting as foolishly as I thought the bird was? How long have I been struggling under the burden of my sin in the vain endeavor to get free, and all the while the door of God's grace has been wide open." Then and there the decision was formed to enter in.— *The Expositor.*

Grace.

"Grace" is a word our fathers understood and loved better than we. It was defined as "favor." And favors even of God are not agreeable to the proud spirit of man. But no common term can ever exhaust, or express, this great and rich idea. "Grace" expresses and denotes at once the feeling that prompts the beneficence that comes of a joy that cannot be uttered, and yet must be expressed, and the joy that cannot bear the sight of pain and misery, and guilt and death, confronting it on this wide earth.— A. M. FAIRBAIRN.

Grace, Beginnings of.

Trace back any river to its source, and you will find its beginnings small. A little moisture oozing through the sand or dripping out of some unknown rock, a gentle gush from some far-away mountain's foot, are the beginning of many a broad river, in whose waters tall merchantmen may anchor and gallant fleets may ride. For it widens and gets deeper, till it mingles with the ocean. So is the beginning of a Christian's or a nation's grace. It is first a tiny stream, then it swells into a river, then a sea. There is life and progression towards an ultimate perfection when God finds the beginning of grace in any man.—J. J. WRAY.

Grace—God's.

For my own part, if my pocket was full of stones, I have no right to throw one at the greatest backslider upon earth. I have either done as bad or worse than he, or I certainly should if the Lord had left me a little to myself; for I am made of just the same materials: if there be any difference, it is wholly of grace.—JOHN NEWTON.

Grace—Growing in.

The only way by which we can grow nearer and nearer to our Lord is by steadfastly keeping beside Him. You cannot get the spirit of a landscape unless you sit down and gaze, and let it soak into you. The cheap tripper never sees the lake. You cannot get to know a man until you summer and winter with him. No subject worth studying opens itself out to the hasty glance. Was it not Sir Isaac Newton who used to say, "I have no genius, but I keep a subject before me"?—A. MACLAREN.

Grace—Growth in.

No man ever suddenly cleared up forty acres of land. A man may begin such a work suddenly. No man ever began to do a thing without making up his mind to do it. No man ever began to be a Christian without a volition; and no volition was ever anything but a flash—an instantaneous thing. But the volition is the beginning. The evolution of Christian character is gradual.—H. W. BEECHER.

Grace—Persistent.

"Hamlet," says Professor Bradley, "usually speaks as one who accepts the received Christian ideas, yet when he meditates profoundly he seems to ignore them." There has been too much of this Hamlet-spirit in the Church. Yet her shortcomings have only thrown into more brilliant relief the quenchless patience of God's love, and the tenacity of His revelation. The vital truths of the faith have refused to be ignored for long. It has been a revelation to the world, as well as to the Church itself, how vital and undying is the sheer grace of God in Christ, often thwarted, often grieved, but never chilled by human imperfections.—J. MOFFATT.

Grace—Power of God's.

It is related that Bishop Kavanagh was one day walking when he met a prominent physician, who offered him a seat in his carriage. The physician was an infidel, and the conversation turned upon religion. "I am surprised," said the doctor, "that such an intelligent man as you should believe such an old fable as that." The bishop said, "Doctor, suppose years ago some one had recommended to you a prescription for pulmonary consumption, and you had procured the prescription and taken it according to order, and had been cured of that terrible disease, what would you say of the man who would not try your prescription?" "I should say he was a fool." "Twenty-five years ago," said Kavanagh, "I tried the power of God's grace. It made a different man of me. All these years I have preached salvation, and wherever accepted have never known it to fail."

Grace,—Silent.

Dew falls insensibly and invisibly. You may be in the field all night and not perceive the dew falling, and yet find great dew upon the grass. So the operations and blessings of God's Word, and graces thereof, are invisible; we feel the work, but the manner of the working is unknown to us. No man can see the conversion of another, nor can well discern his own. The Word works by little and little, like as the dew falls.—B. KEACH.

Grace Sufficient for Trials.

The Rev. Prebendary H. W. Webb-Peploe in one of the Northfield meetings related an experience of his earlier ministry. It was on one of life's dreary days. A much-needed vacation had been cut short by the death of his little child, and he was struggling in weariness and despondency to prepare his sermon for the coming Sabbath. In his extremity he threw himself on his knees, begging God that His grace might be sufficient for his great need. Not yet assured, he opened his eyes, which instantly rested on a wall motto before him, with the words, "My grace is sufficient for thee," so arranged in color scheme that the word "is" stood out vividly. The conviction flashed into his soul that there was no need to beg for that which was divinely assured as a fact. His life from that moment was revolutionized. — *The Sunday School Times.*

Grace—Unmerited.

A Christian lady was visiting a poor sickly woman, and after conversing with her for a little she asked her if she had found salvation yet. "No," she replied; "but I am working hard for it." "Ah, you will never get it that way," the lady said. "Christ did all the working when He suffered and died for us, and made complete atonement for our sins. You must take salvation solely as a gift of free, unmerited grace, else you can never have it at all."—*Clerical Library.*

2. Life—Gift of.

Once there was a brier growing in a ditch and there came along a gardener with his spade. As he dug around it and lifted it out, the brier said to itself, "What is he doing that for? Doesn't he know that I am only an old worthless brier?" But the gardener took it into the garden and planted it amid his flowers, while the brier said, "What a mistake he made! Planting an old brier like myself among such rose trees as these!" But the gardener came once more and with his keen-edged knife made a slit in the brier, and, as we say in England, "budded it" with a rose, and by and by when summer came lovely roses were blooming on that old brier. Then the gardener said, "Your beauty is not due to that which came out of you, but to that which I put into you."—MARK GUY PEARSE.

GOD

A Sleeping Deity.

In China men have conceived of a sleeping Deity. There, lying on his side, with calm face, closed eyes, and head resting upon his hand, is a gilded wooden figure, 30 feet long, and well proportioned. But he does not mind his worshipers. His left arm is resting upon his body, and his bare feet are placed one upon the other. This Buddha is sleeping, while the world goes on. Standing about him are twelve crowned and beautifully dressed images, and in front are the symbols of sacrifice and incense. How unlike Him who neither slumbers nor sleeps!

Agents—God's.

George Stephenson, the inventor of the locomotive engine, was once standing with Dean Buckland, the famous geologist, and others upon the terrace of Sir Robert Peel's mansion at Drayton Manor, when a railway train flashed along in the distance, throwing behind it a long trail of white steam. "Now, Dr. Buckland," said Stephenson, "can you tell me what is the power that is driving that train?" "Well," said the Dean, "I suppose it is one of your big engines." "But what drives the engine?" "Oh, very likely a canny Newcastle driver." "What?" asked the Dean. "It is nothing else," replied the engineer; "it is light bottled up in the earth for tens of thousands of years and now, after being buried in the earth for long ages in the fields of coal, the latent light is again brought forth and liberated; made to work, as in that engine, for great motive purposes." That answer was itself a flash of illumination to the mind of the man of science, and there is more meaning in it than even Buckland or Stephenson himself ever dreams.

For, since that day, not only has light produced by the combustion of coal gas become the chief means of artificial illumination to all civilized nations, but mineral oils derived from the same source are also largely used, and it is the pent-up force of the sunbeam locked up in the coal that drives our motor-cars, and, transformed into heat, generates the power which we transmute again into light in the form of the electric beam. Hundreds of thousands of years ago the light was sown, and now the harvest is being reaped.—J. HALSEY.

Faith in God.

Here is a city perishing from thirst. A great reservoir lies on a hilltop above. Here is a connecting main through which the water rushes from the reservoir to the city below. The dwellers in that city are saved by the reservoir of water, through the pipe which leads down from it. People are never saved from thirst by empty pipes. They are saved by the water through the pipes. A man might have all the faith in the world, but if there were no God in whom to have faith all his faith would be vain. Faith is the supreme condition to receiving salvation; but it is not the Saviour. Wherefore salvation is from God, in Christ through faith.—*Christ Life.*

God's Goodness.

Because colliers live in the bowels of the earth and sometimes do not see the sun rise or set for weeks and months together, or because imprisoned men in dungeons do not witness the changes of the seasons, does it follow that there is no rising of the sun, or that there is neither spring nor summer for the human family? If one avoids the light of the sun, shuts himself out from it, he may miss it, but it is waiting for him: so is God's goodness.—H. W. BEECHER.

God's Goodness Proved.

There is an Indian story of a queen who "proved the truth by tasting the food." The story tells how her husband, who dearly loved her, and whom she dearly loved, lost his kingdom, wandered away with his queen into the forest, left her there as she slept, hoping she would fare better without him, and followed her long afterwards to her father's court, deformed, disguised, a servant among servants, a cook. Then her maidens came to her, told her of the wonderful cooking, magical in manner, marvelous in flavor and fragrance. They are sure it is the long-lost king come back to her, and they bid her believe and rejoice. But the queen fears it may not be true. She must prove it; she must taste the food. They bring her some. She tastes and knows. And the story ends in joy. "O taste and see that the Lord is good."—AMY WILSON CARMICHAEL.

God's Great Gift.

A king who wished to express his affection for a private soldier of his army gave him a richly jeweled cup, his own cup. The soldier, stepping forth to receive the gift, exclaimed shamefacedly, "This is too great a gift for me to receive." "It is not too great for me to give," the king replied. So Christ offers us this infinite gift of the Holy Spirit to cleanse and fill our hearts and to abide with us. Think then how much He must have cared that we receive it.—*The Christian Herald*.

God's Image.

When a Roman penny was made, the image or likeness of Caesar the emperor was stamped upon it, and those who used it were reckoned as his subjects and expected to obey his laws. Ages ago God himself made something and stamped his likeness upon it, as a sign that it belonged to him and must be used in his service. It was not a coin God made. It was a man. And God's image has been stamped upon each of us to show that we were made, not to follow our own pleasure, but to serve him.—*The Intermediate Quarterly*.

God Makes No Mistakes.

There is here a young man of about thirty, of fine talents and capabilities for active life, but for years a cripple, paralytic and helpless. He would starve if left alone. A friend was commiserating his condition, when, with deep earnestness, he exclaimed, as he slowly raised his withered hand, "God makes no mistakes." How noble the sentiment! "Shall not the Judge of all the earth do right?" This is piety. Only a heart divinely taught could thus speak.—DR. TALMAGE.

God Our Refuge.

Once upon a time, at Athens, the Senate was sitting. At their meeting out in the open fields, as the men of Athens were all assembled together deliberating, making laws, a little bird which was just by an oak-tree came flying into the middle of the assembly. And the poor little sparrow came and nestled itself in the breast of one of the Senators. The poor little thing was terribly frightened, and its feathers were all ruffled. As it came and nestled itself in the breast of one of the old Senators, this cruel man took the little bird out of his breast and flung it to the ground, stamped upon it, and killed it. The other Senators said, "It is shocking! He shall never be a Senator again." They said more. They said, "He should die for his cruelty. The man who can kill a little bird in that way is not fit to live. He shall die." And he was actually put to death for his cruelty to the little sparrow! Do you think that those Senators could be so kind to this little sparrow, and that the great God, who loves you, will not receive you when you go to His fatherly, loving breast?

God Our Shield.

Marcus Dods was a probationer for six years before being called to Renfield Church, Glasgow. During these years of waiting he was sometimes so discouraged as to think of giving up the ministry altogether. In a letter to his sister he wrote: "Do these two years and more waiting not show that I am seeking my work in the wrong direction, or why do they not show this, or how long would show this? Possibly you may say, 'Wait till some evident call to some other work arises'; but then, of course, evident calls enough would soon arise were I to put myself in the way of them, e.g., were I to go along to Clark the publisher and ask him for some work, or go out to Harvey of Merchiston and ask him for some; whereas, so long as I keep myself back from such openings they are not a tenth part so likely to arise. But apart from growlery, let me give you a problem. I will give it you in the concrete, as being easier stated and easier apprehended. Is it right of me to wait and see whether I get a call or no, and let this decide whether I ought or ought not to take a charge? To me it seems not (though it's just what I'm doing), and on this ground, because in fact we find that God has often suffered men to enter the Church who were not worthy —because, that is, the call of the people does not always represent the call of God." He was afterwards Professor of Exegesis and Principal of the New College, Edinburgh.

God's Kingdom Stands.

Lessing once related this parable. "Once upon a time a certain king of a great realm built himself a palace, the most gorgeous that ever had been planned, the wonder of the whole earth. A strife arose among certain connoisseurs as to some of the obscure ground-plans upon which the palace was constructed. The conflict lasted through a great many years. While this conflict was going on, it happened upon a time, that a watchman one night cried out, 'Fire!' And the architects began running hither and thither, each with his plan, squabbling as to whether the fire had broken out in this place, or whether it had broken out at that place, and as to what was the best spot to apply the engines. And its friends all took to wrangling. Alas, alas! the beautiful palace will be burned. But it stood there; and presently they discovered that it was not on fire at all. Behind it there was an extraordinary display of northern lights, which shone through it with such brilliancy that the palace itself seemed to be full of flame."

So we say, let knowledge increase, let it run to and fro, let it lighten up the world all it will, it will only illuminate, because it cannot destroy, the city of our God.—S. D. McConnell.

God's Map—No Edge to.

Is there any danger that Christians may have too small a map of the work God would have accomplished in this generation? A big drive was being made during the World War along the British front. The enemy was in retreat and the huge tanks were following up the foe, when one of the tanks stopped dead. It was not disabled, there were no casualties among the crew, and there was plenty of ammunition. Finally an officer came up and with forcible language demanded why the huge beast should halt when the job was as yet unfinished. "The trouble is, Sir," said one of the crew, "we have got to the edge of our way."—*The Sunday School Times*.

God's Watch-Care.

A wild storm was raging round a prairie home one night. The windows were blown in, and no lights could be kept burning. It was only with difficulty that the doors could be braced against the blast. The father was away from home, and the mother, grandmother, and three children sat in the darkness in a room on the sheltered side of the house, fearing that at any moment it might be swept from its foundation by the force of the wind. Suddenly, eleven-year-old Walter was missed. He had been holding a whispered conversation with his grandmother only a few moments before. Frantic with fear, the mother called him at the top of her voice, and receiving no reply, started to grope her way through the darkness of the house. She found the missing boy in bed, fast asleep. And when she asked him how he could go to sleep when they were all in danger of death, he sleepily replied, "Why, grandmother told me God would take care of us, so I thought I might as well go to bed again."

God—A Bearer of.

In the days of Trajan there lived a Saint of God named Ignatius, who sealed his testimony with his blood. Ignatius was commonly known as *Theophoros*—or the Bearer of God. I imagine that there was such a pre-eminent holiness, such a supernatural sanctity in his character that he seemed to be a kind of incarnation of the Divine life. The title given to Ignatius is one to which every Christian who is faithful to his calling may in some degree humbly lay claim. He is a Theophoros, a God-bearer. Christ dwells in him and he dwells in Christ. Christ is "in him the hope of glory."—S. C. Lowry.

God—A False.

Splendid was that festival at Caesarea at which Herod Agrippa, in the pomp and pride of power, entered the theater in a robe of silver, which glittered, says the historian, with the morning rays of the sun, so as to dazzle the eyes of the assembly and excite general admiration. Some of his flatterers set up the shout, "A present god!" Agrippa did not repress the impious adulation which spread through the theater. At that moment he looked up and saw an owl perched over his head on a rope, and Agrippa had been forewarned that when next he saw that bird, "at the height of his fortune," he would die within five days. The fatal omen, according to Josephus, pierced the heart of the King, who with deep melancholy exclaimed, "Your god will soon suffer the common lot of mortality." He was immediately struck, in the language of the sacred volume, by an angel. Seized with violent pains, he was carried to his palace, lingered five days in extreme agony, being "eaten of worms," and so died.—FRANCIS JACOX.

God—A Friend of.

Of no mortal man but Abraham alone does Almighty God ever speak and say, He was My friend. God employs many gracious, beautiful, and endearing names in speaking of the patriarchs, and prophets, and psalmists, and other saints of His in Israel; but it is of Abraham alone that God testifies to Israel and says, Thou art the seed of Abraham, My friend.—A. WHYTE.

God—A Helper.

Gerhardt was exiled from Brandenburg by the Grand Elector in 1659. The said Grand Elector wished to "tune his pulpits." Gerhardt refused to preach save what he found in God's Word. Notice to quit was thereupon promptly served upon the intrepid preacher; he tramped forth a homeless exile, accompanied by his wife and children. Wife and weans at night, wearied and weeping, sought refuge in a wayside inn; Gerhardt, unable to comfort them, went out into a wood to pray. As he prayed, the text, "Commit thy way unto the Lord, trust also in Him and He shall bring it to pass," recurred to his mind, and comforted him so amazingly that he paced to and fro under the forest trees, and began composing a hymn, Englishized by John Wesley, beginning with the verse—

"Give to the winds thy fears.
Hope and be undismayed:
God hears thy sighs and counts
    thy tears;
God shall lift up thy head."

Returning to the inn, he cheered his wife with the text and the hymn, and they went to bed rejoicing in the confident hope that God would take care of them. They had hardly retired before a thunderous knocking at the door aroused them all. It was a mounted messenger from Duke Christian Meresberg, offering him "Church, people, home, and livelihood." So, adds the Chronicle, the Lord took care of His servant.—W. T. STEAD.

God—Acknowledging.

When the Spanish Armada was overthrown by the storm, England caused a medal to be struck, with the inscription, "Afflavit Deus, et dissepantur:" "God blew on them, and they were scattered." On all her coin is stamped, "Dei Gratia." The United States has, since the war of the Rebellion, put on her coin the legend, "In God we trust."

God—Approach to.

The Persian kings took state upon them, and enacted that none should come near to them uncalled, on pain of death. But oh! sirs, the gates of heaven are always open; you have liberty night and day of presenting your petition, in the name of Christ, to the King of the whole earth.—RALPH ERSKINE.

God—Confidence in.

Not long ago a Christian merchant met, unexpectedly, with some very great losses. He began to doubt the wisdom of that Providence which could allow such trials to overtake him. He returned to his home one evening in a gloomy and despairing state of mind. He sat down before the open fireplace in his library, "tossed with the tempest" of doubt and destitute of comfort. Presently his little boy, a thoughtful child of six or seven years, came and sat on his knee. Over the mantel-piece was a large illuminated card containing the words—"His work is perfect." The child spelled out the words, and pointing to them, said, "Papa, what does perfect mean here?" And then, before his father, who was somewhat staggered by the inquiry, could make a reply, there came another question from the little prattler: "Doesn't it mean that God never makes a mistake?" This was just the thought that troubled father needed to have brought before his mind.

God's Existence—Certainty of.

To the wise man, the lightning only manifests the electric force which is everywhere, and which for one moment has become visible. As often as he sees it, it reminds him that the lightning slumbers invisibly in the dewdrop, and in the mist, and in the cloud, and binds together every atom of the water that he uses in daily life. But to the vulgar mind the lightning is something unique, a something which has no existence except when it appears. There is a fearful glory in the lightning because he sees it. But there is no startling glory and nothing fearful in the drop of dew, because he does not know, what the thinker knows, that the flash is there in all its terrors. So, in the same way, to the half-believer a miracle is the one solitary evidence of God. Without it he could have no certainty of God's existence.—F. W. ROBERTSON.

God—Fear and Fascination of.

We have listened to some sweet melody, and we cannot escape from its gracious thraldom. It pervades the entire day. It interweaves itself with all our changing affairs. We hear it in our work and in our leisure; when we retire to rest and when we awake. It haunts us. The analogy may help us to some apprehension of what is meant by the fear of God. The man who fears God is haunted by God's presence. God is an abiding consciousness. God is "continually before him." Everything is seen in relationship to God. The Divine presence prevades the mind and shapes and colors the judgment.—J. H. JOWETT.

God's Honor—Guarding.

A smartly dressed railway guard was bustling about his work on a platform, with a pretty rose in his buttonhole. A man, more than half tipsy, came lurching past, snatched the rose from the guard's buttonhole, and flung it under the train, and then chuckled in his drunken fashion. The guard's face flushed red, but without a word he turned away. As he passed, a man complimented him and said, "You took that splendidly." The guard said, "I am on duty, sir."—JOSEPH TRAILL.

God's Voice.

We once had a trained nurse in our home taking care of a sick woman. She was very fond of her patient and extremely anxious to please her and to see her recover. All day long she would attend to her duties and then lie down at night to rest. What I noticed especially was this; her ears were always open for the ringing of her patient's bell or for the sound of her voice. No matter what she was doing or what other noises were made, she could always hear the call that was meant for her.

Is not that to be our attitude toward the call of God? In the midst of all the noises that surround us, our ears are to be open for one special sound—the sound of God's voice.—S. D. CHAMBERS.

God—Knowing.

Some one came once to an Arab in his tent in the desert, and said to him, "How do you know there is a God?" He said, "How do I know whether it was a man or a camel that went by my tent last night?" How did he know which it was? "By the footprints." The marks in the sand showed whether it was a man's foot, or a camel's foot, that had passed his tent. So the Arab said, "That is the way I know God. I know Him by His footprints. These are His footprints that are all around me."

God—Likeness.

Have not all of us, some time or other, been photographed? And when the proof has arrived, our friends have exclaimed, "Oh, how like you! It is good!" Or else they have said, "That's not a bit like you; you must have your photograph taken again." We are to be God's likenesses or photographs. Men cannot see Him, and many will not take the trouble to read about Him, but they will look at us. Might they say, as we do of some photographs, "If the name were not on, I shouldn't know who it was meant to represent."—*The Sunday School Chronicle.*

God—Moved.

Sometimes a strange thing is seen at sea. The wind and currents and surface ice are all moving in one direction, but a huge iceberg comes along moving against wind and tide and plowing its way through the surface ice on the opposite direction.

What is the explanation? The surface ice floats with the current, but the iceberg has its base down in a deeper and more powerful current and is borne along majestically against all opposition. Most men float with the surface currents, even when these are moving in the wrong direction. But occasionally there comes a man, like Columbus or Luther or Lincoln, who has got his will down into the deeper and more powerful current of God's will, and then all the world must give way before him as he plows his course through. Surface winds and currents have no effect upon such a man; he is in the Gulf Stream of the universe and the very constellations are floating with him. These world-resistors and world-compellers are God-moved and are omnipotent in the Lord and in the power of his might.—*Presbyterian Banner.*

God—Neglecting.

A little boy asked his mother if she thought his father would ever go to Heaven. "Hope so," said his mother, "but why do you ask the question?" "Because," said he, "I am afraid he couldn't leave the store."

God—Praise of.

One of the first acts performed by George III., after his accession to the throne, was to issue an order prohibiting any of the clergy who should be called to preach before him from paying him any compliment in their discourses. His Majesty was led to this from the fulsome adulation which Dr. Thomas Wilson, prebendary of Westminster, thought proper to deliver in the Chapel-Royal, and for which, instead of thanks, he received from his royal auditor a pointed reprimand, His Majesty observing "that he came to chapel to hear the praises of God, and not his own."—*Clerical Anecdotes.*

God—Robbing.

There was once a horse that ran away in the morning and did not return till the evening. When the master upbraided him the horse replied, "But here am I returned safe and sound. You have your horse." "True," answered the master, "but my field is unplowed." If a man turns to God in old age, God has the man, but He has been defrauded of the man's work. And the man himself has been defrauded worst of all.—*The Sunday School Chronicle.*

God the Only Giver.

Earth gets its price for what Earth
  gives us;
 The beggar is taxed for a corner
  to die in,
The priest hath his fee who comes
  and shrives us,
 We bargain for the graves we lie
  in;
. At the Devil's booth are all things
  sold,
Each ounce of dross costs its ounce
  of gold;
 For a cap and bells our lives we
  pay,
Bubbles we buy with a whole soul's
  tasking;
 'Tis heaven alone that is given
  away,
'Tis only God may be had for the
  asking.
                    —LOWELL.

God—Trust In.

A nose and throat specialist had to operate on a poor little girl who was unable to take any anaesthetic. He took a fifty-cent piece out of his pocket and said, "That's for you to spend exactly as you wish. I'm going to hurt you a little, but take a good look at the fifty cents before I begin, and then hold it tight in your hand and remember what you saw while I'm at work,—it won't hurt nearly as much." When it was over the doctor patted her on the head and said, "You're a brave little girl. Tell me what you thought about while I was at work." "I thought of the words," she replied. "The words," said the physician, "the date, you mean?" for he hardly remembered that the coin had any words on it. "No, I mean the words at the top: 'In God we Trust,'" she said quite simply, "it was the first half-dollar I ever saw, so I didn't know they were there; but it's lovely to have them, so the folks who have half-dollars can think about them all the time."—*Youth's Companion.*

Jewels—God's.

In the old castle at Edinburgh, the way to the crown jewels leads through a very humble doorway and through a very dingy and circuitous passage. The humble doorways of common duties are frequently the way to the room where God keeps His jewels.—J. H. JOWETT.

Life—Mysterious Origin of.

Some years ago the engineers engaged in constructing the waterworks of the city of Beyrout set themselves to the task of exploring the caverns from which issues the permanent supply of the Dog River. After great labor and repeated expeditions they succeeded in penetrating to a distance of three-quarters of a mile into the heart of the mountain; but as they passed onward from lake to torrent, now under lofty dome, and again through narrow and tortuous channels, the water was undiminished in its volume, and finally a roaring cataract barred their progress and forbade them to search farther into the secret of the living stream.

So is it that life, after all our inquiries into its nature and origin, remains hidden from us. We are conscious of its existence, we can see its effects, but in itself it is a mystery, even as the great Giver of it, the Fountain of Life, dwells in thick darkness. We can only say, "In his hand is the breath of all living." In Him we "live, and move, and have our being."—J. ROBERTSON.

Will—Accepting God's.

A stage coach was passing through the interior of Massachusetts, on the way to Boston. It was a warm summer day, and the coach was filled with passengers, all impatient to arrive at the city at an early hour in the evening. The excessive heat rendered it necessary for the driver to spare his horses more than usual. Most of the passengers were fretting and complaining that he did not urge his horses along faster. But one gentleman sat in the corner of the stage calm and quiet. The irritation, which was destroying the happiness of all the others, seemed not to disturb his feelings in the least. At last the coach broke down as they were ascending a long steep hill, and the passengers were compelled to alight, and travel some distance on foot under the rays of the burning sun. This new interruption caused a general burst of vexatious feelings. All the party, with the exception of the gentleman alluded to, toiled up the hill, irritated and complaining. He walked along, good-humored and happy, and endeavoring by occasional pleasantry of remark to restore good humor to the party. It was known that this gentleman, who

was extensively engaged in mercantile concerns, had business which rendered it necessary that he should be in the city at an early hour. The delay was consequently to him a serious inconvenience. Yet, while all the rest of the party were ill-humored and vexed, he alone was untroubled. At last one asked how it was that he retained his composure under such vexatious circumstances? The gentleman replied that he could have no control over the circumstances in which he was then placed; that he had commended himself and his business to the protection of the Lord, and that if it were the Lord's will that he should not enter Boston at as early an hour as he desired, it was his duty patiently and pleasantly to submit. With these feelings he was patient and submissive, and cheerful. The day, which to the rest of the party was rendered disagreeable by vexation and complaint, was by him passed in gratitude and enjoyment. And when, late in the evening, he arrived in the city with a serene mind, he was prepared to engage in his duties.

God—Waiting Upon.

It is related of Schwabe the German astronomer that, wishing to determine the relation between sunspots and earth-magnetism, he gave himself to the recording of the varying appearances of the sun's surface. For forty-two years the sun never rose a single morning free of clouds above the flat horizon of the plain at Dessau where Schwabe lived but his patient telescope was there to confront it! The man of science believes in Nature. He waits for it, in the faith that it is, and that it is the rewarder of those that diligently seek it. If only Christian people would realize that it is infinitely more worth their while to wait thus

patiently upon God, what wonders of Spirit-filled lives we should see!
—Archibald Alexander.

God—Strangers to.

Alas, my God, that we should be
  Such strangers to each other!
O that as friends we might agree,
  And walk and talk together!

May I taste that communion, Lord,
  Thy people have with Thee?

Thy Spirit daily talks with them,
  O let It talk with me!

Like Enoch, let me walk with God,
  And thus walk out my day,
Attended with the heavenly Guards,
  Upon the King's highway.

When wilt Thou come unto me,
    Lord?
For till Thou dost appear,
I count each moment for a day,
  Each minute for a year.
        —Thomas Shepherd.

GRATITUDE

Gifts—Reason for.

"I can't get interested in missions!" exclaimed a young girl petulantly, and, if truth must be told, a bit superciliously, as she left a thrilling missionary meeting in company with an older lady, presumably an aunt or other relative. We were near enough to hear the answer. "No, dearie," came the pitying response; "'Tisn't to be expected you should—yet a while. It's just like getting interest in a bank. You have to put in a little something first, and the more you put in, the more interest, time or money or prayers, it doesn't matter which, but something you have to put in, or you never will have any interest. Try it, dearie,—just put in a little something, and you're sure of the interest."—*The King's Own.*

Gratitude.

There was a man in Boston (I know not whether he lives yet,—yes, he lives, but I know not whether he lives in this world) who, though not rich, was accustomed to go into the courts of justice every morning to give bail for culprits that had no friends; and it was his testimony that of all those for whom he gave bail, not one betrayed him, —not one left him in the lurch. And do you suppose that those creatures whom Christ has helped, and whom he has given a hope of eternal salvation, would turn against him, their best friend, and the one to whom they are indebted for their choicest blessings? Would that be human nature? Is there anything on God's earth like gratitude to inspire a soul to act in the right direction?—H. W. Beecher.

HEART

Heart Argument.

No logic or reason would justify George Eliot, who had repudiated Christianity as vigorously as had Harriet Martineau, in reading Thomas á Kempis all her life, and having the immortal meditations of the old monk at her bedside as she died; but the logic of the heart justified her, and we love her for submitting to it. What had she, a woman who thrust aside all the theologies as incredible, to do with a Dinah Morris preaching Christ crucified, upon a village green? Yet she does paint Dinah Morris, and through the lips of the Methodist evangelist she lets her own soul utter a message which her intellect rejected.

Heart—A Careless.

A man can rarely remain unconscious of his special excellence. At last he grows so secure of not failing on this side of his nature that he leaves it to take care of itself. And then, all of a moment, his fortress is taken. The story of the taking of the Castle of Edinburgh has a thousand analogies. The defenders thought it safe where the steep precipice made its strength. All the weak portions of the walls were watched; this was not. Then, one dark night, in storm and driving rain, a band of daring men crept slowly up the angry cliff, and the impossible became a fact. The castle was seized by the foe.—S. A. Brooke.

Heart—A Changed.

"I wish you would change my heart," said the chief Sekomi to Livingstone, "Give me medicine to change it, for it is proud, proud and angry, angry always." He would not hear of the New Testament way of changing the heart; he wanted an outward, mechanical way—and that way was not to be found.—R. F. Horton.

Heart—A Clean.

Describing some of the remarkable conversions among the boatmen who had been induced to attend his Water Street Mission in New York, Jerry McAuley says, "I asked one of them who was saved at that time, when he was testifying, "How do you know you were converted?"

"Well, I'll tell you," he replied: "I went from here to my boat, and, locking the door, just made up my mind never to open it until converted. *And I kept my word!*"

"How could you tell when it was done?"

"Well, I'll have to explain that in my own way," he answered, "but it seems to me the Lord just took, as it were, something like a barnacle-scraper (a keen, sharp-edged, three-cornered piece of steel, fastened to a long handle, and used to scrape off the shell-fish and other deposits that gather on the bottom of vessels) *and scraped my heart all out clean,* and I haven't felt anything wrong there since !"—Jerry McAuley.

Heart—A Generous.

On one of Paderewski's early tours of the United States, he played at San José, California, during Holy Week, which was a bad time for a concert. Two students at Leland Stanford University had guaranteed a fee of $2,000 to the pianist. The box-office receipts were $1,600. In great mental anguish the students told Paderewski's secretary that he must wait for part of the fee—they could turn over at the time not more than $1,600; and the secretary passed the word along. The arrangement did not suit Paderewski at all. He directed that the two students should pay all their expenses from the fund on hand, including the rental of the hall, advertising, and so on; then deduct twenty per cent of the gross receipts for themselves, and turn over the rest. On these terms Paderewski would call it quits. They were the only terms he would accept. One of those students was Herbert Hoover. And through his co-operation thousands of lives were saved in Poland.—*The World's Work.*

Heart—Ice-Bound.

On a winter evening, when the frost is setting in with growing intensity, and when the sun is now far past the meridian, and gradually sinking in the western sky, there is a double reason why the ground grows every moment harder and more impenetrable to the plow. On the one hand, the frost of evening, with ever increasing intensity, is indurating the stiffening clods: on the other hand, the genial rays which alone can soften them are every moment withdrawing and losing their enlivening power. Take heed that it be not so with you. As long as you are unconverted, you are under a double process of hardening. The frosts of an eternal night are settling down upon your souls; and the Sun of Righteousness, with westering wheel, is hastening to set upon you forever more. If, then, the plow of grace cannot force its way into your icebound heart to-day, what likelihood is there that it will enter to-morrow?—R. M. McCheyne.

Heart Ignorance.

An earnest Christian man and faithful reader of the Bible was assailed by an infidel. "I do not understand nor do I believe," said he, "that the blood of Jesus Christ can wash away my sin." "You and St. Paul quite agree on that subject," answered the Bible student. "How?" "Turn to the first chapter of First Corinthians and read the eighteenth verse: 'For the preaching of the cross is to them that perish foolishness; but unto us which are saved it is the power of God.'" The infidel hung his head and began to study the Bible. He soon found it to be God's power unto salvation.—*The Lutheran.*

Heart of Stone.

There is a German folk story of a very poor charcoal burner who had a kind heart and was always doing good turns to people. He often wished that he were rich that he might help still more. One day in the forest a wicked-looking gnome appeared and told him he would make him rich on one condition. He must exchange his heart of flesh for a wonderful mechanical stone heart that the gnome had made and kept in his workshop in a cave underneath the forest. The poor man did not like the condition, but was tempted and consented to the bargain. He was cast into a deep sleep and when he awoke the exchange had been effected and he felt the stone heart working within him with perfect regularity, but it was cold, very cold. When he got back to the village everybody noticed the change. He was harsh, overbearing, a changed man; riches came to him; everything he touched turned to gold, but the richer he grew, the colder seemed the heart, and when old age crept upon him he longed to be poor again and have back his warm human heart. That is a modern way of saying that the man got his request, but leanness came to his soul.—H. Jeffs.

Heart—A Sympathetic.

It is related of St. Elizabeth of Hungary, that in mid-winter, as she carried in her robe a supply of food to some poor people in the mountains, and as she climbed the steep and slippery path, she met her husband returning from the chase. "What hast thou here, my Elizabeth?" said he. "What art thou carrying away now?" And as she stood confused and blushing, he opened her dress and found it full of red and white roses, lovelier than those of earth. So did the Middle Ages invent legends to glorify the sweet charity of this noble woman, who spent her time, strength, and means in caring for the poor people afflicted by famine and plague. Especially she loved children, and built hospitals for them; and they loved her so that they ran after her, calling out "Mother! mother!" The sick children she took into her hospital, washed and dressed their poor little limbs, and bought them toys and gifts to amuse them. For this she was canonized; and she well deserved it, not because of the miracles which they tell of her, but for that which is more Divine than any miracle, her tender heart and love of humanity.—J. F. CLARKE.

Heart—Guarding the.

Visit the electrical power-house of any large town. Watch the whirling dynamo. Here is the energy that drives the car; here is generated the spark that lights the night; here is born the impulse that begets the motion and brightness outside. Musing thus, you will understand what is meant by the heart. Press the illustration further; mark how this monster is guarded and controlled, and then think of the last thunderstorm you can remember.

In the engine-house the power is in subjection, watched with all diligence; outside in the wide universe it is untamed, uncontrolled, wrecking and damaging and contorting. On the one hand, assisting commerce, giving brightness and cheerfulness—the issues of life. On the other, devastation and ruin—the issues of death. Life and death by the same power. Controlled, life; uncontrolled, death. This power is analogous to the heart of man.—J. H. WARD.

Heart,—Hardened.

When I was a soldier I, with others, was drawn out to go to such a place to besiege it; but when I was just ready to go one of the company desired to go in my room, to which, when I had consented, he took my place, and coming to the seige, as he stood sentinel, he was shot in the head with a musket-bullet, and died. Here, as I said, were judgments and mercy, but neither of them did awaken my soul to righteousness; wherefore I sinned still, I grew more and more rebellious against God, and careless of my own salvation.—*Bunyan.*

Heart—Protecting the.

One of the most famous and valuable diamonds in the world is the "Koh-i-nur," or Mountain of Light, which belongs to the British Crown. This gem was exhibited in the Great Exhibition of 1851, and was an object of special interest. It lay upon a little cushion in a case with glass panels, the inside being lighted up with gas. And there was always a group of people crowding to see it. But it was also an object of peculiar care. For while the whole of the Crystal Palace, which contained so many treasures, was well guarded, a special watchman paced to and fro by day and night to guard the "Koh-i-nur." Even so ought every Christian, above all other valuables that he has to guard, to "keep" his heart, for it is the citadel of his life.

Heart-Service.

In crossing over the Atlantic Ocean once, on the second day of the voyage, an unfortunate fellow was pulled up from the hold—a "stowaway." Desiring to go to America, and being too poor to pay his passage, he hid himself on board the ship. But the captain said, "You must work out your passage now that you are here." He was set to wash the decks, and do other rough work on the ship, but I noticed the man had no heart in it; he did it because he was compelled. How different with the true sailors! When they ran up the rigging they sang out with delight, and did their work with all their heart. It did one good to hear the hearty song of the man up near the top of the mast, but the hang-dog look of the stowaway caused gloom in the midst of sunshine. Now, brethren, do your work for Christ with all your heart; put your soul into it; do it with enthusiasm. It is the earnest men only who succeed in temporal things; and it is only God's earnest ones who bring in a plentiful harvest to the heavenly barn.—Wm. Birch.

Life—Fountain of.

Savage tribes not only fight with poisoned arrows; they have been known to creep into another tribe's country, and put poison into the wells, so that when the tired soldier, the thirsting woman and child, and the poor beasts of the forest came to the well to slake their thirst, they drank death in every drop of water that passed their lips. Now,

would you think a chief stern, or too particular, if at war-time he ordered his people to guard the wells? Would not such an order be a kind one? Would not the meaning of it be, "Save your own lives, and the lives of your wives and children?" Well, your heart, your mind, is the well of your life. If that is poisoned, your best life will die, and the Book that bids you guard it well is not a stern book, but a kind, loving book, that wishes you well, and is your best friend.—J. M. Gibbon.

Heart—A Warm.

If the world seems cold to you,
　Kindle fires to warm it!
Let their comfort hide from view
　Winters that deform it.
Hearts as frozen as your own
　To that radiance gather;
You will soon forget to moan,
　"Ah! the cheerless weather!"

If the world's a wilderness,
　Go build houses in it!
Will it help your loneliness
　On the winds to din it?
Raise a hut, however slight;
　Weeds and brambles smother;
And to roof and meal invite
　Some forlorn brother.

If the world's a vale of tears,
　Smile till rainbows span it!
Breathe the love that life endears,
　Clear from clouds to fan it.
Of your gladness lend a gleam
　Unto souls that shiver;
Show them how dark Sorrow's
　　stream
　Blends with Hope's bright river!
　　　　　　　—Lucy Larcom.

Penitent Tears.

At the gateway of the Parthenon in Athens was an altar dedicated to Tears. No sacrifices were consumed, no votive offerings placed upon it; but the sorrowing bowed there and wept out their sorrows. It was the shadowing forth of a great truth; to wit, "The sacrifices of God are a broken spirit; a broken and a contrite heart, O God, thou wilt not despise" (Ps. li, 17.) Dearer to God than all the *misereres* of the chanting Pharisees is the cry of the returning prodigal. He sees him bowed with penitence, and goes out to meet him while he is yet a great way off.—D. J. BURRELL.

HOLY SPIRIT

Comforter—The.

A picture of deap pathos, carrying its own tender suggestion to the heart, appeared in the Academy of 1897. It was painted by Byam Shaw, and entitled "The Comforter." In the interior of a room, upon a bed, there lies a form, the face of which is not seen, only a hand lying upon the silk counterpane with a wedding-ring upon the finger. By the side of the bed there sits a young man, his elbow leaning upon the bed, his head supported by his hand, his face drawn with grief. In his loneliness he sits there while his beloved, with slow and painful breaths, sighs out her little store of life. The picture gives the impression of stillness; pitiful tragedy is working itself out within. But the young man, as he sits there in his unutterable anguish, is not alone; the Comforter has come. Seated beside him is a white figure, unseen to the young man, and in that silent room of death there is another watcher.—J. BURNS.

Holy Spirit Our Guide.

It is said that when John Bunyan was in Bedford jail, some of his persecutors in London heard that he was often out of the prison; they sent an officer to talk with the jailer on the subject, and in order to discover the fact that he was to get there in the middle of the night. Bunyan was at home with his family, but so restless that he could not sleep; he therefore acquainted his wife that, though the jailer had given him liberty to stay till morning, yet, from his uneasiness, he must immediately return. He did so, and the jailer blamed him for coming at such an unseasonable hour. Early in the morning the messenger came, and interrogating the jailer, said, "Are all the prisoners safe?" "Yes." "Is John Bunyan safe?" "Yes." "Let me see him." He was called, and appeared, and all was well. After the messenger was gone, the jailer, addressing Mr. Bunyan, said, "Well, you may go in and out again just when you think proper, for you know when to return better than I can tell you."

Holy Spirit as a Dove.

Of all the birds the dove is the most easily alarmed and put to flight at hearing a shot fired. Remember that the Holy Ghost is compared to a dove; and if you begin to shoot at each other, the heavenly Dove will take wing and instantly leave you. The Holy Spirit is one of love and peace, not of tumult and confusion. He cannot live among the smoke and noise of fire shots: if you would grieve the Holy Spirit and compel Him to retire, you have only to commence firing at one another, and He will instantly depart.

Holy Spirit—Breath of the.

In the times of the Crusaders a band of valiant knights traversed the sunny plains of France, to sail from Marseilles for the Holy Land. There, along with others who were bound on the same enterprise, they embarked on the stately vessel that was to carry them across the sea. But, eager as they were to do, day after day they lay helplessly becalmed. The hot sun beat upon them, and was flashed back from the unbroken surface of the waves. They lounged wearily upon the deck; they scanned the heavens in vain for the signs of an approaching breeze. It seemed as though some adverse fate resolved to hold them back. But in the stillness of an even tide, from a group of warriors assembled at the prow, there rose the swelling strains of the *Veni Creator Spiritus*—"Come, Holy Ghost, our souls inspire." And straightway a breath came upon them from the dying sun; the smooth, shining surface of the sea was ruffled, the cordage rattled, the sails were filled, and the vessel sped joyously over the dancing waves. Whether the story is true or not, it contains a very grand truth. Without the Spirit of Love all is dark and dead.

Come, Holy Ghost, our souls inspire
And lighten with celestial fire.

Holy Spirit—Coming of.

The Holy Spirit comes like a rushing wind upon the disciples, and in an hour they are new men. The jailer hears and believes in a night. Luther, while toiling up the holy stairs of the Lateran, holding to salvation by works, drops that scheme on the way, and lays hold of the higher one of salvation by faith. Ignatius Loyola, in a dream, has sight of the Mother of Christ, and awakes a soldier of Jesus. It is often so. We do not so much grow into the possession of new spiritual truths as we awake to them. Their coming is not relations of things, but is like the lightning, that illuminates earth and sky in one quick flash, and so imprints them for ever on the vision.
—Theodore T. Munger.

Holy Spirit—Misunderstanding.

I know a minister who had to revise his sermon on the Monday, and was rather surprised when he found that having spoken on the Sabbath about the "Afflatus," the reporter had written—what, think you? "Apparatus"! But, brethren,

the reporter was not the only man who has made that mistake. There are thousands in our churches who are substituting human apparatus for the afflatus of the Divine Spirit. Lord, help us never to confuse these two, but to look to Thee alone!—James Russell.

Holy Spirit—Receiving the.

A homely illustration was once used by the old German preacher, Flattish. A lady told him she had been seeking and longing in vain for the presence of the Holy Spirit; this gift of God was her chief desire, but still beyond her attainment. "Dear lady," said Flattish, "the other morning I searched about diligently, but all in vain, for my stocking; I wanted it, but could not find it nowhere. Suddenly I discovered in reality I had it on! Madam, you have what you desire: your seeking and longing prove the indwelling power of God's Holy Spirit, and all you have to do is to cease searching, and be happy in *receiving*." The lady found peace in believing.—*The Quiver*.

Spirit—Quenching the.

A man has lost his way in a dark and dreary mine. By the light of one candle, which he carries in his hand, he is groping for the road to sunshine and to home. That light is essential to his safety. The mine has many winding passages, in which he may be hopelessly bewildered. Here and there marks have been made on the rocks to point out the true path, but he cannot see them without that light. There are many deep pits into which, if unwary, he may suddenly fall, but he cannot avoid the danger without that. Should it go out that mine will be his tomb. How carefully he carries it! How anxiously he shields it from sudden gusts of air, from water dropping on it, from everything that might quench it! The case described is our own. We are like that lonely wanderer in the mine. Does he diligently keep alight the candle on which his life depends? Much more earnestly should we give heed to the warning, "Quench not the Spirit." Sin makes our road both dark and dangerous. If God gave us no light, we should never find the way to the soul's sunny home of holiness and heaven. We must despair of ever reaching our Father's house. We must perish in the darkness into which we have wandered. But He gives us His Spirit to enlighten, guide, and cheer us.—NEWMAN HALL.

Holy Ghost—Sin Against.

This is not a sin which one can commit by accident, and without knowing it. "The unpardonable sin" is not a single act, but a comprehensive state of mind: that is, a sin which applies to the whole condition to which a man has brought himself by repeated perversions, and in which you may say his moral condition is broken down.

No man ever becomes dissipated at once. No man, no matter what his experience may be, can become utterly dissipated in a week—and still less in a day or an hour. But a man can, by days, and weeks, and months, and years, become so dissipated as to have broken down his whole bodily constitution; as to have sapped and sucked dry the brain; as to have impaired every nerve; as to have over-strained every organ. Every part of a man's body may be utterly destroyed by dissipation.

Now, there is a dissipation of the soul which corresponds to the dissipation of the body. It comes on by the perversion of a man's reason; by the perversion of his moral sympathies; by the perversion of his choices; by the perversion of his judgment in respect to things right and wrong. It is a gradually accumulating process. It is not a single act. It is the comprehensive result of a long series of various acts.—H. W. BEECHER.

Temple—A Spiritual.

I have read that some little while back there was discovered in Jerusalem a deep cavern close by the Damascus Gate, and those who have explored it have come to the conclusion that it is the spot from which the stones were taken to build the glorious Temple of Solomon. It was there that the hammering and the cutting were done. It was there that the stones were shaped, and from thence, by some process that we do not now understand, they were brought from their deep grave, and separately placed in position upon Mount Zion. The blocks of stone were taken one by one out of the bowels of the earth and out of darkness, and then carried by mighty power to the temple walls, until, when the last stone was cut out and placed in position, with shoutings of "grace unto it," the whole building was complete. This forms a beautiful illustration of the way in which the Lord builds His spiritual temple. The Spirit of God goes into the deep black quarry of fallen nature, and there hews out the hidden stones, and by His own almighty power bears them to the foundation stone and places them in a living temple to go no more out for ever.—A. G. BROWN.

Humility.

I used to think that God's gifts were on shelves one above the other, and that the taller we grow in Christian character the more easily we should reach them. I find now that God's gifts are on shelves one beneath the other, and that it is not a question of growing taller, but of stooping lower, and that we have to go down, always down, to get His best gifts.—F. B. MEYER.

Humility.

In a church at Copenhagen stands the famous statue by Thorwaldsen, picturing in marble the world's Saviour in the very act of extending the invitation, "Come unto me, all ye that labor and are heavy laden, and I will give you rest." A great scholar came from afar to see this statue and surveyed it critically. What he saw did not seem to satisfy him. A little child, noticing his disappointed face, made bold to address him. "You must go close to it, sir. You must kneel down and look up into his face." The stranger followed the advice of the child, and kneeling there was rewarded by a view of the sculptured face of the Christ so melting in tenderness that it greatly touched his heart. Ah, how impossible it is to come to Christ with pride and the spirit of haughtiness!—EDGAR DE WITT JONES.

Humility—Beauty of.

There is a fable which says that one day a prince went into his garden to examine it. He came to the peach tree and said, "What are you doing for me?" The tree said, "In the spring I give my blossoms and fill the air with fragrance, and on my boughs hang the fruit which men will gather and carry into the palace for you." "Well done," said the prince. Then to the chestnut he said, "What are you doing?" "I am making nests for the birds, and shelter cattle with my leaves and spreading branches." "Well done," said the prince. Then he went down to the meadow, and asked the grass what it was doing. "We are giving up our lives for others, for your sheep and cattle, that they may be nourished"; and the prince said, "Well done." Last of all he asked the tiny daisy what it was doing, and the daisy said, "Nothing, nothing. I cannot make a nesting place for the birds, and I cannot give shelter to the cattle, and I cannot give food for the sheep and the cows —they do not want me in the meadow. All I can do is to be the best little daisy I can be." And the prince bent down and kissed the daisy, and said, "There is none better than thou."—F. B. COWL.

Humility, Knowledge of.

I believe the first test of a truly great man is his humility. I do not mean by humility doubt of his own power or hesitation of speaking his opinions, but a right understanding of the relation between what he can do and say and the rest of the world's sayings and doings. All great men not only know their business, but usually know that they know it, and are not only right in their main opinions, but they usually know that they are right in them only they do not think much of themselves on that account. Arnolfo knows he can build a good dome at Florence; Albert Durer writes calmly to one who has found fault with his work, "It cannot be better done"; Sir Isaac Newton knows that he has worked out a problem or two that would have puzzled anybody else; only they do not expect their fellow-men, therefore, to fall down and worship them. They have a curious under-sense of powerless, feeling that the greatness is not in them but through them; that they could not do or be anything else than God made them; and they see something Divine and God-made in every other man they meet, and are endlessly, foolishly, incredibly merciful.—RUS-KIN.

Humility—Knowledge Through.

Two hundred years ago, a mighty sovereign perceived that his people were rude, ignorant savages—backward in the arts of peace and war. He left, for a season, his realm in the hands of faithful councilors. He threw aside crown and scepter. He arrayed himself in sordid raiment, and traveled to another land. Here as a shipwright he labored with his hands, here he dwelt in a rude wooden cottage, here he mixed with common men. After a season, he returned to his own country, and made it great and powerful by the knowledge and skill he had acquired in the time of his disguise. This was what the patriotism of the Czar Peter of Muscovy induced him to do for the aggrandizement of his country. But a mightier than human kings has worn the disguise of humanity, the aspect of a slave, for us and our salvation!—*Literary Churchman.*

Humility,—Ministerial.

A minister was in company with Mr. Whitefield, and during the interview was very free with reflections on Wesley and his followers. Finally he expressed a doubt concerning Mr. Wesley's salvation, and said to Mr. Whitefield, "Sir, do you think when we get to heaven we shall see John Wesley?" "No, sir," replied Whitefield, "I fear not; for he will be so near the eternal Throne, and we shall be at such a distance, we shall hardly get a sight of him."—*Anecdotes of the Wesleys.*

Humility—Necessity of.

The grandest edifices, the tallest towers, the loftiest spires, rest upon deep foundations. The very safety of eminent gifts and pre-eminent graces lies in their association with deep humility, they were dangerous without it. Great men do need to be good men. Look at this mighty ship, a leviathan on the deep. With her towering masts, and carrying a cloud of canvas, how she steadies herself on the waves, and walks erect upon the rolling waters, like a thing of inherent, self-regulating life! When the corn is waving, and trees are bending, and foaming billows roll before the blast and break in thunders on the beach, why is she not flung on her beam ends, sent down foundering into the deep?

Humility—The Angel of.

And so Vergil and Dante come at last to the Angel-Guardian of the Cornice, against the place of ascent to the next ring—the Angel of Humility, "in his countenance such as a tremulous star at morn appears." He bids them to the steps and beats his wings on Dante's forehead. There comes to Dante's ears the sound of sweet voices singing, "Blessed are the poor in spirit," and he notices that, though mounting steep stairs, he is lighter than when walking on the level below. Why is this? Vergil explains that one of the seven Sin-marks on Dante's brow has been erased by the Angel's wings, the Pride-mark, and that all the remaining six have, at the same time, become much fainter than before; a beautiful indication this of the doctrine that Pride is the deadliest foe of human salvation. When the last Sin-mark is removed Dante will experience not merely no difficulty in mounting but actual delight. Dante feels his brow on hearing this and finds that only six of the marks remain, and Vergil smiles at this. True humility is not even conscious of being humble.—H. B. GARROD.

Revival—Beginning of.

I remember the first revival I had in a church of which I was pastor. I had been laboring at Terre Haute in a revival—the first that I ever worked in—and I came home full of fire and zeal, praying all the way. There was a prayer that began in Terre Haute and ended in Indianapolis, eighty miles apart. I recollect that, when I got home and preached, I gave an account of what I had seen in Terre Haute. The next night I began a series of protracted meetings. The room was not more than two-thirds full, and the people were apparently dead to spiritual things. On the second night I called for persons who would like to talk with me to remain. I made a strong appeal; but only one person —a poor German servant-girl— stopped. All the children of my friends, the young people that I knew very well, got up and went out; all went out except this one servant-girl, who answered to my sermon call. I remember that there shot through me a spasm of rebellion. I had a sort of feeling, "For what was all this precious ointment spilled? Such a sermon as I had preached, such an appeal as I had made, with no result but this!" In a second, however, almost quicker than a flash, there opened to me a profound sense of value of any child of the Lord Jesus Christ. This was Christ's child; and I was so impressed with the thought that anything of His was unspeakably precious beyond any conception which I could form that tear came into

my eyes and ran down my cheeks, and I had the feeling to the very marrow that I would be willing to work all my days among God's people if I could do any good to the lowest and the least creature. My pride was all gone, my vanity was all gone, and I was caught up into a blessed sense of the love of God to men, and of my relation to Christ; and I thought it to be an unspeakable privilege to unloose the shoe-latchets from the poorest of Christ's disciples. And out of that spirit came the natural consequences.—BEECHER.

Stooping to Conquer.

I used to think that God's gifts were on shelves, one above the other, and that the taller we grew in Christian character the easier we could reach them. I find now that God's gifts are on shelves, one beneath the other, and that it is not the question of growing taller, but of stooping lower, and that we have to go down, always down to get his best gifts.—*Alliance Weekly.*

Strength in Weakness.

It is said that the engineer who planned the Brooklyn bridge—one of the most colossal triumphs of scientific skill in the world—was a bed-ridden invalid; and that with the help of a telescope he watched the bridge grow into shape day by day from his couch of paralysis and pain. He triumphed because the great thought in a fragile frame was conjoined with all but exhaustless capital and the illimitable labor that capital could bring into the field.—T. G. SELBY.

Unity—Pleasantness of.

It is related of the Duke of Wellington, that once when he remained to take the sacrament at his parish church, a very poor old man went up the opposite aisle, and, reaching the communion table, knelt down close by the side of the duke. Some one (probably a pew opener) came and touched the poor man on the shoulder, and whispered to move farther away, or to rise and wait until the duke had received the bread and wine. But the eagle eye and quick ear of the great commander caught the meaning of that touch and that whisper. He clasped the old man's hand, and held him, to prevent his rising, and in a reverential undertone, but most distinctly, said "Do not move; we are all equal here."—R. Tuck.

Weakness—Strength in.

Is a sound, strong body a necessary first step to athletic success? It would seem so. But some years ago, there was a young fellow who had to wear metal braces for serious weakness in his legs. He was threatened with lameness that might be a life-long handicap. A physician advised him to exercise his legs regularly, and suggested his trying jumping as something that might strengthen them. The boy did so, and kept up his jumping practice through his school and college years. He found that before he stopped jumping he had broken the world's high jump record by clearing the bar at six feet four inches. There were probably fifty fellows in his class who had stronger leg muscles to start with than had Billy Page. His weakness was the start of his wonderful record. It was not his weakness it was what he did with his weakness.—*The Sunday School Times.*

Humble Paths.

When I am tempted to repine
That such a lowly lot is mine,
There comes to me a voice which
    saith,
"Mine were the streets of Nazareth."

So mean, so common and confined,
And He the Monarch of mankind!
Yet patiently He travelleth
Those narrow streets of Nazareth.

It may be I shall never rise
To place or fame beneath the
    skies—
But walk in straitened ways till
    death,
Narrow as streets of Nazareth.

But if through honor's arch I tread
And there forget to bend my head,
Ah! let me hear the voice which
    saith,
"Mine were the streets of Nazareth."

HYPOCRISY

Appearance—Deceitful.

We cannot always depend upon appearances. When, at the time of the gunpowder plot, the Parliament houses were searched, only coals and fagots were found under the coals and wood, as well as Guy Fawkes with his preparations to blow up the king and his parliament. Many a fine-looking tree is rotten at the core; some who are very healthy in appearance are secretly and fatally diseased; gilding or paint sometimes covers really worthless rubbish; so the lives of some who profess to be "the epistles of Christ" are really a forgery, for they are not what they profess to be.—G. Hughes.

False Teaching.

In the war on the Rhine, in 1794, the French got possession of the village of Rhinthal by a very curious ruse de guerre of one Joseph Werck, a trumpeter. This village was maintained by an Austrian party of six hundred hussars. Two companies of foot were ordered to make an attack on it at ten o'clock at night. The Austrians had been apprised of the intended attack, and were drawn up ready to charge on the assailing party. On perceiving this, Werck detached himself from his own party, and contrived, by favor of the darkness, to slip into the midst of the enemy; when, taking his trumpet, he first sounded the rally in the Austrian manner, and, the next moment, the retreat. The Austrians, deceived by the signal, were off in an instant at full gallop; and the French became masters of the village without striking a blow.—Percy.

Hypocrisy.

You cannot tell by the way a tree looks, whence its roots are sucking sap. There is many a man that wears clean linen, and has good associates, and appears regularly at the house of God, and seems to be a Christian man, who, if you follow down his roots, you will find to be drawing his nourishment from the common sewers.—H. W. Beecher.

JUDGMENT

Ambition—Worldly.

Look to the end of worldly ambition, and what is it? Take the four greatest rulers, perhaps, that ever sat upon a throne. Alexander, when he had so completely subdued the nations that he wept because he had no more to conquer, at last set fire to a city and died in a sense of debauch. Hannibal, who filled three bushels with the gold rings taken from the slaughtered knights, died at last by poison administered by his own hand, unwept, and unknown, in a foreign land. Caesar having conquered 800 cities, and dyed his garments with the blood of one million of his foes, was stabbed by his best friends, in the very place which had been the scene of his greatest triumph. Napoleon, after being the scourge of Europe, and the desolator of his country, died in banishment, conquered and captive. So truly "the expectation of the wicked shall be cut off."—G. S. Bowes.

Censure—Habit of.

It is reported of vultures, that they will fly over a garden of sweet flowers, and not so much as eye them; but they will seize upon a stinking carrion at the first sight. Thus many there are that will take no notice of the commendable parts and good qualities of others; but, if the least imperfection appear, there they will fasten.—Spencer.

Character Building.

Two young masons were building a brick wall—the front wall of a high house. One of them, in placing a brick, discovered that it was a little thicker on one side than the other. "It will make your wall untrue, Ben," the other said. "Pooh!" answered Ben; "what difference will such a trifle as that make? You're too particular." "My mother," replied he, "taught me that 'truth is truth' and ever so little an untruth is a lie, and a lie is no trifle." "Oh," said Ben, "that's all very well; but I'm not lying, and have no intention of lying." "Very true; but you make your wall tell a lie, and I have read that a lie in one's work is like a lie in his character—it will show itself sooner or later, and bring harm, if not ruin." "I'll risk it in this case," answered Ben, and he worked away, laying more brick, carrying the wall up higher, till the close of the day, when they gave up work and went home. The next morning they went to resume their work, when, behold, the lie had wrought out the result of all lies. The wall, getting a little slant from the untrue brick, had got more and more untrue as it got higher, and at last, in the night, had toppled over. Just so with ever so little an untruth in your character; it grows more and more untrue if you permit it to remain, till it brings sorrow and ruin.

Character—Incomplete.

What becomes of those who reach high on the plane of morality, but do not touch the yet higher plane of spirituality? You might just as well ask me what becomes of a marksman who almost hits the mark, but does not hit it. You might just as well ask me what becomes of the anchor that is let out of a ship, and reaches almost to the bottom, but stops short without touching it. You might as well ask me what becomes of a portrait which is splendidly painted, and is almost like the man that it is designed to represent, and yet is not like him.—H. W. Beecher.

Fears—False.

A minister, while crossing the Bay of Biscay, became greatly alarmed as he beheld what he thought was an approaching hurricane. Tremblingly he addressed himself to one of the sailors: "Do you think she will be able to go through it?" "Through what?" inquired the sailor. "That awful hurricane that is coming down upon us." The old sailor smiled and said: "That storm will never touch us. It has passed us already." So, in regard to the believer, judgment as to the penalty of our sins is past. We were tried, condemned, and executed, in the person of our Surety, Jesus Christ.—*The King's Business.*

Glory—Forfeited.

In the long line of portraits of the Doges, in the palace at Venice, one space is empty, and the semblance of a black curtain remains as a melancholy record of glory forfeited. Found guilty of treason against the state, Marino Falieri was beheaded, and his image, as far as possible, blotted from remembrance.

Every one's eye rests longer upon the one dark vacancy than upon any one of the fine portraits of the merchant monarchs; and so the apostates of the Church are far more frequently the theme of the world's talk than the thousands of good men and true who adorn the doctrine of God our Saviour in all things.— SPURGEON.

Judgment Day.

Because sentence against an evil work is not executed speedily, therefore the heart of the sons of men is fully set in them to do evil. Pitt said, "I have no fear for England; she will stand till the day of judgment." Burke answered, "It is the day of no judgment that I dread." —*The Quiver.*

Judgment—Charitable.

Those of us who have read classic history may remember an incident in the history of the Macedonian emperor. A painter was commanded to sketch the monarch. In one of his great battles, he had been struck with the sword upon the forehead, and a very large scar had been left on the right temple. The painter, who was a master-hand in his art, sketched him leaning on his elbow, with his finger covering the scar on his forehead; and so the likeness of the king was taken, but without the scar. Let us put the finger of charity upon the scar of the Christian as we look at him, whatever it may be,—the finger of a tender and forbearing charity, and see, in spite of it and under it, the image of Christ notwithstanding.— DR. CUMMING.

Judgment—Dread of.

A Hungarian king, being sad one day, was asked by his brother the reason of his heaviness of heart. "I have been a great sinner," said he, "and know not how to die, and appear before God in the judgment." His brother laughed at him. It was the custom in that country for the executioner to sound a trumpet before the door of the man who was to be executed. At midnight the trumpet sounded at the door of the king's brother. He arose and came in great haste to the king, and inquired in what he had offended. The king replied, "You have not offended me, but if the sight of my executioner be so dreadful, then shall I not, who have greatly offended, fear to stand in judgment before Christ?"—C. W. BIBB.

Judgment—False and True.

In the raising of flowers I have noted that every one seems to have a weed near it that imitates it in leaf and in habit, sometimes growing quite large and lusty before it is clearly discovered. The portulaca is imitated by the purslane, the aster by the lamb's quarter, the hollyhock by the mallow, the ixia or freesia spike by the spears of lush grass. When very young it is often impossible to distinguish between the flower and the weed, but let both grow together until the harvest! So it is in the church of Christ. The false and the genuine move along side by side, but by their fruits ye shall know them. If a practical horticulturist, as I am, mistakes a weed for a flower, what need there is of the gift of the Holy Spirit to enable us to try the spirits whether they be of God. Paul prays that the Philippians may have the grace of knowledge to try the things that differ.—*Moody Monthly.*

Judgment—Intelligent.

In entering the narrow channel of the Bermudas, the pilot stands not at the helm, but at the bows, looking down into the deep water, clear as crystal, to see the coral reef above which, or rather through which, he is threading his dangerous way. Sometimes there is scarcely twice the ship's own breadth between point and point; yet between those he must go, cannot pause, and ten feet divergence on either side would be shipwreck. He may do his work very awkwardly, and even be conscious of great mistakes; but with the most perfect humility he may utterly disclaim the power of any one standing on the shore to judge his seamanship, who is looking along a smooth, level surface, instead of looking down upon a bed of rocks that lie beneath the surface. No wonder that his tacks, and turns, zigzag eccentricities of course are perfectly unintelligible. "I would have steered direct to that point." "Yes, my good friend, but did you see the rock? and if not, what can you know about the matter? Come up here, and then give me an opinion if you can." Now, the pilot who is up there is not a wiser man than the other, but he has got a different point of view, and from that point he defies all human judgment, until you go and sit beside him.—F. W. ROBERTSON.

Judgment—Personal.

No one can ever persuade himself that wrong can be right. He may wish to do wrong, and please himself by pretending he has convinced himself, but all in vain. He knows at the back of his mind—and especially when he wakes at 3 a. m.—that wrong is wrong and not right.—JOSEPH BELL.

Judgment—Self.

If all other men were but four feet high, a man of five feet would be considered a giant. If he puts his standard low enough, a man always can judge favorably about himself.—H. W. BEECHER.

Judgment—The Lord's.

I do not think that my Master will say my charity is too large, or my inclusiveness too great. Alas! alas! when I see Romanists cursing the Church of England, Evangelicals shaking their heads about the Christianity of Tractarians, Tractarians banning Dissenters, Dissenters anathematizing Unitarians, and Unitarians of the old school condemning the more spiritual ones of the new, I am forced to hope that there is more inclusiveness in the love of God than in the bitter orthodoxy of sects and churches. I find only two classes who roused His Divine indignation when on earth: those who excluded bitterly—the Scribes, and those of a religious name—the popular religious party of the day, who judged frailty and error bitterly—the Pharisees. I am certain that I do not dilute truth, at least what I count truth, nor hold lax views about opinions; but I am certain that men are often better than their creed, and that our Lord's mode of judging of the tree by its fruits is the only true one.—F. W. ROBERTSON.

Lost by Disobedience.

A business in South America ordered a lot of goods from a manufacturer in New York. They gave particular and explicit directions how they must be packed. But that New York manufacturer's folks knew how to pack goods—they did. Didn't require any instructions from South America. So the goods were sent splendidly packed in the New York style, safe enough to go to the moon. Some weeks later that New York manufacturer got a letter advising that because he had failed to pack as directed, all the goods had been destroyed, and he must bear the loss. It seems the goods had to be sent many miles over almost inaccessible mountains on the backs of mules. These mules sometimes lose their footing and roll down the mountain. The goods have to be packed for this contingency. This the manufacturer had neglected to do. The goods were lost. His packing department was entirely too smart! God knows the rough and dangerous paths of life. He knows how you should be packed. Do as He tells you, and save the loss.—*The Sunday School Times.*

Owe No Man Anything.

He (Mahomet) went out for the last time into the mosque, two days before his death; asked, "If he had injured any man? Let his own back bear the stripes. If he owed any man?" A voice answered, "Yes, me; three drachms," borrowed on such an occasion. Mahomet ordered them to be paid. "Better be in shame now," said he, "than at the day of Judgment."—CARLYLE.

Punishment—Eternal.

I do not accept the doctrine of eternal punishment because I delight in it. I would cast in doubts, if I could, till I had filled hell up to the brim. I would destroy all faith in it; but that would do me no good; I could not destroy the thing. . . . I cannot alter the stern fact. The exposition of future punishment in God's Word is not to be regarded as a threat, but as a merciful declaration. If, in the ocean of life, over which we are bound to eternity, there are these rocks and shoals, it is no cruelty to chart them down; it is an eminent and prominent mercy.—BEECHER.

Retribution—Physical.

In that salvation propounded by Christ Jesus, there is amnesty for the past, in so far as it is related to the mind and will of God. The pardon of sin never extends to those transgressions that take hold of natural law. If a man, in drunken fury, has hewn off his hand, the penalty is not averted. If a man in a quarrel has had his face scarred, there is no pardon that restores the comeliness of his countenance. The violation of natural law is inevitably followed by a corresponding penalty.—H. W. BEECHER.

The Desert of Traitors.

Benedict Arnold once asked a loyal captain what the Americans would do with him if they caught him. He replied, "I believe they would first cut off your lame leg, which was wounded in the cause of freedom and virtue at Quebec, and bury it with the honors of war, and afterwards hang the remainder of your body on a gibbet."—FOSTER.

The Master—Judgment of.

I have read somewhere of a young musician listening to the first rendering of his first great composition. He stood up above the orchestra, and as he watched how the music which was the child of his own soul stirred and swayed the hearts of the listening multitude, a strange new emotion swept over his own heart: and yet through all he kept his eye fixed on one who sat there amidst the throng, the face of one who was a past master in the art in which he himself was but a beginner; and every change in the master's face meant more to him than the thunders and plaudits of the crowd.—G. JACKSON.

Judgment—Throne.

"Where have you been, my brother?
    For I missed you from the
        street?"
"I have been away for a night and
        a day
    At the great God's judgment-
        seat."

"And what did you find, my brother,
    When your judging there was
        done?"
"Weeds in my garden, dust in my
        doors,
    And my roses dead in the sun:

"And the lesson I brought back with
        me,
    Like silence, from above—
On the Judgment-Throne there is
        room alone
    For the Lord whose name is
        Love."

        —L. MACLEAN WATT.

LOVE

Enemy—Loving Our.

The story is told of a wounded Scotch Highlander, stroking a German spiked helmet, as he lay upon a cot in a London hospital. A nurse said to him, "I suppose you killed your man?" "No, indeed," was the reply. "It was like this: he lay on the field badly wounded and bleeding, and I was in the same condition. I crawled to him and bound up his wounds; he did the same for me. I knew no German, and he knew no English; so I thanked him by just smiling. He thanked me by smiling back. By way of a token I handed him my cap, while he handed me his helmet. Then, lying side by side, we suffered together in silence till we were picked up by the ambulance squad. No, I didn't kill my man." —*The Christian Herald.*

Guidance—Love's.

A Christian lawyer from Cripple Creek told me once, as we talked over the question of how a man might get his life righted, of an experience of his own years ago, when, in a great deal of perplexity, he had gone to his old pastor to ask him for help as to how he might get his life directed aright. He said the old man simply turned to the 32nd Psalm and read him these two verses: "I will instruct thee and teach thee in the way which thou shalt go; I will counsel thee with mine eye upon thee. Be ye not as the horse, or as the mule, which have no understanding: whose trappings must be bit and bridle to hold them in, else they will not come near unto thee." Then, my friend said, the old man shut up his Bible and turned away. At first he felt no little resentment at his pastor for this curt way of replying to his injury; but when he went away and thought it over he saw that the whole secret of a right life lay just here, that the only way in which God could ever guide a man was not by some mechanical instruction, not by fitting a bit into a man's mouth and pulling him this way and that with a rein, but by planting in his heart His own Spirit and letting that Spirit guide him.— R. E. SPEER.

Heart—A Loving.

While Robert Louis Stevenson's friend, Mataafa, one of the claimants for the throne in Upolo, was imprisoned by the powers along with other chiefs who had sided with him, Mr. Stevenson cheered their captivity with numerous presents of comforts such as they prized. On their release they came to thank him, and declared they must commemorate his kindness by some lasting work. So they decided to make a fine wide road to his house through the bush, a work involving great labor, a thing not loved by an Samoan, and despised as unworthy by a chief. In spite of all this, it was duly finished, and opened with a great feast under the name, "The Road of the Loving Heart." —*Stevenson's Life.*

Love—Influence of.

If you have read a little story for children called "Little Lord Fauntleroy" you have read a magnificent account of the influence of hope on others. You remember how the little lad goes to stay with his grandfather, and that grandfather is one of the most selfish, one of the meanest and most unkind of old men that have ever lived. But the boy believes in him. The boy, only about fourteen, keeps saying to his grandfather, "Oh, grandfather, how they must love you; you are so generous, you are so kind, you are so

considerate to every one you meet."
And the lesson of that beautiful
story is the influence of hope on
character. The old gentlemen cannot withstand the belief of his boy;
and he grows to be the unselfish
generous man that the boy thought
him.

Love Without Arms.

Dr. Maclaren compares human
love to the Venus of Molo, which,
though a statue of most magnificent
qualities as a work of art, has no
arms. It may smile in pity, but has
no arms to aid. It may look on in
sympathy, but has no power to
help. Many a time human love
stands helpless, armless, impotent to
aid. But in Jesus Christ we have
One who is not only matchless in
beauty and grace, but who is mighty
to save.—*Sunday Circle.*

Love Never Faileth.

In Brooklyn one day I met a
young man passing down the
streets. At the time the war broke
out the young man was engaged
to be married to a young lady in
New England, but the marriage was
postponed. He was very fortunate
in battle after battle, until the
Battle of the Wilderness took place,
just before the war was over. The
young lady was counting the days
at the end of which he would return. She waited for letters, but no
letters came. At last she received
one addressed in a strange handwriting, and it read something like
this:—"There has been another terrible battle. I have been unfortunate this time; I have lost both my
arms. I cannot write myself, but
a comrade is writing this letter for
me. I write to tell you you are as
dear to me as ever; but I shall now
be dependent upon other people for
the rest of my days, and I have

this letter written to release you
from your engagement." This
letter was never answered. By the
next train she went clear down to
the scene of the late conflict, and
sent word to the captain what her
errand was, and got the number of
the soldier's cot. She went along
the line, and the moment her eyes
fell upon that number she went to
that cot and threw her arms round
that young man's neck and kissed
him. "I will never give you up,"
she said. "These hands will never
give you up; I am able to support
you; I will take care of you." My
friends, you are not able to take
care of yourselves. The law says
you are ruined, but Christ says, "I
will take care of you."—MOODY.

Love Wrought This.

A century ago, in the north of
Europe, stood an old cathedral, upon
one of the arches of which was a
Sculptured face of wondrous beauty.
It was long hidden, until one day
the sun's light striking through a
slanted window, revealed its matchless features. And ever after, year
by year, upon the days when for a
brief hour it was thus illuminated,
crowds came and waited eager to
catch a glimpse of that face. It had
a strange history. When the cathedral was being built, an old man,
broken with the weight of years and
care, came and besought the architect to let him work upon it. Out
of pity for his age, fearful lest his
failing sight and trembling touch
might mar some fair design, the
master set him to work in the
shadows of the vaulted roof. One
day they found the old man asleep
in death, the tools of his craft laid
in order beside him, the cunning of
his right hand gone, the face up-
turned to this marvelous face which
he had wrought—the face of one
whom he had loved and lost in early

manhood. And when the artists and sculptors and workmen from all parts of the cathedral came and looked upon that face they said, "This is the grandest work of all; love wrought this."—*Christian Advocate.*

Love—Incomplete Knowledge of.

Columbus discovered America; but what did he know about its great lakes, rivers, forests, and the Mississippi valley? He died without knowing much about what he had discovered. So, many of us have discovered something of the love of God; but there are heights, depths, and lengths of it we do not know. That Love is a great ocean; and we require to plunge into it before we really know anything of it.—D. L. MOODY.

Love—Memory of.

There was once, so the story says, a poor musician in Germany who loved a maiden of high degree, and in order to win her went away to distant lands and strove to obtain money and fame. When at last he had obtained both he came back and claimed his bride. They were walking out one evening by the side of the river, and he sought to reach a tuft of little blue flowers for her. In doing so his foot slipped and he fell into the river Rhine; and the story says that, as he was being carried away by the strong current, he flung the bunch of blue flowers to land, crying as he did so, "Forget me not." From that time, and from this story, the little blue flower, known before as the "Mouse's Ear," has been known in Europe everywhere as the "Forget-me-not." It is a much prettier name than the other, and no man has a sweeter memorial raised to him than that poor drowning musician has in

the sweet little flowers that make the face of the earth so beautiful for us year by year.—J. M. GIBBON.

Love—Proof of.

In an engine-room it is impossible to look into the great boiler and see how much water it contains. But running up beside it is a tiny glass tube, which serves as a gauge. As the water stands in the little tube, so it stands in the great boiler. When the tube is half full, the boiler is half full; when the tube is empty, the boiler is empty. Do you ask, How do I know I love God? I believe I love Him, but I want to know. Look at the gauge. Your love for your brother is the measure of your love for God.—*The Sunday School Chronicle.*

Love—Sacrificial.

A poor ignorant woman had been ill-used by her husband, a worthless wretch. She had had to work hard for a precarious livelihood because he refused to work at all. Life was so hard and dark for her that she might have been excused for hating and scorning the man who had made it so. This was Calvary over again, you see; and this child of God was being crucified. The day came when the husband was sentenced to penal servitude for a crime against society. One day the person who tells the story met this woman helping a broken-down man along the street towards her home. It was the released convict, and he looked the brute he was. Her explanation of her action was, "You see, sir, Jim has no one but me now."—R. J. CAMPBELL.

Love—Sacrificial.

Norman Macleod in his Highland Parish tells a wonderful story of love's redemptive sacrifice. Years ago a Highland widow, unable to pay her rent, was threatened with eviction. She set out, with her only child, to walk ten miles over the mountains to the home of a relative. When she started the weather was warm and bright, for the month was May, but before she reached the home of her friend a terrible snow-storm fell upon the hills. She did not reach her destination, and next day a dozen strong men started to search for her. At the summit of the pass where the storm had been the fiercest they found her in the snow, stripped almost to nakedness, dead. In a sheltering nook they found the child, safe and well, wrapped in the garments the mother had taken from her own body. Years afterwards the son of the minister who had conducted the mother's funeral went to Glasgow to preach a preparatory sermon. The night was stormy and the audience small. The snow and the storm recalled to his mind the story he had often heard his father tell, and abandoning his prepared sermon, he told the story of a mother's love. Some days after he was hastily summoned to the bed of a dying man. The man was a stranger to him, but seizing the minister's hand he said, "You do not know me, but I know you, and knew your father before you. Although I have lived in Glasgow many years, I have never attended a church. The other day I happened to pass your door as the snow came down. I heard the singing and slipped into a back seat. There I heard the story of the widow and her son." The man's voice choked and he cried, "I am that son. Never did I forget my mother's love, but I never saw the love of God in giving himself for me until now. It was God made you tell that story. My mother did not die in vain. Her prayer is answered."—*The Expository Times.*

Love—Touch of.

"When did your reformation begin?" was asked of a Christian worker in London who had once been a criminal. "With my talk with Lord Shaftesbury." "What did he say to you?" "I don't remember much, except that he took my hand in his and said, 'Jack, you'll be a man yet.'" It was the touch of his hand, electrified by his soul of love.

Love—Unfailing.

A wealthy business man in Boston, a devout Christian, married a beautiful woman and gave her a beautiful home. She fell, through the besetting sin of drink. One day she left home, never to return, leaving a note behind her saying that her life was not in keeping with her husband's sterling Christian character. He immediately employed men throughout the land to search for her. Copies of her photograph were left in various cities with undertakers, with these instructions, "If her body should ever come to you, buy the finest clothes that money can buy, give her the finest casket possible, bank it with flowers, and send for me." When at last an undertaker called him and he gazed upon the face in the casket, through his tears he said: "Oh, Nellie, if you only knew how I loved you, you would have come back to me." When the funeral was over, he went to the marble works and contracted for a costly monument. When asked what should be inscribed on it, he said, "I want you to engrave on it just one word,—FORGIVEN."—*The Sunday School Times.*

Love—Union of.

When the Forth Bridge was building, the great arms from either side were completed; slowly and steadily they had been built out, and now at the center of the mighty arch all that was needed was the final riveting. But the day fixed was cold and chilly, and in spite of fires set under the iron to expand it the inch or two required, the union could not be completed, and the day's program was a failure. But next morning the sun rose bright, the day was warm and genial; the iron then expanded, the holes came opposite one another, and the riveters had nothing to do but drive the binding bolts home. So love united the brothers of old, and so love unites men still.—*The Sunday School Chronicle.*

Love,—Value of.

A king asked his three daughters how much they loved him. Two of them replied that they loved him better than all the gold and silver in the world. The youngest one said she loved him better than salt. The king was not pleased with her answer, as he thought salt was not very palatable. But the cook, overhearing the remark, put no salt in anything for breakfast next morning, and the meal was so insipid that the king could not enjoy it. He then saw the force of his daughter's remark. She loved him so well that nothing was good without him. —A. C. DIXON.

Love—Winsome.

When the missionary explorer, Frederick Arnot, with his black lads was passing through a clump of grass, a great lion sprang out toward the last lad in the line. Instantly Arnot leaped between them and covered the boy with his own body. The natives fled, and the lion, apparently confused at so much movement, turned and left without doing any harm. The chief of the tribe, upon hearing of this incident, said, "I'd go anywhere with a white man who throws his own body between a lion and a black lad of no account." Such is the spirit of Africa's missionaries. . . . They lay down their lives for her "black lads of no account," and count it a joy to do so.—*The Record of Christian Work.*

Serving in Love.

It is said that when the late M. Gustave Doré was busy painting the face of Jesus in one of his pictures, a lady friend visited his studio, and her attention was immediately riveted upon the face. As she stood there the artist from one corner of the room watched closely the eager face of his lady friend. Suddenly turning around and facing the artist, she said: "M. Doré, why do you look at me so anxiously?" "I wanted to watch the impression that face produced upon you—and I think you like it." "Yes, I do," she replied; "and do you know that I was thinking that you could not paint such a face of Christ unless you loved him." "Unless I loved him!" said Doré. "Well, I trust I do, and that most sincerely—but as I love him more I shall paint him better." Yes, that is true; the more we love the better we serve. The old proverb is quite true: "He who has love in his heart has spurs in his side."—JAMES LEARMOUNT.

Throne—Love on the.

As in the old story, the prince who wooed and won his bride in the disguise of a beggar, brought her to the capital city and the King's palace, took leave of her on some pretext, and caused her to be led all shrinking and solitary into the chamber. When she looked she saw on the throne her lover, her husband, and all fear fled. So the Bride, the Lamb's wife, wooed and won by Him, being found in fashion as a servant, lifts up her eyes and sees on the throne the old face she has learned to love, and is very glad and confident. Her love is made perfect, she has boldness in the day of judgment, and goes to dwell with love for evermore.—W. R. Nicholl.

Truth in Love.

It was a one-man church, and candidates for the pulpit were being heard. An applicant came and preached on the text, "The wicked shall be turned into hell." The rich man turned thumbs down on him. This preacher was followed by another, who by strange coincidence used the same text. The rich man said, "He'll do, call him." Folks were amazed. "Why, he had the same text as the other minister," they said. "True," replied the rich man, "he preached that the wicked would be turned into hell all right, but he was oh, so sorry, but the the other man was glad of it."—*The Sunday School Times.*

Love—Remembering.

Just to recollect His love,
  Always true;
Always shining from above,
  Always new.
Just to recognize its light
  All-enfolding;
Just to claim its present might,
  All-upholding.
Just to know it as thine own,
  That no power can take away.
Is not this enough alone
  For the gladness of the day?
     —F. R. Havergal.

Love—The Call of.

My God, I love Thee; not because
  I look for Heaven thereby,
Nor yet because who love Thee not
  Are lost eternally.

Thou, O my Jesus, Thou didst me
  Upon the Cross embrace,
For me didst bear the nails and
    spear,
  And manifold disgrace.

Then why, O blessed Jesus Christ,
  Should I not love Thee well,
Not for the sake of winning Heaven,
  Or of escaping Hell,

Not with the hope of gaining aught,
  Not seeking a reward;
But as Thyself has loved me,
  O ever-loving Lord?

Even so I love Thee, and will love,
  And in Thy praise will sing,
Solely because Thou art my God,
  And my eternal King.

Love—Touch of.

Love touch'd my eyes—these eyes
  which once were blind,
  And, lo! a glorious world reveal'd
    to view,
A world I ne'er had dream'd so fair
  to find.
  I sang for gladness—all things
    were made new.

'Twas Love unstopp'd my ears, and
  every sound
  Borne through the silence seem'd
    a psalm of praise:
Bird-song, child-laughter—yet o'er
  all I found
  They voice the music of my happy
    days.

Love chang'd life's draught and
  made the water wine,
  And through my languid senses
    seem'd to flow

Some pow'r enkindled by the fire
  divine,
  Some inspiration I can ne'er fore-
    go.

Love rais'd the dead to life—and
  never more

Can many waters quench th'
  eternal flame.
Love open'd wide the everlasting
  door,
And bade us enter, called by His
  name.

—Una, *In Life's Garden.*

NEUTRALITY

Character—A Negative.

Mr. Sankey, the evangelist, once said of a man, who was always objecting to things, that he was like Sanballat and Geshem in the Book of Nehemiah, who said, "Come, let us meet together in . . . the plain of Ono" (see chap. 6). A writer speaks of a man who was so unwilling to say Yes to anything that, when he tried a new pen or fresh ink, he wrote the word No several times through pure impulse. This is the answer of human nature to God's will. The meaning of "If we confess our sins" is that we agree with what God says about them. Were the people true to their Amen? Thank God for 2 Corinthians 1:20: "For all the promises of God in him are yea, and in him Amen."—MRS. COWARD.

Life-Service.

There is a story of a horse that ran away one morning and came back in the evening. When the master upbraided him, the horse replied, "But here am I, returned safe and sound. You have your horse." "Yes," returned the master, "but my field is not plowed." So, when boys and girls refuse to begin the Christian life, and wait until they are grown up, they fail to serve the Master, and they harm themselves, for they cannot return safe and sound.

MINISTERS

A Minister's Fears.

At one point in Dr. Bang's ministry he became greatly discouraged, and attempted to leave his work. A significant dream relieved him. He thought he was working with a pickaxe, on the top of a basaltic rock. His muscular arm brought down stroke after stroke for hours, but the rock was hardly indented. He said to himself at last, "It is useless; I will pick no more." Suddenly a stranger of dignified mien stood by his side, and said, "You will pick no more?" "No." "Were you not set to do this task?" "Yes." "Why then abandon it?" "My work is in vain; I make no impression." Solemnly the stranger replied, "What is that to you? Your duty is to pick, whether the rock yields or not. Your work is in your own hands; the result is not. Work on." He resumed his task. The first blow was given with almost superhuman force, and the rock flew into a thousand pieces. He awoke, returned to his work, and a great revival followed.—A. STEVENS.

Dead—Arousing.

Do you remember De Quincey's dream—how in his dream he saw the great chariot rushing down the vast aisles of a cathedral, past the storied tombs of kings and warriors, on which were the sculptured forms of the mighty dead, and yet upon the pavement in the very track of the chariot was a little child stooping down and playing with a flower, heedless of the approaching death? So terrible and imminent was the tragedy, that at the moment when the horse's feet were about to crush the life out of the little one, the figure of a trumpeter that was lying on a tomb started up from his stony sleep and blew a blast of warning, while an angel hand stretched forth to snatch the little one from its awful death!—J. M. GIBBON.

Doctrine and Deed.

A prelate, since deceased, was present whose views were not favorable to the doctrine of Election. "My lord," said he, addressing the Archbishop, "It appears to me that the young clergy of the present day are more anxious to teach the people high doctrine than to enforce those practical duties which are so much required." "I have no objection," said His Grace, "to high doctrine if high practice be also insisted upon; otherwise it must, of course, be injurious."—*Life of Archbishop Whately.*

Duty—Path of.

Among modern soldiers there is not a more honored name than Henry Havelock. In the words of the Governor-General of India, "He was every inch a soldier, and every inch a Christian." From the time of his religious decision he was not ashamed to own his heavenly Father, but was concerned only to talk worthy of Him. Show him the path of duty, and he held consequence as light as air. He had only one object of fear, and that was sin. Personal danger was as the idle wind. When the deliverance of our Indian Empire from a fearful rebellion seemed to depend on the success of the army which he led, he could find time before the earliest march to commune with his God in prayer, and in the reading of His word, and thus to strengthen himself for the terrible work he had in hand. His motto was, "As for me, I will serve the Lord."

Engine Trouble.

The Jewish train came to a dead stop in A.D. 70. A faulty engine rendered it useless, and it had to be shunted to a siding. God then requisitioned the Gentile train to fulfill his purposes. It had been in course of preparation since 606 B.C. After twenty-five hundred years the same engine trouble has developed. The times of the Gentiles are fulfilled, and the Jewish express, to which God is fitting new engines, will be on the main line once again. What is wrong with the Gentile engine? The same old Jewish fault —unbelief. "Have any of the rulers . . . believed on him?" (John 7:48.) Do not many of our leaders, professors, popular preachers, bishops, and scientists deny the Christ who bought them? "The utterances of Jesus are unreliable," we are told; but the utterances of a German professor are evidently reliable! The same engine trouble.— JEWISH ERA.

Evangelical Simplicities.

Berry told some of his Bolton friends, at the time, how startled and disappointed he had been at finding himself powerless for a while to give help and comfort to a woman who was dying, amid tragic and squalid surroundings, in one of the lowest parts of the town. He had been called upon to minister to her, but as he unfolded the Christian message, as he was wont to preach it then—the doctrine of the Divine Fatherhood and the Eternal Love—as he told the story of the Prodigal and the Magdalene, her heart gave no response, and she looked up with eyes which seemed to him to ask if that was all he had to say to a lost and dying woman. Under a new afflatus, that came he knew not whence, he began with

trembling voice to speak on evangelical simplicities, to tell of Christ's death for a world's sin, and to point her to the Cross for pardon. To his joy and wonder he found that in response to words as simple as those he heard at his mother's knee, the sinful one found rest and peace. —J. S. DRUMMOND.

Good Fruit.

A preacher had been speaking of the joy of full surrender and the possibilities of the holy life, drawing a beautiful picture of what home life would be if everybody acted according to the Bible teaching. He closed his address by making an appeal for men and women to give themselves wholly to Christ. A woman in his audience turned to the woman by her side. "That is excellent preaching," she said, smiling, "but I wonder if such a life is possible?" The other woman smiled back at her. "Well, I know the preacher lives such a life," she said. "I happen to be his wife."—*Christian Herald.*

Gospel Ministers.

Gospel ministers should not only be like dials on watches, or milestones upon the road, but like clocks and larums, to sound the alarm to sinners. Aaron wore bells as well as pomegranates; and the prophets were commanded to lift up their voice like a trumpet. A sleeping sentinel may be the loss of the city. —BP. HALL.

Guides—Ignorant.

Mr. Huxley, it is said, was once on his way to a meeting of the British Association in Dublin, and, arriving late at the station, he threw himself into a jaunting-car and called out to the coachman, "Drive fast." Away went the cab, jolting over the streets, until Mr. Huxley inquired, "Do you know where you are going?" and the driver answered, "No, I don't know where we are going, but anyway I'm driving fast." Is that not a picture of the modern life,—driving fast, but going nobody knows where: a speed without purpose, a restlessness without end or peace?—FRANCIS PEABODY.

Life—A Fruitful.

A Moravian missionary named George Smith went to Africa. He had been there but a short time and had only one convert, a poor woman, when he was driven from the country. They found this man dead one day. He had died praying for the Dark Continent. Failure? And yet when they celebrated the one hundredth anniversary of the founding of that mission, they learned that company, accidentally stumbling upon a place where he had prayed, had found the copy of the Scriptures he had left. They also found one aged woman who was his convert. They sought to sum up his brief life, and reckoned more than thirteen thousand living converts that had sprung from that life which seemed such a failure.—A. J. GORDON.

Marching Orders.

The Duke of Wellington was once asked, "Is it any use to preach the Gospel to the Hindu?" The Duke said, "What are your marching orders?" "Oh!" was the reply, "our marching orders undoubtedly are to 'preach the gospel to every creature.'" "Very well," was the withering answer, "You must obey the command. You have nothing to do with results."—T. LLOYD WILLIAMS.

Messenger—The Needed.

It is said of a famous preacher that he always preached "as a dying man to dying men." It is such preaching that is always effective. A minister visiting a penitentiary one Saturday was invited by the Christian warden to speak to the inmates the next day. That evening the minister felt impressed to go to the penitentiary and learn the details regarding the service. Noting two chairs draped in black in the main assembly room he inquired as to the reason. Said the warden, "These two chairs are draped for death. Your sermon will be the last these men will ever hear." You can realize that Browning and Emerson figured very little in the sermon that was delivered on that occasion. There are chairs in most audiences draped for death.—*Toronto Globe.*

Minister—Helping the.

Dr. Alexander Whyte, of Edinburgh, tells us of an interview he had with Dr. Carmen, of Glasgow, one of the finest and most successful men in the city, and munificent in his liberality to every good cause. God had prospered him, and he had tried to do well by any poor creature who came to him. Dr. Whyte had been doing some church business with him, and when they had finished he looked at the doctor with great blazing eyes, and said, "Now, ha'e ye any word for an old sinner?" "It took my breath away," says Dr. Whyte. "He was an old saint! But it is the paradox of grace that the greatest saints feel they are the greatest sinners. So I just rose up and held out my hand to him—a strong man's hand was his—and I said to him, 'He delighteth in mercy.' I had nothing else to say, and escaped out of the room.

Next morning I got a letter from him. I have it in my desk. It read: 'Dear Friend, I will never doubt Him again—the sins of my youth. I was near the gates of hell, but that word of God comforted me, and I will never doubt Him again. I will never despair again. If the Devil casts my sin in my teeth, I will say, "Yes, it is all true, and you cannot tell the half of it, but I have to do with One who delighteth in mercy."' "I can show you the paper, says Dr. Whyte; "it sanctifies my desk. It may touch the tongue of some of my sons years hence to preach the same gospel the old father has tried to preach to you to-day."—*The Sunday School Times.*

Neglecting Christ's Work.

One evening I was told that a minister's son was to be present in my congregation, and that though he professed to be a Christian he did not work much at it. I watched for him and selected the man in the audience who I thought was he, and selected the right man. At the close of the service I hurried to the door by which he would leave, and shook hands with different ones as they passed out. When he came I took his hand and said, "Good evening! I am glad to see you; are you a friend of Jesus?" "Yes," he replied heartily, "I consider myself a friend of Jesus," "Jesus says," I replied, "'Ye are my friends, if ye do whatsoever I command you.'" His eyes fell. "If those are the conditions, I guess I am not."—R. A. TORREY.

Preacher's Foundation.

A short man wanted to drive a nail in a wall to carry a big picture. He stood on a chair, he was not high enough. His wife put on a small box, and, balancing himself precariously, he began to give the nail hesitating taps with the hammer. His wife said, "Why don't you give a brave blow or two, and settle it?" He replied, "How can a man give a brave blow or two when he is standing on a foundation like this?" That settles the question of certainty or uncertainty. It depends upon the foundation on which the preacher or teacher is standing. One need have no note of uncertainty if he believes the Bible has "Thus saith Jehovah" for all he preaches and teaches.—J. A. CLARK.

Preacher—A Patient.

The "Letters of Marcus Dods" tell of his bitter experience in enduring more than five years' waiting between his being licensed by the Presbytery and getting a church. In one of these letters he likens himself to the cripple at the Pool of Bethesda who, when the Angel gave healing virtue to the water, was unable because of his handicap to avail himself of his opportunity. But, says Dods significantly, "One thing I did not do, I did not throw mud at the Angel." In other words, he did not gird at circumstances, nor fling gibes at the omissions of Providence. With every fiber of his brain and will did he dig into the ores of knowledge, saying to himself: "A church I may never get, but if I do, I will be ready for the church." And when waiting had done its work, Providence opened up to him the mighty purpose for which he had been girded. The God who kept Marcus Dods waiting those trying years was the God who made him "chief among the brethren."

Preacher—A Persistent.

More than one hundred years ago, Robert Morrison set out for China as a missionary. Just as he was established in Canton, a Chinese law was passed making it illegal to print Christian books or preach the gospel. A man of less resolute purpose would have returned home. But he secured employment as translator for the East India Company, giving his business hours to the work for which he was paid, meanwhile compiling a dictionary and translating the Gospels, and waiting for the time when his work should have an open door. Suffering from incessant study and overwork, and compelled at times to stop and rest, he nevertheless in the course of years, with the aid of Dr. Milne, published the entire Bible in the Chinese language. Mr. Morrison returned to England to be greatly honored. In spite of poor health, Chinese hatred of England, and other difficulties, he had won the respect of the people among whom he labored, secured the confidence of great business interest and enlisted their support, paved the way for a coming civilization, and given a nation the Word of God.— *The Sunday School Times.*

Preacher an Obstacle.

The story is told of a well-known Welsh preacher who went to deliver the address at the burial of a pious and venerable village minister in South Wales. Hundreds of miners assembled in silence around the grave, and these were the first words that fell upon their ears: "My brethren, the greatest obstacle on your road to hell has been removed!" Can you conceive of a greater honor than to be such an obstacle as was that village minister?—*The King's Business.*

Preacher,—A Tireless.

On Saturday, September 29, 1770, Mr. Whitefield rode from Portsmouth (New England) to Exeter, fifteen miles, in the morning, and preached there to a very great multitude in the fields. It is remarkable that before he went out to preach what proved to be his last sermon, Mr. Clarkson, observing him more uneasy than usual, said to him, "Sir, you are more fit to go to bed than preach"; to which Mr. Whitefield answered, "True, sir"; but turning aside he clasped his hands together and, looking up, spoke—"Lord Jesus, I am weary in Thy work, but not to Thy work. If I have not yet finished my course, let me go and speak for Thee once more in the fields, and come home and die." During the night—his last upon earth—his servant said to him that he wished he would not preach so often. His reply was, "I had rather wear out than rust out." Then he sat up in bed and prayed that God would bless his preaching where he had been, and on the coming day, that more souls might be brought to Christ. He lay down, slept a while, woke again, and in an hour or so was dead.

Preacher—An Unusual.

On the whole, poor Irving's style of preaching was sufficiently surprising to his hide-bound Presbyterian public; and this was but a slight circumstance to the novelty of the matter he set forth upon them. Actual practice: "If this thing is true, why not do it? You had better do it; there will be nothing but misery and ruin in not doing it!"—that was the gist and continual purport of all his discoursing; —to the astonishment and deep offense of hide-bound mankind.— CARLYLE.

Preaching—Constant.

The good St. Francis of Assisi once stepped down into the cloisters of his monastery, and laying his hand on the shoulder of a young monk, said, "Brother, let us go down into the town and preach." So they went forth, the venerable father and the young man. And they walked along their way, conversing as they went. They wound their way down the principal streets, round the lowly alleys and lanes, and even to the outskirts of the town, and to the village beyond, till they found themselves back at the monastery again. Then said the young monk, "Father, when shall we begin to preach?" And the father looked kindly down upon his son, and said, "My child, we have been preaching; we were preaching while we were walking. We have been seen, looked at; our behavior has been remarked; and so we have delivered a morning sermon. Ah! my son, it is of no use that we walk anywhere to preach unless we preach as we walk."—Paxton Hood.

Preaching—Effective.

Lord Guthrie, according to The British Weekly, said in a recent address that one Sunday when he was on his way to church in London he passed a lay-preacher addressing a crowd in the open air. "I have not been to college, but I have been to Calvary," he heard the speaker say. That day he heard Canon Liddon, Dr. Oswald Dykes, and C. H. Spurgeon. After the lapse of many years he found himself unable to recall a single sentence uttered by any of the celebrated preachers on that day, but there still remained with him the words of the earnest layman.—The Sunday School Times.

Preaching,—Interesting.

A minister who was finding fault with one of his elders for falling asleep so often in church said to him, "You should take a pinch of snuff, and it would help to keep you awake." His elder's answer was, "It would be far better, I think, sir, if you would put a pinch o' snuff in your sermons."—James Douglas.

Preaching—Pleasing.

A young man had just become pastor of a large church. At a reception given him by his people, one of the gossips, a woman with a dangerous tongue, came up and said: "I do not understand how you dared attempt the task of pleasing seven hundred people." Quick as a flash the Lord gave him the answer. He replied: "I did not come to this city to please seven hundred people. I have to please only One; and if I please Him all will be well."—The Watchman-Examiner.

Preaching—Red-Hot.

Richard Sheridan used to say, "I often go to hear Rowland Hill because his ideas come red-hot from the heart." Dr. John M. Mason was asked what he thought was the forte of Dr. Chalmers. After a moment's consideration, Dr. Mason replied, "His blood-earnestness." A Chinese convert once remarked, in a conversation with a missionary, "We want men with hot hearts to tell us of the love of Christ."

Scoffer Turned Preacher.

One evening a young man who had been educated for a barrister was seated with some gay companions in a London tavern, when his companions, knowing he was a clever mimic, requested him to go and hear Mr. Wesley preach, and then come and mimic the whole affair for their amusement. He went.

The text, "Prepare to meet thy God," frightened him like a bursting shell, and conviction deepened during the sermon. On his return to his friends they inquired, "Well, have you taken him off?" He replied, "No gentlemen; but he has taken me off." He left his companions, gave his heart to God, and became one of Mr. Wesley's most useful preachers.—*The Evangelist.*

Sermons, Controversial.

A Christian brother of some originality was once asked when coming out of church whether he had been edified by the sermon. He replied, "It was very fine and orthodox, and the minister seemed to be filled with holy indignation. First he made war upon the wicked Darwin, then the blows came down upon Hauckel and Schleiermacher. Thereupon he inveighed against the spirit of the time and against certain abuses. But as for me and all the poor servant-girls, the workmen and the busy house wives, who had had quite a job to get ready for church, we were waiting for bread from heaven—and it never came. We had to go home a-hungering, and were poorer than we had been before."—PASTOR FUNCKE.

Sermons—Likes in.

"You have no 'likes' in your sermons. Christ taught that the kingdom of heaven was 'like' to leaven hid in meal; 'like' to a grain of mustard-seed etc. You tell us what things are, but never what they are like." Such was a criticism of Robert Hall on a brother minister. In every age of the Church's history, the most effective preachers have been those who have imitated the manner of Christ's teaching.

Sermons—Purpose of.

A minister once had the celebrated Andrew Fuller as a hearer. After service both were invited to a neighboring house for refreshment. The preacher, who evidently thought he had made no failure, was desirous to ascertain Mr. Fuller's opinion of his effort. The veteran divine seemed unwilling to be drawn out upon that subject, and for some time took no notice of his younger brother's allusions and hints. At length a remark was made of so inviting a character as that Mr. Fuller could not well avoid making some reply. He said, "I gave close attention to your sermon, and tried to ascertain at what you were aiming it; what was your object?" Several years afterwards that preacher referred to Mr. Fuller's inquiry as a cutting reproof which he deeply felt, and which had the effect of changing essentially the character of both his motives and his labors.—*Clerical Library.*

Sermons—Repeating.

A poor, juiceless sermon should never be preached the first time; but a nutritious, savory discourse may be made all the better on a second delivery. Dr. Addison Alexander preached his glorious sermon on the "Faithful Saying," until he wore out the manuscript; and Dr. Griffin repeated his elaborate discourse on the "Worth of the Soul" ninety times. He never wearied of it; nor did his audience either. His congregations change constantly, and memories are leaky. A first-rate practical sermon ought to be repeated (with extempore improvements) about once in five years. Fewer sermons and richer should be a settled pastor's aim. Whitefield attained great finish and power by giving the same discourse over again through all his missionary tours.—T. L. CUYLER.

Sermon—The First.

There is a world of difference between the beginning of the life of Livingstone and the end of it. Blaikie writes thus: "He was sent to preach one Sabbath evening at a place called Stanford Rivers. He took his text, read it very deliberately, and then—then—his sermon had fled. Midnight darkness came upon him, and he abruptly said, 'Friends, I have forgotten all I had to say,' and, hurrying out of the pulpit, left the chapel. He never became a preacher, and in the first letter I received from him from Elizabeth Town in Africa he says, 'I am a very poor preacher, having a bad delivery, and some of them said if they knew that I was to preach again they would not enter the chapel.'" This was at the beginning—notice what Punch writes at the close:

"Open the Abbey doors and bear him in
   To sleep with king and statesman, chief and sage,
The missionary come of weaver-kin,
   But great by work that brooks no lower wage.

He needs no epitaph to guard a name
   Which men shall prize while worthy work is known;
He lived and died for good—be that his fame:
   Let marble crumble: this is Living-stone."
—*From "Blaikie's Life of Living-stone."*

Statistics and Service.

We are told of a minister in Scotland, who was called to task by some of the Church officers because of his want of success. And he had to confess that during the whole year only one young man had joined the Church, so that his heart was sick within him. But that very night the same young man spoke to his pastor of his intention of becoming a missionary. Then the pastor's grief was turned to joy, and he thought that the work would be judged by quality rather than by quantity. The young man was Robert Moffat, who afterwards became famous by his mission work in the dark continent. The year of his conversion was not barren in the annals of that country parish after all.—H. C. WILLIAMS.

Unconverted Minister.

Dr. Chalmers became a preacher, alas! before he became a Christian. It is said that after his first settlement, and when botany had proved to him an all-engrossing pursuit, he was followed one Sunday morning by his beadle, and reminded of the fact he had forgotten, that it was the hour for public worship. Dr. Chalmers hastened into the pulpit, and as he took off his hat the flowers he had been culling fell out upon his face, exhibiting the evident indications of the manner in which he had been just engaged. After his settlement at Kilmany his preaching ran mainly upon moral properties, and he was ignorant of the great peculiarities which the gospel enshrines and discovers. Here, however, it pleased God to meet with him, and for the rest of his ministry few men could have been more faithful to central truth than he.

Unconverted Minister.

The Rev. Solomon Stoddard, the predecessor of the far-famed President Edwards, was engaged by his people on an emergency. They soon found themselves disappointed, for he gave no indications of a renewed and serious mind. In this difficulty their resource was prayer. They agreed to set apart a day for special fasting and prayer, in reference to their pastor. Many of the persons meeting for this purpose had necessarily to pass the door of the minister. Mr. Stoddard hailed a plain man whom he knew, and addressed him, "What is all this? What is doing to-day?" The reply was, "The people, sir, are all meeting to pray for your conversion." It sank into his heart. He exclaimed to himself. "Then it is time I prayed for myself!" He was not seen that day. He was seeking in solitude what they were asking in company; and, "while they were yet speaking," they were heard and answered. The pastor gave unquestionable evidence of the change; he labored among a beloved and devoted people for nearly half a century, and was for that period, deservedly ranked among the most able and useful of Christian ministers.

What Ministers Must Preach.

In a village church in one of the Tyrolese valleys, we saw upon the pulpit an outstretched arm, carved in wood, the hand of which held forth a cross. We noted the emblem as full of instruction as to what all true ministry should be, and must be—a holding forth of the cross of Christ to the multitude as the only thrust of sinners. Jesus Christ must be set forth evidently crucified among them. Lord, make this the aim and habit of all our ministers.—C. H. Spurgeon.

Sermons—Defective.

"I have had to interline your sermon all through and through with the name of Christ," was the criticism which an aged parishioner once passed upon the discourse of a young pastor. Said the lamented M'Cheyne, "Some speculate on doctrines about the gospel, rather than preach the gospel itself." "I see a man cannot be a faithful minister, until he preached Christ for Christ's sake."—*Christian Treasury.*

Words and Deeds.

At a country village in England a number of persons had congregated together in a small place of worship to attend a meeting, of which due notice had been given. The chapel was full and overflowing, and many persons, who were anxious to hear, were obliged to remain outside; these crowded around the open doors and windows. After reading, singing, and prayer, a speaker commenced addressing the meeting. He had not proceeded far when a voice was heard from without, "Speak louder, we cannot hear; remember those outside." Those words at once furnished a good motto for the meeting; it was indeed the very object for which the assembly had congregated, to stir up one another to "remember those outside"; those who were outside the church, at a distance from the means of grace—those who knew nothing of God and salvation by Jesus Christ.—*Moody Monthly.*

PARDON

Conviction and Pardon.

In the International Exhibition of 1862 were two pictures. The first was called "Waiting for the Verdict." At the door of a room where a trial was going on, there was a little gathering of people. A woman, (oh what agony was in her look!) and a dear little child lying against her asleep; another, who looked like the grandmother, holding the youngest child; the grandfather, with one hand fallen down between his legs, the other covering his face, from which the big tears were rolling; the dog, looking up and wondering; the elder sister standing there against the door, all anxiety,—what meant it all? Before the bar in that court of justice the father was standing; and they were "waiting for the verdict." In the second picture, the same people were standing at the same place; only one is among them we did not see before. A man is sitting on the bench, his wife, with joyful look, embracing him; the dog licking his hand; the grandmother, with eyes swollen with weeping, only they are tears of joy now, holding up a dear little child for a kiss from the father, who, a few minutes before, had been standing before that bar. Why are they all so changed? Why joy where there was sorrow, happiness where there was misery? A "word only" had done it all. "Not guilty," "The Acquittal." —*Biblical Treasury.*

Foundation—Defective.

In the city of Brooklyn, two or three years ago, a detective went into a drug store, laid his hand upon the shoulder of a man, and said, "You're wanted." He admitted his crime and asked to be allowed to go home and say good-by to his wife and child. They went to his home. He met his wife and little child in the parlor and said: "Wife, haven't I been a kind husband? Haven't I been a good father and worked hard to make a living?" She replied, "Yes; what do you mean?" "I mean that I am an escaped convict from the penitentiary." He was all right with his wife and child and neighbors, but all wrong with the State of New York. You may be all right with your friends and neighbors, but all wrong with God. —A. C. DIXON.

Offenses—Forgiving.

George IV, wishing to take the sacrament, sent for the Bishop of Winchester to administer it. The messenger having loitered on his way, considerable time elapsed before the bishop arrived, and some irritation had been manifested by the king. On the arrival of the prelate, his delay was complained of and its cause explained. His Majesty immediately rang his bell, and commanded the attendance of the messenger. On his entering the room he rebuked him sharply, and dismissed him from his service. Then, turning to the bishop, he said, "Now, my Lord, if you please, we will proceed." The bishop, with great mildness, but at the same time with firmness, refused to administer the sacrament while any irritation or anger toward a fellow-creature remained in the mind of the king, who, suddenly recollecting himself said, "My Lord, you are right." He then sent for the offending person, whom he forgave and restored to favor in terms of great kindness and condescension.—*The Free Methodist.*

Pardon and Praise.

Dr. Doddridge, on one occasion, interested himself in behalf of a condemned criminal, and at length succeeded in obtaining his pardon.

On announcing to him the joyful intelligence, he prostrated himself at the doctor's feet, and exclaimed, "Oh, sir, every drop of my blood thanks you, for you have had mercy on every drop of it! Wherever you go, I will be yours!" With how much greater propriety may the Christian prostrate himself at the feet of Christ, and make use of similar language!—*Clerical Library.*

Pardon—A Surprising.

A man was severely attacked by another, who thought to kill him. The face of the injured man was badly scarred for the rest of his life. He cherished no enmity, however, against the person who made the attack, and later sought to have him pardoned. Then he asked the privilege of taking the pardon down to Joliet himself. But the criminal, as he took the pardon in his hands, said, "I want something more than pardon, sir; I want friendship." "What kind of friendship do you want?" asked the other. The prisoner replied, "I can do without anybody else's friendship but that of the man I injured." The man with the scars on his face, which he bore for life, made the pardoned prisoner happy by assuring him both of forgiveness and friendship. And that is exactly what our wounded Christ offers to us.— F. W. Gunsaulus.

Pardon—Christ's.

Only the rightful king or ruler can issue a pardon. In Sir Walter Scott's "Ivanhoe," the story is told of Richard the Lion Hearted, in disguise, coming upon a sheriff and his men who were about to execute a prisoner. Reining in his horse and raising his hand Richard exclaimed, "Hold! I spare that man's life." But his very act of mercy revealed his identity, for instantly the men recognized that this one with authority to pardon must be none other than Richard himself. . . . Who is he that forgiveth sins? It is the co-equal with the Father. —*Sunday School Times.*

Pardon Needed.

A strange thing came to light in the aftermath of the "Maine" disaster. Some years before a young man residing in Omaha became wild and wayward. He went from bad to worse until he was convicted of burglary and sentenced to fifteen years. On his way to the penitentiary he escaped and made his way to Boston, enlisted in the Navy under an assumed name, and was assigned to the "Maine." He was among the few survivors of the explosion which destroyed the great battleship. A letter to his parents told of his experiences in the wreck, and application was made to the Governor of Nebraska for a pardon. No man can bury his sin. Somewhere a man must face his record. Until it is pardoned it stands forever against him. Only in Jesus Christ is there safety and peace.— *Anecdotes and Morals.*

Pardon—The Forgotten.

A pastor friend of mine, in talking to a group of ministers on "Evangelism," related a story of a man who was sent by the governor to bring a pardon to a man in prison. He visited the prisoner and began commenting on his prison life, speaking of the meals, the daily routine, his family at home, of messages sent by his friends, and the fruits and flowers he himself had brought. In fact, he talked about everything except the one thing he went for, and finally, he left the prison without delivering the pardon, which would have meant freedom. He remembered it later, of course, but so often, when talking with sinners, we who have a pardon for them from God, never mention it, and, sad to say, we fail to remember it even after leaving them, and they go out to a Christless eternity.—HOWARD M. GREEN.

Pardon—Withholding A.

What would we think of a man who, being in debt, and able to pay, took advantage of the fact that his creditors, poor and ignorant folk, did not know of the money due to them and let them perish by non-payment? One of the best governors of the Isle of Man was impeached for treason in the Civil Wars, and sentenced to death. The king granted a pardon; but it fell into the hands of a bitter enemy of the governor, who never delivered it, and the governor was executed. We hold in our hands the pardon of the world: shall we hold it back?—D. M. PANTON.

The Great Purifier.

There is a lonely little pool of water in a hollow on the mountainside near Tarbet, Loch Lomond, called the Fairy Loch. If you look into it you will see a great many colors in the water, owing to the varied nature of the materials that form its bottom. There is a legend about it which says that the fairies used to dye things for the people round about, if a specimen of the color was left along with the cloth on the brink of the pool at sunset. One evening a shepherd left beside the Fairy Loch the fleece of a black sheep, and placed upon it a white woollen thread to show that he wished the fleece dyed white. This fairly puzzled the good folk. They could dye a white fleece any color: but to make a black fleece white was impossible. In despair they threw all their colors into the loch, giving it its present strange look, and disappeared for ever.—HUGH MACMILLAN.

PEACE

Trust in the Lord.

Paul Gerhardt, the German poet and preacher, after ten years of pastoral work in Berlin, was deprived of his charge by the King of Prussia, and expelled from the country. He turned towards Saxony, his native land, accompanied by his wife and little children, all on foot, without means and without prospect. They stopped at a village inn to pass the night, and there the poor woman naturally gave way to a burst of sorrow and anxiety. Her husband endeavored to comfort her, especially dwelling upon the words of Scripture, "Trust in the Lord with all thine heart, and lean not to thine own understanding; in all thy ways acknowledge Him, and He shall direct thy paths." The same evening two gentlemen entered the inn parlor, and mentioned that they were on their way to Berlin to seek the deposed clergyman, Paul Gerhardt, by order of Duke Christian, of Merseburg, who desired to settle a considerable pension on him as a compensation for the injustice from which he had suffered.—*Fifteen Hundred Illustrations.*

Trust—A Fixed.

I see the wrong that round me lies,
  I feel the guilt within;
I hear, with groan and travail-cries,
  The world confess its sin.

Yet, in the maddening maze of things,
  And tossed by storm and flood,
To one fixed trust my spirit clings;
  I know that God is good!

Not mine to look where cherubim
  And seraphs may not see,
But nothing can be good in Him
  Which evil is in me.

The wrong that pains my soul below
  I dare not throne above:
I know not of His hate,—I know
  His goodness and His love.

I dimly guess from blessings known
  Of greater out of sight,
And, with the chastened Psalmist, own
  His judgments too are right.
                              —J. G. WHITTIER.

Peace in Quietness.

"Does it hurt you severely?" one asked of a friend who lay with a broken arm. "Not when I keep still," was the answer. This is the secret of much of the victoriousness we see in rejoicing Christians. They conquer the pain and the bitterness by keeping still. They do not ask questions, or demand to know why they have trials. They believe in God, and are so sure of His love and wisdom that they are pained by no doubt, no fear, no uncertainty. Peace is their pillow, because they have learned just to be still. Their quietness robs trial of its sharpness, sorrow of its bitterness, death of its sting, and the grave of its victory.
—J. R. MILLER.

Rest—Pictures of.

Two painters each painted a picture to illustrate his conception of rest. The first chose for his scene a still lone lake among the far-off mountains. The second threw on his canvas a thundering waterfall, with a fragile birch tree bending over the foam; at the fork of the branch, almost wet with the cataract's spray, a robin sat on its nest. The first was only stagnation; the last was rest. For in rest there are always two elements—tranquillity and energy; silence and turbulence; creation and destruction; fearlessness and fearfulness. Thus it was in Christ.—HENRY DRUMMOND.

Peace—Plural.

Professor Johnston Ross relates that he once visited a furniture-dealer's shop in West London. The man was a Jew, and, noticing that his visitor wore clerical dress, he began to talk on religious matters. After an interesting conversation the Professor mounted his bicycle, saying, "Good-bye," when the dealer called out in Hebrew, "Peace be unto you"—using the plural form. The Professor's curiosity was aroused, and he asked: "Why do you put it so? Is there another that you wish peace to?" "Yes," replies the Jew, "Peace be to you and to the angel over your shoulder."

Quiet Places.

Just as an eagle, which has been drenched and battered by some fierce storm, will alight to plume its ruffled wings, so, when a great soul has "passed through fire and through water," it needs some safe and quiet place in which to rest. . . . Like almost every great soul in ancient or modern times, to whom has been entrusted the task of swaying the destinies by molding the convictions of mankind—like Sakya Mouni, like Mahomet in the cave of Hira, like St. Francis of Assisi in his sickness, like Luther in the monastery of Erfurt, Paul would need a quiet period in which to elevate his thoughts, to still the tumult of his emotions, to commune in secrecy and in silence with his own soul.—F. W. FARRAR.

Trust—Lack of.

A man on a dark night, rolling down a steep place, caught a bush growing out of the rocks and held on in the grimness of despair. His muscles strained, and his grip was maintained with frenzy. At length endurance reached its limit. In despair he let go and dropped—just six inches. Some people worry and struggle, with nerves at the utmost tension, when all the time they only need to let go to find the Everlasting Arms beneath them.—*The Sunday School Times.*

PERSONAL WORK

Beattitudes.

The Beatitudes are in reality Be-attitudes; they are attitudes that come not from doing, but from be-ing.—WILLIAM LYON PHELPS.

Disciples—Making.

"Some years ago I was preaching in an American city. Among my audience I noticed a young lawyer whom I knew, and at the close of the meeting I made my way down to where he was sitting, stepped up to him and said, 'Good evening. Are you a Christian?' 'Yes,' he said, 'I consider myself a Christian.' 'Are you bringing others to Christ?' I asked. 'No, sir, I am not,' replied he; 'that is not my business, it's yours. I am called to practise law—you are called to preach.' I opened my Bible to Acts 8: 4, and said, 'Will you please read what the Word of God says about it?' He read, 'They that were scattered abroad went everywhere preaching the word.' 'Oh, but those were the Apostles,' he objected. I said, 'Will you be kind enough to read the first verse.'—'And they were all scattered abroad . . . except the Apostles.' He had nothing more to say; what could he say? Your great Captain's command is Go out and make disciples. Are you doing it?"—DR. TORREY.

Effort—Aggressive.

"Brother," said a dying man, "Why have you not been more pressing with me about my soul?" "Dear James," replied the brother, "I have spoken to you several times." "Yes," was the answer, "you are not to blame; but you were always so quiet over it; I wish you had gone on your knees to me, or had taken me by the neck and shaken me, for I have been careless, and have nearly slept myself into hell."—C. H. SPURGEON.

Joy in Unselfishness.

A poor man came home one day and brought five peaches: nice beautiful peaches. He had four sons; he gave one to each and one to his wife. He did not say anything, but just gave them. At night he came home again, and then he said, "How were the peaches—all nice?" I will tell you what each of the four boys said.

The eldest boy said, "Oh yes, father, delicious. I ate my peach, and then I took the stone very carefully, and went and planted it in the garden, that we may have another peach-tree some day." "Well," said the father, "very prudent; look out for the future."

Then the little boy said, "Oh, father 'twas exceedingly nice. I ate all mine, and mother gave me half hers, and I threw away the stone." "Well," said the father, "I am glad you liked it, but perhaps if you had been a little older, you would have acted differently."

The second boy said, "Yes, father, I will tell you what I did with mine; I picked up the stone my little brother threw away, broke it, and ate the kernel; I enjoyed that exceedingly; but I did not eat my peach, I sold it. I could buy a dozen peaches with what I got for it." The father said, "That may be right, but I think it was a little covetous."

Then he said to the third boy, "Well, Edward, what did you do with your peach?" Edward came forward reluctantly; but in answer to his father, he replied, "I took it to poor little George, who is sick down the lane. He would not take it, so I left the peach on his bed and ran away."

163

Which of the four peaches was the sweetest? "Taste and see" the way to enjoy anything.—JAMES VAUGHAN.

Leadership—Personal.

It was a dark, stormy night, and a little child, lost in the streets of the city, was crying in distress. A policeman, gathering from the child's story enough to locate the home, gave directions after this manner: "Just go down this street half a mile, turn and cross the big iron bridge, then turn to your right and follow the river down a little way, and you'll see where you are." The poor child only half comprehending, chilled by the wind, and bewildered by the storm, was turning about blindly, when another voice spoke, and said in a kindly tone. "Just come with me." The little hand was clasped in a stronger one, and the corner of a warm cloak was thrown over the shoulders of the shivering child. The way home was made easy. The first one had *told* the way; this one condescends to *be* the way.—*The Expositor*.

Opportunities—Missed.

It seems a somewhat ridiculous story, but it conveys an important lesson to relate how a great life insurance company in New York invited all its agents throughout the country to a business conference in New York, and while in attendance one of the agents from the West insured the barber, the elevator man, and a waiter in the restaurant, all of whom had been employed for years by the insurance company in its great building. No one had thought to offer policies to these men in the home office building! Exactly so. That is the reason the professional evangelist sweeps in so many; he simply improves the chance that has been there all the time. But why must we wait for him? Why be like that insurance company?—*Central Christian Advocate*.

Patience,—Perfect mark of.

Some years ago, in a manufacturing town in England, a young lady applied to the superintendent of a Sunday school for a class. He told her he had no vacant classes, but that if she liked to go out and hunt up a class of boys for herself, he would be glad to have her help. She did so, and gathered a class of poor ragged boys. Among these, the worst and most unpromising boy was one named Bob. The superintendent told these boys to come to his house during the week, and he would get them each a new suit of clothes. They came and got their clothes. After two or three Sundays Bob was missing. The teacher went after him. She found that his new clothes were torn and dirty. She invited him back to school. He came. The superintendent gave him a second new suit. After attending once or twice Bob's place was empty again. Once more the teacher sought him out. She found that the second suit of clothes had gone the same way as the first. She reported the case to the superintendent, saying she was utterly discouraged about Bob, and must give him up. "Please don't do that," said the superintendent; "I can't but hope that there is something good in Bob. Try him once more. I'll give him a third suit of clothes if he'll promise to attend regularly." Bob did promise. He received his third suit of clothes. He did attend regularly after that. He got interested in school. He became an earnest and persevering seeker after

Jesus. He found Him. He joined the Church. He was made a teacher. He studied for the ministry, and the end of the story is, that that discouraging boy—that dirty, ragged, runaway Bob—became the Rev. Dr. Robert Morrison, the great missionary to China, who translated the Bible into the Chinese language.— REV. RICHARD NEWTON.

Personal Work Difficult.

Dr. Trumbull was often spoken of as being a man of exceptional "tact." He practised pretty constantly at individual soul-winning from the time when he first found his Saviour, at twenty-one, until his death more than fifty years later. People who knew him and his ways, and his lifelong habit, have said of him, "Oh, it was 'second nature' to Dr. Trumbull to speak to a man about his soul. He simply couldn't help doing it, it was so easy for him. *I* never could get *his* ease in the work." And in so saying they showed how little they knew of him or of the demands of this work upon every man. The book on Individual Work was written after its author was seventy years of age. Hear what he had to say as to the "ease" which his long practice had brought him: "From nearly half a century of such practice, as I have had opportunity day by day, I can say that I have spoken with thousands upon thousands on the subject of their spiritual welfare. Yet, so far from my becoming accustomed to this matter, so that I can take hold of it as a matter of course, I find it as difficult to speak about it at the end of these years as at the beginning. Never to the present day can I speak to a single soul for Christ without being reminded by Satan that I am in danger of harming the cause by introducing it just now.

If there is one thing that Satan is sensitive about, it is the danger of a Christian's harming the cause he loves by speaking of Christ to a needy soul. He (Satan) has more than once, or twice, or thrice, kept me from speaking on the subject by his sensitive pious caution, and he has tried a thousand times to do so. Therefore my experience leads me to suppose that he is urging other persons to try any method for souls except the best one."—C. G. TRUMBULL.

Personal Work—Hesitancy in.

Gideon Ouseley, telling of his call to preach, would say, as Mr. Hay tells, "The voice said, 'Gideon, go and preach the gospel!'" But he so felt his ignorance and unworthiness that he pleaded, "Lord I am a poor ignorant creature. How can I go?" Then it would rush into his mind, "Do you not know the disease?" "Oh, yes, Lord, I do." "And do you know the cure?" "Oh, yes, glory be to thy name! I do." "Go then and tell them these two things, the disease and the cure; never mind the rest; the rest is only talk." —*Life of Gideon Ouseley. By* W. ARTHUR.

Service—True.

A beautiful story is told about Sir Bartle Frere, an English nobleman, who was once the governor of Bombay in India and of Cape Colony in Africa. He went away from his home on a trip, and on his return his wife went down to the railroad station to meet him. She took with her a servant who had never seen her husband. When they arrived at the railway station, she said to the servant, "Now you must go and look for Sir Bartle." "But how shall I know him?" asked the servant. "Oh," answered the lady, "look for a tall gentleman helping somebody." The answer was sufficient, for when the servant went to look for Sir Bartle he found a tall man helping an old lady from the car, and this tall man proved to be Sir Bartle himself.—*The Northern Messenger*.

Soul-Winning,—Patience in.

Dr. Judson labored diligently for six years in Burmah before he baptized a convert. At the end of three years he was asked what evidence he had of ultimate success. He replied, "As much as there is a God who will fulfill all His promises." A hundred churches and thousands of converts already answer his faith.

Success of Personal Work.

An American bishop, speaking of the personal love and earnestness which in Christian work prove, with God's blessing, so successful, related that a youth belonged to a Bible-class, but at last the time came when he thought fit to discontinue his attendance, and to otherwise occupy his time. The class assembled, but his place was empty, and the leader looked for the familiar face in vain. He could not be content to conduct the Bible-reading as usual, ignorant as to the condition and whereabouts of the missing one. "Friends," he said, "read, sing, and pray; my work is to seek and find a stray sheep"; and he started off on the quest. "The stray sheep is before you," said the bishop to his hearers. "My teacher found me, and I could not resist his pleading; I could not continue to wander and stray while I was sought so tenderly."—*The Quiver*.

Without a Goal.

There is such a thing as futile speed. Never before in all history were people in such a hurry as now to get nowhere.—*The Toledo Blade*.

Word In Season.

One day, as Felix Neff was walking in a street in the city of Lausanne, he saw, at a distance, a man whom he took for one of his friends. He ran up behind him, tapped him on the shoulder before looking in his face, and asked him, "What is the state of your soul, my friend?" The stranger turned. Neff perceived his error, apologized, and went his way. About three or four years afterwards a person came to Neff, and accosted him, saying he was indebted to him for his inestimable kindness. Neff did not recognize the man, and begged he would explain. The stranger replied, "Have you forgotten an unknown person whose shoulder you touched in a street in Lausanne, asking him, 'How do you find your soul?' It was I; your question led me to serious reflection, and now I find it is well with my soul." This proves what apparently small means may be blessed of God for the conversion of sinners, and how many opportunities for doing good we are continually letting slip, and which thus pass irrecoverably beyond our reach. One of the questions which every Christian should propose to himself on setting out upon a journey is, "What opportunities shall I have to do good?" And one of the points on which he should examine himself on his return is, "What opportunities have I lost?" "Have I done all the good that I could?"— John Angell James.

Workers, Not Observers.

Pythagoras was once asked contemptuously by a Greek tyrant who he was and what was his particular business in the world. The philosopher replied that at the Olympic games some people came to try for the prizes, some to dispose of their merchandise, some to enjoy themselves and meet their friends, and some to look on. "I" said Pythagoras, "am one of those who come to look on at life." Bacon, in telling the story, adds: "But men must know that in this theater of man's life it is reserved only for God and angels to be lookers-on.—J. Moffatt.

PRAISE

Joy—Reason for.

A detachment of the American Army had just entered a small French village from which the enemy had fled. In an ecstacy of joy the few remaining inhabitants flocked out to greet them, singing, dancing, shedding tears of gladness as they approached. "Well, I'm glad to help save these people," exclaimed a young officer thoughtlessly, "but I don't see why they have to get so crazy over it." "Ah, m'sieur," an old lady who had overheard him replied, "that's because you don't know what you've saved us from!" Perhaps the reason many people do not get more joy and happiness out of Christ is because they do not realize what He has saved them from. . . . Christians, you must not forget "the rock whence ye were hewn, and the hole of the pit whence ye were digged." —*Forward.*

Light and Noise.

A man who knew little about electricity had his house wired and a battery installed for the ringing of various bells. He thought that if a battery could ring a bell it could make a light, and so he proceeded to run wires up into his study. Then he adjusted a globe in the fashion of an electric light, turned on the current, and was greatly disappointed to find that he got no light. About that time an electrician came in, and, seeing his predicament, said, "What is the matter?" "I don't know. I have a battery here that has been ringing all the bells for a long time, and it has never failed me. So I thought that it would light my study. I tried and failed." The electrician looked at him and said, "Don't you know that it takes more power to make a light than it does to make a noise?"—LEN BROUGHTON.

Music in the Storm.

There is an old German tale which might be a parable of the purpose in our life of the unintelligible things. The story is told of a baron who, having grown tired of the gay and idle life of the Court, asked leave of his King to withdraw from it. He built for himself a fort on a rugged rock, beneath which rolled the Rhine. There he dwelt alone. He hung wires from one wing of the fort to the other, making an Aeolian harp, on which the winds might play to solace him. But many days and nights had passed, and winds had come and gone, yet never had there been music from that harp. And the baron interpreted the silence as the sign of God's unremoved displeasure. One evening the sky was torn with wild hurrying clouds, the sun was borne away with a struggle, and as night fell a storm broke out which shook the very earth. The baron walked restlessly through his rooms in loneliness and disquiet. At length he went out into the night, but stopped short upon the threshold. He listened, and behold the air was full of music. His Aeolian harp was singing with joy and passion high above the wildness and the storm. Then the baron knew. Those wires, which were too thick to give out music at the call of common days, had found their voice in a night of stress and storm.—JOHN A. HUTTON.

No Music in Unbelief.

Christianity came into the world on the wings of song. Unbelief has no music, no anthems, no hymns, no oratorios, no symphonies. When Robert Ingersoll died the printed notice of his funeral said: "There will be no singing."—Hugh Tomson Kerr.

Praise—Deserved.

A short time ago, one of our blind soldiers was playing the piano in the convalescent ward of a London hospital. Presently some visitors entered the room, but he was used to such interruptions, and played on, filling the long ward with a lovely melody. When the music ceased, a gentleman walked over to the piano and said, "Well done, my friend!" The surprised soldier, thinking it was one of his comrades, swung round on the stool, and with a smile said, "And who are you?" Quick as a flash, and as startling, came the reply, "Your king!" In an instant the man was on his feet with his hand at salute, his whole being instinct with pleasure at the honor accorded him by the royal word of praise. A slight story, but a very sweet parable.— *Sunday Strand.*

Praise—Unrestrained.

A good Presbyterian minister in old Scotland, of the staid and orthodox type, had in his congregation a poor old woman who was in the habit of saying "Praise the Lord," "Amen," when anything particularly helpful was said. This practice greatly disturbed the minister, and one New Year's day he went to see her. "Betty," he said, "I'll make a bargain with you. You call out 'Praise the Lord' just when I get to the best part of my sermon, and it upsets my thoughts. Now if you will stop doing it all this year, I'll give you a pair of wool blankets." Betty was poor, and the offer of the blankets looked very good. So she did her best to earn them. Sunday after Sunday she kept quiet. But one day a minister of another

type came to preach—a man bubbling over with joy. As he preached on the forgiveness of sin and all the blessings that follow, the vision of the blankets began to fade and fade, and the joys of salvation grew brighter and brighter. At last Betty could stand it no longer, and jumping up she cried, "Blankets or no blankets, Hallelujah!"—J. Linton.

Servant—A Faithful.

From old crusading times comes this story: A certain king, on his way back from the Holy Land, was captured by enemies and cast into prison—where, none of his friends knew. The king had a favorite minstrel, who determined to find his master. He went throughout the country, pausing before the door of every prison, singing the songs he had been wont to sing in the palace of his king. He hoped thus to find the captive monarch. Long he journeyed in vain, but at last, as he stood before a prison window and sang, he heard a voice within, the voice of him he sought. The old songs sung at the prison window were heard by the captive, who was soon released. So the messengers of Christ should go through this world singing the song of Christ's love before every prison door.

Singing His Song.

Bjornsen, the Norwegian poet, was once asked what incident in his life had given him the most pleasure. He replied that it was on one occasion when he had done something that had aroused the displeasure of the Storthing, the Norwegian Parliament. Some members of that body had made their way to his house, just outside Christiana, and they broke the house windows of the poet. Then they marched away singing the Norwegian National Anthem, "Yes, we love this land of ours," and Bjornsen chuckled, for he was the author of their song. They had smashed his windows, but they had to sing his song. The world to-day is not very friendly to Jesus. So many offer him a sham allegiance that is not worthy of the name of discipleship. The peace he offers gets little consideration from those who need it so badly, but the world shall yet sing his song.—*United Methodist Magazine.*

Singing the New Song.

It is related of Peter Mackenzie, the Durham miner, who became the noted Wesleyan preacher and lecturer, that when he first started out on his career as an evangelist his purpose was to get a crowd of people together for others to preach to. He would gather the crowd himself, and then get somebody to speak to them. But one day he had a large crowd but no speaker, so they forced him into speaking. He said, "If I must preach, give me my subject," and they said, "Preach about heaven." "Very well," said Peter Mackenzie, and thereupon launched out in a characteristic description of heaven. Right in the middle of his sermon someone shouted out, "Peter, what do they do in heaven?" He paused for a moment, and then said: "One thing they do is to sing. I expect one day to walk only the streets of the eternal city, and come face to face with David playing an accompaniment on his harp to his own great song, 'The Lord is my Shepherd, I shall not want.' I expect some day I shall lead the choir in heaven, and if ever I do, there are two songs I am going to give out. One is No. 749 in the Wesleyan Hymn-book, 'My God and Father, while I stray'; but if I ever give out that song in heaven, half the angels in the choir will say, 'Peter, you are in heaven, and you

cannot stray.' Then if I give that out, and they cannot sing it, I will try another, No. 651, in the Wesleyan Hymn-book, 'Though waves and storms beat o'er my head'; and then, not half the angels, but the whole choir will be on their feet, saying, 'Peter Mackenzie, this is heaven; there are no storms here.' Then I think I shall stand in wonder and amazement, and say, 'What shall we sing?' and from every angel in the skies will come the answer, 'Sing the New Song!' 'Sing the New Song!' Then all the redeemed in heaven, from the least unto the greatest, will join in singing an ascription of praise unto Him who hath loved us and washed us from our sins in His own precious blood."—J. WILBUR CHAPMAN.

The Persistent Note.

A German with a trained musical ear came a stranger into an American city. He heard the voice of song, and following the sound, found himself where they were singing psalmody in a nasal and discordant way. After he had entered, he wished he were outside, and he did not know whether he ought to put his hands over his ears and so show his disgust, or rush out of the hall; but being too well bred to do either, he determined to endure it as best he could. And while he was sitting there, he discerned a woman's voice, clear and sweet, singing in exact tune. She was not trying to drown all the rest; nor, on the other hand, was she at all disturbed or her melody at all marred by the discords around her; she just kept singing that sweet, pure note of concord, until at last it became infectious, and the others began to fall in with it; and it was not long before the whole company was singing in perfect harmony, in-

fluenced by the example of that one
voice.

The Old Hymns.

There's lots of music in 'em—the
    hymns of long ago,
And when some gray-haired brother
    sings the ones I used to know,
I sorter want to take a hand—I
    think of days gone by,
"On Jordan's stormy banks I stand
    and cast a wistful eye!"

There's lots of music in 'em—those
    dear sweet hymns of old,
With visions bright of lands of light
    and shining streets of gold,
And I hear 'em ringing—singing
    where memory dreaming stands,
"From Greenland's icy mountains to
    India's coral strands."

They seem to sing forever of holier,
    sweeter days,
When the lilies of the love of God
    bloomed white in all the ways;
And I want to hear their music from
    the old-time meetings rise,
"Till "I can read my title clear to
    mansions in the skies."

We never needed singin' books in
    them old days—we knew
The words, the tunes of every one—
    the dear hymn book through!
We didn't have no trumpets then, no
    organs built for show;
We only sang to praise the Lord
    "from whom all blessings flow."

And so I love the good old hymns
    and when my time shall come
Before the light has left me, and my
    singing lips are dumb,
If I can hear 'em sing them then,
    I'll pass without a sigh
To "Canaan's fair and happy land,
    where my possessions lie."

        —FRANK L. STANTON.

PRAYER

Angels—The Two.

There is a legend about St. Peter sending out two angels from the door of heaven, each with a basket to gather what we would call flowers—that is, they were the prayers of God's people. One was the Angel of Thanksgivings and one was the Angel of Petitions. When they returned to Peter each one "seemed to be in trouble sore"; the Angel of Petitions had in addition to his overflowing basket a bag bound upon his back which was "cram full." The Angel of Thanksgivings blushed with shame when he showed only three little prayers of thanksgiving rattling around in his big basket.

Childish Prayer.

A little boy, whose conduct made his mother say that she feared he did not pray, replied, "Yes, I do: I pray every night, that God will make you and pa like my ways better."

Enemy—Prevailing Against the.

I remember a wonderful mural painting. It depicts the Jews brought into subjection to the heathen. To the left stands Pharaoh, exquisite, effeminate, deadly cruel. In one hand he lifts the scourge, and with the other he grasps the hair of the captives. On the right is the Assyrian king, duller, heavier, with knotted limbs. He presses down the yoke on the poor prisoners. But supplicating hands are raised up to heaven, and Jehovah lends His ear to the cry of His people. The cherubim fly before Him, their wings a glowing crimson. They hide His face; but from behind the wings issue His arms. The slender Pharaoh He represses by the mere impact of His fingers. The brute force of the Assyrian He holds in a grasp of tremendous power.

Fear not, O trembling heart: when Jesus presents your prayers before the throne, no enemy can prevail against you.—A. Smellie.

Prayer and Revivals.

The great revival in New York in 1858-9 began in answer to the earnest believing prayers of one man. After long waiting upon God, asking him to show him what He would have him to do, and becoming more and more confident that God would show him the way through which hundreds might be influenced for their soul's good, he at last began a noon-day prayer-meeting. The first half-hour no one came, and he prayed through it alone. At half-past twelve the step of a solitary individual was heard on the stairs; others came, until six made up the whole company. His record of that meeting was, "The Lord was with us to bless us." Of those six, one was a Presbyterian, one a Baptist, another a Congregationalist, and another a Reformed Dutch."—*The Power of Prayer.*

Prayer Answered.

When the season has been cold and backward, when rains fell and prices rose, and farmers desponded, and the poor despaired, I have heard old people, whose hopes resting on God's promise did not rise and fall with the barometer nor shifting winds, say we shall have harvest after all; and this you can safely say of the labors and fruits of prayer.—T. Guthrie.

Prayer Changes Things.

Mr. S. D. Gordon imagines a conversation between Christ and the angel Gabriel, soon after the Ascension. Gabriel is asking Jesus what plans he had made to let all the world know how he lived and died and rose again. And the Master is supposed to reply: "I asked Peter and James and John, and some more of them down there, just to go and make it the business of their lives to tell the others. And the others are to tell others, and the others yet others, and still others beyond, till the last man in the farthest reach has heard the story and has been caught, thrilled and thralled by the power of it." But Gabriel looks as if he could see difficulty in the Master's plan, and he says, "Yes, Master, suppose after a while Peter forgets. Suppose John loses his enthusiasm and simply doesn't tell the others. Suppose their successors away down there in the twentieth century get so busy about things, some of them good things—church things maybe —suppose they get so busy that they do not tell the others. What then?" And back came that quiet voice of the Lord Jesus. He says, "Gabriel, I haven't made any other plans. I am counting on them."— EDGAR DE WITT JONES.

Prayer in Jesus' Name.

"It is the name at the foot of the check," says the Rev. T. G. Selby, "which gives it value when passed over the counter of the bank, and he is a poor simpleton indeed who imagines that the check for a sum in four figures will be dishonored unless he drive there in carriage and pair. And yet some of us are just as whimsical and uninformed upon the subject of prayer. We assume that God will respond more richly and readily to the supplications of prophets, apostles, famous saints, those who belong to brilliant spiritual hierarchies, than to yours and mine. Prayer becomes priceless through the name in which it is presented, however poor and mean and ignoble the petitioner himself.—*Sunday at Home.*

Prayer-Book—the Lost.

A worthy minister of the gospel, in North America, was pastor of a flourishing church. He was a popular preacher, but gradually became less to his hearers, and his congregation very much decreased. This was solely attributed to the minister; and matters continuing to get worse, some of his hearers resolved to speak to him on the subject. They did so; and when the good man had heard their complaints, he replied, "I am quite sensible of all you say, for I feel it to be true; and the reason of it is, that I have lost my prayer-book." They were astonished at hearing this, but he proceeded: "Once my preaching was acceptable, many were edified by it, and numbers were added to the church, which was then in a prosperous state. But we were then a praying people. . . ." They took the hint. Social prayer was again renewed and punctually attended. Exertions were made to induce those who were without to attend the preaching of the Word. And the result was, that the minister became as popular as ever, and in a short time the church was again as flourishing as ever.—*Clerical Library.*

Prayer—Alone in.

A man was standing in a telephone booth trying to talk, but could not make out the message. He kept saying, "I can't hear, I can't hear." The other man by-and-by said sharply, "If you'll shut the door you can hear." His door was not shut, and he could hear not only the man's voice, but the street and store noises too. Some folks have gotten their hearing badly confused because their doors have not been shut enough.

Man's voice and God's voice get mixed in their ears. They cannot tell between them. The bother is partly with the door. If you'll shut that door you can hear.—S. D. GORDON.

Prayer—Answer to.

Lord Bolingbroke once asked Lady Huntington how she reconciled prayer to God for particular blessings with absolute resignation to the Divine will. "Very easy," answered her ladyship; "just as if I were to offer a petition to a monarch of whose kindness and wisdom I have the highest opinion. In such a case my language would be, 'I wish you to bestow on me such a favor; but your majesty knows better than I how far it would be agreeable to you or right in itself to grant my desire. I therefore content myself with humbly presenting my petition, and leave the event of it entirely to you."

Prayer—Delayed Answer to.

A poor woman stood at a vineyard gate and looked over into the vineyard. "Would you like some grapes?" asked the proprietor. "I should be very thankful," replied the woman. "Then bring your basket." Quickly the basket was brought to the gate. The owner took it and was gone a long time among the vines, till the woman became discouraged, thinking that he was not coming again. At last he returned with the basket heaped full. "I have made you wait a good while," he said, "but you know the longer you have to wait the better grapes and the more." So it sometimes is in prayer. We bring our empty vessel to God and pass it over the gate of prayer to Him. He seems to be delaying a long time,

and sometimes faith faints with waiting. But at last He comes, and our basket is heaped full with luscious blessings. He waited long that He might bring us a better and a fuller answer.—*From "Making the Most of Life," by* J. R. MILLER.

Prayer—Delayed Answers to.

At sixty years of age Dr. Pierson was not too old to learn, and, with humility and an eager thirst after knowledge, he listened as Mr. George Müller of Bristol gave detailed testimony to show God as a hearer and answerer of prayer. In one of these interviews he asked Mr. Müller if he had ever petitioned God for anything that had not been granted.

"Sixty-two years, three months, five days and two hours have passed," replied Mr. Müller with his characteristic exactness, "since I began to pray that two men might be converted. I have prayed daily for them ever since and as yet neither of them shows any signs of turning to God."

"Do you expect God to convert them?"

"Certainly," was the confident reply. "Do you think God would lay on His child such a burden for sixty years if He had no purpose for their conversion?"

Not long after Mr. Müller's death, Dr. Pierson was again in Bristol, preaching in Bethesda Chapel—the meeting-place of the Brethren. In the course of his sermon, he told of this conversation, and as he was going out at the close of the service a lady stopped him and said: "One of those two men, to whom Mr. Müller referred, was my uncle. He was converted and died a few weeks ago. The other man was brought to Christ in Dublin."—*Life of A. T. Pierson, 277.*

Prayer—Deliverance in.

A pastor related in our hearing how he once had under his care a church blessed with many innocent women. One of the best of these, who had overworked herself, suddenly became, as she supposed, "a castaway." She sent for her pastor, and confided to him her deplorable condition. She could not pray. To read the Bible was a hated task; she must be a castaway. The pastor considered for a while; then he said, "Have you confidence enough in me to do exactly what I tell you?" "Certainly," she replied; she had full confidence in her pastor's judgment. "Put your hand in mine," he said. She obeyed. "Now give me your solemn promise never to open a Bible or attempt to pray until I give you leave." After a moment's hesitation she made the required promise, and the minister took his leave. I think it was that very day—perhaps the day after—that a messenger came in hot haste for the minister to hurry to the good sister's house. With a quiet smile the pastor turned to that errand. As he showed his face at the door the sister rushed to him, crying, "Release me! release me quick, or I shall pray! I must pray, I will pray!—you shall not hinder me!" "Do pray," said her pastor; and that was the last of her being "a castaway."—*Christian Age.*

Prayer,—Faith in.

It is said that a man once asked Alexander to give him some money to portion off a daughter. The King bade him go to his treasurer and demand what he pleased. He went and demanded an enormous sum. The treasurer was startled, said he could not part with so much without an express order, and went to the King, and told him that he thought a small part of the money the man had named might serve for the occasion. "No," replied Alexander; "let him have it all. I like that man; he does me honor; he treats me like a king, and proves, by what he asks, that he believes me to be both rich and generous." Let us go to the throne of grace, and put up such petitions as may show that we have honorable views of the riches and bounty of our King.—NEWTON.

Prayer—Foolish.

If I am to talk to my friend on the telephone, after I have rung him up, I must wait for an answer. It is not a bit of use to ring up and then put the instrument down. I must wait until I hear the "Hello!" or "Are you there?" from the other end. Now, it is exactly like that with prayer—we must give God time to reply. It is not a bit of use to offer up a prayer and then ring off. That is a mistake people often make in prayer.—J. D. JONES.

Prayer—Humility in.

Artabanus, one of the military officers of the Athenians, was applied to by a certain great man, who told him that he desired an audience of the king. He was answered that before it was granted, he must prostrate himself before him, for it was a custom of the country for the king to admit no one to his presence who would not worship him. That which was an arrogant assumption in an earthly king, is a proper condition of an approach to the King of kings. Humility is the foundation of an intercourse with Him. We must bow before His throne. No sinner who is too proud to yield obedience to this law need expect any favors from His hands.

Prayer—Information of.

You looked out of the window and saw the whole little history; but when the children come in to tell the tale of joy, you assume that you know nothing about it. Why? Because you want to hear it from their lips. You say, "What is it?" though you know as well as they do. You enjoy hearing them rehearse it.

God knows all; but he loves to hear his children talk to him.—H. W. BEECHER.

Prayer—Instant in.

"Once there was a king, who employed his people to weave for him. The silk and patterns were all given by the king. He told the workers that, when any difficulty arose, they should send to him, and he would help them, and never to fear troubling him.

"Among many men and women at the looms there was one little child who worked cheerfully, though often alone. One day, when the men and women were distressed at the sight of their failures—their silks were tangled and their weaving unlike the pattern—they gathered round the child, and said:

"'Tell us how it is that you are so happy in your work. We are always in difficulties.'

"'Then why do you not send to the king?' said the little weaver. 'He told us that we might do so.'

"'So we do, night and morning.'

"'Ah!' said the child, 'but I send directly when I find I have a little tangle.'

"So let us take all our wants and troubles directly to the Lord in prayer. He invites us so to do, and promises to help us."—*The Wellspring.*

Prayer—Listening to.

A poor old woman had often in vain attempted to obtain the ear of Philip of Macedon to certain wrongs of which she complained. The King at last abruptly told her he was not at leisure to hear her. "No!" exclaimed she; "then you are not at leisure to be king." Philip was confounded; he pondered a moment in silence over her words, then desired her to proceed with her case; and ever after made it a rule to listen attentively to the applications of all who addressed him.—*Percy Anecdotes.*

Praying Warriors.

When Ethelred, the Saxon king of Northumberland, invaded Wales, and was about to give battle to the Britons, he noticed, near the enemy, a host of unarmed men. He inquired who they were, and what they were doing. He was told that they were the monks of Bangor, praying for the success of their countrymen. "Then," said the Saxon king, "they have begun the fight against us. Attack them first."

Prayer, A Constant Privilege.

In the vestibule of St. Peter's, at Rome, is a doorway which is walled up and marked with a cross. It is opened but four times in a century; on Christmas eve, once in twenty-five years, the Pope approaches it in princely state, with the retinue of cardinals in attendance, and begins the demolition of the door by striking it thrice with a silver hammer. When the passage is opened the multitude pass into the nave of the cathedral, and up to the altar by an avenue which the majority of them never entered thus before, and never will enter thus again. Imagine that the way of the throne of grace were like the Porta Santa, inaccessible save once in a quarter of a century, on the 25th of December! With what solicitude we should wait for the coming of the holy day!—*Clerical Library.*

Prayers—Recorded.

A characteristic letter from Henry Ward Beecher is found in the archives of the Grand Army of the Republic. It was written in reply to a request for a copy of a prayer of his for publication:—"PEEK-SKILL, July 11, 1878.—Gen. H. A. Barnum, Grand Marshal. You request me to send you my prayer made on Decoration Day evening. If you will send me the notes of the oriole that whistled from the top of my trees last June, or the iridescent globes that came in by millions on the last waves that rolled in on the beach yesterday, or a segment of the rainbow of last week, or the perfume of the first violet that blossomed last May, I will also send you the prayer that rose to my lips with the occasion and left me for ever. I hope it went heavenward and was registered; in which case the only record of it will be found in heaven.—Very truly yours, HENRY WARD BEECHER.

Prayer—Relying on.

I shall never forget what the late Dr. A. C. Dixon, of Spurgeon's Tabernacle, once said when speaking upon this theme of prayer. I cannot quote him verbatim, but the substance was this: "When we rely upon organization, we get what organization can do; when we rely upon education, we get what education can do; when we rely upon eloquence, we get what eloquence can do, and so on. Nor am I disposed to under-value any of these things in their proper place. But," he added impressively; "when we rely upon prayer, *we get what God can do*."—*The European Harvest Field.*

Prayer—Safety in.

You remember the story of the godly family whose home lay across the track a returning army was expected to follow, when flushed with victory and athirst for rapine and blood. "Be a wall of fire unto us, O God," was the prayer which the father put up as he knelt at the household altar ere retiring for the night, and having thus committed himself and his circle to the hands of a preserving God, he and they together laid them down in peace, and took their quiet rest, knowing who it was that made them dwell in safety. The night-watches hastened on, morning came, and the family awoke. All was unwontedly dark and still when they rose. There was no light from chink or from window nor sound of stirring life around. Noiselessly, and all unseen, the hand whose protection they craved stole forth from the wintry heavens, not, indeed, in the shape of a wall of fire, but in something as sufficient and safe—in wreath upon wreath of driven snow. Meanwhile the foe had passed by, and had gone on his way, and those whom he threatened breathed freely, for they knew that their tabernacle was at peace.—W. A. GRAY.

Prayer—Secret.

A man was standing in a telephone box trying to talk, but he could not make out the message. He kept saying: "I can't hear, I can't hear." The other man by and by said sharply: "If you'll shut the door you can hear." The door was not shut, and he could hear, not only the man's voice, but the street and shop noises too! A great many Christians are going lean and hungry on the way, because they do not shut the door more frequently that shuts them up with God, and silences for a while the din of worldliness. Jesus makes the shut door the condition of peculiar blessings from God.—*Selected.*

Prayer,—Strength in.

There is an old story of mythology about a giant named Antæus, who was born by the earth. In order to keep alive this giant was obliged to touch the earth as often as once in five minutes, and every time he thus came in contact with the earth he became twice as strong as before. The Christian resembles Antæus. In order to become and continue a truly-living Christian, the disciple of Christ must often approach his Father by prayer.—*Preacher's Lantern.*

Prayer—True.

Preaching recently in London, the Bishop of Chelmsford suggested that some Christians got into the habit of compiling a list of things they wanted God to give them, and they never knelt in prayer without asking for one of them. It reminded him of the time when his little girl used to come into his study—knowing that he kept a bag of sweets there, and that she would doubtless get one or two of them. But once she looked in, and when asked what she had come for, she replied: "Nothing; I've just come to see you, daddy." Have you ever knelt down before God with the feeling that you just wanted to be near Him and to see Him and speak to Him, and to listen for His words to you? If you have, you may be sure you are getting into the spirit of true prayer.—*The Sunday School Chronicle.*

Prayers—Unanswered.

We do not wait on the Lord enough in day-and-night praying. The story is told of a woman who dreamed that she died and went to heaven. As one of the angels was showing her about the rooms of that glorious place, she was brought to a large room where many bundles were piled in a corner. Finding her name on several bundles, she asked for an explanation, saying as she did so, "I remember praying for those very things when I was down on the earth." The angel replied, "Yes, when any of God's children make requests to Him, preparations are made to give the answer, but the angels are told if the petitioner is not waiting for the answer to return it, and store it in this room." Does not this account for our failure many times to receive answers to our prayers?—Norman H. Camp.

Prayer—Value of United.

I often think of the negro woman who was once asked by the governor of Surinam why she and her fellows always prayed *together*. Could they not do it each one for himself? He happened to be standing at the time before a coal-fire, and the woman answered: "Dear sir, separate these coals from each other, and the fire will go out; but see how brisk the flame when they burn together." From the mere circumstance that when in fellowship with others our hearts grow warm, we can easily understand what the Saviour means when He says, "Where two or three are gathered together in my name, there am I in the midst of them." And again, "If two of you shall agree on earth as touching anything that they shall ask, it shall be done for them of my Father which is in heaven." This, says a devout man, is as when the whole children of a family take heart, and with one accord beseech the father for a boon. It is then far harder for him to refuse.—A. Tholuck.

Prayer-Meeting.

A crowded gathering of distinguished scientists had been listening, spellbound, to the masterly expositions of Michael Faraday. For an hour he held his brilliant audience enthralled as he demonstrated the nature and properties of the magnet. He brought his lecture to a close with an experiment so novel, so bewildering, and so triumphant that, for some time after he resumed his seat, the house rocked with enthusiastic applause. And then the Prince of Wales, after King Edward the Seventh, rose to propose a motion of congratulation. The resolution, having been duly seconded, was carried with renewed thunders of applause. But the uproar was succeeded by a strange silence. The assembly waited for Faraday's reply; but the lecturer had vanished! What had become of him? Only two or three of his most intimate friends were in the secret. They knew that the great chemist was something more than a great chemist; he was a great Christian. He was an elder of a little Sandemanian Church, a church that never boasted more than twenty members. The hour at which Faraday concluded his lecture was the hour of the midweek prayer-meeting. That meeting he never neglected. And, under cover of the cheering applause, the lecturer had slipped out of the crowded hall and hurried off to the little meeting house.—F. W. Boreham.

The Shut Door.

Whoever has pondered long over a plan which he is anxious to accomplish, without distinctly seeing at first the way, knows what meditation is. It was in this way that one of the greatest of English engineers, a man uncouth, and unaccustomed to regular discipline of mind, is said to have accomplished his most marvelous triumphs. He threw bridges over almost impracticable torrents, and pierced the eternal mountains for his viaducts. Sometimes a difficulty brought all the work to a pause; then he would shut himself up in his room, eat nothing, speak to no one, abandon himself intensely to the contemplation of that on which his heart was set, and at the end of two or three days would come forth serene and calm, walk to the spot, and quietly give orders which seemed the result of superhuman intuition.—L. W. Bacon.

Prayer for Peace.

I do not ask, O Lord, that life may be
    A pleasant road;
I do not ask that Thou would'st take from me
    Aught of its load;

I do not ask that flowers should always spring
    Beneath my feet;
I know too well the poison and the sting
    Of things too sweet.

For one thing only, Lord, dear Lord, I plead;
    Lead me aright—
Though strength should falter, and though heart should bleed—
    Through peace to light.

I do not ask, O Lord, that Thou
    should'st shed
  Full radiance here;
Give but a ray of peace, that I may
    tread
  Without a fear.

I do not ask my cross to understand,
  My way to see—
Better in darkness just to feel Thy
    hand,
  And follow Thee.

Joy is like restless day; but peace
    divine
  Like quiet night;
Lead me, O Lord—till perfect day
    shall shine,
  Through peace to light.

      —ADELAIDE ANNE PROCTER.

Prayer—Answered.

Unanswered yet, the prayer your
    lips have pleaded,
  In agony of heart these many
    years?
Does faith begin to fail? Is hope
    departing,
  And think you all in vain those
    falling tears?
Say not the Father hath not heard
    your prayer;
You shall have your desire some-
    time, somewhere.

Unanswered yet, though when you
    first presented
  This one petition at the Father's
    Throne,
It seemed you could not wait the
    time of asking,
  So urgent was your heart to have
    it known?
Though years have passed since
    then, do not despair;
The Lord will answer you some-
    time, somewhere.

Unanswered yet? Nay, do not say
    ungranted;
  Perhaps your part is not yet
    wholly done;
The work began when first your
    prayer was uttered,
  And God will finish what He has
    begun.
If you will keep the incense burn-
    ing there,
His glory you will see sometime,
    somewhere.

Unanswered yet? Faith cannot be
    unanswered,
  Her feet are firmly planted on the
    rock;
Amid the wildest storms she stands
    undaunted,
  Nor quails before the loudest
    thunder shock.
She knows Omnipotence has heard
    her prayer,
And cries, It shall be done—some-
    time, somewhere.

PROCRASTINATION

Delay—Danger of.

"Serious things to-morrow," said a distinguished individual against whose life a plot was laid. One of the confederates, relenting, had sent a notice of the plot by a messenger who had particular instructions to deliver it personally, and to state that the letter must be read immediately, as it was on a very serious matter. The messenger, however, found the person against whose life the plot was laid in the midst of a convivial feast. The letter and message were both faithfully delivered; but the man of mirth and wine laid it aside, saying, "Serious things to-morrow!" The morrow he never saw, for that night the assassin plunged the deadly weapon into his heart. So many put away from them the serious warnings of the gospel, and perish in their sins.

Delay—Danger of.

A Christian tradesman bethought him that he had never spoken to a certain regular customer about his soul, though the man had called at his shop for years. He determined to plead earnestly with him the next time he came in his way. There was no next time; his customer died suddenly, so that he saw him no more.—C. H. Spurgeon.

Delay—Danger of.

What do you wait for? Do you wait for youth to pass? When I would bring to a friend a pleasant gift from my garden I do not wait till the rose sheds its leaves, and pluck the remainder for that friend: I give it to him while it is in its highest state of freshness and beauty. And would you bring to God, the greatest, the dearest, the noblest, the best of friends, your soul after the bloom of youth is dropped and you have come into the years of decay?—H. W. Beecher.

Delay—Dangers of.

Often it is said of the penitent thief on the cross that one such case is recorded in the Scripture, that none may despair of repentance on a death-bed; and but one, that none may presume. It is like crossing Niagara over the rapids on a tight-rope. One Blondin out of forty millions may have done it, and reached the hither shore in safety; but would you or I risk it for that?—Professor Phelps.

Delay—Dangerous.

Mission services were being held in a certain district in Ireland. After one of these services, two women were discussing them in the local grocery shop. The one woman, a Christian, was telling the other her need of Christ. The other woman could not see her need, but replied: "Oh, well, I must turn over a new leaf." "But," said the Christian woman, "you might be at the end of the book, there will be no more to turn over." There was silence after that.—*Christian Herald.*

Delay—Fatal.

J. M. Barrie has given us in A Window in Thrums a very pathetic picture of Jamie's homecoming. When some of the neighbors saw Jamie prowling about in the gloaming near the old home, his face seemed to them like that of a man who had come "straucht frae hell." He had gone back to the old home. He meant to go back in penitence to find safety and rest, at the old fireside, and in the shelter of a mother's wounded but forgiving and tender love; but he was too late. The door of the old cottage was shut upon all that, and father and mother and sister were gathered to God, and he was alone.

Delay—No Time for.

A man was once shut up in prison, loaded with chains, and condemned to be hung. He had been taken a prisoner in war by a cruel tyrant, and knew that there was no hope for him if he could not in some way make his escape. In the dead hour of night, when all his guards were sound asleep, and not a footstep was to be heard around his prison, the door of his dungeon was opened, his general entered and took off his chains, and said to him, "Haste thee, escape from this place. I have, at immense expense and terrible exposure of my life, entered this prison to save you. Follow me, and I will guide you safely. But you have not a moment to lose. An hour's delay may prove for ever too late." What will you think when I tell you that the prisoner said, "Let me think about it—wait a little while"; and then actually refused to go with him? Who was to blame for that man's death, but himself? This is precisely the way that sinners, condemned and bound by Satan to be shut up in the dark prison of despair, act when Jesus, the great Captain of our salvation, comes to set them free.—BISHOP MEADE.

Danger—Playing with.

Two boys were playing on a narrow ledge, worn smooth in the face of a seaside cliff. Some twenty feet beneath, the deep sea-green water lapped against the rock. One of the boys was the miller's son. He had been warned again and again of the peril of the path. He had been caught and chastized. This day a careless step to the edge

paid its penalty and he fell into the smooth, deep water below. Death seemed to be his just fate. But his keen cry was heard in the near-by mill, and his father ran out with anger on his face. But when he saw his son struggling with death the frown became a spasm of anguish, and at the risk of his own life he plunged in and rescued him. As the boy lay in his exhaustion, tended by loving care, he knew how far it was true that our sins find us out. He understood the Psalmist's profounder word, "He hath not dealt with us after our sins, nor rewarded us after our iniquities." He knew that the world which seems to be all law, is really all love, and that mercy rejoices against judgment.—W. M. CLOW.

"First" Means First.

At the cashier's desk of a large store there was a notice that read something like this: "Don't delay for a minute charging up goods that you have sold. No matter who is calling you, the rule of the house is to enter the charge first. The charge has the right of way here. In spite of clerks or customers, or anybody else, charge the goods. If the house is afire, get out quickly, but charge the goods. Business is business." Our Master's charge is "Seek ye first the kingdom." No matter what else may call, "seek first the kingdom."—*Record of Christian Work.*

Indecision—Terrace of.

Travelers tell us that there is, near the Jaffa gate at Jerusalem, a small terrace on the top of a hill, called the "Terrace of Indecision." The ground is so level that the rain, falling upon it, seems at a loss which way to go. Part of it is carried over the west side, where it flows into the Valley of Roses, and gives life, fertility, beauty, and fragrance to the Sharon lilies and roses. The rest flows down the east side into the Valley of Tophet and onward to the Dead Sea. Every life has its terrace of indecision. On the decision of each one hangs his future of helpful life or of death.— *Record of Christian Work.*

Invitations—Delayed.

Wu Ting Fang, Chinese ambassador to the United States, always praised Confucianism as being far above Christianity. He spent his last Sunday in New York City before leaving America. The Rev. Huio Kin, a Chinese pastor, phoned Mr. Wu and asked him to attend church service. Mr. Wu replied: "When I was a boy in China I was acquainted with some Christian people and thought highly of Christianity. When I was appointed to America, I decided that I wanted to throw in my lot with Christian people there, and made up my mind that I would accept the first invitation that was given me to attend a Christian service." Then after a moment's pause, he added: "This is the first invitation I have had!"— *Christian Herald.*

Life—Renewed.

The best made road wants looking after if it is to be kept in repair. What would become of a railway that had no surfacemen and platelayers going along the line and noticing whether anything was amiss? I remember once seeing a bit of an old Roman road; the lava rocks were there, but for want of care, here a young sapling had grown up between two of them and had driven them apart, there were many split by the frost; here was a great ugly gap full of mud, and the whole thing ended in a jungle. How shall a man keep his road in repair? "By taking heed thereto." Things that are left to go anyhow in this world have a strange knack of going one how. You do not need anything else than negligence to ensure that things will come to grief.—A. MACLAREN.

Lingering—Folly of.

When a man hath to go over a river though he ride once and again into the water and come out, saying, I fear it is too deep for me, yet, considering that there is no other way for him, he resolves to venture, for, saith he, the longer I stay the higher the waters will rise, and there is no other way for me— I must go through at the last, why not at the first? And so he ventures through.

Opportunities,—Laziness and.

The Russians have a fable about a miller who was too lazy to repair the leak in his dyke, through which the water escaped which should have turned his mill, but who flies into a passion with his fowls and kills them because he catches them drinking the water. So men lose the opportunities of life, and salvation, let them all slip by one by one, and then lay the blame upon some insignificant thing, and quarrel with themselves and the world about that, as if it were a matter of vital importance.—B.

Opportunity—Lost.

It is said if you take one of a migratory flock of birds out of the line which the God-given instinct has formed and is guiding to its distant home, and cage it behind iron bars, it will beat its wings against the cage in its frantic efforts to rise and go on its journey. But let the season pass in which birds migrate, then open the cage; your bird will not go now. You may take it in your hand and toss it high into the air; it will be of no use; the instinct for motion has passed; the bird returns heavily to the same spot. So decisions for Christ may be delayed until there is no desire to be His.—*The Christian Endeavor World.*

Procrastinate.

Many persons come to the right point in conversion; but they never shove off. I question them about their state, and I find all as it should be; but they are waiting for something, they know not what; standing still in thought and feeling.—BEECHER.

Procrastination,—Cause of.

Philidas purposely invited the chiefs of the oligarchy and the Spartan commanders to a magnificent supper, where he promised to regale his guests with the company of some of the handsomest of the Theban courtesans. While the guests, warm with wine, eagerly called for the introduction of the ladies, a courtier arrived from Athens and brought a letter to Archias, the chief governor, desiring it to be read as containing important business (news of the plot). "This is no time," said the voluptuary, "to trouble us with business; we shall consider of that to-morrow." Meantime Pleopidas and his companions, dressed in female attire, entered the hall, and each drawing a dagger from under his robe, massacred the governor and the whole of the Spartan officers before they had time to stand upon their defense.—TYTLER.

Procrastination—Origin of.

A minister of the gospel determined on one occasion to preach on the text, "Now is the accepted time; now is the day of salvation." Whilst in his study, thinking, he fell asleep, and dreamed that he was carried into hell, and set down in the midst of a conclave of lost spirits. They were assembled to devise means whereby they might get at the souls of men. One rose, and said, "I will go to the earth, and tell men that the Bible is all a fable, that it is not divinely appointed of God." "No, that would not do. Another said, "Let me go: I will tell men that there is no God, no Saviour, no heaven, no hell"; and at the last words a fiendish smile lighted upon all their countenances. "No, that will not do: we cannot make men believe that." Suddenly one arose, and with a wise mien, like the serpent of old, suggested, "No: I will journey to the world of men, and tell them that there is a God, that there is a Saviour, that there is a heaven,—yes, and a hell too,—but I'll tell them there is no hurry; to-morrow will do, it will be 'even as to-day.' " And they sent him.—*Biblical Treasury.*

The Danger of Delay.

"Serious things to-morrow," said a distinguished individual against whose life a plot was laid. One of the confederates, relenting, had sent a notice of the plot by a messenger who had particular instructions to deliver it personally, and to state that the letter must be read immediately as it was on a very serious matter. The messenger, however, found the person against whose life the plot was laid in the midst of a convivial feast. The letter and message were both faithfully delivered; but the man of mirth and wine laid it aside, saying, "Serious things to-morrow!" The morrow he never saw, for that night the assassin plunged the deadly weapon into his heart. So many put away from them the serious warnings of the gospel, and perish in their sins.

The Folly of Lingering.

When a man hath to go over a river, though he ride once and again into the water and come out, saying, I fear it is too deep for me, yet, considering that there is no other way for him, he resolves to venture, for, saith he, the longer I stay the higher the waters will rise, and there is no other way for me—I must go through at the last, and why not at the first? And so he ventures through. Thus it is with you. You say, "Oh, but my heart is not humbled; oh, but I am a great sinner; and should I venture upon Jesus Christ?" Will this heart be more humbled by keeping from Jesus Christ, and wilt thou be less a sinner by keeping from Him? No, certainly, for the longer you stay from Christ, the harder it will be to venture on Him at the last.—W. Bridge.

Time—None to Lose.

The poor needle-woman with her inch of candle has work to finish. See how her fingers fly, for she fears lest she should be left in darkness, and her work undone.—C. H. Spurgeon.

REPENTANCE

Conviction and Repentance.

Conviction is not repentance. It is one thing to be awakened at five o'clock in the morning and it is another thing to get up.—*The Christian Endeavor World.*

Penitence and Pardon.

Across the river Zambesi, below Victoria Falls, is a bridge spanning the widest chasm and overlooking the most terrible turmoil of waters to be seen on any river in the world. That bridge was made by building out an arm from either shore, and uniting the two outstretched arms in the center over the roaring stream; neither could have reached the opposite bank by itself; the two were needed to meet each other. Penitence and pardon form the bridge across the tumultuous stream and those stupendous falls which seem to separate the soul from God. Pardon without penitence is impossible, and penitence without pardon is useless.—R. F. HORTON.

Repentance—Continual.

There was once at Westminster School a singularly innocent boy whose name was Philip Henry. Though he was a Nonconformist the stern royalist headmaster, Dr. Busby, loved him, and severe as he was he never chastised him but once, and then with the words, "And thou, too, my child." A holier boy, a holier man, never lived. A contemporary said of him, "Should angels come from heaven it is my sense they would not be heard with greater reverence. We praise all virtues in admiring him." Yet when Philip Henry was far advanced in years a young man said to him, "Mr. Henry, how long do you mean to go on repenting?" "Sir," he meekly answered, "I hope to carry my repentance to the very gates of heaven."—*Ibid.*

Repentance,—Death-Bed.

Do not trust a death-bed repentance, my brother. I have stood by many a death-bed, and few indeed have there been where I could have believed that the man was in a condition physically (to say nothing of anything else) clearly to see and grasp the message of the gospel. I know that God's mercy is boundless. I know that a man, going—swept down that great Niagara—if, before his little skiff tilts over into the awful rapids, he can make one great bound with all his strength, and reach the solid ground—I know he may be saved. It is an awful risk to run. A moment's miscalculation, and skiff and voyager alike are whelming in the green chaos below, and come up mangled into nothing, far away down yonder upon the white turbulent foam. "One was saved upon the cross," as the old divines used to tell us, "that none might despair; and only one that none might presume."—MACLAREN.

Repentance—Death-Bed.

Often it is said of the penitent thief on the cross that one such case is recorded in the Scripture, that none may despair of repentance on a death-bed; and but one, that none may presume. It is like crossing Niagara over the rapids on a tightrope. One Blondin out of forty millions may have done it, and reached the hither shore in safety; but would you or I risk it for that? —PROFESSOR PHELPS.

REGENERATION

Born Again.

Michael Angelo carved his celebrated statue of David from a block of marble which had received so deep an indentation as to be quite unserviceable under a less daring chisel. So Christ deals with humanity. No other hand but his could shape the saint, who is to stand faultless at last before the presence of the glory of God, out of man as we see him in the world around us. —B.

Cleansing—Divine.

Once, when in Leicester, I was paying parochial calls, and dropped in on a washerwoman who had just got out a line of clothes. I congratulated my friend because they looked so white. So, very much encouraged by her pastor's kind words, she asked him to have a cup of tea, and we sat down. While we were taking the tea the sky clouded, and there was a snowstorm, and as I came out the white snow lay everywhere, and I said to her: "Your washing does not look quite as clean as it did." "Ah," she said, "the washing is right enough, but what can stand against God Almighty's white?"—F. B. Meyer.

Converts—Man's.

A man lying drunk was accosted by Dr. Kidd, who asked him what he was and why he was lying there. "Do you not know me, Doctor? I am one o' your converts," was the reply. "Very like my handiwork," rejoined the Doctor; "for if God had converted you, you wouldn't be where you are."—James Stark.

Cure—Internal.

You might as well try to cure smallpox by scenery as to try to save the world by improvement of environment.—*The Christian Observer.*

Immediate Obedience.

As when a general commands his army to march, if, then, the soldiers should stand upon terms, and refuse to go except they have better clothes, their pay in hand, or the like, and then they will march;—this would not show them an obedient, disciplined army; but if, at the reading of their orders, they presently break up their quarters, and set forth, though it be midnight when the command come, and they without money, or clothes on their backs, leaving the whole care of themselves for these things to their general, and they only attend how they may best fulfill his commands, —these may be said to march in obedience.—H. G. Salter.

Life—Aim of.

I can understand how a man may go to burn down a house or a city wickedly, and yet, on the march, help up a companion if he falls down, give him food if he is hungry, and do a thousand kind acts. But the wrong thing for which he is marching is not modified by these incidental kindnesses on the road. You may have a great many moralities, a great many excellent traits; and yet, if the great end of your life is not divine, is not tending towards immortality, you are under condemnation.—H. W. Beecher.

Man—Reform of.

The Sailor's Home, in Liverpool, was once on fire in the dead of the night, and a great cry of "Fire!" was raised. When the people assembled they saw in the upper stories some men crying for help.

187

The fire escape did not nearly reach where the men were. A long ladder was brought and put against the burning building; but it was too short. A British sailor in the crowd, seeing the state of affairs, is said to have rushed up the ladder, balanced himself on the uppermost round with his foot, and seized the window-sill with his hands, saying: "Quick men, scramble over my body, on the ladder, and down you go." One by one the men came down until all were saved, and then the sailor came down, his face burned, his hair singed, and his fingers blistered; but he had saved the men. That ladder went a long way; but before the men could be saved it needed the length of a man. Your franchise, your land reform, your temperance reform go a long way, but for the uplifting of men, to give men that peace of mind that passeth knowledge, they need the length of a man—the man Christ Jesus whom we preach.—CHARLES LEACH.

New Birth.

"Socialism," declared a street orator, "can put a new coat on a man!" "Jesus Christ," cried a voice in the crowd, "can put a new man in the coat, and that is better still!"—*Onward.*

New Birth,—Necessity of.

A man has bought a farm, and he finds on that farm an old pump. He goes to the pump and begins to pump. And a person comes to him and says, "Look here, my friend, you do not want to use that water. The man that lived here before, he used that water, and it poisoned him and his wife and his children—the water did." "Is that so?" says the man. "Well, I will soon make that right. I will find a remedy." And he goes and gets some paint, and

he paints up the pump, putties up all the holes, and fills up the cracks in it, and has got a fine-looking pump. And he says, "No I am sure it is all right." You would say, "What a fool, to go and paint the pump when the water is bad!" But that is what sinners are up to. They are trying to paint up the old pump when the water is bad. It was a new well he wanted. When he dug a new well it was all right. Make the fountain good, and the stream will be good. Instead of painting the pump and making new resolutions, my friend, stop it, and ask God to give you a new heart. —MOODY.

New Birth—Necessity of.

Sin is a dreadful, positive, malignant thing. What the world in its worst part needs is not to be developed, but to be destroyed. Any other talk about it is shallow and mischievous folly. The only question is about the best method and means of destruction. Let the sharp surgeon's knife do its terrible work, let it cut deep and separate as well and thoroughly as it can, the false from the true, the corrupt from the uncorrupt; it can never dissect away the very principle of corruption which is in the substance of the blood itself. Nothing but a new reinforcement of health can accomplish that.—PHILLIPS BROOKS.

Punishment—Failure of.

It might be thought that one such flood as this would keep the world in order for ever, whereas men now doubt whether there ever was such a flood, and repeat all the sins of which the age of Noah was guilty. You would think that to see a man hanged would put an end to ruffianism for ever, whereas history goes to show that within the very shadow of the gallows men hatch the most detestable and alarming crimes. Set it down as a fact that punishment, though necessary, even in its severest forms can never regenerate the heart of man.—Joseph Parker.

Regeneration—Necessity of.

None go to heaven but they that are made meet for it. As it was with Solomon's temple, so it is with the temple above. It was "built of stone, made ready before it was brought thither," namely of "living stones, wrought for the self-same thing"; for they cannot be laid in that glorious building just as they came out of the quarry of depraved nature. Jewels of gold are not meet for service, and far less jewels of glory for unrenewed sinners. Beggars in their rags are not meet for kings' houses, nor sinners to "enter into the king's palace," without the "raiment of needlework." What wise man would bring fish out of water to feed on his meadows? or send his oxen to feed in the sea? Even as little are the unregenerated meet for heaven, or is heaven meet for them.—Thomas Boston.

RELIGION

Foundations of Sand.

Reports that the foundations of Grant's tomb, on Riverside Drive, have been undermined by water, that the magnificent mausoleum is in danger of collapse, are to be thoroughly investigated by an official commission. Attention has been called to the fact that frequent crackings of the pavement around the tomb, and breaking off of parts of the steps, and a noticeable settling of the entire structure, are to be plainly seen. It is a well known fact that the tomb is not built on a rock, but is reared on a sandy mound.

Unless character is built upon the foundation of religious principles, it will not only totter, but eventually fall. This incident strongly suggests the old story of the house that was built upon the sand.

Godliness—Genius for.

Thoreau spoke of men whose pretence to be Christian was ridiculous, for they had no genius for it. Matthew Arnold said of John Wesley that he had "a genius for godliness." But nothing can be more misleading than to use such terms as these. They are a distinct denial of Christ's great truth that God's revelation of grace is made not to the wise and prudent, but to babes. There have been men of a real genius for morality, but there is no such thing as a genius for religion. The most reckless and godless atheism, about whom Thoreau and Matthew Arnold would say that he had a genius for devilry, has become a splendid and glorious saint. Wherever there is a soul there is a genius for godliness. But that soul must have come nakedly and openly under the power of God. Then and not till then does it pass into Christ's society.—W. M. Clow.

Kingdom—Unable to Stop the.

An acquaintance met Horace Greeley one day, and said: "Mr. Greeley, I have stopped your paper." "Have you?" said the editor. "That's too bad," and he went his way. The next morning Mr. Greeley met the man again, and said, "I thought you had stopped the Tribune?" "So I did." "Then there must be some mistake," said Mr. Greeley, "for I just came from the office and the presses were running, the clerks were as busy as ever, the compositors were hard at work, and the business was going on the same as yesterday and the day before." "Oh," ejaculated the man, "I didn't mean I had stopped the paper. I stopped my copy of it, because I didn't like your editorials." "Oh, is that all? It wasn't worth taking my time to tell me such a trifle as that." We may think, if we don't like God's plan or take his views, that if we withdraw ourselves it is all going to cease; but "of the increase of his government and of peace there shall be no end."—*The Success.*

No Religion.

The worst kind of religion is no religion at all, and these men living in ease and luxury, indulging themselves in the amusement of going without religion, may be thankful that they live in lands where the gospel they neglect has tamed the beastliness and ferocity of the men, who, but for Christianity, might long ago have eaten their carcasses like the South Sea Islanders.

I fear that when we indulge ourselves in the amusement of going without a religion, we are not, perhaps, aware how much we are sustained at present by an enormous mass all about us of religious feeling and religious convictions; so that, whatever it may be safe for us to think—for us who have had great advantages, and have been brought up in such a way that a certain moral direction has been given to our character—I do not know what would become of the less favored classes of mankind if they undertook to play the same game.—JAMES RUSSELL LOWELL.

Religious Problems.

Matthew Arnold well expressed the modern spirit when he wrote: "An age which has its face towards the future, and in which men are full of plans for the welfare of the world, is not an age that has lost its faith. Its temper of mind is constructive; it is eager for new institutions, keen for new ideas, and has already a half-belief in a future in which all things will be new." With these hopeful words ringing in our ears, let us attempt to face the religious problems of the present age.—G. F. TERRY.

Religion—Attractive.

At an exhibition of pictures it was discovered that a masterpiece by a famous artist was quite unnoticed because it was poorly framed and hung in a shadowed corner very high. The man in charge reframed and rehung the picture, and then everybody acknowledged its beauty. We are to do with the Christian religion what that man did with the picture—present it in the best light and give it a chance to be known. Those who look upon Church work and Christian duties as burdens to be shirked, if possible, and those who in bitterness criticize the minister and Christian people and their work are not an example of adorning the doctrine.

Religion—Constancy of.

I have read of a waterfall in a nobleman's garden, beautiful in its construction, but the water was never turned on unless his lordship was there. That is like much of the religion existing in the present age. It is only turned on when there is some one to see and applaud. Our service must not be kept for mere effect and display.—R. VENTING.

Religion—Half Way.

It is said of Redwald, King of the East Saxons, that he had in the same church one altar for the Christian religion and another altar for the service of the devil; and of Rufus that he painted God on one side of his shield, the devil on the other side, with this inscription: "I am ready for either." This is the attitude and temper of thousands to-day. They have just enough religion to rob them of the pleasures of the world and make them miserable. They sail their life-boat along the coast of the world, encountering its storms and risking destruction on its rocks, instead of sailing out heroically and joyfully on the boundless ocean of God's unspeakable love. —*The Sunday School Chronicle.*

Religion—No Time For.

"Sir," said one to an evangelist, "I have not time to serve God." Prompt and pertinent was the reply —"God wants no more of your time to serve Him than that which you give to serve the devil."—JOHN GUTHRIE.

Religion—Testing.

A jeweler gives, as one of his surest tests for diamonds, the "water test." He says: "An imitation diamond is never so brilliant as a genuine stone. If your eye is not experienced enough to detect the difference, a simple test is to place the stone under water. The imitation diamond is practically extinguished, while a genuine diamond sparkles even under water, and is distinctly visible. If you place a genuine stone beside an imitation under water, the contrast will be apparent to the least experienced eye." Many seem confident of their faith so long as they have no trials, but when the waters of sorrow overflow them, their faith loses its brilliancy; it is then that true servants of God, like Job, shine forth as genuine jewels of the king.—*Christian Age*.

Religion—Understanding.

"One should think," said a friend to the celebrated Dr. Samuel Johnson, "that sickness and the view of death would make men more religious." "Sir," replied Johnson, "they do not know how to go to work about it. A man who has never had religion before, no more grows religious when he is sick than a man who has never learned figures can count when he has need of calculation."

Voice of Common Sense.

Napoleon, making a forced march accompanied by his chiefs of staff, came to a river and asked the engineer how wide it was. The officer explained that his instruments had not yet come to the front. The emperor asked him again, rather sharply, for the width of the river. The officer then brought his military cap to the level of his eyes and marked where the line of vision fell on the opposite bank; fixing his attention on that distance he turned carefully and marked where that line fell on the bank where they were standing; he stepped the distance off and gave the emperor the width of the river. Thus in the absence of instruments of precision, he fell back on common sense. In the absence of more stirring commanding voices, let us listen to the voice of our own common sense on this matter of religion.—R. MACKENZIE.

Wheelbarrow Religion.

Richard Baxter said a good thing when he said of some who lived in his day, that they had a "wheelbarrow religion." They "went when they were shoved."

REWARD

Crown—Obtaining a.

It is recorded in history that Bernadotte, one of the generals of Napoleon, became a Lutheran in order that he might become King of Sweden. A fellow-officer of Bernadotte's became a Christian, and some of his companion soldiers began to tease him on account of his change. He answered, "I have done no more than Bernadotte, who has become a Lutheran." "Yes," they replied, "but he became so to obtain a crown." "My motive is the same," said the officer, "we differ only as to the place. The object of Bernadotte was to obtain a crown in Sweden; mine is to obtain a crown in heaven."—J. AITCHISON.

Encouragement—Example of.

The Emperor of Rome, one day during the childhood of Galba, took him by the chin, and said, "Thou, Galba, shalt one day sit upon a throne." A like promise from a higher power has every true Christian.

Instant in Season.

Charles M. Schwab, the steel magnate, once said: "I know a young New York fellow who has built for himself a big business. He used to be a poorly paid clerk in a department store. One rainy day, when customers were few, the clerks had gathered in a bunch to discuss baseball. A woman came into the store wet and disheveled. The baseball fans did not disband; but this young fellow stepped out of the circle and walked over to the woman. 'What can I show you, madam?' he asked courteously. She told him. He got the article promptly, laid it before her, and explained its merits smilingly and intelligently. In short, he treated the woman just as his employer would have treated her under similar circumstances.

"When the woman left she asked for his card. Later the firm received a letter from a woman ordering complete furnishings for a great estate in Scotland. 'I want one of your men, Mr.——,' she wrote, 'to supervise the furnishing personally.' The name she mentioned was that of the clerk who had been courteous. 'But, madam,' wrote the head of the firm in response, 'this man is one of our youngest and most inexperienced clerks. Hadn't we better send Mr. ——?' 'I want this young man and no other,' wrote the woman. 'Large orders impose their own conditions.' So our courteous young clerk was sent across the Atlantic to direct the furnishing of a great Scotch palace. His customer that rainy day had been Mrs. Andrew Carnegie. The estate was Skibo Castle."

Memory—the Best.

Forget each kindness that you do
　As soon as you have done it;
Forget the praise that falls to you
　The moment you have won it;
Forget the slander that you hear
　Before you can repeat it;
Forget each slight, each spite, each sneer,
　Wherever you may meet it.

Remember every kindness done
　To you whate'er its measure;
Remember praise by others won
　And pass it on with pleasure;
Remember every promise made
　And keep it to the letter;
Remember those who lend you aid
　And be a grateful debtor.

Remember all the happiness
　That comes your way in living;
Forget each worry and distress,
　Be hopeful and forgiving;

193

Remember good, remember truth,
Remember heaven's above you,
And you will find, through age and
    youth,
That many hearts will love you.

Old Age—Fruit of.

A young man came to a man of
ninety years of age and said to
him, "How have you made out to
live so long and be so well?" The
old man took the youngster to an
orchard, and, pointing to some large
trees full of apples, said, "I planted
these trees when I was a boy, and
do you wonder that now I am permitted to gather the fruit of them?"
We gather in old age what we plant
in our youth. Sow to the wind and
we reap the whirlwind. Plant in
early life the right kind of a Christian character, and you will eat
luscious fruit in old age, and gather
these harvest apples in eternity.—
Dr. Talmadge.

Reward—Royal.

It is said that the Emperor
Napoleon III. was desirous of bestowing the cross of the Legion of
Honor upon Rosa Bonheur, the
eminent artist, but hesitated, fearing the popular judgment might
condemn the giving of it to a
woman. Leaving home in the summer of 1865 for an excursion, he left
the empress as Regent. From the
imperial residence at Fontainebleau
it was only a short drive to By.
The countersign at the gate was
forced, and unannounced the empress entered the studio where Rosa
was at work. She rose to receive
her visitor, who threw her arms
about her neck and kissed her. It
was only a short interview. The
imperial vision had departed, the
rumble of the carriage and the
crack of the outriders' whips were
lost in the distance. Then, and not
till then, did the artist discover that
as the empress had given the kiss,
she had pinned upon her blouse the
cross of the Legion of Honor!

Work—the End Crowns.

Tennyson was in his 81st year
when he wrote "Crossing the Bar."
He showed the poem to his son,
who exclaimed, "That is the crown
of your life's work." "It came in a
moment," was the aged poet's reply.
Yes, but however instantaneous was
the inspiration, the hymn had behind it a lifetime of careful, painstaking, even fastidious work.

Serving by Waiting.

The Master knows; He can but see
How willingly, how joyfully
I would within His vineyard stay
To bear the burden of the day,
And yet He bids me stand apart
With folded hands and longing
    heart.
I see at morn the happy throng
Pass by my door with jest and song.
They seem so glad, they seem so
    gay,
So ready for the busy day.

And when at eve they homeward go
Sometimes with weary steps and
    slow,
But laden with the sweet new wine,
And purple clusters of the vine,
And precious sheaves of golden
    grain
To recompense their toil and pain;
But that the Lord doth choose for
    me,
I fain within their ranks would be.

Yet though I can but hope and wait,
I am not sad or desolate.
For every day with bounty free
The Master bringeth gifts to me.
From out His life there seems to
    shine
A wondrous glory into mine.

My life! how dark and how unclean,
How poor and fruitless has it been.
But sure the seed He planted there
That should have grown so tall and
　　fair
Must now, at last, begin to spring
Beneath such heavenly nourishing.

And if, perchance, I fail to see
The thought of God concerning me,
I leave in peace my fallow field
Till love divine shall make it yield.
And when at last the corn and wine
Of all His harvests shall be mine,
Then shall I know, or soon, or late,
They also serve who stand and wait.

Waiting.

Serene I fold my hands and wait,
　　Nor care for wind, nor tide, nor
　　　sea;
I rave no more 'gainst time or fate,
　　For lo! my own shall come to me.

I stay my haste, I make delays,
　　For what avails this eager pace?

I stand amid the eternal ways,
　　And what is mine shall know my
　　　face.

Asleep, awake, by night or day,
　　The friends I seek are seeking me;
No wind can drive my bark astray,
　　Nor change the tide of destiny.

What matter if I stand alone?
　　I wait with joy the coming years;
My heart shall reap where it hath
　　sown,
　　And garner up its fruits of tears.

The waters know their own, and draw
　　The brook that springs in yonder
　　　heights;
So flows the good with equal law
　　Unto the soul of pure delights.

The stars come nightly to the sky;
　　The tidal wave unto the sea;
Nor time, nor space, nor deep, nor
　　high,
　　Can keep my own away from me.

　　　　　　　　—JOHN BURROUGHS.

Good Deeds Exempt.

A Jew who had done a worthy act on the Sabbath, which others refused to do, was reproached for it, and replied, "Good deeds have no Sabbath."—*Christian Herald.*

Sabbath Day Holy.

Dr. Charles R. Brown, in the Congregationalist says:

When I was a pastor in Boston twenty-five years ago one of my deacons had a draying business. One Saturday afternoon a customer came requesting that teams and men be furnished to haul to the cold storage warehouse on Sunday morning a cargo of fish which would arrive that night. The deacon declined the business on the ground that they did not work on Sunday. But the fish dealer insisted that the fish would spoil and he would thereby incur loss unless the cargo was moved on Sunday forenoon.

The deacon finally consented, saying, "I will not ask my men to work, but my two sons and I will come over and do it for you ourselves." The dealer was very grateful and next morning the deacon was absent from his accustomed place in Winthrop church. When the end of the month came the fish dealer received his bill for draying during the preceding thirty days but he noticed that no charge had been made for hauling that particular cargo of fish. When he called to pay the bill he called the attention of the firm to this omission. Then our good Deacon Wiley said: "There is no charge for that. We do not do business on Sunday. My sons and I did it for you as an act of accommodation to save the food."

If no Sunday labor were paid for it would change the Sunday problem.

Sabbath, Appointed of God.

The Governor Turnusrupis once asked Rabbi Akiba, "What is this day you call the Sabbath more than any other day?" The Rabbi responded, "What art thou more than any other person?" "I am superior to others," replied he, "because the Emperor has appointed me governor over them." Then said Akiba, "The Lord our God, who is greater than your Emperor, has appointed the Sabbath-day to be holier than the other days."—TALMUD.

Sabbath—Blessing of the.

A Jewish rabbi's parable tells of seven brothers who lived together. Six worked and the seventh cared for the house, having the meals ready and the house bright for his brothers in the evening. But the six said that the seventh must work, too. So in the evening they returned home and found the house dark and no meal prepared. Then they saw how foolish they had been, and quickly restored the old way. The Sabbath is a day among the seven which provides light, comfort, and good for the others. If it is driven out to work, the other days will all miss its blessing.—J. R. MILLER.

Sabbath—Gain of.

Lord Hatherley, who rose to be Lord High Chancellor of England, testified, at a public meeting in Westminster, that many lawyers who were in the habit of Sunday study or practice of law have failed in mind and body—not a few of them becoming inmates of lunatic asylums; and that, within his experience, the successful and long-living lawyers are those who, like himself and Lords Cairns and Selborne, have always remembered the

Sabbath Day to keep it holy. If you wish to get the full good of your mind, you will give it the rest which its Creator indicates; you will give it sleep; you will give it the Sabbath. The mind is not an artesian well, but a land-spring. The supply is limited. If you pump continually, the water will grow turbid; and if, after it grows turbid, you continue to work it, you will not increase the quantity, and you will spoil the pump. There is a difference of intellectual activity, but the most powerful mind is a land-spring after all; and those who wish to preserve their thoughts fresh, pure, and pellucid, will put on the Sabbath padlock. In the subsequent clearness of their views, in the calmness of their judgment, and in the free and copious flow of ideas, they find their speedy recompense.

Sabbath—Need of.

Lord Macaulay, in his speech before the House of Commons on the Ten Hours' Bill, spoke thus: "The natural difference between Campania and Spitzbergen is trifling when compared with the difference between a country inhabited by men full of mental and bodily vigor, and a country inhabited by men sunk in bodily and mental decrepitude. Therefore it is we are not poorer, but richer, because we have, through many ages, rested from our labors one day in seven. That day is not lost. While industry is suspended, while the plow lies in the furrow, while the Exchange is silent, while no smoke ascends from the factory, a process is going on quite as important to the wealth of nations as any process which is performed on more busy days. Man, the machine of machines—the machine compared with which all the contrivances of the Watts and the Ark-

wrights are worthless—is repairing and winding up, so that he returns to his labors on the Monday with clearer intellect, with livelier spirits, with renewed corporeal vigor."—G. D. BOARDMAN.

Sabbath, Seeing on the.

When a gentleman was inspecting a house in Newcastle, with a view to hiring it as a residence, the landlord took him to the upper window, expatiated on the extensive prospect, and added, "You can see Durham Cathedral from this window on a Sunday." "Why on a Sunday above any other day?" inquired our friend, with some degree of surprise. The reply was conclusive enough. "Because on that day there is no smoke from those tall chimneys." Blessed is the Sabbath to us, when the earth-smoke of care and turmoil no longer beclouds our view; then can our souls full often behold the goodly land and the city of the New Jerusalem.—SPURGEON.

The Pilgrim's Sabbath.

The "Mayflower," a name now immortal, had crossed the ocean. It had borne its hundred passengers over the vast deep, and after a perilous voyage had reached the bleak shores of New England, in the beginning of winter. The spot which was to furnish a home and a burial-place was now to be selected. The shallop was unshipped, but needed repairs, and sixteen weary days elapsed before it was then sent out, with some half a dozen pilgrims, to find a suitable place where to land. The spray of the sea, says the historian, froze on them, and made their clothes like coats of iron. Five days they wandered about, searching in vain for a suitable landing-place. A storm came on; the snow and the rain fell; the sea swelled; the rudder broke; the mast and the sail fell overboard. In this storm and cold, without a tent, a house, or the shelter of a rock, the Christian Sabbath approached, the day which they regarded as holy unto God; a day on which they were not to "do any work." What should be done? As the evening before the Sabbath drew on they pushed over the surf, entered a fair sound, sheltered themselves under the lee of a rise of land, kindled a fire, and on that little island they spent the day in the solemn worship of their Maker. On the next day their feet touched the rock, now sacred as the place of the landing of the pilgrims. Nothing more strikingly marks the character of this people than this act, and I do not know that I could refer to a better illustration, even in their history, showing that theirs was the religion of principle, and that this religion made them what they were.—BARNES.

SACRIFICE

Amputation Needed.

A man who suffered from a grievance, and who could talk of little else, was one day having a chat with a doctor. "I suppose your experience tells you it is possible to cure almost anything by careful nursing?" he asked. The doctor, who had a deep sense of humor, looked quickly at his questioner. "One thing can never be cured by nursing," he said emphatically. "What might that be?" "A grievance," said the doctor, with a laugh.—*The (London) Christian Herald.*

Deliverance Through Sacrifice.

On the 10th of June, 1770, the town of Port-au-Prince, in Hayti, was utterly overthrown by a dreadful earthquake. From one of the fallen houses the inmates had fled except a negro woman, the nurse of her master's infant child. She would not desert her charge, though the walls were even then giving way. Rushing to its bed-side, she stretched forth her arms to enfold it. The building rocked to its foundation; the roof fell in. Did it crush the hapless pair? The heavy fragments fell indeed upon the woman, but the infant escaped unharmed: for its noble protectress extended her bended form across the body, and, at the sacrifice of her own life, preserved her charge from destruction.

Healing—Permanent.

If a person with a deadly disease were told that he could go to a hospital and there come under the treatment of the greatest physician in the world, who had never lost a patient suffering from that disease; that all the expenses would be paid, and the treatment would be without personal suffering or risk, and he could count on being discharged from the hospital with a complete and permanent cure, would such a patient say that this offer, and this experience if he went through it, was a great hardship? Or would he look back on that hospital experience with unspeakable gratitude as the most blessed time of his life? That is a faint and inadequate suggestion of what the cross is to the Christian.—*Sunday School Times.*

Life in Renunciation.

Nearly half a century after *Sartor Resartus* was written, Carlyle addressed the students of Edinburgh University as their Lord Rector, and then again, after having tested its worth in a life of heroic labor, he deliberately referred to Goethe's interpretation of the moral significance of Christianity and doctrine of the reverence due by man to his God, to his brethren, and to himself, as what he would rather have written than any other passage in recent literature. "It is only with renunciation," says the great poet and philosopher, who is supposed to have been hewn from ice, and to have had no object in life but to polish himself up, so that the ice might show to advantage, "it is only with renunciation that life, properly speaking, can be said to begin. —P. Bayne.

Power of the Cross.

The other night a friend of mine witnessed a drunken brawl. There was a man there who continued in the brawl, and his wife came out of the crowd and said: "I will go and fetch baby to him; that will bring him out if anything will." Ah! she was a philosopher, though she did not know it. She wanted to get to the deepest part of the man's nature. She did not talk of policemen and prison; she wanted to bring the innocent one before him, as much as to say, "Will you make a thorny couch for this little one to lie upon? Will you forge a dagger with which to pierce this little one's heart?" And in a measure she came in the spirit of the gospel; for the gospel comes to make us hate sin by showing that another suffered and died for it.— C. VINCE.

Sacrifice—Fragrant.

A king once planted in his garden a beautiful rose-tree, and bade his gardener so tend and train it as to make its flowers the richest and loveliest possible. The tree grew and flourished, and year by year blushed into blossoms of manifold beauty. But it sent out so many shoots, formed so many buds, that its very fertility threatened to injure the quality of its flowers. So the gardener removed the shoots, pruned away the buds, till the tree seemed to bleed all over in loss and pain; but the wounds healed, the sap and strength ran up to those buds that were spared, and when the season of ripeness was come, the roses were lovelier and sweeter than ever—most meet of all in the garden to be carried into the palace of the great king, to fill its galleries and chambers with delicious and grateful fragrance.

Sacrifice—Progress by.

When upon one occasion the Emperor Justinian was about to surrender to the clamorous claims and the harsh and violent demands of the mob, his wife Theodora is represented to have said to him that it was better to meet and go down to death as the avowed ruler of all than purchase life for a little while by

yielding to the unworthy exactions of the unrighteous few; and empire, she tells him, "is the best winding-sheet." Empire, universal empire, throughout all the world, throughout all the ages, is the winding-sheet of Jesus Christ. Victorious in the wilderness, victorious in Gethsemane, before that worldly-minded Governor in the judgment hall, victorious on the Cross, because His eye looked not upon the unworthy demands of the immediate occasion, but upon the everlasting years, upon all future times, and wrapped around in the winding-sheet of empire does He die.—D. H. GREER.

"Shadow of the Cross."

Those who have seen Holman Hunt's "Shadow of the Cross," will remember how Mary is employed when she gets the first awful premonition of what her Child's fate is to be. She is engaged—so the painter fancies her—looking into a coffer, where the gifts of the wise men are preserved, feasting her eyes on the beautiful crowns and bracelets and jewels, so prophetic, as she thinks, of what her Son's afterdestiny is to be. And then she turns, and what a contrast! There, in shadow on the wall, imprinted by the western light, she sees her Son stretched on a cross! What a sight for a mother to see! As she looks, the solemn, mysterious words of Simeon flash through her heart, "Yea and a sword shall pierce through thine own soul." Against that awful destiny her mother's heart rises up in arms, and it was, I believe, this love, this misguided love, that led her to seek to keep back her Child from His mission, and point Him into a path of glory, not of shame; of royalty, not of sacrifice; of a crown, not of a cross. —W. M. MACKAY.

Hero of the Race.

I saw them start, an eager throng
All young, and strong and fleet;
Joy lighted up their beaming eyes,
Hope sped their flying feet.
And one among them so excelled
In courage, strength and grace
That all men gazed, and smiled, and
  cried:
"The winner of the race."

The way was long, the way was
  hard;
The golden goal gleamed far
Above the deep and distant hills—
A shining pilot star.
On, on they sped, but while some
  fell,
Some faltered in their speed;
He upon whom all eyes were fixed
Still proudly kept the lead.

But ah! What folly! see, he stops
To raise a fallen child,
To place it out of danger's way
With kiss and warning mild.
A fainting comrade claims his care,
Once more he turns aside;
Then stays his strong young steps
  to be
A feeble woman's guide.

And so wherever duty calls,
Of sorrow or distress,
He leaves his chosen path to aid,
To comfort and to bless.
Though man may pity, blame or
  scorn,
No envious pang may swell
The soul who yields for love the
  place
It might have won so well.

The race is o'er. Mid shouts and
  cheers
I saw the victors crowned;
Some wore fame's laurels, some
  love's flowers
Some brow's with gold were bound,
But all unknown unheeded stood—
Heaven's light upon his face,
With empty hands and uncrowned
  head,
The winner of the race.

SALVATION

Feeling in Salvation.

D. L. Moody told the story of a conversation he had with a man in Manchester. "Are you a Christian?" the evangelist had asked. "No, but I wish I were." Then Moody proceeded to quote passages from the Bible, but the man said they did not meet his case. "The fact is, I cannot feel that I am saved." "Was it Noah's feelings that saved him, or was it the ark?" asked Moody. The man thought a while, and then said, "Good-night, Mr. Moody, it's all settled."—*The Christian Herald.*

Lacking One Thing.

I have in my possession a watch, and by competent judges it is pronounced to be one of great excellence. Gold, chains, pivots, stones, are of the first order. Yet if it lacked *one thing*—the main-spring—it would be of no service to me, in the sense in which a watch is expected to serve, namely, recording the time of day. The mainspring is only "one thing," but that one thing is all-important to the value and usefulness of my watch.

No Safety in Our Works.

In the twenty-eighth year of the Emperor Tan Kwang, the rise of the river Yangtze was higher than it had been for a hundred years or more. The loss of property was incalculable. Old Doctor Tai, who well remembers the occurrence, gave me the account. "Were there many lives lost?" I asked. "Numbers," said he. "It was something like obtaining salvation from sin," he continued. "The rich, who had well-built houses, trusted to them, and went to the upper story, thinking themselves safe. But the flood increased. The foundations gave away; and the house to which they trusted, fell and buried them in its ruins, or in a watery grave. But the poor, knowing that their mud-built huts could not stand the rising flood, fled in time to the neighboring hills; and though they lost all, yet they themselves were saved."—S. Martin.

Salvation All of Grace.

Mr. McLaren and Mr. Gustart were ministers of the Tolbooth Church, Edinburgh. When Mr. McLaren was dying, Mr. Gustart paid him a visit, and put the question to him, "What are you doing, brother?" His answer was, "Doing! I'll tell you what I am doing, brother. I am gathering together all my prayers, all my sermons, all my good deeds, all my evil deeds; and I am going to throw them all overboard, and swim to glory on the plank of free grace."—E. Foster.

Salvation is for All.

I remember when the Master Street Hospital, in Philadelphia, was opened, during the war, a telegram came saying, "There will be three hundred wounded men to-night, be ready to look after them," and from my church went thirty men and women to look after the wounded. No one asked from whence they came; there was a wounded man, and the only question was, how to treat him the most gently. And when a soul comes to God, He does not ask where he came from. Healing is there for all his wounds, pardon for all his guilt.—Dr. Talmage.

Salvation Provided.

Here is an illustration of a man who was very much burdened with care on account of his soul, and who had this care cured by the salvation which Jesus provides. Many years ago there was a very celebrated preacher, whose name was the Rev. George Whitefield. He went traveling all over England and this country preaching the gospel, and did a great deal of good in this way. One day a brother of Mr. Whitefield's heard him preach. The sermon led him to see what a sinner he was, and he became very sorry on account of his sins. He was burdened with care because he thought his soul could not be saved; and for a long time it seemed as if he could get no relief from this burden. And the reason of it was that he was not willing to believe the word of Jesus. It is only in this way that we can be saved. When we read the promises of Jesus in the Bible, we must believe that He means just what he says. We must trust His word, and then we shall be saved. Well, one evening this brother of Mr. Whitefield was taking tea with the Countess of Huntingdon. This was an earnest Christian lady, who took a great interest in all good ministers, and the work they did for Jesus. She saw that the poor man was in great trouble of mind, and she tried to comfort him as they took their tea by talking to him about the great mercy of God to poor sinners through Jesus Christ. "Yes, my lady," said the sorrowful man, "I know what you say is true. The mercy of God is infinite. I am satisfied of this. But, ah! my friend, there is no mercy for me. I am a wretched sinner, a lost man." "I am glad to hear it, Mr. Whitefield," said Lady Huntingdon. "I am glad in my heart that you have found out that you are a lost man." He looked at her with great surprise. "What, my lady!" he exclaimed, "glad, did you say? glad at heart that I am a lost man?" "Why, certainly I am, Mr. Whitefield," said

she; "for you know, Jesus Christ came into the world 'to seek and to save them that are lost.' And if you feel that you are a lost man, why, you are just one of those that Jesus came to save." This remark had a great effect on Mr. Whitefield. He put down the cup of tea that he was drinking, and clapped his hands together, saying, "Thank God for that! Thank God for that!" He believed God's promise then. That cured his care. It took away his trouble. It saved his soul.—C. H. SPURGEON.

Salvation Rejected.

What would you think if there were to be an insurrection in a hospital, and sick man should conspire with sick man, and on a certain day they should rise up and reject the doctors and nurses? There they would be—sickness and disease within, and all the help without! Yet what is a hospital compared to this fever-ridden world, which goes swinging in pain and anguish through the centuries, where men say, "We have got rid of the Atonement, and we are rid of the Bible"? Yes, and you have rid yourselves of salvation.—BEECHER.

Salvation—Assurance of.

A theological student once called on Archibald Alexander in great distress of mind, doubting whether he had been converted. The old doctor encouraged him to open his mind. After he was through, the aged disciple, laying his hand on his head, said, "My young brother, you know what repentance is—what faith in Christ is. You think you once repented and once believed. Now don't fight your doubts; go it all over again. Repent now; believe in Christ—that's the way to have a consciousness of acceptance with God. I have to do both very often. Go to your room and give yourself to Christ this very moment, and let doubts go. If you have not been His disciple, be one now. Don't fight the devil on his own ground. Choose the ground of Christ's righteousness and atonement, and then fight him."

Salvation—Selling.

A Methodist layman visited a great city church during a business trip. After the service he congratulated the minister on his service and his sermon. "But," said the keen business man, "if you were my salesman I'd discharge you. You got my attention by your appearance, voice, and manner; your prayer, reading, and logical discourse aroused my interest; you warmed my heart with a desire for what you preached; and then you stopped, without asking me to do something about it! In business, the important thing is to get them to sign on the dotted line."—*Methodist Times.*

Salvation—the Most Wonderful.

When Gypsy Smith was holding a testimony meeting at one time, a man got up and said: "I have spent twenty years in prison for murder, but God has saved me." Another said: "I have been a drunkard for twenty years, and God has saved me." Another said: "I have been a coiner of counterfeit money, and the Lord has saved me." Then Gypsy Smith got up and said: "Men, listen. God has done wonders for you, but don't forget he did more for this gypsy boy than for all of you put together. He saved me before I got there."—*Sunday School Times.*

Salvation—Uttermost.

There is a story told of the great Dr. Doddridge. During his Northampton ministry an Irishman was convicted of sheep-stealing and, according to the cruel custom of the time, condemned to death. Doddridge did everything he could to save him, but in vain. When the man was being drawn in the death-cart to the place of execution, he asked that they should stop at Dr. Doddridge's house, and they did. Then he said: "Dr. Doddridge, every drop of my blood loves you, every vein of my heart loves you because you tried to save me." And how shall we carry ourselves to Christ, who died and lives to save us? Say to Him, "Shall I not love Thee back again for all the miracle of Divine love Thou has brought to me?" For He is able to save to the uttermost them that come unto God by Him, seeing He ever liveth to make intercession for us.—W. Robertson Nicoll.

Saved, by Destruction of Works.

As is well known, Sir Thomas Thornhill painted the inside of the cupola of St. Paul's cathedral. After having finished one of the compartments, he gradually retired backwards, to see how it looked at a distance. Intent on the painting, he had approached to the very edge of the scaffolding, and was in the utmost danger of falling from it, when a person, perceiving his situation, and fearing to alarm him by calling out, snatched up a brush and disfigured his painting. The artist sprang forward in great displeasure, but was soon impressed with gratitude, when he discovered the danger in which he had been placed, and saw that, by this way, his life had been preserved.

Saved—Almost.

In an October day a treacherous calm on the northern coast is suddenly followed by one of the fiercest storms within the memory of man. Without warning signs a squall comes sweeping down the main, and the ocean leaps in its fury like a thing of life. The heavens seem to bow themselves, and form a veil of mirk and gloom; and above the voices of the storm is heard the cry of those on shore, "O God of mercy, send us those we love!" But, alas! there are those for whom that prayer cannot now avail; for floating spars and bodies washed ashore from which all life is sucked tell too plainly that some home is desolate, some spirit crushed. And now a mighty shout is heard, and all eyes again turn towards the sea, for through the darkness of the storm a boat is seen struggling towards the shore, now lost to sight, and again borne on the crest of the wave, nearer and yet nearer the harbor's mouth. The climax now approaches in this wild race for life; and hearts are high with hope or chilled with fear, for the next wave must either bear them into safety or send them to their doom.

See! there it comes, threatening in its vastness and twisting in its progress like some hideous thing of night. A cold sweat breaks out on those on shore, for the boat is lifted on its boiling crest and dashed with resistless fury against the stonework of the pier; and as a mighty cry of anguish rises, the men clinging to the wreck wave to their friends a last adieu, who, close at hand, stand agonized spectators of the scene! Yes, they have surmounted all the dangers which have proved fatal to their fellows, only to miss the friendly hands stretched out to save, and perish before the eyes, and be washed up lifeless at the very feet, of those they love. In all such cases the grief of onlookers and of all who mourn their loss, is augmented by the thought that though so near to safety they yet were lost. Remember that to be near the harbor-mouth is not to be safe in its shelter—that though near to the kingdom of heaven you may never enter therein; and that, in so far as your final salvation is concerned, being near to Christ is no better than being far away, if it never leads to a complete surrender of your heart to Him.—W. LANDELS.

Antichrist—Teaching of.

In the frescoes of Signorelli we have "The Teaching of Antichrist" —no repulsive figure, but a grand personage in flowing robes, and with a noble countenance, which at a distance might easily be taken for the Saviour. To him the crowd are eagerly gathering and listening, and it is only when you draw close that you can discover in his harder and cynical expression, and from the evil spirit whispering in his ear, that it is not Christ.—Augustus J. C. Hare.

Devil—Fighting the.

"If you go to Wartburg they will show you a dark spot on the old walls which they say was caused by the breaking of the ink bottle that Martin Luther threw at the Devil. Now, I know that people say it was not the Devil, but rats in the wall that Luther heard. But this thing I know: Luther *thought* it was the Devil, and he just let it drive. I wish there were more men to-day who would fling their ink at the Devil, whether by the bottleful or in drops from the pen's point."— Charles L. Goodell.

Devil—Resisting.

D. W. Whittle tells of a man who came to Mr. Finney and said: "I don't believe in the existence of a devil." "Don't you?" said the old man. "Well, you resist him for a while, and you will believe in it."— *The Sunday School Times.*

Judas Honored.

It was M. Halling-Koehler's lot to travel to the small town of Sviashsk, near Kazan, on the occasion of nothing less than the unveiling there of a statue to Judas Iscariot. . . . On arrival at Sviashsk, Mlle. Dolly donned a sailor's cap, a white coat, breeches, and high tan boots, and led a Parade of the Red (rouge) Army, made up of two hundred Hungarians, captured during the war, and a sprinkling of Russians. Before the great draped statue stood a red-bearded Soviet leader, who delivered the inauguratory speech. He declared that the committee had hesitated between three candidates to statuehood— Lucifer, Cain, and Judas Iscariot. "On closer investigation," said the man, "it was seen that the views of Lucifer were not quite in accord with Soviet principles, and it was decided that Cain was only semi-mythical, so the statue was decreed for Judas." Thereon the girl pulled a string, and the assembled crowd saw a plaster-cast figure with its fist raised to heaven. The peasants gathered wonderingly, and, by the grace of Heaven, understanding nothing, crossed themselves in reverence as before the statue of a great saint.—*The Jewish Era.*

Satan's Commentary.

Said a quaint New England preacher: "Beware of Bible commentators who are unwilling to take God's words just as they stand. The first commentator of that sort was the devil in the Garden of Eden. He proposed only a slight change —just the one word 'not' to be inserted—'Ye shall not surely die.' The amendment was accepted, and the world was lost." Satan is repeating that sort of commentary with every generation of hearers. He insists that God couldn't have meant just what he said. To begin with, Satan induced one foolish woman to accept his exegesis; now he has theological professors who are of his opinion on these points; and there are multitudes of men and women who go on in the ways of sin because they believe Satan's word, and do not believe the Word of God.

Satan's Language.

During the Arian controversy, at a general meeting of the ministers of London at Salter's Hall, Mr. Thomas Bradbury had been contending that those who really believed the doctrine of Christ's deity should openly avow it; when, to bring it to the test, he said: "You who are not ashamed to own the deity of our Lord, follow me into the gallery." He had scarcely mounted two steps before the opposite party hissed him. Turning around, he said, "I have been pleading for Him who bruised the serpent's head; no wonder the seed of the serpent should hiss.—*Christian Herald.*

Satan's Servants.

We saw in the museum at Venice an instrument with which one of the old Italian tyrants was accustomed to shoot poisoned needles at the objects of his wanton malignity; we thought of gossips, backbiters, and secret slanderers, and wished that their mischievous devices might come to a speedy end. Their weapons of innuendo, shrug, and whisper appear to be as insignificant as needles, but the venom which they instil is deadly to many a reputation.—C. H. SPURGEON.

Satan—Evil Influences of.

I remember standing in the front of the Cathedral of Notre Dame, in Paris, admiring its beautiful statuary. As I did so a Parisian approached me and said, "Do you not see something amusing up there?" "No!" I said, "it seems to be all religious." Inwardly I was asking myself, "Is this an Atheist, or is he making a fool of me?" "Do you

see those figures?" he inquired, pointing to a group representing a soul being weighed to see if it should be found wanting. "You observe that there is an angel standing on the one side and Satan on the other. Satan seems as if he were just watching to see that there was fair play." "Yes," I answered, "but I fail to see anything amusing in that." "Just look under the scales!" he replied. I looked, and there underneath was a little imp pulling down the scale. That is the way Satan gives fair play. A man says, "I will reform. I'll mend my life. I'll give up drink." "All right," says Satan, and he seems to stand aside and give fair play. Do not trust him. He has some unseen imp hanging on against you. If it be not strong drink, it will be some other sin. The only way to get clear of all these is to get Christ beside you; His power and grace will outweigh all the evil influences of Satan.—*Christian Herald.*

Satan—Exposed.

Milton relates, how that, suspecting Satan to be in the garden of Eden, two angels instituted a search. They found a toad at the ear of Eve, as she, together with her husband, reposed in one of its bowers, whispering evil in her ear. One of the angels (Ithuriel) touched the toad with his spear; and up rose, in all his fallen grandeur and malignity, the Tempter, the Devil. We are exposed to evil: when we would do good, evil is present with us. It is sometimes difficult to detect; but touch it with the sword of the Spirit, that is more powerful than Ithuriel's spear, and the evil will appear in its true colors.—*Biblical Treasury.*

The Devil in Print.

We are informed that the wretched man who took the life of

President Carnot lived an apparently harmless, decent life for a good many years, until he came into contact with anarchist publications, which so saturated his mind with the evil thoughts, schemes, and ideas that at length he was capable of the awful crime he committed. He was defiled, ruined, and destroyed by the word of falsehood which he read. It has again and again been shown in courts of justice that thieves and robbers have had the thoughts of such a life put into their heads by the tales of highwaymen and the like which are sown broadcast in print. The same principle holds true conversely, and it holds good with regard to the Word of God. The Bible has a sanctifying influence: it is a holy book—it sets before us holy examples, it exhorts us to a holy course of life, it furnishes us with holy doctrines, it points us to a holy Saviour.—E. MOORE.

The Devil's Inheritance.

It is reported that the Finish courts have upheld the title of the will of an atheist who bequeathed his farm, on his death, to the Devil. In accordance with the finding of the court, the wish of the deceased is to be carried out by leaving the land absolutely untouched by human hands and allowing it to revert to the wilderness condition. We confess to being somewhat startled by the question that arose in our minds as we read the account. Do things that are left to themselves naturally and of necessity go to the Devil? To let farms, and some much more valuable things, go to the Devil, all that is needed to be done is to let them run wild.—*The Sunday School Times.*

The Devil's Business.

Men don't believe in a devil now,
  As their fathers used to do;
They've forced the door of the broadest creed
  To let his majesty through;
There isn't a print of his cloven foot,
  Or a fiery dart from his bow,
To be found in earth or air to-day,
  For the world has voted so.

But who is mixing the fatal draft
  That palsies heart and brain,
And loads the earth of each passing year
  With ten hundred thousand slain?
Who blights the bloom of the land to-day
  With the fiery breath of hell,
If the devil isn't and never was?
  Won't somebody rise and tell?

Who dogs the steps of the toiling saint,
  And digs the pits for his feet?
Who sows the tares in the field of time
  Wherever God sows His wheat?
The devil is voted not to be,
  And of course the thing is true;
But who is doing the kind of work
  The devil alone should do?

We are told he does not go about
  As a roaring lion now;
But whom shall we hold responsible
  For the everlasting row
To be heard in home, in Church, in State,
  To the earth's remotest bound,
If the devil, by a unanimous vote,
  Is nowhere to be found?

Won't somebody step to the front forthwith,
  And make his bow and show
How the frauds and the crimes of the day spring up?
  For surely we want to know.
The devil was fairly voted out,
  And of course the devil is gone;
But simple people would like to know
  Who carries his business on.

Hidden Treasure.

John Wilkerson says: "The Church is the Gospel express train, stopping at a few stations to pick up a few passengers, the train 'Israel' being sidetracked to let the express go by. When Christ comes, the train 'Israel' will be switched back upon the main line, stop at all stations, and take on the world."— *The Sunday School Times.*

Lord—Watching for the.

When Shackleton was driven back from his quest of the South Pole, he left his men on Elephant Island, and promised to come back to them. Working his way as best he might to South Georgia, he tried to get back to fulfill his promise, and failed; tried again and failed. The ice was between him and the island; he was not able to come, but he could not rest; though the season was adverse, and they told him it was impossible, yet in his little boat "Yalcho" he tried it again. It was the wrong time of year, but strange to say he got nearer the island; there was an open avenue between the sea and the place where he had left his men; he ran his boat in at the risk of being nipped, got his men, all of them, on board, and came out again before the ice crashed to. It was all done in half an hour. When the excitement was partly over he turned to one of the men and said, "Well, you were all packed and ready!" and the man said, "You see, boss, Wild (the second in command) never gave up hope, and whenever the sea was at all clear of ice he rolled up his sleeping-bag, and said to all hands, 'Roll up your sleeping-bags, boys; the boss may come to-day.'" "And so it came to pass," said Shackleton, "that we suddenly came out of the fog, and from a black outlook; in an hour all were in safety, homeward bound."— *Christ Life.*

Ticket—Round Trip.

A Christian woman was once talking to a servant of Christ about the assurance of her safety in the Saviour, and said, "I have taken a single ticket to glory, and do not intend to come back." Whereupon the man of God replied, "You are going to miss a lot. I have taken a return ticket, for I am not only going to meet Christ in glory, but I am coming back with him in power and great glory to the earth.—J. A. CLARK.

Sins,—Attractive.

It is notable that nearly all the poisonous fungi are scarlet or speckled, and the wholsome ones brown or gray, as if to show us that things rising out of darkness and decay are always most deadly when they are well dressed.—RUS-KIN.

Faults—Hidden.

A relief lifeboat was built at New London thirteen years ago. While the workmen were busy over it, one man lost his hammer. Whether he knew it or not, it was nailed up in the bottom of the boat. Perhaps if he found it out, he thought the only harm done was the loss of one hammer. The boat was put to service, and every time it rocked on the waves that hammer was tossed to and fro. Little by little it wore for itself a track, until it had worn through planking and keel, down to the very copper plating, before it was found out. Only that plate of copper kept the vessel from sinking. It seemed a very little thing in the start, but see what mischief it wrought. So with a little sin in the heart. It may break through all the restraints that surround us, and but for God's great mercy, sink our souls in endless ruin. A few evil words in a child's ear have rung in his soul for twenty years, and brought untold harm. It is the sin hidden in the heart that we should most fear. There are none who do not need to pray "Cleanse Thou me from secret faults."—T. BROOKS.

Guilt—Indirect.

Wickedness which a man can prevent, and which he does not prevent, inculpates him. Men are responsible for the mischief which they could hinder. If you put the torch to your neighbor's house, you are guilty in one way; but if another puts the torch to that house, and you go by, and see the flames, and say, "It is not my business; I did not kindle that fire; and, besides, he is an enemy of mine," you are as culpable as if you had set fire to the house yourself.—H. W. BEECHER.

Original Sin.

Now he who would deny original sin must contradict all experience in the transmission of qualities. The very hound transmits his peculiarities, paces, taught by art, to his offspring, as a part of their nature. If it were not so in man, there could be no history of man as a species; no tracing out the tendencies of a race or nation; nothing but the unconnected repetitions of isolated individuals, and their lives. It is plain that the first man must have exerted on his race an influence quite peculiar; that his acts must have biased their acts. And this bias or tendency is what we call original sin.—F. W. ROBERTSON.

Sinners Called.

In John Bunyan, God calls the bold leader of village reprobates to preach the gospel—a blaspheming tinker to be one of England's famous confessors. . . . From the deck of a slave-ship He summons John Newton to the pulpit; and by hands defiled with Mammon's foulest and most nefarious traffic, brings them that are bound out of darkness, and smites adamantine fetters from the slaves of sin. In Paul, the Apostle of the Gentiles, He converts Christ's bitterest enemy into His warmest friend; to the man whom a trembling Church held most in dread she comes to owe, under God, the weightiest obligations. . . . How much better for these three stars to be shining in heaven than quenched in the blackness of darkness!—better for the good of mankind, better for the glory of God.—GUTHRIE.

Sinner Needs God.

Your sinfulness is not a reason why you should keep away from God. It is the very reason why you should go to him. He is to your soul what the physician is to your body. When your body is racked with pains, you go to the physician. And so, the consciousness of your sin, and of the hatefulness of it, is the very reason why you should go to God.—H. W. BEECHER.

Sin's Burden.

As an Indian evangelist was preaching, a flippant youth interrupted him. "You tell about the burden of sin. I feel none. How heavy is it? Eighty pounds? Ten pounds? The preacher answered, "Tell me, if you laid a four-hundred-pound weight on a corpse, would it feel the load?" "No, because it is dead," replied the youth. The preacher said, "That spirit, too, is dead which feels no load of sin."— *Record of Christian Work.*

Sin in the Heart.

Some malady which you do not understand troubles and alarms you. The physician is called. Thinking that the illness proceeds from a certain inflammatory process on a portion of your skin, you anxiously direct his attention to the spot. Silently but sympathizingly he looks at the place you have bidden him look, and because you have bidden him look there, but soon he turns away. He is busy with an instrument on another part of your body. He presses his trumpet-tube gently to your breast, and listens for the pulsations which faintly but distinctly pass through. He looks and listens there, and saddens as he looks. You again direct his attention to the cutaneous eruption which annoys you. He sighs and sits silent. When you reiterate your request that something should be done for the external eruption, he gently shakes his head, and answers not a word. From this silence you would learn the truth at last; you would not miss its meaning long. Oh, miss not the meaning of the Lord when He points to the seat of the soul's diseases: "Ye will not come." These, His enemies, dwell in your heart.—DR. ARNOT.

Sins Forgotten.

There are persons who live largely in re-hashing their sins and their sense of guilt. Why, did you not repent of them? When a man has repented of his sins, that is enough. Put them out; do not keep them like so many mummies in the house. When you have done wrong and found it out, and have changed to right, and have rectified all the ways in which your wrong-doing has affected anybody else, that is the end; you have no business to come back and sit down on your old gravestones.—H. W. BEECHER.

Sins of Neighbors.

"In a certain village in Scotland there lived a half-witted man whose coat presented a most curious appearance. All down the front it was covered with patches of various sizes, mostly large. When asked why the coat was patched in such a remarkable way, he answered that the patches represented the sins of his neighbors. He pointed to each patch, and gave the story of the sin of some one in the village, then went on to another, until he had related the sins of all in the village. On the back of his coat there was a small patch, no bigger than a three-penny piece. On being asked what it represented, he said, 'That's my ain sin, and I cannot see it!' Is not this a fair picture of the attitude of the Pharisees in Christ's time? And how about our own attitude to-day?"—*Sunday School Chronicle*.

Sin—A Habitual State of.

An old divine says: "A sheep and a sow may each fall into the same quagmire; but the sow will wallow in it, whilst the sheep will bleat piteously, until she is extricated and cleansed." Such is the difference between the ungodly and the children of God. "Whosoever abideth in him sinneth not"; that is, sin can never become his normal and habitual state.—F. B. Meyer.

Sin—Bondage of.

The stags in the Greek epigram, whose knees were clogged with frozen snow upon the mountains, came down to the brooks of the valleys, hoping to thaw their joints with the waters of the stream; but there the frost overtook them, and bound them fast in ice, till the young herdsmen took them in their stranger snare.—Jeremy Taylor.

Sin—Clinging to.

Luther was one day seated in the confessional at Wittenburg. Many of the townspeople came successively and confessed themselves guilty of great excesses. Adultery, licentiousness, usury, ill-gotten gains —such are the crimes acknowleged. . . . He reprimands, corrects, instructs. But what is his astonishment when these individuals reply that they will not abandon their sins! . . . Greatly shocked the pious monk declares that, since they will not promise to change their lives, he cannot absolve them. The unhappy creatures then appeal to their letters of indulgence; they show them, and maintain their virtue. But Luther replies that he has nothing to do with these papers, and adds, "Except ye repent, ye shall all likewise perish." They cry out and protest; but the doctor is immovable. They must cease to do evil and learn to do well, or else there is no absolution.—D'Aubigne.

Sin—Covered.

Certain great iron-castings have been ordered for a railway bridge. The thickness has been calculated according to the extent of the span and the weight of the load. The contractor constructs his molds according to the specification, and when all is ready pours in the molten metal. In the process of casting, through some defect in the mold, portions of air lurk in the heart of the iron, and cavities, like those of a honey-comb, are formed in the interior of the beam; but all defects are hid, and the flaws are effectually concealed. The artisan covered his fault, but he will not prosper. As soon as it is subjected to a strain the beam gives way. Sin has covered his fault, but he will not a human soul, and when the strain comes the false gives way.—W. Arnot.

Sins—Danger of Small.

A gentleman crossing the English Channel stood near the helmsman. It was a calm and pleasant evening, and no one dreamed of a possible danger to their good ship, but a sudden flapping of a sail, as if the wind had shifted, caught the ear of the officer on watch, and he sprang at once to the wheel, examining closely the compass.

"You are a half point off the course," he said sharply to the man at the wheel. The deviation was corrected, and the officer returned to his post.

"You must steer very accurately," said the looker-on, "when only half a point is so much thought of."

"Ah! half a point in many places might bring us directly on the rocks," he said.

So it is with life. Half a point from strict truthfulness strands us upon the rocks of falsehood. Half a point from perfect honesty, and we are steering for the rocks of crime. And so of all kindred vices. The beginnings are always small. No one climbs to the summit at one bound, but goes the one little step at a time. Children think lightly of what they call small sins. These rocks do not look so fearful to them. —*Sailor's Magazine.*

Sin—Deceitfulness of.

It is not only a crime that men commit when they do wrong, but it is a blunder. "The game is not worth the candle." The thing that you buy is not worth the price you pay for it. Sin is like a great forest tree that we sometimes see standing up green in its leafy beauty, and spreading a broad shadow over half a field; but when we get round on the other side there is a great dark hollow in the very heart of it, and corruption is at work there. It is like the poison-tree in travelers' stories, tempting weary men to rest beneath its thick foliage, and insinuating death into the limbs that relax in the fatal coolness of its shade. It is like the apples of Sodom, fair to look upon, but turning to acrid ashes on the unwary lips. It is like the magician's rod that we read about in old books. There it

lies; and if tempted by its glitter or fascinated by the power that it proffers you, you take it in your hand, the thing starts into a serpent, with erect crest and sparkling eyes, and plunges its quick barb into the hand that holds it, and sends poison through all the veins.—A. MACLAREN.

Sin—Detracting Power of.

Ruskin was never weary of telling that, whatever faults an artist may have, they are always reproduced in his work. He declares that the fumes of wine and the stain of sensuality mentally leave dark shadows upon the artist's masterpiece. He cannot indulge his lower nature without in some degree clouding and marring his genius. But if everybody can see that in a man's physique and in a man's genius, is it not just as certain that sin will spoil a man's lordlier self, his moral and spiritual being? A man can never commit a transgression but it has blinded the eyes of his spiritual understanding. A man never violates a commandment of God but he has done an injustice to his conscience. —W. L. WATKINSON.

Sin—Disguised.

Some of you know the old Greek story describing how Ulysses slew the monster Proteus. You know how he had been forewarned that it would be of no use to kill it only in its first form, because the monster would change itself from shape to shape, appearing now as a seal, now as a lion, now as a bear. Only by recognizing it in its first form, and killing it in each different shape, could he hope to conquer it in the end. And you remember how, by following this advice, Ulysses was able to conquer, though only after a very long struggle.

It is only an old Greek legend, I

know; but perhaps it will bring out more clearly what we mean by sins "in disguise." Sometimes a temptation to sin comes to you—so small that it seems hardly worth your while to fight against it. But if you do not recognize it as a sin in its first form, and try to overcome it at once, then it, too, will change from shape to shape, until at last it will become a giant sin, bearing, perhaps, no likeness at all to the first little sin which as boys you allowed to enter your mind, but a giant sin so huge that you cannot cast it out.— F. DE W. LUSHINGTON.

Sin—Gradual Growth of.

There is an old bridge in the highlands of Scotland. It was built by General Wade at the time of Jacobite risings in order to reach the Highland clans more easily. It was a massive structure, rising high above the rocky cleft over which it stretched, and it was in use from its building until a few years ago when it was pronounced unsafe and closed for traffic. And this is why. A tiny birch-seed has ruined that bridge. One day a gust of wind had caught that seed and landed it in a small opening above the keystone. It sank into the moldy lime, and there it germinated in the winter rain. It grew into a sapling, so small at first that a child's hand could have pulled it out. But that was not done. The people crossing it never thought. And it was allowed to grow into a tree. And now with its deep and strong roots, it has wrenched the solid masonry apart. And in a few years at the most, the arch will fall and the bridge be a complete ruin. All owing to a seed so small that it could be lifted by a gust of autumn wind, all owing to a sapling that people saw quite plainly, but they never thought of its growing into a tree.

Unlike that bridge destroyed by the tree, there is no sin too powerful to be got rid of, no matter how deep and strong are its roots. If our cry be, "O wretched man that I am, who shall deliver me?"—the Gospel answers, "Through Jesus Christ our Lord."—ANDREW MUTCH.

Sin—Grip of.

I knew of one who, while wandering along a lonely and rocky shore at the ebb of tide, slipped his foot into a narrow crevice. Fancy his horror at finding he could not withdraw the imprisoned limb! Dreadful predicament! There he sat, with his back to the shore and his face to the sea. . . . How he shouted to the distant boat! how his heart sank as her yards swung round and she went off on the other tack! how bitterly he envied the white sea-mew her wing, as, wondering at this intruder on her lone domains, she sailed above his head, and shrieked back his shriek! how at length, abandoning all hope of help from man, he turned his face to heaven and cried loud and long to God! All that God only knows. But as sure as there was a terrific struggle, so sure, while he watched the waters rising inch by inch, these cries never ceased till the wave swelled up, and washing the dying prayer from his lips, broke over his head with a melancholy moan. There was no help for him. There is help for us, although fixed in sin as fast as that man in the fissured rock.—GUTHRIE.

Sin—Growth of.

The Arabs have a fable of a miller, who was one day awakened by having the nose of a camel thrust into the window of a room where he was sleeping. "It is very cold out here," said the camel: "I only want to get my nose in." The miller granted his request. After a while, the camel asked that he might get his neck in; then his fore feet; and so, little by little, crowded in his whole body. The miller found his companion troublesome; for the room was not large enough for both. When he complained to the camel, he received the answer, "If you do not like it, you may leave: as for myself, I shall stay where I am."

Sins—Little.

Thieves, when they go to rob a house, if they cannot force the doors, or that the wall is so strong that they cannot break through, then they bring little boys along with them, and these they put in at windows, who are no sooner in, but they unbolt the doors and let in the whole company of thieves. And thus Satan, when by greater sins he cannot tell how to enter the soul, then he puts on and makes way by lesser, which, insensibly having got entrance, set open the doors of the eyes and the doors of the ears, and then comes in the whole rabble: there they take up their quarters, there, like unruly soldiers, they rule, domineer, and do what they list, to the ruin of the soul so possessed.— J. SPENCER.

Sin—Physician for.

A great warrior was once persuaded by his enemies to put on a beautiful robe which they presented him. Not suspecting their design, he wrapped himself tightly in it, but in a few moments found that it was coated on the inside with a deadly poison. It stuck to his flesh as if it had been glued. The poison entered into his flesh so that in trying to throw off the cloak he was left torn and bleeding. But did he for that reason hesitate about taking it off? Did he stop to think whether it was painful or not? Did he say, "Let me wait and think about it awhile?" No, he had more sense than that. He tore it off at once, and threw it from him, and hastened away from it to the physician.

Sin—Punishment of.

As you stood some stormy day upon a sea-cliff, and marked the giant billow rise from the deep to rush on with foaming crest, and throw itself thundering on the trembling shore, did you ever fancy that you could stay its course, and hurl it back to the depths of ocean? Did you ever stand beneath the leaden lowering cloud, and mark the lightning's leap, as it shot and flashed, dazzling athwart the gloom, and think that you could grasp the bolt and change its path? Still more foolish and vain his thought, who fancies that he can arrest or turn aside the purpose of God, saying, "What is the Almighty that we should serve him? Let us break his bands asunder, and cast away his cords from us!" Break his bands asunder!—How he that sitteth in the heavens shall laugh!— GUTHRIE.

Sin—Redeeming from.

On one occasion, when our ancestors in the New England colonies were threatened by Indians, they built stockades around their settlements for protection. They placed in each stockade, on a high pole, an iron receptacle which held pine-knots and other inflammable material, which, in case of danger from the Indians was to be lighted as a signal. There was one certain group who built their stockade apart from the rest, and one day they found themselves surrounded by Indians with poisoned arrows. They thought of lighting the signal fire, but for any one to climb the tall pole would mean certain death. So they determined to fight on as best they could. Finally one of the members said, "Brethren, if the torch were lit our friends would know we are in danger; I will go up and light the signal." Climbing the pole, he succeeded in lighting the signal, but immediately fell back lifeless, shot through by poisoned arrows. The neighbors saw the signal and came to the rescue, and every life was saved except the man who lit the signal fire. The rescued people placed on the hero's tomb these words, "He died for us." He saved others; himself he could not save.—*The Sunday School Times.*

Sin—"Palace of Art" and.

In Tennyson's "Palace of Art" we have the story of how a soul tried to satisfy herself with an environment completely beautiful. Art and Literature were drawn upon lavishly to make her a meet dwelling-place. But into this paradise of all beauty despair crept, and made havoc. Fear fell like a blight, and the question of questions came to be

What is it that will take away my sin,
    And save me lest I die?

At last, come to her true self, and awake to her need of God,

"Make me a cottage in a vale," she said,
"Where I may mourn and pray."

Yet Tennyson had too wide a vision of the truth to make an end there. He honors the "first needs" in his poem, but he is careful to leave room for all that enriches life. And so he makes his penitent soul ask as a last request,

Yet pull not down my palace towers, that are

So lightly, beautifully built:
Perchance I may return with others there
When I have purged my guilt.
                    —Arch. Alexander.

Sins—Perils of Secret.

In some waters a man may drive strong piles, and build his warehouses upon them, sure that the waters are not powerful enough to undermine his foundations; but there is an innumerable army of minute creatures at work beneath the water, feeding themselves upon those strong piles. They gnaw, they bore, they cut, they dig into the poled wood, and at last a child might overthrow those foundations, for they are cut through and eaten to a honeycomb. Thus by avarice, jealousy, and selfishness men's dispositions are often cut through, and they don't know it.—H. W. Beecher.

Sin of Presumption.

Daedalus was a skillful artificer, who built the famous labyrinth for King Minor of Crete, but afterwards fell under his displeasure, and was not allowed to leave the island. He then designed and formed wings of wax and feathers, for himself and his son Icarus, that, if they could not escape by sea, they would defy the king by flying through the air. He equipped himself and then his son for flight, giving him the following directions: "Icarus, my son, I charge you to keep at a moderate height; for if you fly too low, the damp will clog your wings; and if too high, the heat will melt them. Keep near me, and you will be safe." They rose, and flew through the air, and the plowmen beneath mistook them for gods. At length the boy Icarus grew confident and exultant, and, leaving his father's care, soared upward. The sun's blaze softened the wax that held the feathers of his wings in place, and they fell out. His arms moved, but would not sustain him; and down, down he fell, and was drowned in the sea beneath.

Sins—Presumptuous.

During the Franco-Prussian War a regiment of Prussian soldiers was deploying from the shelter of a wood, in full face of French fire. The appearance of the regiment as seen from a distance, said one of the war correspondents, was like that of some dark serpent creeping out from beneath the wood. The far-stretching figure seemed to leave a dark trail in its path. The correspondent looked carefully through his glass, and this trail resolved itself under close inspection into patches of soldiers who had fallen under French fire. Some of them were seen to get on to their feet, stagger on a few paces, and fall again. The passion of battle was upon them, and they were scarcely conscious of their wounds. And is it not thus with us? We are intoxicated by the passion of life's battle, the battle for bread and place and power and conquest of every kind; and we stagger on, unconscious of the fact that we are pierced with many a hidden wound. The excitements that are in the air whirl us along, and we are all but insensible to the moral disaster He sees who watches the battle from afar. Our slowness to recognize the hurt that has overtaken us may be the sign that the pulse of vitality is fluttering itself out. "Keep back Thy servant also from presumptuous sins."—T. G. Selby.

Sin—Seeing Our.

The coming of the Son of God made a sin possible that was not possible before; light reveals darkness. There are Negroes in Central Africa who never dreamed that they were black until they saw the face of a white man and there are people who never knew they were sinful until they saw the face of Jesus Christ in all its whiteness and purity.—A. J. Gordon.

Sin—Senseless.

According to Æsop, an old woman found an empty jar which had lately been full of prime old wine, and which still retained the fragrant smell of its former contents. She greedily placed it several times to her nose, and drawing it backwards and forwards said, "Oh, most delicious! How nice must the wine itself have been when it leaves behind, in the very vessel which contained it, so sweet a perfume!"

Men often hug their vices when their power to enjoy them is gone. —Spurgeon

Sin—Sorrow Over.

There is a pathetical story of Origen,—that when he had fallen into a foul apostasy, and, after some recovery from it, came into a congregation, and was desired to preach; he took the Bible, and opened it accidentally at the Fiftieth Psalm, and his eye fell first to read these words in the sixteenth and seventeenth verses of it:—"But unto the wicked God saith, What hast thou to do to declare my statutes, or that thou shouldest take my covenant in thy mouth? Seeing thou hatest instruction, and casteth my words behind thee." Upon reading the words, he remembered his own fall, and instead of preaching, he fell a weeping, and wept so bitterly, that he caused all the con-

gregation to weep with him.—J.
LIGHTFOOT.

Sin—Wreck of.

Did you ever look upon that wild
sea-piece of Stanfield's which he has
called "The Abandoned?" The sky
is dark and lowering, with a forked
flash of lightning shooting athwart
it; the ocean is angry, and all over
it lies a dreary loneliness that makes
the spectator almost shudder. The
one solitary thing in sight is a huge
hull, without mast or man on board,
lying helpless in the trough of the
sea. The men who stood by her as
long as it was safe have been picked
up by some friendly vessel now entirely unseen, and there that battered, broken thing floats on at the
mercy of the winds and waves. That
is sad enough; but what is it after
all in comparison with the condition
of an abandoned man, abandoned by
friends, abandoned by himself, abandoned, it may be even, like Saul, by
God, and drifting on the ocean of
life all dismantled and rudderless,
tossed hither and thither by every
wind of appetite or impulse, and
soon to disappear beneath the waters!—TAYLOR.

Sinner—Hopeful for.

A celebrated physician who always entered the sick room with a
smile upon his lips was asked how
he could be living among so many
terrible diseases and yet not be over-
whelmed by them. He replied: "I
always look upon disease from a
curative standpoint." The heart of
Christ would have broken long before He reached the cross had He
not looked upon sinning humanity
from the "curative standpoint." If
we would have His joy in us let
us take His view of evil.—*Record of
Christian Work.*

Sinner—Only Hope for.

Sinner, this is the way you must
treat your sins if you would be
saved. And do it now. "Now is the
accepted time; now is the day of
salvation." A sprightly boy, who
was the pride of his master, who
was loved by all his fellow-servants,
once came to me to talk about his
soul's salvation. He had heard that
to live in sin was to live in rebellion
against God and in great danger.
He felt that he was a sinner. He
knew that he ought to forsake his
sins. He talked freely with me about
himself. Before we parted he
promised to begin the service of
God the next day. He went off to
his business. I saw no more of him
for about three months. As I was
riding along one day his master met
me and asked me to go in and see
William, for that was his name,
who was very sick. I found him
very ill, and about to die. Surely,
said I to myself, he is prepared and
willing to go, for I remembered his
promises and good resolutions to
begin the next day. I said to him,
"William, I hope Christ is precious
to you now?" "Oh! sir," said he,
"I have no hope in Christ! I fear
I am lost. I resolved when I saw
you last to repent and be a Christian the next day. But the next day
brought something that prevented
me, and caused me to put it off till
the next day. But every day passed
on and closed in the same way. And
here I am yet, a hardened sinner,
and in the arms of death." I tried
to tell him about Jesus as his Saviour.
I prayed for him. And while I was
repeating some precious promises
from the Word of God, he turned to
me and said, "Oh! sir, it is too late;
I am lost. I cannot be saved now.
Tell my fellow-servants not to put
off another day making their peace
with God." Scarcely had he given
this testimony of the danger of de-

lay, when he was overcome by stupor and delirium, and thus died in darkness and impenitence.—BISHOP MEADE.

Sin—Root of.

A pious minister, having preached on the doctrine of original sin, was afterwards waited on by some persons, who stated their objections to what he had advanced. After hearing them, he said, "I hope you do not deny actual sin too?"—"No," they replied. The good man expressed his satisfaction at their acknowledgment; but, to show the folly of their opinions in denying a doctrine so plainly taught in Scriptures, he asked them, "Did you ever see a tree growing without a root?"—J. G. WILSON.

Son—Unrecognized.

"Yes'm, he stopped right there at the gate, speakin' to some one, and I just give a glance at him, and never thought who it was," said the old woman, telling of her absent son's return. "All them long weeks and months I'd been waitin' and prayin' for him to come, and then didn't know him when he stood right outside the gate! Sorter wondered to myself, fretty like, who was comin' in to hinder my work." The answers to many of our prayers stand unrecognized just outside our gate. The trouble with most of us is not that so many of our prayers are unanswered, as we faithlessly complain, but that we do not know the answers when they come.—FORWARD.

Sin—Mark of.

I bear upon my brow the sign
    Of sorrow and of pain;
Alas! no hopeful cross is mine,
    It is the brand of Cain.

The course of passion, and the fret
    Of Godless hope and fear,—
Toil, care, and guilt,—their hues
        have set,
    And fix'd their sternness there.

Saviour! wash out the imprinted
        shame;
    That I no more may pine,
Sin's martyr, though not meet to
        claim
    Thy cross, a saint of Thine.
                    —J. H. NEWMAN.

Body—Care of.

If one should send me from abroad a richly carved and precious statue, and the careless drayman who tipped it upon the sidewalk before my door should give it such a blow that one of the boards of the box should be wrenched off, I should be frightened lest the hurt had penetrated further, and wounded it within. But if, taking off the remaining boards and the swathing-bands of straw or cotton, the statue should come out fair and unharmed, I should not mind the box, but should cast it carelessly into the street. Now, every man has committed to him a statue, molded by the oldest Master, of the image of God; and he who is only solicitous for outward things, who is striving to protect merely the body from injuries and reverses, is letting the statue go rolling away into the gutter, while he is picking up the fragments, and lamenting the ruin of the box.—H. W. BEECHER.

Lost Souls.

Travelers sometimes find in lonely quarries, long abandoned or once worked by a vanished race, great blocks squared and dressed, that seem to have been meant for palace or shrine. But there they lie neglected and forgotten, and the building for which they were hewn has been reared without them. Beware lest God's grand temple should be built up without you, and you be left to desolation and decay.—MACLAREN.

Martyr Souls.

To speak of Abel as the first martyr to righteousness is to recall a striking incident in which the same word was used of Mazzini, the Italian patriot. Carlyle was out of touch with some of Mazzini's aspirations, and indeed they had recently quarreled over them. Yet when Mazzini was unfairly attacked in England, Carlyle wrote to the Times in his defense. This is the letter: "Whatever I may think of his practical insight and skill in worldly affairs, I can with great freedom testify to all men, that he, if I have ever seen such, is a man of genius and virtue, a man of sterling veracity, humanity, and nobleness of mind, one of those rare men, numerable unfortunately but as units in this world, who are worthy to be called martyr souls; who in silence, piously in their daily life, understand and practice what is meant by that."—BOLTON KING.

Soul—A Dead.

The unregenerate man may be said to be made up of two parts—a living body and a dead soul. In states of disease and injury we sometimes find something analogous, in one part of the body being full of life, and another part of it palsied and dead. I have seen a person after injury of the lower part of the neck surviving for a time; the head perfectly alive and well, but the body and limbs perfectly motionless. In the last fatal duel fought near Edinburgh a bullet struck the spine of the challenger. I have often heard this unhappy man's physician tell that when he first visited him, some hours afterwards, and asked him how he felt. "I feel," he replied, "exactly what I am—a man with a living head and a dead body mysteriously joined together." Every unbelieving man consists of a dead soul mysteriously joined to a living body.—SIR JAMES SIMPSON.

Soul—A Generous.

Early in the Civil War, before General Robert E. Lee had proved his preeminence as a general, he was severely criticized on more than one occasion by a General Whiting. Whiting had stood at the head of his class at West Point, and was considered a bright and capable man. One day President Davis, wishing an officer for some important command, called upon General Lee for advice. "What do you think of Whiting?" Lee answered without hesitation, commending Whiting as one of the ablest men in the army, well qualified in every way for even the most responsible place. One of the officers present was greatly surprised, and at the first opportunity drew Lee aside. "Don't you know what unkind things Whiting has been saying about you?" he inquired. "I understood," Lee answered, "that the president desired to know my opinion of Whiting, not Whiting's opinion of me."—*The Christian Herald.*

Soul—A Restored.

The Rev. John Newton, the fame of whose piety fills all Christendom, while a profligate sailor on shipboard, in his dream thought that a being approached him and gave him a very beautiful ring, and put it upon his finger, and said to him, "As long as you wear that ring you will be prospered; if you lose that ring you will be ruined." In the same dream another personage appeared, and by a strange infatuation persuaded John Newton to throw that ring overboard, and it sank into the sea. Then the mountains in sight were full of fire and the air was lurid with consuming wrath. While John Newton was repenting of his folly in having thrown overboard the treasure, another personage came through the dream, and told John Newton he would plunge into the sea and bring the ring up if he desired it. He

plunged into the sea and brought it up, and said to John Newton, "Here is that gem, but I think I will keep it for you, lest you lose it again"; and John Newton consented, and all the fire went out of the mountains, and all the signs of lurid wrath disappeared from the air. John Newton said that he saw in his dream that that valuable gem was his soul, and that the being who persuaded him to throw it overboard was Satan, and that the One who plunged in and restored that gem, keeping it for him, was Christ. That dream makes one of the most wonderful chapters in the life of that most wonderful man.—T. De Witt Talmage.

Soul—Bankruptcy.

I have seen men, that had lived with a great circuit of prosperity, disbranched by commercial revulsions, who yet stood, in adversity, nobler, riper, better than ever they were with all their environments of wealth. And I have seen persons who have come to bankruptcy, and sold their houses, and their musical instruments, and their very cradles, and were stripped of everything without; but, oh, woe! that was as nothing to the bankruptcy within. All courage gone; all hope gone; all faith gone; no sweetness; no love; no trust; only whining, querulous despondency! Of all bankrupties in the world, that of a man's soul and disposition is the most pitiful.—H. W. Beecher.

Soul—Battling for the.

Some of you may have seen the celebrated painting by Retsch, in which, with wondrous skill, he has portrayed a game of chess between Satan and a young man, who has staked his soul on the issue. The truth and vivid power of the representation; the different expression in the faces of the players; the gay, heedless look of the young man, all unconscious of his peril; and the cunning, hellish leer of the Fiend, as the chances seemed to turn in his favor, can never be forgotten by any who have once beheld them. But how much more graphic and solemn is the scene which the Divine pencil has drawn—Christ and Satan battling for the soul of man! Nor is it picture merely; it is real. The contest is actually going forward, going forward now, going forward in your own spiritual history. Intrenched within your heart, "the Prince of the Power of the Air" plied all his weapons of falsehood and delusion and worldly enchantments to maintain his fatal mastery over you; while at the door stands the crucified One—pity in His eye and salvation in His hands —summoning you to thrust out the deceiver, and yield the palace to the sweet control of His love.—Dr. G. B. Ide.

Soul—Cramping the.

A recent writer upon the London Zoological Gardens refers to "the spacious aviary" provided for the eagles. Spacious aviary! One would like to know what the eagles think of that. Surely the amplest artificial horizon is narrow and the loftiest dome mean to creatures born to range the skies and seek the sun. The noble birds must feel in dull, strange ways the loss of their native heaven; the most spacious aviary can only grievously and mysteriously fret them. So the world, and the things of the world, painfully cramp the creature in whose heart God has set eternity; his cage is narrow even when the stars are its gilded wires. It is said that a bird of the north, confined in a yard, and longing for his arctic haunts, has been known in spring to migrate from the southern to the northern side of his narrow confines. And, however men doom themselves to the straitened life of sense, the instinct of eternity pathetically asserts itself within absurd limits, and distracts the soul with morbid repinings.—W. L. Watkinson.

Soul—Cleansing the.

While walking down a street one day, I passed a store where a man on the pavement was washing the large plate-glass shop-window. There was one soiled spot which defied efforts to remove it. After rubbing hard at it, using much soap and water, and failing to remove it, he found out the trouble. "It's on the inside," he called out to someone in the store. Many are striving to cleanse the soul from its stains. They wash it with tears of sorrow; they scrub it with the soap of good resolves; they rub it with the chamois of morality, but still the consciousness of it is not removed. The trouble is, "It's on the inside." Nothing but the blood of Jesus, applied by the mighty hand of the Holy Spirit, can cleanse the inside, for there God's Spirit alone can reach.—*The Wellspring.*

Souls—Foolish.

Some years ago there was a bridge at Bath in so crazy a condition that cautious persons chose rather to make a long circuit than run the risk of crossing it. One day, however, a very nervous lady, hurrying home to dress for the evening, came suddenly upon the spot without, till that moment, remembering the danger. The sight of the bridge reminded her of its ruinous state, just as she was about to set her foot upon it. But what was she to do? If she went on the frail arch might give way under her; to go round would be fatiguing and attended with much loss of time. She stood for some minutes trembling in anxious hesitation; but at last a lucky thought occurred to her. She called for a sedan-chair, and was carried over in that conveyance! You may laugh, perhaps, at this good lady's odd expedient for escaping danger by shutting out the view of it. But is not something of the same kind happening around you every day? Those people who are alarmed and perplexed at the danger of having to judge for themselves in religious matters think to escape that danger by choosing to take some guide as an infallible one, and believe or disbelieve as he bids them. What is this but crossing the crazy bridge in a sedan-chair?—Excelsior.

Souls—Kingly.

There is an Eastern story of a king who built a great temple at his own cost, no other one being allowed to do even the smallest part of the work. The king's name was put upon the temple as the builder of it. But, strange to say, when the dedication day came it was seen that a poor widow's name was there in place of the king's. The king was angry and gave command that the woman bearing the name on the scroll should be found. They discovered her at last among the very poor and brought her before the king. He demanded of her what she had done toward the building of the temple. She said, "Nothing." When pressed to remember anything she had done, she said that one day when she saw the oxen drawing the great stones past her cottage, exhausted in the heat and very weary, she had in pity given them some wisps of hay. And this simple kindness to dumb animals, prompted by a heart's compassion, weighed more

in God's sight than all the king's vast outlay of money. What we truly do for Christ and in love is glorious in His sight.—J. R. MILLER.

Souls—Repairing.

"A bruised reed shall He not break." In one of his sermons Mr. William Birch says, "I remember some years ago, while riding over one of the deserts of northern Africa, meeting with a company of Arab travelers, and dining with them in the primitive way of sitting on the sand. After dinner one of the men brought out his pipes to play. These pipes were two reeds, something like the tin whistles on which boys sometimes play, but made of cane. The man put the end of the reeds in his mouth and played Arab tunes with them, the music thus produced being soft and tremulous. When he had finished playing he placed the reeds on the ground, and a horse happening to tread on one it was injured. I at once thought of the passage of Scripture, referring to Christ, which says, 'A bruised reed shall He not break,' and I wondered for a moment what this Arab would do. He took up the reed, and though it was bruised he did not throw it away, but sat down on the ground, and for probably half-an-hour tried gently and patiently to straighten and repair it, so that he might be able to use it again for his cheering tunes, as it was the only instrument of music in that little caravan."

Soul—Restoration of.

I remember meeting a man who, though a Christian, had fallen into sin. The church of which he had been a member had exercised discipline in his case; and for twelve years he had been in this condition. In answer to my inquiry he replied, "I was a Christian once, but I fell." "Well, but," I rejoined, "have you never been restored?" "No," he replied; "I have been utterly miserable about it, and would give anything to be what I once was." "Would you like to be restored at this moment?" I asked; "for as surely as God lives you may be." He looked at me in amazement. To help his mind I said, "suppose that you had a daughter who had sinned against you, and given you great sorrow; last night, however, she came and threw her arms about her mother's neck, saying, 'O mother, I am so ashamed of myself for having given you and dear father such anxiety and sorrow; do forgive me.' I ask, can your daughter restore herself, or must her restoration be your act?" "Mine," he replied. "Now, how soon would you restore her—in twelve years?" "Surely no," he added. "Well, in twelve months?" "No," he replied, "Well, in three?" "No," he said. "Then how soon would you restore her?" I asked. "Why, at once," he rejoined. "What!" I said, "are you prepared at once to restore your child, and do you think that our Father in heaven is not prepared upon confession to Him to restore immediately?" Opening my Bible, he read the first clause of the third verse of the Twenty-third Psalm: "He restoreth my soul." "Notice," I remarked, "that the word restoreth is in the present tense," . . . I can never forget the joy with which, after prayer, my friend was filled. "Thank God," he replied, "for this night. I see it clearly now. It is God that restores."—HENRY VARLEY.

Souls,—Seeking.

Sportsmen must not stop at home and wait for the birds to come and be shot at; neither must fishermen throw their nets inside their boats and hope to take many fish. Traders go to the markets; they follow their customers, and go out after business if it will not come to them; and so must we.—SPURGEON.

Souls—Trusted with.

The providence of God sent across my path some years ago a thief who had been in prison above twenty times, and who had been twice in penal servitude. I could find no work for him here, because he was well known, and therefore I sent him across the ocean to America, but his character followed him, and he was returned to England. At length we obtained work for him out of Manchester; and he turned out to be a faithful servant. One day the manager of the works was removing his goods to a new house, and the mistress—who did not know what the man had been—called him, saying, "John, this basket contains all our silver; will you please be very careful about it, and carry it to the new house." I said to the man, "And what did you do?" He replied, "When I got outside, I looked into the basket and saw the silver shining. I lifted it up, and it felt very heavy." "Well, what did you do then?" He said, "I cried, because I was trusted." Of course, he carried it safely. Brethren, God knows the past sin of our lives, yet He takes us into His service and trusts us with human souls, bidding us to take them to the mansion in heaven.—WM. BIRCH.

Soul—Value of.

A book is an invention by which men live after they are dead, so far as this world is concerned. A hymn or song that deserves to live is lifted above persecution. The tyrant or despot cannot touch it. But oh!

neither book, nor hymn, nor song, nor any product of the human mind, is to be compared with the immortal life itself; and ye that save one soul, and lift it, by the power of your instrumentality, blessed of God, into the sphere of immortality and glory, shall shine as the stars in the firmament!—H. W. BEECHER.

Soul—Value of One.

Some years ago the king of Abyssinia took a British subject prisoner. They carried him to the fortress of Magdala, and in the heights of the mountains put him in a dungeon, without cause assigned. Britain demanded his instantaneous release. King Theodore refused, and in less than ten days ten thousand British soldiers were on shipboard and sailing down the coast. They marched seven hundred miles beneath the burning sun up the mountains to the very dungeon where the prisoner was held, and there they gave battle. The gates were torn down, presently the prisoner was lifted upon their shoulders, carried down the mountain, and placed upon the white winged ship which sped him in safety to his home. It cost the English government $25,-000,000 to release that man. I belong to a better kingdom than that, and do you suppose that earthly powers will protect their subjects and God will leave me without help? —J. WILBUR CHAPMAN.

Souls—Sleepy.

There was an old turnpike man in a quiet country road whose habit was to shut his gate at night and take a nap. One dark, wet midnight I knocked at his door, crying "Gate! Gate!" "Coming," said the voice of the old man. Then I knocked again, and once more the voice replied, "Coming." This went on for some time, till at length I grew quite angry, and, jumping off my horse, opened the door and demanded to know why he cried "Coming" for twenty minutes, but never came. "Who's there?" said the old man in a quiet, sleepy voice, rubbing his eyes. "What d'ye want, sir?" Then awakening, "Bless yer, sir, and yer pardon; I was asleep. I get so used to hearing 'em knock that I answer 'Comin'' in my sleep, and take no more notice about it." So it is with too many hearers of the gospel, who hear by habit, and answer God by habit, and at length die with their souls asleep.—*The Sunday School Chronicle.*

Character—A Sterling.

When Governor Charles E. Hughes was beginning his heroic campaign to secure the passage of his anti-racetrack gambling bills many of his so-called friends warned him of the violent attacks he would certainly be subjected to were he to adopt such a course. "The opposition will stop at nothing; they will defame your character, they will ruin you politically." "Gentlemen," said the governor, "there is only one man in this world who can harm Charles E. Hughes, and that man is Charles E. Hughes."—*The Sunday Circle.*

Destroying Self.

Some time ago, in India, two little children were asleep in a bungalow, when a tiger came out of the jungles after something to eat. He scented the children, and broke into the bungalow after them. But the first thing the tiger saw was a looking-glass, and in the looking-glass he saw a tiger. The tiger did not know it was himself, so he growled and grew angry; and the tiger in the looking-glass growled and grew angry. That made him furious, and he sprang at the tiger in the glass, which, of course, smashed the glass into a thousand pieces; and it frightened the tiger so that he was glad to run off.

Destruction—Personal.

Julian the apostate had for his coat of arms on his escutcheon an eagle struck through the heart with a shaft feathered from her own wing, with the motto, "Our death flies to us with our own feathers, and our wings pierce us to the very heart." The moral is, that, if a man receives injury, he alone has caused it, and is alone to blame.

Divided Allegiance.

Reader, watch a weighing machine. You may step on the platform, but it moves not. Step on again and put in the money, and you are instantly weighed. So, many try to satisfy God's claim by giving themselves alone, or their money only, but cannot.—*Heart and Life Bulletin.*

Duty—Call of.

The pangs of pity which Dante's sensitive soul feels for the forlorn and tormented spirits in the *Inferno* serve to show how intense is his conviction that nothing can set aside the laws of eternal right. Francesca will arouse in him infinite and overwhelming compassion, but Francesca must face the withering tempest which her fault has aroused against her. Mr. J. A. Symonds expressed his wonder that Dante should be so hard and pitiless in his judgment upon the weaklings who hesitated to identify themselves on either side in the great battle of all time. Others may have felt that the harsh contempt expressed by the poet was out of proportion to a fault which might be called weakness, but never vice; but to Dante the cowardice which refused the call of high duty or noble ideal was sin almost beyond forgiveness: it revealed a spirit dead to righteousness through the paralyzing influence of self-interest.—W. Boyd Carpenter.

Enemy—Our Worst.

When Abraham Lincoln was candidate for the Presidency, some one asked him what he thought of the prospect. With characteristic humor he answered, "I do not fear Breckinridge, for he is of the South, and the North will not support him; I do not much fear Douglas, for the South is against him. But there is a man named Lincoln I see in the papers of whom I am very much afraid. If I am defeated, it will be by that man."—*Gospel Herald.*

Looking-Glasses.

A man was complaining of his neighbors. "I never saw such a wretched set of people," he said, "as are in this village. They are mean, greedy of gain, selfish, and careless of the needs of others. Worst of all they are forever speaking evil of one another." "Is it really so?" said an angel who happened to be walking with him. "It is indeed," said the man. "Why, only look at this fellow coming toward us! I know his face, though I cannot just remember his name. See his little, shark-like, cruel eyes darting here and there like a ferret's, and the lines of covetousness about his mouth! The very droop of his shoulders is mean and cringing, and he slinks along instead of walking." "It is very clever of you to see all this," said the angel, "but there is one thing which you did not perceive." "What is that?" asked the man. "That it is a looking-glass we are approaching," said the angel.—*Baptist World.*

Punishment of Self.

When Gregory the Great was Bishop of Rome, a beggar once died of hunger in the streets of the Eternal City. Am I my brother's keeper? he asked himself. He felt he could not avoid the true answer. One of the sheep committed to his care had been starved to death; his charity was shocked; his vigilance had failed; his sense of responsibility was outraged; and he imposed a severe penance on himself, and for many days actually lay under his own sentence of excommunica-

tion, performing no priestly act. This is the man who won the title of Great; this is the man who attained to the brilliant company of the Saints.—S. E. COTTAM.

Self—Ashamed of.

A young convert tried to preach in the open air. He could not preach very well, but he did the best he could. Some one interrupted him and said: "Young man, you cannot preach; you ought to be ashamed of yourself!" Said the young man: "So I am, but I am not ashamed of my Lord." That is right. Do not be ashamed of Christ—of him who bought us with his own blood.—*The Christian Herald (London).*

Self-Control.

People say to me, "Oh religion —it is all about limitations and restrictions. It means that a man is to be reined in, and not allowed the legitimate use of his natural passions and appetites." Not at all. I have lately had an opportunity of seeing some of the dark and erratic ways of motor-cars, and one of the great things they say of a car is, "I have got it under complete control." Well, what does it mean? That it won't go? You don't suppose that the man who has got a motor-car at the side of a road, which absolutely will not move, is inclined to say, "My car is under such perfect control." The ideal of a car that is subject to perfect control is that it will travel easily at its highest speed, that it will do exactly what is required of it, and do it easily without stress or strain. That is the complete ideal.—C. SYLVESTER HORNE.

Self-Control and Tact.

"A man evidently crazed by a drug was talking vociferously and blasphemously in an elevated car. Finally the brakeman's attention was called to the disturbance. The brakeman went up to the man and said, gently, "Aren't you a little too profane, my friend?" The offender quieted down and stopped talking. A rough word would have set the man on fire. It was a surprising exhibition of self control and tact on the part of the train hand. In fact, I have heard a Sunday-school superintendent use a far more imperious tone in rebuking the children for being out of time in singing, 'I want to be an angel.' "

Self-Conquering.

Years ago Sir Edwin Arnold visited America and spoke to the students of our oldest university. One memorable and ever unforgettable sentence seized the memory of every hearer. He gave a succinct and epigrammatic description of the great wars of our past and of the greater contest of the future: "Gentlemen of Harvard," he said, in 1776 and in 1812 you conquered your fathers. In the years from 1861 to 1865 you conquered your brothers. Will you permit an Englishman to say that your next victory must be over yourself?" It approaches the heart of our present American problem.—BISHOP E. H. HUGHES.

✓ Self-Discovery.

There is a Nothern legend, told in the proem of one of Hall Caine's books, of a man who thought he was pursued by a monster. His ricks were fired, his barns unroofed, his cattle destroyed, his lands blasted, his first-born slain. So he lay in wait for the monster where it lived in the chasms near his house, and in the darkness of night he saw it. With a cry he rushed

upon it, and gripped it about the waist, and it turned upon him, and held him by the shoulder. Long he wrestled with it, reeling, staggering, falling and rising again; but at length a flood of strength came to him, and he overthrew it, and stood over it, covering it, conquering it, with its back against his thigh, and his hand set hard at its throat. Then he drew his knife to kill it; and the moon shot through a wrack of cloud, opening an alley of light about it, and he saw its face, and lo, the face of the monster was *his own*.

Self-Effacement.

Upon leaving Rome, S. Francis traveled to the seaport of Ancona, where he found a ship on the point of setting sail for Venice. Finding that the captain was willing to take him on board, he engaged his passage, and paid his fare. At the moment of departure, however, a lady of rank made her appearance, and perceiving S. Francis, who had already taken his place, in an angry tone desired the captain to order him out, as she had engaged the whole vessel for herself and her attendants. Upon this, S. Francis, coming forward, stated his case respectfully to the lady, and begged that he might be allowed to keep his place, as he should not be at all in her way, and was very anxious to pursue his journey. The lady, however, rudely persisted, and almost gave orders to have his luggage thrown overboard. S. Francis submitted to the affront with his usual meekness, and, when the ship set sail, remained on shore trying to pacify his angry attendants. While he was speaking the clouds gathered, a violent storm arose, and the ill-fated vessel sank, before their eyes, with every soul on board, at

the very entrance of the harbor.—
S. J. Eales.

Self-Effacing.

As Michael Angelo wore a lamp
on his cap to prevent his own shadow from being thrown upon the picture which he was painting, so the
Christian minister and servant needs
to have the candle of the Spirit always burning in his heart, lest the
reflection of self and self-glorying
may fall upon his work to darken
and defile it.—A. J. Gordon.

Self-Righteousness.

When Morales, the painter, was
invited by Philip the Second to
court, he came in such a magnificent
costume that the King, in anger,
ordered a sum of money to be paid
him, and so dismissed him. The
next time they met he appeared in a
very different dress, poor, old and
hungry, which so touched the heart
of the King, that he immediately
provided him with a revenue which
kept him in comfort for all the
future. So when men come to the
throne of grace it is not their mag-
nificence but their very want which
touches the heart of God.

Self—Giving of.

When the King of Greece came
over to this country, a member of
his suite had a most beautiful dog,
which during the voyage fell overboard. His master entreated the
captain to stop the ship and rescue
the dog; but the captain did not
deem the matter of so much importance, and having the King on board,
refused to stop. What did the master do? He asked, "Would you stop
the ship if it had been a man?"
"Certainly." And before they could
hinder him he had flung himself into
the sea. The ship was stopped, and
not only the man but the dog was
rescued too. And all because the
man, devoted to the dog, identified
himself with him in his peril, and
braved even death itself to save him.
Even a King was stopped by such
devotion. How much better is a
man than a dog! Go thou and do
likewise.—W. Y. Fullerton.

Self—Love of.

A young artist had produced an
exquisite picture, the most successful of all his efforts, and even his
master found nothing in it to criticize. But the young artist was
so enraptured with it that he ces-
santly gazed at his work of art, and
really believed that he would never
be able to excel what he had already
produced. One morning, as he was
about to enjoy anew the contemplation of his picture, he found his
master had entirely erased his work
of art. Angry, and in tears, he ran
to his master and asked the cause
of this cruel treatment. The master answered, "I did it with wise
forethought. The painting was good,
but it was at the same time your
ruin." "How so?" asked the young
artist. "My beloved pupil," replied
the master, "you love no longer your
art in your picture, but only yourself. Believe me, it was not perfect,
even if it did appear so; it was only
a study, and attempt. Take your
pencil and see what your new creation will be, and do not repent of
the sacrifice." The student seized
his pencil and produced his masterpiece, "The Sacrifice of Iphigenia."
His name was Timanthes.—*Christian
Age.*

STEWARDSHIP

Avarice—Danger of.

A servant of an Indian rajah was ordered to keep away from a cave near the rajah's residence, and to keep all others away. The servant began to consider the probable reason of his having been forbidden to enter the cave. He made up his mind that his master must have great treasure hid there, and resolved to get it. Taking a fellow-servant with him to secure the coveted prize, they rolled away the stone at the mouth of the cave, when a tremendous tiger sprang upon them, and tore them to pieces.

Benevolence.

An eminent layman, in making a platform missionary speech said, "I have heard of churches starving out from a saving spirit; but I have never heard of one dying of benevolence. And if I could hear of one such, I would make a pilgrimage to it, by night, and in that quiet solitude, with the moon shining and the aged elm waving, I would put my hands on the moss-clad ruins, and gazing on the venerable scene would say. 'Blessed are the dead who die in the Lord.'"

Bled to Death.

Some good people, who proudly call themselves "loyal," say that the churches are being bled to death by their offerings for missions. One of their own number says that as long as their offerings for missions average only seven cents a member, it is amusing to talk of being bled to death. A people that cannot give seven cents each in a year without being bled to death must be somewhat anaemic.—*Missionary Intelligence.*

Charity—Beauty of.

I like so much the legend of St. Elizabeth of Hungary, who did all for charity's sake—that is, for love's sweet sake. You know that the heavy load of bread which she was carrying, trying to conceal it from her husband's eye, all turned to roses, red and white, when he commanded her to open the pack which she was bringing to the poor. Gentle deeds of charity always turn fragrant and beautiful in our hands, even when custom or authority, or fashion, or prudence rebukes us for bestowing gifts. You give a loaf, and you let an angel into your heart.—ANNIE H. RYDER.

Charity—Parade of.

It is related of Father Taylor, the sailor missionary of Boston, that on one occasion, when a minister was urging that the names of the subscribers to an institution (it was the missionary cause) should be published, in order to increase the funds, and quoted the account of the poor widow and her two mites, to justify this trumpet-sounding, he settled the question by rising from his seat, and asking in his clear, shrill voice, "Will the speaker please give us the name of that poor widow?"—*Christian Age.*

Checks—Worthless.

Only the one who went all the way received the blessing. Says Russell Sewall: "I carried a check halfway to the bank. Did the bank therefore pay me half the value of the check? Nay; the bank didn't pay me a cent till I went all the way to the paying teller's window. And then the check was paid in full. Half-trust in God is no trust at all, and gets no reward; and that is why so many Christians lead flabby lives."—*Christian Union Herald.*

Destruction—Escape From.

It is related that once the city of Pleurs stood in a quiet valley of the Alps, beneath the shadow of the snow-covered mountains, a pleasant and prosperous town. Above it hung the avalanche threatening destruction. One night a wakeful man heard the ominous sound breaking on the still air, which heralds the descending mass of ice. Starting from his repose, he awoke his daughter, and with her hastened towards the city gate. There she recollected that her casket of jewelry had been left in the house, and turned back to secure the treasure. In another moment the overwhelming deluge of the avalanche fell with the voice of thunder between father and daughter, burying the city beneath it. When the morning dawned, the spires of the churches alone arose above the cold, white grave of the just before busy town. The maiden perished with her idol, while he who sought to save her escaped.—*Tract Journal.*

Evil—Prolific Root of.

In Brailsford's book, *The Spiritual Sense in Sacred Legend,* we are told that Noah had a vision of coming calamity and that he and Methuselah went to Enoch for an explanation. Enoch detailed the sins that had deserved the flood, and among others mentioned the forging into weapons of war of the metals which had been discovered, and the molding of them into coinage, and the finding of jewels and polishing them, from pride and luxury. We are told later that the love of money is a root of all kinds of evil, but it is strange to hear that the prolific

root was planted so early.—Archibald Alexander.

Gift—The Best.

A rich man was down at the water front waiting the departure of an ocean liner. He was joined by an acquaintance, who said to him, "You seem to be much pleased about something." "Yes," said the rich man, "I do feel unusually good to-day. Do you see that vessel at anchor in the North River? Well, I have on that vessel ten thousand dollars worth of equipment for a hospital in China, and I just came down to see the vessel safely off." "Well, that is interesting, and I am glad you made that gift," said the friend. "But you know I also have a gift on that ship. My only daughter is on that vessel, going to China to give her life as a missionary." The wealthy man looked touchingly into the eyes of his friend and exclaimed, "My dear brother, I feel as though I have given nothing as I think of what this sacrifice means to you!"—John Roach Straton.

Giving and Receiving.

"I can't get interested in missions!" exclaimed a young girl petulantly, and, if truth must be told, a bit superciliously, as she left a thrilling missionary meeting in company with an older lady, presumably an aunt or other relative. We were near enough to hear the answer. "No, dearie," came the pitying response; "'tisn't to be expected you should—yet a while. It's just like getting interest in a bank. You have to put in a little something first, and the more you put in, the more interest, time or money or prayers, it doesn't matter which, but something you have to put in, or you never will have any interest. Try it, dearie,—just put in a little something, and you're sure of the interest."—*The King's Own.*

Giving Our Best.

The story told of Mary of Bethany is that she went to a shop to buy a box of ointment. The man in charge showed her a box, but she said that she must have something better. He showed her a second box, but even that was not good enough. The third box, costly as it was, did not seem sufficiently worthy. Then the merchant said, "I have a box, but its price is so high that I do not dare to show it to you." "That is what I want," she said; "there is nothing too good for my Lord."—J. G. K. McCLURE.

Giving—Growth in.

A well-known writer on Christian stewardship says, "Giving is not just a way of raising money. It is God's way of raising men."—*Christian Herald.*

Giving—Ways of.

Some men give so that you are angry every time you ask them to contribute. They give so that their gold and silver shoot you like a bullet. Other persons give with such beauty, that you remember it as long as you live; and you say, "It is a pleasure to go to such men." There are some men that give as springs do: whether you go to them or not, they are always full; and your part is merely to put your dish under the ever-flowing stream. Others give just as a pump does where the well is dry, and the pump leaks.—BEECHER.

Gold and the Grave.

A cartoon in a paper not long ago showed a man in his shirt sleeves in a gutter picking up gold. Behind him as far as could be seen were bags of money—gold he had picked up. Just ahead of him was a cemetery. There he was with the sweat pouring from his brow, working as hard as he could to gather up his riches, but always coming nearer and nearer to the cemetery. This is a true picture of many a man, using hands and mind and strength gathering gold, but on the way to the cemetery.—MRS. M. WATTS.

Greed of Gold.

Midas, the Phrygian king, asked a favor of the gods, and they agreed to grant him whatever he should desire. The monarch, overjoyed, resolved to make the favor inexhaustible. He prayed that whatever he touched might be turned into gold. The prayer was granted, and bitter were the consequences. Whatever the poor king touched did turn to gold. He laid his hand upon a rock, and it became a huge mass of gold of priceless value; he clutched his oaken staff, and it became in his hand a bar of virgin gold. At first the monarch's joy was unbounded, and he returned to his palace the most favored of mortals. Alas for the short-sightedness of man! He sat at table, and all he touched turned in mockery of his wish to gold—pure, solid gold. Then the conviction came rushing upon his humbled mind, that he must perish from his grasping wish—die in the midst of plenty; and remembering the ominous saying he had heard, "The gods themselves cannot take back their gifts," he howled to the sternly smiling Dionysius to restore him to the coarsest, vilest food, and deliver him from the curse of gold.

Inheritance Withheld.

If your father left in his will an inheritance for you and your brother, and your brother, being at a distance, could receive his inheritance only if you sent it to him, would you feel free to decide whether to send it to him or not? And if you did send it to him, would you take considerable credit to yourself for doing so? That is like foreign missions. People talk complacently about the "poor heathen." Why "poor?" Because the heathen have not received their share of the inheritance which the Father left us to give them.—J. A. CLARK.

Key of Loyalty.

"Somewhere I remember reading of a strange Christmas gift once received by a young woman. The young woman had expected some valuable present. She had set her heart on a piece of jewelry which she had reason to believe would be given to her by a very dear friend, a charming woman, the hospitality of whose home she had often enjoyed and highly prized. But when Christmas day dawned and the young woman opened the gift from this friend it turned out to be just an ordinary door key, tied with a piece of ribbon on which was a little card. The young woman was at first so disappointed that she did not even read the inscription on the card; but when she did, this is what she saw: "The key to the door of the house of a friend. It is yours to use. Use it every day if you wish." The lovely significance of the gift then broke fully upon the young woman; that lovely home with the special guest chamber in which she had on several occasions rested in peace and comfort—this home open whenever she minded to use the key!

O beautiful symbol! To let the Great Guest into our hearts but once a week or once a year is not often enough. Give him the key—the key of loyalty and love! Let him in—let him in to stay. "I will come and sup with thee and thou with me," said Jesus. Let the blessed Saviour into your life, and the spirit of Christmas will abide forever and ever.—EDGAR DE WITT JONES.

Offering—Unprepared for.

A little boy, sitting next to a lady in church, noticed that she had nothing for the collection-plate. His own collection was in his hand; but as the collector approached, the little fellow seemed greatly disturbed because his seatmate seemed entirely unprepared for the offering. When the steward got within a few pews' distance he handed over his silver piece to the lady, as he whispered in her ear: "Take this, and I will get under the seat till he goes by." Such sensitive souls as this boy are exceedingly rare.—IDA R. SAUSSER.

Poor—Friends of the.

Tolstoy, the Russian socialist, has said that "the rich are willing to do anything and everything for the poor, except get off their backs!" Through a similar but universal perversity, the unconverted man is willing, more or less, to do anything and everything toward God that might lie in his power—heathen-like—except to yield Him real heart-friendship!—G. E. FABER.

Prosperity—Shadow of.

It is said of the soldiers of a certain king, in ancient times, that they lost a great battle by mistaking the shadows for the persons of their enemies. They discharged their arrows at the empty resemblance, instead of the living and moving ranks of men. How many make a similar mistake with regard to prosperity! They mistake the shadow for the substance; and thus they take a wrong aim. All their energies and all their efforts are directed to something short of the mark.—C. Overton.

Purse and Piety.

In Southern France, where attar of roses is distilled, a very curious ailment imperils the workers. The very abundance of the rose-leaves induces a sort of sleeping sickness. And surely it is even so in the abundances that are sometimes given to man. They are prone to sink him into the sleep of spiritual forgetfulness. A man's devotion is apt to dwindle as he becomes more successful. Our piety does not keep pace with our purse. Absorption in bounty makes us forgetful of the Giver. We can be so concerned in the pasturage that the Shepherd is forgotten. Our very fulness is apt to become our foe. Our clearest visions are given us in the winter-time when nature is scanty and poor. The fulness of the leaf blocks the outlook and the distance is hid. And the summertime of life, when leaves and flowers are plentiful, is apt to bring a veil. And the very plentifulness impedes our communion.—J. H. Jowett.

Riches—Fleeting.

Croesus, whose name is a synonym for great wealth, was himself taken captive, stripped of all his treasures, and in old age was supported by the charity of Cyrus.

Riches—Wishing for.

"I wish I were rich, I would buy everything," cried Charlie. "The sun, moon, and stars?" inquired William. "No; everything that can be had for money." "That's not happiness," said William. "Get your hat Charlie, and come with me to Mr. Morrison's," said his father. "Oh, please not, papa, he is such a disagreeable, miserable old man, with his cross looks and gouty foot, hobbling about and groaning." "I think you would like to live with him," said his father. "I, papa? I would rather live down a coal-pit!" "With him you would have all that can be bought with money. Be content with as much of it as God gives and seek to use it aright."

"The fear of God and sweet content
Yield riches that will ne'er be spent."

Stewardship—Fritz Kreisler's.

"I was born with music in my system. I knew musical scores instinctively before I knew my ABC's. It was a gift of Providence. I did not acquire it. So I do not even deserve thanks for music. Music is to sacred to be sold. And the outrageous prices the musical celebrities charge to-day truly are a crime against society. I never look upon the money I earn as my own. It is public money. It is only a fund entrusted to my care for proper disbursement. I am constantly endeavoring to reduce my needs to the minimum. I feel morally guilty in ordering a costly meal, for it deprives some one else of a slice of bread—some child, perhaps, of a bottle of milk. My beloved wife feels exactly the same way about these things as I do. You know what I eat; you know what I wear. In all these years of my so-called success in music, we have not built a home for ourselves. Between it and us stand all the homeless in the world!"—Fritz Kreisler.

Tithing or Tipping.

While we were bowling over the roads Henry said to his friend in a casual way, "How would you like to be a porter?" Timothy busy with driving, shook his head decidedly. "Why not?" persisted his friend. "Mostly tips. When I deal with a man I want him to pay me my due, eye to eye; not slip anything into my hand behind my back." "I wonder if that is the way the Lord feels about it?" quietly remarked Henry. "Just what do you mean?" asked Timothy. "Only this. When we give to the Lord without any fixed rule, just when we please and just as we please, I wonder whether he doesn't feel a bit like a heavenly porter. And perhaps we come to feel like the passengers and fall into the habit of giving him whatever spare bit of change we may have handy. I wonder if it wouldn't be better for the Lord and for us if we just looked him in the eye and give him according to some fixed rule."—W. S. WOODHULL.

Treasures—Seeking.

It was rumored that underneath a certain piece of ground there was iron to be found, and two men were appointed to go and inspect the land and see whether there was really iron there. One man, a scientist and mineralogist, was very conscious of his own limitations; and knowing his own weakness, he took with him some scientific instruments. The other man, who was buoyant and self-confident, said, "I believe what I can see, and what I can't see I won't believe"; and so he walked over the field, and got over it in no time. He said, "Iron? nonsense! I see no iron; there is no iron here." This man went to the syndicate and said, "There is no iron there: I walked all over the field and I could not see a trace of it." The other man did not trust to his eye at all. He carried in his hand a little crystal box, and in that little crystal box there was a needle, and he kept watching that needle. He paused, for the needle in that crystal box had pointed down like the very finger of God, and he said, "There is iron there." He passed on, until again that needle pointed down, and he said, "There is iron there," and when he handed in his report he said, "From one end of the field to the other there is iron." "Oh!" said one of the adherents of the first man, "how do you know, when you did not see it?" "Because," he said, "that which cannot be seen with the eye can be magnetically discerned."—A. G. BROWN.

Giving—Unselfish.

A farmer went to hear John Wesley preach. The farmer was not converted; he cared little about religion; on the other hand, he was not what we call a bad man. His attention was soon excited and riveted. John said he should take up three topics of thought—he was speaking greatly about money. His first head was, "Get all you can." The farmer nudged a neighbor and said, "This is strange preaching. I never heard the like of this before. This is very good. Yon man has got things in him; it is admirable preaching." John discoursed of "Industry," "Activity," "Living to purpose," and reached his second division, which was, "Save all you can." The farmer became more excited. "Was there ever anything like this?" he said. Wesley denounced thriftlessness and waste, and he satirized the willful wickedness which lavishes in luxury; and the farmer rubbed his hands, and he thought, "All this have I been from my youth up"; and what with getting, and what with hoarding, it seemed to him that "salvation had come to his house." But Wesley advanced to his third head, which was, "Give all you can." "Ay dear, ay dear," said the farmer; "he has gone and spoiled it all." There was now no further point of contact, no interest in the farmer's mind.—*Preacher's Lantern.*

Giving—Greatness in.

There are loyal hearts, there are spirits brave,
  There are souls that are pure and true;
Then give to the world the best you have,
  And the best shall come back to you.

Give love, and love to your heart will flow,
  A strength in your utmost need;
Have faith, and a score of hearts will show
  Their faith in your word and deed.

For life is the mirror of king and slave,
  'Tis just what you are and do;
Then give to the world the best you have
And the best will come back to you.
                    —MADELINE S. BRIDGES.

God the Only Giver.

Earth gets its price for what Earth gives us;
  The beggar is taxed for a corner to die in,
The priest hath his fee who comes and shrives us,
  We bargain for the graves we lie in;
At the devil's booth are all things sold,
Each ounce of dross costs its ounce of gold;
  For a cap and bells our lives we pay,
Bubbles we buy with a whole soul's tasking;
  'Tis heaven alone that is given away,
'Tis only God may be had for the asking.
                    —LOWELL.

TEMPTATION

Character—Testing.

The Rev. J. Stuart Holden says, in "Supposition and Certainty": "One of our great Scotch novelists, George MacDonald, put these words into the mouth of one of his characters who had been buffeted by inexplicable circumstances, and who, complaining to a friend about the hardness of her life, said in anger: 'Oh, I would to God I had never been made.' 'Why,' replied her friend, 'my dear child, you are not yet made; you are only being made, and you are quarreling with God's processes.'"

Made Strong by Trials.

A bee-keeper told me the story of a hive,—how, when the little bee is in the first stage, it is put into a hexagonal cell, and honey enough is stored there for its use until it reaches maturity. The honey is sealed with a capsule of wax, and when the tiny bee has fed itself on the honey and exhausted the supply, the time has come for it to emerge into the open. But, oh, the wrestle, the tussle, the straining to get through that wax! It is the strait gate for the bee, so strait that in the agony of exit the bee rubs off the membrane that hid his wings, and on the other side is able to fly! Once a moth got into the hive, and fed on the wax capsules, and the bees got out without any strain or trouble. But they could not fly; and the other bees stung them to death. Are you congratulating yourself on having an easy time? No hardness, no difficulties, no cross? Beware lest, like the bees, you lose your wing-power, and perish miserably in the dust.— F. B. MEYER.

Temptation—Courting.

There is a deep lesson to be read in a strange picture by Burne Jones, called "The Depths of the Sea." A mermaid, beautiful in face, but hideously repellent in her scaly train, has flung her arms around a youth, and is dragging him down through the green waters to her cave. In her face is the intense malignity of cruel triumph and cruel scorn; in the youth's face is the agony of frustration and of death. And the motto below is "Habes totâ quod mente petisti, Infelix!"—"Thou hast what thou soughtest with all thy soul, unhappy one." Oh that it were in my power to preach to all young men a sermon of meaning so intense as that picture! The mermaid, like the Siren of mythology, like the strange woman of the Proverbs, is the harlot Sense. She is the type of carnal temptation, ending in disillusion, shame, anguish, death. It is the meaning of the saying of the rabbis, "The demons come to us smiling and beautiful: when they have done their work, they drop their mask." It is the meaning of Solomon: "But he knoweth not that the dead are there, and that her guests are in the depths of hell." God has granted to that youth his heart's desire, and sent leanness withal into his bones. He has got what he passionately longed for, and it is—death!—F. W. FARRAR.

Temptation—Fighting.

A believer's watchfulness is like that of a soldier. A sentinel posted on the walls, when he discerns a hostile party advancing, does not attempt to make head against them himself, but informs his commanding officer of the enemy's approach, and leaves him to take the proper measures against the foe. So the

Christian does not attempt to fight temptation in his own strength; his watchfulness lies in observing its approach, and in telling God of it by prayer.—W. Mason.

Temptations—Little.

One of the men who accompanied Commodore Peary to the North Pole has since been drowned in a canoe in some waters near his home. After escaping the perils of cracks in the polar ice, and giving the most human account of the dash to the north, George Borup lost his life in what he must have considered quite a negligible peril, compared with those he had passed through. It is so in the moral life. Souls that can brave successfully the big outstanding perils are often the victims of the small ones. A temptation to be dishonorable in a big matter is easily overcome; but many yield to the temptation to be unduly angry over small things.—*Sunday at Home.*

Temptation—Resisting.

A sentinel posted on the walls, when he sees a party of the enemy advancing, does not attempt to make head against them himself, but at once informs his commanding officer of the enemy's approach, and awaits his word as to how the foe is to be met. So the Christian does not attempt to resist temptation in his own strength, but in prayer calls upon his Captain for aid, and in His might and His Word goes forth to meet it.

Testings—Severe.

I remember, some years ago, when I was at Shields, I went into a glass-house; and, standing very attentive, I saw several masses of burning glass of various forms. The workman took a piece of glass and put into one furnace, then he put it into a second, and then into a third. I said to him, "Why do you put it through so many fires?" He answered, "Oh, sir, the first was not hot enough, nor the second; therefore we put it into a third, and that will make it transparent."—WHITE-FIELD.

Trials—Blessing in.

A visitor to a famous pottery establishment was puzzled by an operation that seemed aimless. In one room there was a mass of clay beside a workman. Every now and then he took up a large mallet and struck several smart blows on the surface of the lump. Curiosity led to the question, "Why do you do that?" "Wait a bit, sir, and watch it," was the answer. The stranger obeyed, and soon the top of the mass began to heave and swell. Bubbles formed upon its face. "Now, sir, you see," said the man, with a smile, "I could never shape the clay into a vase if these air bubbles were in it, therefore I gradually beat them out." Is not the discipline of life just a beating out of the bubbles of pride and self-will, so that the Master may form a vessel of earth to hold heavenly treasures?—*The Sunday at Home.*

TESTING

Adversity—Blessing in.

"Blessed be the name of the Lord." God is a wonderful organist, who knows just what heart-chord to strike (says a famous preacher). In the Black Forest of Germany a baron built a castle with two lofty towers. From one tower to the other he stretched several wires, which in calm weather were motionless and silent. When the wind began to blow the wires began to play like an Aeolian harp in the window. As the wind rose into a fierce gale, the old baron sat in his castle and heard his mighty hurricane-harp playing grandly over the battlements. So, while the weather is calm and the skies clear, a great many of the emotions of a Christian's heart are silent. As soon as the wind of adversity smites the chords the heart begins to play, and when God sends a hurricane of terrible trial you will hear strains of submission and faith, and even of sublime confidence and holy exultation, which we never could have heard in the calm hours of prosperity.

Beauty—Secret of.

The Brussels lace is superior to all other lace; so beautiful, so multiform, so expensive. All the world seeks it. Do you know how it is made? The spinning is done in a dark room, the only light admitted through a small aperture, and that light falling directly on the pattern. And the finest specimens of Christian character I have ever seen are those to be found in lives all of whose windows have been darkened by bereavement and misfortune save one, but under that one window of prayer the interlacing of divine workmanship went on until it was fit to deck a throne.—*Christian Herald.*

Blessings Hidden.

There is a beautiful figure in one of Wordsworth's poems of a bird that is swept from Norway by a storm. And it battles against the storm with desperate effort, eager to wing back again to Norway. But all is vain, and so at last it yields, thinking that the gale will carry it to death—and the gale carries it to sunny England, with its green meadows and its forest glades. Ah, how many of us have been like that little voyager, fretting and fighting against the will of God! And we thought that life could never be the same again when we were carried seaward by the storm. Until at last, finding all was useless perhaps, and yielding to the wind that bloweth where it listeth, we have been carried to a land that was far richer, where there were green pastures and still waters.—G. H. MORRISON.

Blessings—Trampling On.

One day in the town of Sonora, in the southern mines of California, after a very heavy rain and freshet, a man was leading his mule-cart up the steep principal street, when his foot struck upon a large stone; he stooped down to remove it, and found it was a solid lump of gold, about twenty-five pounds' weight, which had been exposed by the storm, and many hundreds of people had passed over it daily. So do we daily trample on blessings richer than all the wealth of California. There is the goodness we misconstrue. We count sublime things commonplace and reckon as losses and disappointments the discipline which brings incorruptible treasure. The "benefits" of God are not the pleasant things merely, but all the things of pain and tears.—W. L. WATKINSON.

Burdens and Blessings.

In one of Schiller's poems a beautiful story is told to this effect: When God made the birds He gave them gorgeous plumage and sweet voices, but no wings. He laid wings on the ground and said, "Take these burdens and bear them." They struggled along with them, folding them over their hearts. Presently the wings grew fast to their breasts and spread themselves out, and they found that what they had thought were burdens were changed to pinions.—A. T. PIERSON.

Duty and Pleasure.

I heard sometime since of an oculist who was very fond of cricket. But he had given it up, much as he enjoyed it, for he found that it affected the delicacy of his touch; and for the sake of those whom he sought to relieve he sanctified himself and set himself apart. That is what we want—that there shall come into our lives a force that prompts us always to be at our best and readiest for service, our fullest and richest to help, a tree that is always in leaf and always in bloom and always laden with its fruit, like the orange tree, where the beauty of the blossom meets with its fragrance the mellow glory of the fruit. —MARK GUY PEARSE.

Guidance—Providential.

On the place where we live chicks are kept, and it has fallen to the writer's lot to be the one to look after them. Every night they would be shut in securely, and early in the morning they could be seen pecking away at the window of their house, and for a while there would be a running to and fro, and a fumbling, and a peeping, and a pushing for some egress before the appointed time. But the owner, who had shut them in lest harm befall them from some marauder, knows best when it is time to open the door.

Thus are God's dealings with His children. Oft indeed they are shut in, and within it does now and then seem dark, and eagerly enough do men peck away at where the light is seen to stream in, and gladly would they escape before the time. But He who watches even over each hair of their heads knoweth best when it is time to open the door.— IVAN PANIN.

Guides—Pasts Recalled.

To her friend Miss Nicholson, whose sympathy brought her much strength and peace, Florence Nightingale wrote in 1846: "My imagination is so filled with the misery of this world that the only thing in which to labor brings any return, seems to me helping and sympathizing *there;* and all that poets sing of the glories of this world appears to me untrue: all the people I see are eaten up with care or poverty or disease. I know that it was God who created the good, and man the evil, which was not the will of God, but the necessary consequence of His leaving free-will to man. I know that misery is the alphabet of fire, in which history, with its warning hand, writes in flaming letters the consequences of Evil (the Kingdom of Man), and that, without its glaring light, we should never see the path into the Kingdom of God, or heed the directing guideposts."—SIR EDWARD COOK.

Life—Love of.

A young officer doing duty with an Indian cavalry regiment went tiger shooting one day, "missed his mark," and soon found himself in the tiger's clutches. It was an anxious moment—few of his friends being at hand. As a sportsman of experience the young man knew well that his best course was to lie quietly and sham death. The tiger surveyed his prey, looked around, and thinking all was safe, set to work to make its meal. Taking the young officer's hand in his mouth he deliberately devoured it, and the arm was eaten to the elbow before help arrived. Had the victim moved, or uttered even a groan, the tiger would have put an end to his existence before going on with his repast. Of course, the shattered arm had to be removed from the shoulder, but that brave officer lives, and holds at this present moment a post of honor under the Government. Now imagine the suffering endured by him while lying, quite conscious, in the power of a voracious "man-eater"! Why do I tell you this? To ask you what it was that strengthened him to such an act of heroism. It was love of life—it was "for his life"!—J. B. C. MURPHY.

Music in the Storm.

There is an old German tale which might be a parable of the purpose in our life of the unintelligible things. The story is told of a baron who, having grown tired of the gay and idle life of the Court, asked leave of his King to withdraw from it. He built for himself a fort on a rugged rock, beneath which rolled the Rhine. There he dwelt alone. He hung wires from one wing of the fort to the other, making an Æolian harp, on which the winds might play to solace him. But many days and nights had passed, and winds had come and gone, yet never had there been music from that harp. And the baron interpreted the silence as the sign of God's unremoved displeasure. One evening the sky was torn with wild hurrying clouds, the sun was borne away with a struggle, and as night fell a storm broke out which shook the very earth. The baron walked restlessly through his rooms in loneliness and disquiet. At length he went out into the night, but stopped short upon the threshold. He listened, and behold the air was full of music. His Æolian harp was singing with joy and passion high above the wildness and the storm. Then the baron *knew*. Those wires, which were too thick to give out music at the call of common days, had found their voice in a night of stress and storm.—JOHN A. HUTTON.

Pain—Blessing Through.

A skilled physician about to perform a delicate operation on the ear said reassuringly to the patient. "I may hurt you, but I will not injure you." How often the Great Physician speaks to us that same message, if we would only listen? Richer life, more abundant health, for every child of His, is His only purpose. Why defeat that purpose? —*The Sunday School Times*.

Providence and Inheritance.

The celebrated Richard Boyle, Earl of Cork, who rose from a humble station in life to the highest rank, and passed through strange and trying vicissitudes, used these words as his motto, and ordered them to be engraved on his tomb: "God's providence is my inheritance."— *Old Testament Anecdotes*.

Sorrow—Blessing in.

It is said, that gardeners sometimes, when they would bring a rose to richer flowering, deprive it for a season of light and moisture.

Silent and dark it stands, dropping one fading leaf after another, and seeming to go down patiently to death. But when every leaf is dropped, and the plant stands stripped to the uttermost, a new life is even then working in the buds, from which shall spring a tender foliage and a brighter wealth of flowers. So, often, in celestial gardening, every leaf of earthly joy must drop before a new and divine bloom visits the soul.—Mrs. H. B. Stowe.

Sorrow—Ministry of.

The late Sir Arthur Sullivan had long admired the words of "The Lost Chord," and had made up his mind to set them to music. Relating the circumstances of the composition of the best-known sacred solo of the day, Sir Arthur said, "One night I was in the room next to that in which my brother lay dying. I had been watching at his bedside, and was thoroughly tired out and weary. I chanced to sit down in the room and there the noble words were before me. I did not rise from the seat until I had composed the music." The lovely strains were composed in the hour of sorrow. The dark night gave birth to the sweet song. Perhaps we do not know what we are producing when we travel the rough road—we are only conscious of the pains, and not of the products. But we may rest assured that our Father knows the ministry of every circumstance through which He makes us pass. —J. H. Jowett.

Sorrow—Sanctified.

On the rocky coast of Maine stands a lighthouse, built some distance from the land on a small rock. The lighthouse-keeper and his wife lived alone, visited every two months by a relief boat. On one occasion in the middle of winter they saw a small bark in distress obviously battling to find an entrance into the narrow mouth of the harbor, and the husband conceived it his duty to launch his boat to help them, to give them the guidance and bearings they needed. Ere he reached the bark his wife saw his boat swamp and her husband go down. There she was alone, alone amid that howling waste of wintry water. What did she do? She went and kept the light trimmed. At night she lighted the lamp, realizing that her private sorrow must not be allowed to extinguish the light which guided mariners from destruction into safety. For three weeks before the packet-boat came she lived alone with her sorrows and cares, and she kept the light shining.—J. Stuart Holden.

Sorrow—Transformed.

A traveler entered Milan Cathedral at the dawn of day. The sunbeams fell on the eastern windows. Every pane of glass revealed its beauty. The images of apostle, prophet, angel, and Christ were seen in all their glory. The sun swept on to his zenith and then drove his chariot behind the western Alps. As he did so he flung his beams upon the western windows of the great shrine. Then the glories they contained appeared. Not a figure remained without its light. All the richness of color and symbolism appeared. So the passing of time and the shining of the consolations of faith into a life transforms sorrow into joy and gloom into glory.—F. Smith.

Spirits—Ministering.

Every one knows the history of Raphael's "Madonna di San Sisto," at Dresden. Its background is composed of clouds. For many years the picture, begrimed with dirt, remained uncleaned, and the background of clouds looked dark and threatening; when the picture was cleaned and carefully examined, it was discovered that the supposed clouds were not dark atmospheric clouds but multitudes of angel faces luminously massed together. It is ever thus. His clouds are ministering spirits, angel faces; the heavy masses of Earth's dust, which look so dark and unangelic, are His veil; in them He comes, seeking the heart, striving to eradicate selfishness, to quench passion, to melt obstinacy, to wean from earthly things.—B. WILBERFORCE.

Spiritual Beauty.

You showed me a beautiful leaf in the summer-time, its color rich, its veins exquisitely penciled, its tints matchless in their prettiness and delicacy. But where is its beauty now? It is commingled with the dust, and is trodden under foot of men. And that beautiful flower that you gave me? I tended that with scrupulous care, I protected it from every blast; I suffered not the sun to scorch it by day, nor the frost by night; but I could not save it from decay. One morning I found it faded, and a little later, the petals scattered upon the floor. Is it not so with all mortal beauty? The bloom on the cheek, the roseate hue, the human face divine flushed with beauteous fire. How soon that bloom fades! One night's deep grief suffices to destroy it forever. How soon the eye loses its youthful luster! How soon the forehead has lines cut right across it! How soon the cheeks fall back! And, when we are not thinking of it, old Father Time passes by and sprinkles on our heads a handful of snow, to tell us that the autumn has come and that winter is nigh.—E. D. SOLOMON.

Stepping-Stones.

The bone that is broken is stronger, they tell us, at the point of junction, when it heals and grows again, than it ever was before. And it may well be that a faith that has made experience of falling and restoration has learned a depth of self-distrust, a firmness of confidence in Christ, a warmth of grateful love which it would never otherwise have experienced.—A. MACLAREN.

Suffering—Perfected in .

The great musician, Beethoven, had always a great horror of deafness, and his feelings may be imagined when he found that he was becoming "hard of hearing." When the first symptoms of the infirmity became apparent, he became the prey of an anxiety bordering on despair. Doctors and quacks alike were consulted, and the Royal Library at Berlin possesses a collection of ear trumpets and similar instruments which he made in the vain hope of assisting his weakening sense. But the deafness increased until at last he conversed only by means of writing. Yet it was after he was dead to all sense of sound without that Beethoven wrote his grandest music. Out of a calamity came forth sweet music.—*The Home Messenger.*

Testing Times.

The nineteenth century produced three famous persons in this country who contributed more than any of their contemporaries to the relief of human suffering in disease: Simpson, the introducer of chloroform; Lister, the inventor of antiseptic surgery; and Florence Nightingale, the founder of modern nursing. The second of the great discoveries completed the beneficent work of the first. The third development—the creation of nursing as a trained profession—has co-operated powerfully with the other two, and would have been beneficent even if the use of anæsthetics and antiseptics had not been discovered. The contribution of Florence Nightingale to the healing art was less than that of either Simpson or Lister; but perhaps, from its wider range, it has saved as many lives, and relieved as much, if not so acute, suffering as either of the other two.—Sir Edward Cook.

Testing to Reveal.

In the Napoleon wars, it is said that once the emperors of Austria and Russia and the king of Prussia were discussing the relative absolute, unquestioning obedience of their soldiers. Each claimed the preeminence, in this regard, for his own soldiers. They were sitting in a room in the second story. To test the matter, they agreed that each in turn should call up the sentinel at the door, and command him to leap out of the window. First the Prussian monarch called his man. "Leap out of the window," was the order. "Your Majesty," said the soldier, "it would kill me." He was then dismissed, and the Austrian soldier was called. "Leap out of that window," commanded the emperor. "I will," said the man, "if you really mean what you say." He was in turn dismissed, and the Czar called his man. "Leap out of that window," cried the Czar. Without a word in reply the man crossed himself, and started to obey, but of course was stopped before he had reached the window.

Thorn in the Flesh.

A man met a little fellow on the road carrying a basket of blackberries, and said to him, "Sammy, where did you get such nice berries?"

"Over there, sir, in the briers!"

"Won't your mother be glad to see you come home with a basket of such nice, ripe fruit?"

"Ye' sir," said Sammy, "she always seems glad when I hold up the berries, and I don't tell her anything about the briers in my feet."

The man rode on. Sammy's remark had given him a lesson, and he resolved that henceforth he would try and hold up the berries and say nothing about the briers.

Trouble—Mission of.

It is the mission of trouble to make earth worth most and heaven worth more. I suppose sometimes you have gone to see a panorama, and the room has been darkened where you were sitting—this light put out, and that light put out, until the room was entirely darkened where you sat. Then the panorama passed before you, and you saw the towns and villages, the cities and the palaces. And just so God in this world comes to us and puts out this light of joy, this light of worldly prosperity, and this light of satisfaction; and when He has made it all dark around us, then He makes to pass before our souls the palaces of heaven and the glories that never die.—Dr. Talmage.

VISION

Blindness—Blessing in.

When only twenty-three, Dr. Moon of Brighton was struck with total blindness. When prayer for cure failed, he cried, "I thank thee for the talent of blindness; may I so invest it that at the coming of the Lord Jesus, he may receive his own with usury." He at once applied his cultured intellect to devising the Moon system for the blind, now used in 492 languages and dialects, and by which thousands of the sightless are said to have found their way to Heaven.—*Dawn.*

Eyes Opened.

A Christian worker in Arizona tells of a fierce looking cowboy who came to him asking for copies of Mark's Gospel, and who told him this story: "I went to San Francisco and threw away much money in rough revelry. I slept late after a night of dissipation. When I awoke I saw a little Book on the table near my bed: the Gospel of Mark. I angrily threw it on the floor. I did the same thing the second morning. Awaking the third morning, I saw that same little Book. This time I took it with me to a near-by park and began to examine it. I spent the day reading it. I heard the Son of God say to a leper, 'Be thou clean.' I heard him say to a paralytic, 'Thy sins be forgiven thee.' I heard him commend the widow for her mite. I saw him take little children in his arms and bless them. I heard him say, 'Couldst thou not watch one hour?' I saw him die. It broke my heart and changed my life. I am a different man. Now, Stranger, I spend much time giving away copies of the Gospel of Mark."—*Winona Echoes.*

Eyes,—Blinded.

A man said to Mr. Dawson, "I like your sermons very much, but the after-meetings I despise. When the prayer-meeting begins I always go up into the gallery and look down, and I am disgusted." "Well," said Mr. Dawson, "the reason is, you go on the top of your neighbor's house, and look down his chimney to examine his fire, and, of course, you get only smoke in your eyes!" —Talmage.

Eyes That See Not.

I have read of a woman who worked hard with her pen, and at last found her eyes troubling her. The oculist whom she consulted told her that her eyes needed rest and change. From the windows of her home there was a grand view of some distant hills, and the doctor told her, when her eyes were tired with work, to look out of the window and gaze on the distant hills. It is good for us all to look out of the window sometimes. If we are always looking at the rooms where we live, the shop where we trade, the farm or the counting-house, we begin to think there is nothing else. Our little bit of ground is all this world and the next; we never see anything beyond our own handiwork, we are blind to all else, like the horse in the coal-mine.—H. J. Wilmot-Buxton.

"Expectation Corners."

A little book, "Expectation Corners," tells of a king who prepared a city for some of his poor subjects. Now far from them were large storehouses where everything they could need was supplied, if they but sent in their requests. But on one condition—they should be on the lookout for the answer, so that when the king's messengers came with the answers to their petitions they should always be found waiting and ready to receive them. The sad story is told of one desponding one who never expected to get what he asked, because he was too unworthy. One day he was taken to the king's storehouse, and there, to his amazement, he saw, with his address on them, all the packages that had been made up for him and sent. They had been to his door, but found it closed; he was not on the lookout.—*Christ Life.*

Light for Others.

There is a story of a man who was walking down a dark street and met another man with a staff and a lantern. The striking thing, as the stranger noticed it, was that the man was feeling his way with his staff, and apparently making no use of the light. When asked if he were not blind, the man replied that he was, but he knew the street well, and had no difficulty in making his way with his staff. "But," asked the stranger, "why do you carry a lantern?" "To keep other people without lanterns from stumbling over me," was the blind man's answer. To be able only to tell others where not to go is a small gift, but it is something. Not every one can be a brilliant beacon in the world, but the humblest person can keep himself from being a stumbling-block.—*The Youth's Companion.*

Light not Shining.

One night a man in a trap was run down at a level crossing. Consequently the old signalman in charge had to appear in court. After a severe cross-examination he was still unshaken. He said he had waved his lantern frantically, but all to no avail. The following day the superintendent of the line called him into his office. "You did wonderfully well yesterday, Tom," he said. "I was afraid at first that you might waver." "No, sir," replied Tom, "but I was afraid that old lawyer was going to ask me whether my lantern was lit!" How tragic it is that so many Christians are "waving the lantern" in the same way—and lives are lost.—*The Sunday Companion.*

Light—A Useful.

The words are somewhat sharply spoken by the conductor of an evening train, "Keep your lantern by you. If anything should happen, you would be at one end of the car and your lantern at the other." The brakeman was a new hand who had just come on duty. The conductor met him at the rear of the last car, when the above words were spoken. We glanced forward as the brakeman passed toward the front end, and there, to our own surprise indeed, we saw his lantern hung up in a corner. There are people who seem to be shining lights in the church, but who do not take their religion with them in daily life. Do you leave your lantern hung up where it can do little good in a special hour, or do you let your light so shine at all times that men, seeing your good works, glorify your Father which is in heaven?—*The Christian Observer.*

Light—Going Against.

One morning about twelve hundred dead birds were found around the statue of Liberty. They had beaten their bodies up against the great light, making no impression on the light, but killing themselves. Just so do some people try to battle against the light of the Gospel, going against its teachings, and they

are the ones who are being injured.
—*Sunday School Chronicle.*

Light—Hiding the.

David Rittenhouse, of Pennsylvania, the great astronomer, was skillful in measuring the size of the planets and determining the position of the stars. But he found that, such was the distance of those orbs, a silk thread stretched across the glass of his telescope would entirely cover a star; and, moreover, that a silk fiber, however small, placed upon the same glass, would not only cover the star, but would conceal so much of the heavens that the star, if a small one and near the pole, would remain obscured behind that silk fiber several seconds. Thus a silk fiber appeared to be larger in diameter than a star. There are times when a very small self-gratification, a very little love of pleasure, a very small thread, may hide the light. The little boy who held the sixpence near his eye said, "O mother, it is bigger than the room!" and when he drew it still nearer he exclaimed, "O mother, it is bigger than all out doors!" And in just that way the worldling hides God, and Christ, and judgment, and eternity from view, behind some paltry pleasure, some trifling joy, or some small possession which shall perish with the using, and pass away with all earth's lusts and glory, in the approaching day of God Almighty. —H. L. HASTINGS *(abridged).*

Light—Life Giving.

The Rev. A. H. Lash, of South India, in an earnest missionary speech, told an anecdote of a young officer who many years ago was dying of yellow fever. As the physicians stood helplessly around his bed, one whispered to him, "Is there anything you would like?" "Yes," he replied, "put me in the opposite bed that I may die in the sun." His wish was granted, but he did not die. The ebbing tide of life was arrested, and began to flow again until there was complete recovery. "That officer," said Mr. Lash, "was my father. When I was a little boy he told me this incident, and, like my father, I have tried all my life to live in the sun. It is only by living in the sunshine of God's presence that workers can obtain strength for their task."

Light—Missing the.

A Hibernian sailor was once left in charge of the helm, with directions from the captain to keep his eye on a certain star, and steer the vessel directly towards it, which he promised faithfully to do. The captain went below, and fell asleep. After awhile he awoke, went on deck, and found the vessel sailing in a course exactly opposite to that in which he had directed the helmsman to steer. "What does all this mean, Patrick?" "Faith, Captain, ye must pick me out another star, for I've sailed clear by that one!" Just so, many have turned their back on God, and heaven, and light, and peace, and think they have sailed by all the revelations of God, and want some one to pick them out another star.—H. L. HASTINGS.

Light—Plenty of.

A gentleman was working by the light of a lantern which went out. Things went wrong, and he could not find what he wanted. Then a boy came in. "Why don't you turn on the light?" he said; and sure enough the gentleman had forgotten all about the newly-installed electric light plant, and that all that was necessary was to turn a button, and the room would be flooded with light. Many grope in darkness all their lives because they do not seek God and turn on the light.—*Sunday School Times.*

Light—Progressive.

"If we live up to our light, we are doing all that can be expected of us, I reckon," said Silas. "I don't know about that," answered Aunt Hannah. "The first thing that might be expected of a good many of us might be that we should have a much better light. If I get a cheap lamp and poor oil to save money, and use an untrimmed wick and a smoked chimney, because I am too careless or too lazy to put them in order, it isn't much excuse for poor work to say that I am doing it according to my light. My grandmother did her work by a tallow-dip—the best work she could do by the best light she could get,—but I have no right to be doing tallow-dip work in this age of illumination."— J. R. MILLER.

Light—Protection of.

Some of the great jewelers have discovered a more effective method of securing their establishments than by the old-fashioned methods of bolts and bars and iron shutters; all through the night the lights are left brilliantly burning, and the gold and gems are found to be most secure in the simple shelter of the light. It is true also that the ultimate and absolute security for all the splendid treasures of our human nature and life will be found, not in the bolts and bars of an external prudential preservation of character, but in that divine light and glory which invests the character whenever the heart is full of love and purity.—W. L. WATKINSON.

Light—Receiving.

A passer-by one day asked of an Irishman, whom he observed breaking a large hole in the wall of an old cellar, what he was doing. The answer of Barney was prompt, "Shure, an' I'm lettin' out the dark." Whether the darkness be that of uncivilized ignorance, or infidel prejudice, let us shine in the light of the glorious Gospel, and the darkness will fly.—W. LUFF.

Light—Sufficient.

Late at night a man who had sought counsel of a minister was starting for his home a mile away. He was feeling discouraged because he could not see far enough ahead in the pathway of life. The minister asked him why he carried the lantern. "To light my way, because it is so dark," he replied. "But can you see your way home from where you stand?" was asked. "Oh, no, it is very dark just ahead." "Of what use, then, is the light?" "It will light the path as I go the same as it does here." The minister responded: "God's Word is a light unto your path. Walk in the light you have, and go on doing so, and it will shine around you all the way as you need to see.—WILLIAM S. BOWDEN.

Light—The World's.

In that famous picture which Holman Hunt has painted of this wonderful scene and utterance in the Saviour's life, there is one fatal blunder, as it appears at least to those who read Jesus with clearest eyes. The Saviour stands in the encircling gloom, lamp in hand, through which rays of light stream out upon the dusky archways of the Temple, upon the shadowy forms in the background, and upon His

own sad, beautiful face. But it is
from the lamp which He carries that
the illumination comes. That is the
mistake. It ought to have been
shown as the irradiation from His
own person, the glory of His own
face, the sunlight of His own matchless purity, grace, and love. He
Himself is the light of the world—
not what He taught, but what He
was and did. His very incarnation
is the world's light.—J. G. GREEN-
HOUGH.

Look—The Backward.

The ancients told a fable about
Orpheus who, they said, could move
men and beasts, birds and fishes,
and even trees and rocks by his
wonderful music; that when his wife
Eurydice was bitten by a serpent
and had died, then Orpheus followed
her into the infernal regions and
there played his music with such
exquisite skill that even Pluto (who
was said to be the stern and inexorable king of hell) and his grave
wife Prosperpina were moved to
such pity that they gave Orpheus
leave to take his wife back to the
world again on condition that he
did not look around while they
ascended. As, however, they were
rising, the fable says that he looked
round, either from love, or doubt,
or forgetfulness. The result was he
saw his much-loved wife for a moment, but then she vanished from
his sight for ever. If we look and
turn back to the world or sin, we
shall lose God's favor and blessings,
and we may lose our soul for ever.

Seeing into the Depths.

It is a fact well known to seamen
that objects under water, such as
shoals and sunken rocks, become
visible, or more visible, when viewed
from a height; and it is customary
at sea, when a sunken object is

suspected of lying in a vessel's
course, but cannot be seen from
the deck, to send a man aloft, when
the higher he can climb the mast
the farther will his vision penetrate
beneath the waves. From the top
of a lofty cliff the depth is seen better still; while the elevation of a
balloon enables the spectator to see
most perfectly beneath the surface,
and to detect sunken mines, tor-
pedoes, and the like which may be
concealed there. Now, just as there
is an optical reason why the depth
is best penetrated from the height,
so there is a moral reason why the
holy God best knows the plagues
and perils of the human heart. He
who from the pure heaven of eternal light and purity looks down into
the depths of the heart is cognizant
of its defects long before they report themselves in the creature-
consciousness.—W. L. WATKINSON.

Spiritual Vision Blurred.

The spiritual field glasses through
which we come to see God's will
for our lives are double-barreled.
Side by side are two lenses: the
one, "I trust," the other, "I will."
When a man can hold both of these
to his eyes, he will see God's will
with unclouded clearness. But suppose a man says to God, "I doubt."
Then a veil falls over that lens of
faith. And suppose he says, "I will
not." Then a veil falls over the
other, the lens of the will, of choice.
Straightway that man's spiritual
vision is in eclipse.—JAMES H.
McCONKEY.

Vision—A Clear.

The story is told of a little boy
whose family was very poor. He
received no gifts at Christmas-time,
but he spent what time he could
looking in the store windows at the
pretty things other little boys could

have, but he couldn't. One day he was run over by a car and taken to a hospital. One of the nurses brought him a toy, a troop of soldiers. As he touched them, what do you think he said? "There isn't any glass between!" So some day the glass will be removed between us and the pleasures and beauties of heaven.—*The Christian Herald.*

Vision—A Glorious.

A very popular picture of Watts which usually holds the spectator spellbound is taken from the Arthurian Epic. Riding through the forest, with its tangled vegetation graphically painted, Sir Galahad had suddenly caught a glimpse of the mystic Sangreal, which was concealed from all ordinary vision.

The times
Grew to such evil that the holy cup
Was caught away to Heaven, and disappear'd.

The Knights of King Arthur had gone in search of this hidden treasure. At the same time and in the same place, one could see it and another could not. The knights had the vision of the Grail in proportion to their purity. To some of them who saw it, it appeared veiled with a luminous cloud. But Sir Galahad, the knight of pure heart and unselfish living, who lost himself to save himself, beheld the glorious thing itself, clear and distinct. It is at this supreme moment when the heavenly vision appears to him that he is painted by the artist. He dismounts from his white horse, and stands bareheaded with fascinated eyes gazing upon the glorious vision revealed to him in the luminous sky through a break in the trees, and lighting up his face and armor. . . . The inner meaning of the subject will come to us as the view

of the Grail came to Sir Galahad, when our eye is single and our heart is pure, suddenly and unexpectedly; and we shall find that the idea which underlies the whole picture, and makes it lovely with a loveliness far surpassing that of hue and form so vividly delineated, is an intensely modern one, and as applicable to our day as to the far-off times of King Arthur.—Hugh Macmillan.

Vision Blurred.

There is an old fable of a man who for some crime or injustice was cursed with the power of seeing other human beings, not in their beauty of flesh and blood, but as skeletons gaunt and grisly. Much of the sorrow of the world comes from the fact that too many of us have this miserable faculty, and go about stripping off every worthy charm and beauty with which men and women are clothed, trying to find and expose some ugly trait or passion underneath.—Louis Albert Banks.

Vision—Defective.

Many of the faults and failings of our neighbors exist only in our own disordered minds. If you have a flaw in your window glass, the loveliest view seen through it will be ugly and distorted. So much depends upon our way of looking at things. I heard of a man who, coming home late one night, complained that he had been followed by an ill-looking person. It turned out that this was his own shadow. —*Sunday Companion.*

Vision—The Unerring.

It is written in one of the Eastern legends that somewhere in the deserts of Arabia there stood a mass of jagged rock, the surface of which was seamed and scarred by the elements; but whenever any one came to the rock in the right way he saw a door shape itself in the sides of the barren stone, through which he could enter in and find a store of rich and precious treasures which he could carry away with him. There are some things in God's universe that seem as barren and unattractive as bare and fissured rocks, but which contain an inwardness of warmth and sweetness inconceivable. The inner holies of God are fast concealed from those who will not come aright, with a heart of love and trust, but open to all who are willing to see and to hear.—*Christian Age.*

Vision—Value of.

There is a story of an old mason whose work day by day was the mixing of the mortar for use in the erection of a beautiful building. It was this old man's custom to contemplate the plan of the finished building as displayed outside the contractor's office. He said it helped him to mix his mortar so much better if he could keep before his mind the lovely thing that the architect had planned. The Bible is the rule of Faith, the character-builder's "Vade Mecum." It pictures the Perfect Temple, Christ Jesus. It says that we shall be like Him. And he that hath this hope in him, purifieth himself even as He is pure.— E. J. PADFIELD.

Vision—A Full.

Anoint my eyes that I may see
Through all this sad obscurity,
This worldly mist that dims my sight,
These crowding clouds that hide the light.

Full vision, as perhaps have they
Who walk beyond the boundary way,
I do not seek, I do not ask,
But only this,—that through the mask,

Which centuries of soil and sin
Have fashioned for us, I may win
A clearer sight to show me where
Truth walks with faith divine and fair.

        —NORAH PERRY.

Angel—A Ministering.

A little princess' recovery from a dangerous illness was the occasion for setting apart a special day of quiet thanksgiving by the king, in which none of the peasants were to stir from their homes. Slipping unobserved from the castle with a basket under her arm, the little princess went among the peasants distributing her gifts among the needy. A strange guard halted her and in a gruff voice said, "Don't you know this is the special thanksgiving day, when no one is allowed on the streets?" She turned in childish glee, exclaiming, "Yes, but I am the princess, and this is my day."—J. A. CLARK.

Confessing Christ—Duty of.

St. Augustine, in his Confessions, relates an excellent story of one Victorinus, a great man at Rome, that had many great friends that were heathens. But it pleased God to convert him to the Christian religion; and he comes to one Simplicianus, and tells him secretly that he was a Christian. Simplicianus answers, "I will not believe thee to be a Christian till I see thee openly profess it in the church." At first, Victorinus derided his answer, and said, "What! do the churchwalls make a Christian?" But afterwards, remembering that saying of our Saviour, "He that is ashamed of me before men," etc., he returns to Simplicianus, and professeth himself openly to be a Christian.—SPENCER.

Confession—Reason for.

If I am working beside a man, and I see that he tries to shirk and shift his labor upon me, I am angry with him. But if he says to me, "I am wounded, and cannot work"; or,

"I am lame" or "sick,"—then the thought comes to me at once, "You shall not work: I will help you." And so, if a man says to us, "I know I did wrong, but I am weak; blame me as little as you can, but help me as much as you can,"—that very confession disarms us, and we think better of him than we did before. Therefore it is that God so exhorts us to confess our sins to him.—BEECHER.

Example—A Holy.

In far-away China, a young father brought his baby son to the missionary to be christened and dedicated to the Lord. He asked that the name "Moo Dee" be given the child. The missionary had never heard a Chinese name like that, and questioned the father about its origin. "I have heard of a great man who love Jesus and obey his words," he replied. "Missionary call him 'Moody.' In our language 'Moo' means 'love' and 'Dee' means 'God.' Want my child too, love God and keep his commandments." No one can truly love the Lord Jesus and not have regard for the things he asks him to do. God grant that we may all so "Moo Dee" that all may see by our lives that we are indeed his followers.—*The King's Business*.

Fidelity to Duty.

On that great day when the nobility of England assembled in Westminster Abbey before the open tomb in which the body of David Livingstone was to be laid, all eyes were fixed on the quiet, black man, Jacob Wainwright, who stood at the head of the coffin. He was the Zanzibar servant who with his companions had brought his master's body back from the swamp in the heart of Africa where he died, and had delivered him to the representative of the Queen at the seacoast, and had asked as his sole recompense the privilege of attending the body until he could deliver it to his friends in the distant home. Now the service was completed; and as England arose to pay her tribute of honor to the heroic man who had given his life to close the open sore of the world, all eyes were turned to the faithful servant who stood at the head of his grave.—H. A. STIMSON.

Life—Abundant or Anemic.

An embankment is to be thrown up, or a cutting to be dug out. You want laborers. Here are your spades, and your picks, and your wheelbarrows, but the men are required. See a number of persons offer themselves for hire. They are very thin, they have singularly bright eyes, sunken cheeks, and hollow churchyard coughs—they are a choice company from the Consumptive Hospital. Will you hire them? Why do you look so dubious? These men have life. "Oh, yes," you say, "but I wish they had it more abundantly: they cannot do such work as I have to offer them."—C. H. SPURGEON.

Loyalty—Power of.

In the battle of Sadowa, after the Prussians had gained the victory over the Austrians, a young Austrian officer was found mortally wounded in a wet ditch. When the Prussian ambulance officers tried to remove him he besought them with such terrible earnestness to let him lie where he was and die in peace, that at last, seeing he had but a few hours to live, they yielded to his entreaties; and there, in that wet ditch, he died. When they moved the body they discovered the reason of his earnestness to be left where

he lay. Underneath the body were found hidden the colors of his regiment. Rather than they should fall into the hands of the enemy he had covered them with his dying body. The noble foe forebore to touch them. They wound them round the young hero's body, and buried him in that shroud with military honors.—ELLICE HOPKINS.

Providence—Guidance of.

A gunner, describing the intense moment just before the new recruits came up under Blucher that turned that decisive battle of modern times, said that moment seemed ages, and the dust and smoke of the battle were so thick and intense that the gunner, as he stood on the height on which he had been placed by the commanding officer, could not see five yards in front of him. He felt the swaying tides of the battle move this way and that, and he did not know at one time whether he was among friend or foe. Some one asked him: "Well, my friend, what did you do in that supreme hour of darkness and solitude?" "I stood by my guns," said he. That is all you and I have to do. We are not responsible for the swaying tides of battle: we are not responsible for apparent defeat or apparent failure. The question is, Am I where God puts me, and do I do as God would have me do?—A. T. PIERSON.

Redemption—Discovering.

Some time ago an evangelist, traveling on the cars, was singing to himself the song, "I've been Redeemed." A fellow passenger, hearing, joined him in the song. After singing, the evangelist put the question to the stranger, "Have you been redeemed?" "Yes, praise the Lord," was the answer. "May I ask you how long since?" "About nineteen hundred years ago," came the reply. The astonished evangelist echoed in surprise, "Nineteen hundred years ago?" "Yes," was the reply, "but I'm sorry that it's not more than a year that I've known it."—*The Expositor.*

Saints—Transparent.

A wee tot, the child of Quaker parents, whose aunt had for the first time taken her to a great cathedral, sat wondering at the glory that poured through the magnificent windows. At length curiosity got the better of her, and she whispered, "Aunt May, who are those people on the windows?" "They are saints," the aunt replied. Then in a voice audible to those near, the child said, "Now I know what saints are. They are not people who wear ugly clothes and bonnets. They are people who let the light shine through."—*"Love's Immensity."*

Testimony—Bearing.

Discoverers in the natural world frequently, for prudential reasons, keep silence as to their discoveries. When Galileo first turned his glass on the planet Saturn he saw, as he thought, that it consisted of three spheres close together, the middle one being the largest. Being not quite sure of his fact, he was in a dilemma between his desire to wait longer for further observation, and his fear that some other observer might announce the discovery if he hesitated. To combine these, Galileo wrote a sentence, "I have observed the highest planet to be triple." He then jumbled the letters together and made the sentence into one long monstrous word, and published this, which contained his discovery, but under lock and key. He had reason to congratulate himself on his prudence, for within two years two of the supposed bodies disappeared, leaving only one; and for nearly fifty years Saturn continued to all astronomers the enigma which it was to Galileo, until in 1856 it was finally made clear that it was surrounded by a thin flat ring which, when seen fully, gave rise to the first appearance in Galileo's small telescope, and when seen edgeways disappeared from view altogether. With an instinct that makes the newly saved Christian long that others may share his joy, he, however, goes everywhere saying, "We have found the Messias: this is the Christ."

Testimony—Cheerful.

It does my soul good to hear (at a church prayer-meeting) such cheerful testimony to the value of Christ's presence and blessing in affliction. At night, when a railroad train, having stopped at a station, is about to start again, in order that the conductor may know that everything is as it should be, the brakeman on the last car calls out through the darkness, "All right here!" and the next man takes up the word, "All right here!" and the next echoes, "All right here!" and so is passes along the line, and the train moves on.—BEECHER.

Tongue—A Loose.

"When this pen flows too freely," run the instructions given with a fountain-pen, "it is a sign that it is nearly empty, and should be filled." The caution would seem to apply also to human beings. Gossip, slander, idle chatter, all testify to the emptiness of the mind, and are a damaging sign.—*Forward.*

Water of Life.

In Flanders there is a pretty legend told of a place called Temsche. A clear fountain was in a farmer's field. He was a churlish man, and would not let the villagers go into his field to draw water from it one hot summer, when the land was parched and all the wells were dry. Then a holy maiden, living there, went and filled a sieve with water, and shook it over the neighboring common, and wherever a drop fell there sprang up a living fountain. Now the old Jewish nation was much like that farmer, that would keep divine grace for itself alone. It would have the living fountain of spiritual life for its own use only, and deny it to the Gentile world. But then came the apostles, who took up the living water given them by Christ, and scattered it over all the wide earth.—Quoted from BARING-GOULD.

Water of Life.

Some years ago, a young man of New England entered college. He was associated with other students in numerous wild pranks. One night they stood before the bar of a low drinking saloon. He was the leading spirit of the party, and the man at the bar said, "Young man, you never tasted anything better than that in your life." A poor, bloated, blear-eyed drunkard, half asleep, croaked out from his corner, "Except the water you drank from your father's well." It was too much for the young man. He set down his glass and asked to be excused. When next day the company met him they did it by invitation, and he read to them a poem which he had composed as his apology for having misled them. "The Old Oaken Bucket" may be familiar to you as a popular selection, but perhaps you did not know its history.—*The Expositor.*

Witnessing for Christ.

It became the most sacred duty of a new convert (among the early Christians) to diffuse among his friends and relations the inestimable blessing which he had received, and to warn them against a refusal that would be severely punished as a criminal disobedience to the will of a benevolent but all-powerful Deity. —GIBBON.

Witness—A Fearless.

Robley D. Evans will scarcely go down in fame as a diplomat; but in all his stirring career, remarks the *New York Sun*, he never rendered a greater service to this country than during that trying time in the harbor of Valparaiso when his little gunboat, the Yorktown, was the sole representative of our naval power in Chilean waters. Insult after insult was coolly heaped upon the young captain's hot-tempered head, and diplomacy was needed. Evans lay in the harbor with nine Chilean war vessels about him. The Chileans were celebrating some independence day or other with fireworks and searchlight drills. The white beams from the Chilean vessels had an impudent way of swinging occasionally on the little Yorktown, where she lay within machine-gun range of the Chilean cruisers. As the cruiser Cochrane fired her salute she let off a flight of war-rockets, and one of the heavy bombs barely missed the Yorktown. "I at once hoisted a large American flag," reads Evans' log, "and turned both my searchlights on it, so that if any one really wanted to hit me he could know just where I was. I was determined if trouble came there should be no ground for saying we had accidentally been struck in the dark. When the searchlights a few minutes later lighted us up they showed the crew of the Yorktown standing at their quarters and the guns all ready for business." No more rockets came our way.—*The Literary Digest.*

Witness—An Honorable.

A case was on trial in a Kentucky court-room. An old man of somewhat shabby appearance had just given important testimony; and the lawyer, whose cause suffered by his statements, strove in every way to confuse and trip him, but in vain. The witness stuck to his story, and did not lose his temper, in spite of the irritating manner in which the cross-examination was conducted. Finally, in the hope of breaking down the credibility of the witness, the lawyer at a venture asked, "Have you ever been in prison?"

"I have," replied the witness.

"Ah!" exclaimed the attorney, with a triumphant glance at the jury, "I thought as much. May I inquire how long you were there?"

"Two years and three months," answered the witness, quietly, with a manner that was interpreted by the lawyer as indicating chagrin at an unexpected exposure.

"Indeed," said the delighted lawyer, feeling his case already won, "that was a heavy sentence. I trust the jury will note the significance of the fact. Now, sir, tell the jury where you were confined."

"In Andersonville," replied the old man, drawing himself up proudly.

There was a moment of silence. The jurors looked at each other; and then the court-room rang with cheers which the court officers were powerless to check, and in which some of the jury joined. It is scarcely necessary to add that that lawyer lost his verdict.

Witness—Most Efficient.

When some one asked Sir Joshua Reynolds how long it had taken him to paint a certain picture, he answered, "All my life." "If I omit one day's practice," Rubenstein is reported to have said, "I know it the next day, the critics know it the day after, and the public the day after that." If, then, it be true that—

The heights by great men reached
  and kept
Were not attained by sudden
  flight;
But they, while their companions
  slept,
Were toiling upward in the
  night;

how is it to be supposed that it can be otherwise with great Christians? Our Lord bids us "strive to enter in at the strait gate," literally, to agonize to do it; and St. Paul declares: "By the grace of God I am what I am," yet immediately adds, "and his grace which was bestowed upon me was not in vain; but I labored more abundantly than they all." So in this matter of witnessing he will succeed best who takes most pains.—W. A. N. HALL.

Workers—Unknown.

A commercial traveler, named Rigby, was compelled to spend a week-end every quarter in Edinburgh. He always worshiped in Dr. Alexander Whyte's church and always tried to persuade some other visitor to accompany him. On one occasion, having taken a Roman Catholic traveler there who thereby accepted Christ, he called on Dr. Whyte to tell him of the conversion. The doctor then asked his name, and on being told that it was Rigby, he exclaimed: "Why, you are the man I've been looking for for years!" He then went to his study and returned with a bundle of letters from which he read such extracts as these: "I was spending a week-end in Edinburgh some weeks ago, and a fellow-commercial named Rigby invited me to accompany him to St. George's. The message of that service changed my life." "I am a young man, and the other day I came to hear you preach at the invitation of a man called Rigby, and in that service I decided to dedicate my life to Christ." Dr. Whyte went on to say that twelve of the letters were from young men, of whom four had since entered the ministry.—*Record of Christian Work.*

Workers—Unknown.

The whole world knows how Sir Walter Raleigh threw down his cloak at the crossing for Queen Elizabeth to tread on; but no one knows aught of those who cast their garments in the way before the Man of Nazareth. However, God remembers; some of those names are doubtless written on the palms of his hands.—David James Burrell.

FATHER

Father—Acknowledging His.

While Octavius was at Samos after the battle of Actum, which made him master of the universe, he held a council to examine the prisoners who had been engaged in Antony's party. Among the rest there was brought before him an old man, Metellus, oppressed with years and infirmities, disfigured with a long beard, a neglected head of hair, and tattered clothes. The son of this Metellus was one of the judges; but it was with great difficulty he knew his father in the deplorable condition in which he saw him. At last, however, having recollected his features, instead of being ashamed to own him, he ran to embrace him, and begged Caesar that they might be put to death together.

Father's Example.

A young man, when about to be ordained as a Christian minister, stated that at one period of his life he had been nearly betrayed into the principles of infidelity. "But," he added, "there was one argument in favor of Christianity which I could never refute—the consistent conduct of my own father."—*Innes's Domestic Religion.*

Father-Hearted.

I was told once of an old man in a Yorkshire village, whose son had been a sore grief to him. One day a neighbor inquired how the lad was doing. "Oh, very bad!" was the answer. "He's been drinking again, and behaving very rough." "Dear, dear!" said the neighbor. "If he was my son, I would turn him out." "Yes," returned the father, "and so would I, if he was yours. But, you see, he's not your's; he's mine."—*Ibid. p. 189.*

Father—Joy of.

As the Rev. Joseph Davis, an excellent Baptist minister in London, was walking along one of the crowded streets of that city his attention was arrested by the circumstance that a carriage with several horses was just about to pass over a little girl who was slowly crossing the road. He strongly felt the danger of the child, and forgetting his own, he ran, snatched her up in his arms, and hastened with her to the side-path, when the thought struck him—how would the parents of this dear child have felt had she been killed! At this moment he looked in the face of the little girl, which had been concealed from his view by her bonnet, and imagine, if you can, what his feelings were when he discovered that she was his daughter !—Arvine.

Father—Love of.

I remember to have heard a story of a bad boy who had run away from home. He had given his father no end of trouble. He had refused all the invitations his father had sent him to come home and be forgiven, and help to comfort his old heart. He had even gone so far as to scoff at his father and mother. But one day a letter came, telling him his father was dead, and they wanted him to come home and attend the funeral. At first he determined he would not go, but then he thought it would be a shame not to pay some little respect to the memory of so good a man; and so, just as a matter of form, he took the train and went to the old home, sat through all the funeral services, saw his father buried, and came back with the rest of the friends to the house, with his heart as cold and stony as ever. But when the old man's will was brought out to be read the ungrateful son found that his father had remembered him along with all the rest of the family, and had left him an inheritance with the others, who had not gone astray. This broke his heart in penitence. It was too much for him, that his old father, during all those years in which he had been so wicked and rebellious, had never ceased to love him.—Moody.

Guide—Father as.

I sometimes think of it as of a child sitting in a boat. The child does not know the coast, and it very little understands how to row. If the child were left to itself, pulling upon the oars, its right hand being a little stronger than the other, it would be all the time veering the boat to the right, and the boat would be constantly turning round and round. The child would, perhaps, make its way out of the harbor and into the ocean, and it would be carried away and lost, if there were no guiding power in the boat except its own. But there in the stern sits the father. The uneven strokes of the child would carry the boat this way or that way out of its course; but the steady hand of the father overcomes those uneven strokes; and all the mistakes with the oars are rectified by the rudder, and the boat keeps the right course. So that the force exerted by the child, though misdirected, all works for good when the father guides.— Beecher.

Memorials—Intimate.

It happened once that a family had a father who was a benefactor to the State, and did such service that after his death a statue was erected in a public place to his memory, and on the pedestal his virtues were engraven that all might read his name and revere his memory. His children mingled with the people as they stood in that square and listened to their father's praise with pride. But their eyes were dry. This figure with civic robes, cut in stone, was not the man they had known and loved. Within the home were other memorials more intimate, more dear, more living—a portrait, a packet of letters, a Bible. All he had done for the big world was as nothing to what he had done for his own. In the Last Supper we have sweet memorials of what Jesus has done for us.—John Watson.

MOTHER

Face—A Beautiful.

Do you remember the scene in Roderick Hudson, a story written by Henry James? The hero, who is a young artist, has wandered to Rome, and there drifted into a life of selfish indulgence. But far away from the old American home a mother's prayers had followed him. Her absent boy made her forget self in those moments when she kneeled at the throne of Grace; then face and soul become strangely plastic. She was conscious of no change as the years sped, but when at last she crossed the ocean in search of her son, and they met in the foreign city, the artist asked in surprise: "What has happened to your face? It has changed its expression." "Your mother has prayed a great deal," she replied. "Well, it makes a good face," answered the artist. "It has very fine lines in it."—A. G. MACKINNON.

God's Good Woman.

A child stood at the window of a baker's shop, looking in with hungry eyes. A lady passing by took compassion on her. The little one received the purchased dainties without a word, until at parting she quaintly and pathetically said, "Be you God's wife?" There was profound philosophy at the bottom of that. All true kindness proceeds from the best and noblest—yes, from God within us.—D. J. BURRELL.

Like Mother.

If ever there was a child of many prayers, Samuel was he. His life was an answer to the fervent supplication of his mother, by whom he was dedicated before his birth to the holy service of Jehovah. For weal or for woe a mother's influence is infinitely great. We are not surprised to learn that Byron's mother was proud, ill-tempered, and violent; or that Nero's was a murderess. On the other hand, we need not be astonished that Sir Walter Scott was a lover of poetry; or those of Wesley, Augustine, Chrysostom, Basil, and others, remarkable for their intelligence and goodness. Like mother, like child. This is what led the good Lord Shaftesbury to exclaim, "Give me a generation of Christian mothers, and I will undertake to change the face of society in twelve months."—E. MORGAN.

Love for Mother.

A pleasant-faced woman boarded a trolley car with her two small sons during the busy noon hour of the holiday season. The smaller boy sat with his mother upon one side of the car, while the other, who was about four years old, took a seat opposite. It interested him to look out of the window, but frequently he glanced across at his mother. At length he called softly, "Mother!" "Mother!" This time it was said a bit louder, and the mother looked over and smiled. The boy's eyes lighted, and he whispered: "Mother! I love you." The mother turned a glorified face upon her small son and men and women in the car looked tenderly from one to the other. The trolley car had suddenly become a place of blessing because a little boy had voiced this everbeautiful sentiment: "Mother, I love you."—*Zion's Herald.*

Love—Mother's.

The late Professor William James, Harvard's famous psychologist, would frequently illuminate a misty subject with a homely anecdote. Discussing motherhood once, Professor James said: "A teacher asked a boy this question in fractions: 'Suppose that your mother baked an apple pie, and there were seven of you—your parents and five children. What part of the pie would you get?' 'A sixth, ma'am,' the boy answered. 'But there are seven of you,' said the teacher. 'Don't you know anything about fractions?' 'Yes, teacher,' replied the boy, 'I know all about fractions, but I know all about mother, too. Mother would say she did not want any pie.'"

Melody in the Soul.

There came to Glasgow, not so long ago, a pianist of an excellent reputation. I read the *Herald's* criticism on him, and there was one thing in it that I noted specially. The *Herald* said that he had always been brilliant—always been wonderful as an executant—but now there was a depth of feeling in him that had never been present in his work before. A day or two afterwards, preaching in a suburb, I met a relative of the pianist. And we fell to talk of him, and of the *Herald*, and of the *Herald's* criticism on him. And he said to me, "Did you notice that? And do you know what was the secret of the change? *It was the death of his mother eighteen months ago.*" He was the only son, unmarried, and he had been simply devoted to his mother. And then she died, and he was left alone, and all the deeps were broken up in him. And now he played as only he can play who knows what life and death are, and what sorrow is.—G. H. Morrison.

Mother an Impartial.

Another manifest principle observed by Mrs. Wesley in the education and training of her family, was that of thorough impartiality. There was no pet lamb in her deeply interesting flock; no Joseph among her children to be decked out in a coat of many colors, to the envy of his less loved brethren. It was supposed by some of her sisters that Martha was a greater favorite with Mrs. Wesley than the rest of her children, and Charles expressed his "wonder that so wise a woman as his mother could give way to such a partiality or did not better conceal it." This, however, was an evident mistake. Many years afterwards, when the saying of her brother was mentioned to Martha, she replied, "What my sisters call partiality was what they might all have enjoyed if they had wished it, which was permission to sit in my mother's chamber when disengaged, to listen to her conversation with others, and to hear her remarks on things and books out of school-hours." There is certainly no evidence of partiality here. All her children stood before her on a common level, with equal claims, and all were treated in the same way.—J. Kirk.

Mother's Covenant.

My mother, when she had a large family of children gathered around her, made a covenant with three neighbors, three mothers. They would meet once a week to pray for the salvation of their children until all their children were converted—this incident was not known until after my mother's death, the covenant then being revealed by one of the survivors. We used to say: "Mother, where are you going?" and she would say, "I am just going out for a little while; going over to the neighbors." They kept on in that covenant until all their families were brought into the Kingdom of God, myself the last, and I trace that line of results back to an evening many years before, when my grandmother commended our family to Christ, the tide of influence going on until this hour, and it will never cease.—Dr. Talmage.

Mother's Devotion.

My grandmother's son, Walter, had gone forth from her, in prosecution of his calling, had corresponded with her from various counties in England, and then had suddenly disappeared; and no sign came to her, whether he was dead or alive. The mother-heart in her clung to the hope of his return; every night she prayed for that happy event, and before closing the door, threw it wide open, and peered into the darkness with a cry, "Come hame, my boy Walter, your mither wearies sair"; and every morning, at early break of day, for a period of more than twenty years, she toddled up from her cottage door, at Johnsfield, Lockerbie, to a little round hill, called the "Corbie Dykes," and, gazing with tear-filled eyes towards the south for the form of her returning boy, prayed the Lord God to keep him safe and restore him to her yet again. Always, as I think upon that scene, my heart finds consolation in reflecting that, if not here, then for certain there, such deathless longing love will be rewarded, and, rushing into long-delayed embrace will exclaim, "Was lost and is found."—John G. Paton.

Mother's Face.

J. M. Barrie has a beautiful chapter in Margaret Ogilvy, entitled, "How my Mother got her Soft Face." It is a suggestive exposition of a sweetness of life that came through suffering and bereavement. The "wild beasts" tear our life and strive for the mastery, but we have the angel ministry to keep the soul in perfect peace. And in our day

we have a great example in General Booth. What has he not suffered from the "wild beasts?" What shall we say of the hate and malice and persecution that he has borne? He has been in the wilderness with the foes and come out more than conqueror. It is the same story in each case, and apostles, martyrs, saints, humble mothers, and all sacrificial and sainted lives are proof of it.— F. R. Brunskill.

Mother's Faithfulness.

It is interesting to read the testimony of men at once great and good, to parental fidelity and affection. Said Lamartine, the celebrated French author: "The future state of the child depends in a great measure upon the home in which he is born. His soul is nourished and grows, above all, by the impressions which are there left upon his memory. My father gave me the example of a sincerity carried even to scrupulousness; my mother, of a goodness rising to devotion the most heroic. . . . I drank deep from my mother's mind; I read through her eyes; I felt through her impressions; I lived through her life." Further on, he says: "I know that my mother wished to make me a happy child, with a healthy mind and a loving soul, a creature of God, not a puppet of men." Again, he adds: "Our mother's knee was always our familiar altar in infancy and in boyhood. She elevated our thoughts to God as naturally as the plant stretches upward to the air and light. When she prayed along with us and over us, her lovely countenance became even sweeter and gentler than before, and when we left her side to battle with the world, we never forgot her precepts." The child of the wisest and best may go wrong, for there are seeds of evil in every heart. But the rule is that

God's blessing on affectionate fidelity secures a happy and useful life here, with the assurance of heavenly awards in the hereafter.— HENRY M. GROUT.

Mothers Help God.

A little boy who was told by his mother that it was God who makes people good, replied, "Yes, I know it is God, but mothers help a lot."— *The Christian Guardian.*

Mother—Honoring.

There lived in a Scotch village a very little boy, Jamie by name, who set his heart on being a sailor. His mother loved him very dearly, and the thought of giving him up grieved her exceedingly, but he showed such an anxiety to go and see the distant countries which he had read about that she finally consented. As the boy left home, the good woman said to him, "Wherever you are, Jamie, whether on sea or land, never forget to acknowledge your God. Promise me that you will kneel down, every night and morning, and say your prayers, no matter whether the sailors laugh at you or not." "Mother I promise you I will," said Jamie; and soon he was on shipboard bound for India. They had a good captain, and as several of the sailors were religious men, no one laughed at the boy when he kneeled down to pray. On the return voyage things were not quite so pleasant. Some of the sailors having run away, their places were supplied by others, and one of these proved to be a very bad fellow. When he saw little Jamie kneeling down to say his prayers, this wicked sailor went up to him, and giving him a sound box on the ear, said in a very decided tone, "None of that here, sir." Another seaman who saw this, although he swore

sometimes, was indignant that the child should be so cruelly treated, and told the bully to come up on deck, and he would give him a thrashing. The challenge was accepted, and the well-deserved beating was duly bestowed. Both then returned to the cabin, and the swearing man said, "Now, Jamie, say your prayers, and if he dares to touch you, I will give him another dressing." The next night the devil tempted Jamie to do a very foolish thing. He does not like to have any one say his prayers, or do right in any way, and so he put it into the little boy's mind that it was quite unnecessary for him to be creating such a disturbance in the ship, when it could easily be avoided, if he would only say his prayers very quietly in his hammock, so that nobody would observe it. Now, see how little he gained by this cowardly proceeding. The moment that the friendly sailor saw Jamie get into the hammock, without first kneeling down to pray, he hurried to the spot, and dragging him out by the neck, he said, "Kneel down at once, sir! do you think I am going to fight for you, and you not say your prayers, you young rascal?" During the whole voyage back to London, this reckless, profane sailor watched over the boy as if he had been his father, and every night saw that he knelt down and said his prayers. Jamie soon began to be industrious, and during his spare time studied his books. He learned all about ropes and rigging, and when he became old enough, about taking latitude and longitude. Several years afterwards, the largest steamer ever built—the Great Eastern—was launched on the ocean, and carried the famous cable across the Atlantic. A very reliable, experienced captain was required for this important undertaking, and who should be chosen but the little Jamie of whom I have been telling you!

When the Great Eastern returned to England, after this successful voyage, Queen Victoria bestowed on him the honor of knighthood, and the world now knows him as Sir James Anderson.—J. N. Norton.

Mother's Letter.

Frederick, King of Prussia, one day rung his bell, and nobody answering, he opened his door, and found his page fast asleep in an elbow chair. He advanced towards him and was going to awaken him, when he perceived part of a letter hanging out of his pocket. His curiosity prompting him to know what it was, he took it out and read it. It was a letter from this young man's mother, in which she thanked him for having sent her a part of his wages to relieve her misery; and finished with telling him that God would reward him for his dutiful affection. The king, after reading it, went back softly into his chamber, took a bag full of ducats, and slipped it with the letter into the page's pocket. Returning to the chamber, he rang the bell so loudly, that it awakened the page, who instantly made his appearance. "You have had a sound sleep," said the king. The page was at a loss how to excuse himself; and putting his hand into his pocket by chance, to his utter astonishment, he there found a purse of ducats. He took it out, turned pale, and looking at the king, shed a torrent of tears without being able to utter a single word. "What is that," said the king, "what is the matter?" "Ah, sire," said the young man, throwing himself on his knees, "somebody seeks my ruin! I know nothing of this money which I have just found in my pocket." "My young friend," replied Frederick, "God often does great things for us, even in our sleep. Send that to your mother; salute her on my part, and assure her that I will take care of both her and you."—*Moral and Religious Anecdotes.*

Mother's Prayer.

Another great teacher, Professor George Wilson of Edinburgh, Scotland, who succeeded in putting himself into the life of his students in a marvelous way, in spite of the pain that tortured him all through his professional life, liked to tell lovingly of his debt to his mother. One of his first memories was of the evening visits paid by her to the bed in which he slept with his twin brother. As she bent over the boys, she would whisper the prayer of Jacob: "The God who hath fed me all my life long unto this day, the angel who hath redeemed me from all evil, bless the lads!" George was fascinated by the words, which he heard one night when the mother thought he was asleep. After that he used to lie awake, pretending to be asleep, that he might hear the earnest prayer. The thought of the petition so often repeated was a benediction to him throughout his life.—John T. Farris.

Mother's Prayers.

I tried when I was a boy to be an infidel, but there was one thing I could never get over. I never could answer my mother's love and character. My father was an intemperate man, and my mother, when made miserable by his brutal treatment, would lead my little brother and myself to a spot under a hillside, and kneeling there, would commend us to God. Hardship and her husband's harshness brought her to her grave. At the age of twenty-one I was vicious, hardened, utterly impenitent. Once I found myself, near the home of my boyhood, and felt irresistibly moved to take another look at the little hollow under the hill. There it was as I left it; the very grass looked as if no foot had ever trod it since the guide of my infant years was laid in her early grave. I sat down. I heard again the voice pleading for me. All my bad habits and my refusals of Christ came over me and crushed me down. I did not leave the spot till I had confidence in my Saviour. My mother's prayers came back in answers of converting grace, and I stand to-day the living witness of a mother's faithfulness, of a prayer-hearing God.—Richard Cecil.

Mother's Strong Boy.

A little boy declared that he loved his mother "with all his strength," and he was asked to explain what he meant by the expression. After some little time spent in reflection, he said: "Well, I'll tell you. You see, we live up here on the fourth floor of this tenement, and there's no elevator, and the coal is kept 'way down in the basement. Mother is dreadfully busy all the time, and she isn't very strong, so I see to it that the coal hod is never empty. I lug all the coal up four flights all by myself, and the hod is pretty big. It takes all my strength to get it up here. Now, isn't that loving mother with all my strength?" The boy's heart was open, and the sunshine of love came out. Once he was a cross and crying baby. His mother took him to the warm heart of her love, loved him and loved him, until she opened his heart. He loved his mother because she first loved him.—Edwin H. Byington.

Mother's Traits.

Sir Walter Scott's mother was a superior woman, well educated, and a great lover of poetry and painting. Byron's mother was proud, ill-tempered, and violent. The mother of Napoleon Bonaparte was noted for her beauty and energy. Lord Bacon's mother was a woman of superior mind and deep piety. The mother of Nero was a murderess. The mother of Washington was pious, pure, and true. The mother of Patrick Henry was marked by her superior conversational powers. The mother of John Wesley was remarkable for her intelligence, piety, and executive ability, so that she has been called "the mother of Methodism." It will be observed, that, in each of these examples, the sons inherited the prominent traits of the mother.

Mother Waiting.

Bianconi, the introducer of the car system into Ireland, in leaving his home in Italy, found his most trying leave-taking in separating from his mother. She fainted as he left her. Her last words were words which he never forgot—"When you remember me, think of me as waiting at this window watching for your return."—Smiles.

Mothers, Influence of.

"Of sixty-nine monarchs who have worn the French crown," a French writer says, "only three have loved the people, and all those three were reared by their mothers without the intervention of pedagogues. A Bossuet educated the tyrant Louis XIV.; his mother did not train him. St. Louis was trained by Blanche, Louis XII, was trained by Maria of Cleves, and Henry IV. was trained by Jane of Albret; and these were really the fathers of their people."

Mother—Memory of.

Many a son who has stood unmoved by the tears of a living

mother—his mother by whom he lives, who has cherished him as her own soul, who has forgiven and forgiven and forgiven him, who has toiled and prayed, and watched for him—though he has hardened himself against her looks of imploring love and turned carelessly from her entreaties and burst through all the fond cords and snares by which she has sought to keep him, has yet broken down before the calm, unsolicitous, resting face of the dead. Hitherto he has not listened to her pleadings, and now she pleads no more. Hitherto she has heard no word of pure love from him, and now she hears no more. Hitherto he has done nothing for her of all that a son may do, and now there is nothing he can do. All the goodness of her life gathers up and stands out at once, and the time for gratitude is past. He sees suddenly, as by the withdrawal of a veil, all that that worn body has passed through for him, and all the goodness these features have expressed, and now they can never light up with joyful acceptance of his love and duty. Such grief as this finds its one alleviation in the knowledge that we may follow those who have gone before us; that we may yet make reparation. —M. Dods.

Mother—Memoirs of.

The music of that silver-toned voice we again hear from the spirit-land, singing some soothing melody, or telling in simple language "that sweet story of old," till forgotten were all our childish sorrows. And now, in the strife and tumult of life, when the cold world frowns darkly upon us, her gentle words come back, bidding us "look above." Who can fathom the depth of a mother's love? No friendship so pure, so devoted. The wild storm of adversity and the bright sunshine of prosperity are all alike to her: however unworthy we may be of that affection, a mother never ceases to love her erring child. Often, when alone, as we gaze up to the starry heaven, can we in imagination catch a glimpse of the angels around the "great white throne"; and among the brightest and fairest of them all is our sweet mother, ever beckoning us onward and upward to her celestial home. —R. Smith.

Woman—A Great.

We are told that, throughout the strain of the civil war in America, Abraham Lincoln found a true priest in the godly and much-suffering woman who had charge of his children. He, who became more powerful than any monarch of modern times through the reverence of his countrymen for the man he was, tells us how he was sustained in that awful crisis of national calamity and personal sorrow by the prayers in his behalf of this stricken, yet believing woman. She knew God, Lincoln felt, so she became God's priest to Lincoln. He resorted to her for intercession on his behalf— he who would, as one truly remarks, have treated with "courteous and civil incredulity a proffer of sacerdotal good offices from Cardinal Gibbons."—A. Shepherd.

A Cradle Rocking.

Like a cradle rocking, rocking
  Silent, peaceful, to and fro,
Like a mother's sweet looks dropping
  On the little face below,
Hangs the green earth, swinging, turning
  Jarless, noiseless, safe and slow;
Falls the light of God's face bending
  Down, and watching us below.

And as feeble babes that suffer,
Toss and cry, and will not rest,
Are the ones the tender mother
Holds the closest, loves the best;
So when we are weak and wretched,
By our sins weighed down, dis-
tressed,
Then it is that God's great patience
Holds us closest, loves us best.

O great heart of God! whose loving
Cannot hindered be nor crossed;
Will not weary, will not even
In our death itself be lost—
Love divine! of such great loving
Only mothers know the cost—
Cost of love which, all love passing,
Gave a Son to save the lost.

—SAXE HOLM.

CHILDREN

Acts—Good.

A pretty story is told of Leonardo da Vinci's boyhood. The little fellow was accustomed to buy such caged birds as he saw exposed for sale on the streets of Florence that he might set them free. The little Leonardo early learned the lesson that there is more genuine pleasure in a good act than in a good possession. There are, in the path in which each of us walk, many caged birds which we can set free. Of all keys to unlock the prison captives sympathy is the best. A kind word of praise, a hearty expression of good-will, a little help offered at the right time—none of these things cost much, but each may make the difference, to many a sad heart, between joy and sorrow.

Ambition—Worldly.

On the accession of Claudius, Agrippina was restored to her rank and fortune, and once more undertook the management of her child (Nero). His beauty made him an object of special pride to his mother. From this time forward it seems to have been her one desire to elevate the boy to the rank of Emperor. In vain did the astrologers warn her that his elevation involved her murder. To such dark hints of the future she had but one reply—"Occidat dum imperit!" "Let him slay me so he do but reign." (He put her to death afterwards.)—Farrar.

Both Knees.

A lecturer recently declared at the outset of his lecture that he "received his moral training at the knee of a devout mother and across the knee of a determined father." One wonders how many of the oncoming generation will be enabled to make such a statement.—*King's Business.*

Boy Foreshadows the Man.

Once there was at Oxford University a little bootblack named George. He was bright and active. The boys liked him very much. At length one of them said: "A boy who can black shoes well can study well." The other boys agreed, and banded together to educate the little fellow. The bootblack became a learned man; and, better than that, a man of very beautiful character. He was George Whitefield, the great preacher.—*Home Department Quarterly of International Sunday School Lessons.*

Boys—Kindness to.

I remember when I first went away from home. It was only twelve miles; but I've never been so far since as that seemed to me then. I had left my mother and sisters for the first time in my life, and if I ever needed a kind word or a word of cheer, it was then. I was walking down the street with my brother, who had gone there a year before; and as we were going along my brother said, pointing out an old gentleman, "There's a man that will give you a cent. He gives every new boy that comes to this town a cent. He gave me one, and I know he will you." I looked at him. I thought he was the finest-looking man I ever saw. When he came up to us he said to my brother, "Why, this is a new boy in the town, isn't it?" And he said, "Yes, sir. He's just come." He wanted him to be sure I hadn't got the cent. The old man took off my hat, and put his trembling hand on my head, and said, "Well, God bless you, my boy! I am told your father is dead; but you've got a Father in heaven."

He gave me a brand-new cent I don't know what has become of the cent; but I can feel the pressure of the old man's hand upon my head to-day. He gave me what I wanted so much—a kind and cheering word.—MOODY.

Child—Generosity of.

A certain business man has a curious little charm for his watch chain. Business acquaintances often joke him about it, for it is nothing but a queer little copper two-cent piece, bright, it is true, through frequent polishing, but plainly showing its value. Its value, indeed! The man wouldn't sell it for a thousand dollars. "I had lost every cent I had in the world, practically," he told some one with tears in his eyes, "and there at my desk, my head on my arms, I was thinking of a possible way to end it, when my little girl came up to me and asked a question: 'What does ruined mean, papa?' and then I knew I had been groaning loud enough to be heard and understood. 'You said "ruined," papa. What does ruin mean?' 'It means I haven't any money baby. Papa's a poor man.' The little feet pattered away, and then back again, and here on my watchchain is what she gave me. Not a great fortune—no, but the foundation of one. Whatever I've got since came from it, for it gave me courage."—*The Expositor.*

Child Sower.

"I was wont when very young to follow my father, who was a skilled agriculturist, into the field. Knowing well how much a child is gratified by being permitted to imitate a man's work, he sometimes hung the seed bag with a few handfulls in it upon my shoulder, and sent me into the fields to sow. I contrived in some way to throw the grain away and it fell among the clods. But the seed which fell from an infant's hand, when it fell in the right place, grew as well and ripened as fully as that which had been scattered by a strong and skillful man. Even so a child may spread the knowledge of the word."—ARNOT.

Children—Care of.

In a Chinese Christian family at Amoy, a little boy, the youngest of three children, on asking his father to allow him to be baptized, was told that he was too young; that he might fall back if he made a profession when he was only a little boy. To this he made the touching reply, "Jesus has promised to carry the lambs in His arms. I am only a little boy; it will be easier for Jesus to carry me." This logic of the heart was too much for the father. He took him with him, and the dear child was ere long baptized. The whole family, of which this child is the youngest member— the father, mother, and three sons— are all members of the Mission Church at Amoy.

Children and Christ.

Robert Hall, the prince of Baptist preachers, was converted at twelve years of age. Matthew Henry, the commentator, who did more than any man of his century for increasing the interest in the study of the Scriptures, was converted at eleven years of age; Isabella Graham, immortal in the Christian Church, was converted at ten years of age; Dr. Watts, whose hymns will be sung all down the ages, was converted at nine years of age; Jonathan Edwards, perhaps the mightiest intellect that the

American pulpit ever produced, was converted at seven years of age; and that father and mother take an awful responsibility when they tell their child at seven years of age, "You are too young to be a Christian," or, "You are too young to connect yourself with the church." That is a mistake as long as eternity.—TALMAGE.

Children—Conversion of.

Many persons are afraid of children's conversion. As though the conversion of a child that is free from the cares and burdens which you carry like a hump on your back was not more likely to be genuine than yours, if you give it fair play! When little children think they are converted people say, "What, converted so small? Christians so young? Let us be careful. We will not take them into the church yet. It will not do to bring them along too fast. If they hold out we will receive them."

Suppose, a child being born, the doctor should say, "My dear father and mother, it is uncertain whether or not this child will live, and I advise you to put it out on the front door-steps and leave it over night. If it lives in the open air in January you may be sure that it has a good constitution, and you will be warranted in bringing it in and taking care of it." Thus you do a devilish work, and hope that God will do a good one. Those periods when children feel drawings toward higher things, and hear the call of God, are just the periods when you should take care of them. It is not hard to make a tree grow right if you begin to train it when it is young, but to make a tree grow right after you have allowed it to grow wrong till it is old is not an easy matter.— H. W. BEECHER.

Children—Early Conversion.

On the mantelpiece of my grandmother's parlor was an apple in a vial. It entirely filled the body of the bottle, and my childish wonderment constantly was, "How could it have got there?" I climbed a chair to see if the bottom would unscrew, or if there had been a joint throughout the length of the vial. But neither of these proved to be the case, and the apple remained to me a mystery. One day, walking in the garden, I saw it all. There on a tree, in the garden, was a vial tied, and within it a tiny apple growing. The apple was put into the bottle while it was little, and it grew there. So we must capture the boys and girls and introduce them within the influence of the church, and let them grow up therein.—The Sunday School Times.

Children—Faith in.

The Booth children were left in no mist of doubt as to their future. There was an end, a point, a purpose, in their life. They grew up in an atmosphere of decision. Many children are made timid, diffident, ineffective by their training. They are constantly told how naughty they are, till they begin to believe that they are good for nothing. The Booth parents acted on a different principle. They had faith in their children and for their children. When Katie was still a little girl in socks, her mother would say to her, "Now, Katie, you are not here in this world for yourself. You have been sent for others. The world is waiting for you."—J. STRAHAN.

Children in the Fold.

A good old Scotch elder, who was deeply concerned because his pastor persistently refused to allow children to be admitted to church fellowship, invited him to his house. After tea the elder took the pastor out to see his large flock of sheep put into the fold. Taking his stand at the entrance to the sheepfold the elder allowed the sheep to enter, but as the little lambs came up he roughly pushed them back with a heavy stick. The pastor became very indignant, and exclaimed: "What are you doing to the lambs? They need the shelter far more than the sheep!" "Just what you are doing to the children of the church," was the prompt reply. The object-lesson did its work. Never again did the pastor attempt to shut out from the fold of the church one of Christ's little ones.—*The Expositor.*

Children—Influence Over.

The mother of a family was married to an infidel, who made jest of religion in the presence of his own children; yet she succeeded in bringing them all up in the fear of the Lord. I asked her one day how she preserved them from the influence of a father whose sentiments were so opposed to her own. This was her answer: "Because, to the authority of a father, I do not oppose the authority of a mother, but that of God. From their earliest years, my children have always seen the Bible upon my table. This holy book has constituted the whole of their religious instruction. I was silent, that I might allow it to speak. Did they propose a question, did they commit a fault, did they perform a good action, I opened the Bible, and the Bible answered, reproved, or encouraged them. The constant reading of the Scriptures has wrought the prodigy which surprises you."—A. MONOD.

Children—Obedient.

Years ago a famous children's specialist said to me: "When it comes to a serious illness, the child who has been taught to obey stands four times the chance for recovery that the spoiled and undisciplined child does." Those words made a lasting impression upon me. Up to that time I had been taught that one of the ten commandments was for children to obey their parents. Never had it entered my mind that a question of obedience might mean the saving or losing of a child's life.—*Herald and Presbyter.*

Children—Value of.

Socrates once said, "Could I climb to the highest place in Athens, I would lift my voice and proclaim—Fellow-citizens, why do ye turn and scrape every stone to gather wealth, and take so little care of your children, to whom one day you must relinquish it all?"—*Family Circle.*

Early Conversions—Importance of.

There was an abbot who desired a piece of ground that lay conveniently for him. The owner refused to sell it, yet, with much persuasion, was contented to let it. The abbot hired it for his rent, and covenanted only to farm it with one crop. He had his bargain, and sowed it with acorns,—a crop that lasted three hundred years. Thus Satan begs but for the first crop. Let him sow thy youth with acorns: they will grow up with thy years to sturdy oaks, so big-bulked and deep-rooted, that they shall last all thy life.—T. ADAMS.

Early Piety—Importance of.

The most important ten years of human life are from five to fifteen years of age. The vast majority of those who pass twenty irreligious are never converted at all. Dr. Spencer tells us, that, out of two hundred and thirty-five hopeful converts in his church, one hundred and thirty-eight were under twenty years, and only four had passed their fiftieth year. I have been permitted, during my ministry, to receive nearly one thousand persons into the church on confession of their faith; and not one dozen of these had outgrown their fiftieth year. I did, indeed, once baptize a veteran of eighty-five; but the case was so remarkable, that it excited the talk and wonder of the town. Such late repentances are too much like what the blunt dying soldier called "flinging the fag-end of one's life into the face of the Almighty."—T. L. CUYLER.

Early Repentance.

If a man sets about climbing a steep cliff when he is young and active, and has the free use of his limbs, he has a great advantage: the old and the crippled are pretty sure to fail. So it is with repentance. The young can mount the hill, if they set about it in good earnest, with much less evil. But they who are old in sin; they whose souls have become stiff through years of wickedness, and have grown double, so to say, by always looking earthward,—how can they make the efforts which are needed for such a task? Of all hopeless miracles, the miracle of a death-bed repentance seems one of the most hopeless.—A. W. HARE.

Envy—Wicked.

When Sir Walter Scott was a boy at school, his efforts to gain a prize seemed all to no purpose, on account of the superior memory of one of his companions, who never failed to say his lessons perfectly. Walter did well, but now and then he would make a slip. In vain he strove to be first; he was always second, but could not oust his school-fellow from the top place. One day, watching his rival repeating a long task without mistake or hesitation, Walter noticed that his fingers were perpetually fidgeting a particular button on his waistcoat. A thought struck the envious lad. Could it be? He would see. An opportunity soon occurred, and he cut off that button from that waistcoat while its owner was asleep. Next day the class stood up. Number one began, and as the first words left his lips, his fingers might be seen feeling for the familiar button. They felt for it in vain; and the hapless boy stopped, then stammered, then stopped again, and broke down altogether. Utterly unconscious of the cause, he racked his memory in despairing amazement, but he could not remember a line, and Walter stepped to the top of the class. Not a very serious trick, many boys will say. I choose it on this very account, as an illustration of what envy will lead to.—E. STOCK.

Faith as a Child.

A poor woman, holding the hand of her little boy, recently said to the preacher, "Sir, the word 'Jehovah-jireh' has been a great comfort to us through this child. Owing to my husband's long illness we were in great want. But one Sunday Robert came running home and said: 'Cheer up, father and mother, the Lord will be sure to provide; Jehovah-jireh!' And often after that, when we have been in trouble, he has said: 'Come, let us sing a verse of Jehovah-jireh—

' "Though troubles assail and danger affright,

Though friends should all fail,
and foes all unite,
Yet one thing secures us, what-
ever betide,
The Scripture assures us—The
Lord will provide." '

"Once, when we had no food
left, he again told us not to forget
Jehovah-jireh. He went out, but
came back in a few minutes holding
up a shilling he had found on the
pavement, and saying: 'Here's Jehovah-jireh, mother; I was sure He
would provide!'" Who will say
this betokened childish ignorance
and not Christian wisdom? Might
not our philosophy be more sound,
if we were more as "little children"?
We know who said, "Out of the
mouth of babes and sucklings Thou
hast perfected praise."—NEWMAN
HALL.

Girl—a Good Shepherd.

Here is a little story that comes
to us from France. A girl of twelve
was tending sheep on the bare,
peaked hills of Auvergne with a dog
she had known only a day or two
—a surly and suspicious dog. As
evening came on, and the little
shepherdess thought of returning to
the farm, the dog sprang at her and
savagely gashed her cheek. The
plucky little maid herded the sheep
together and led them home, where
she explained what had happened,
and added: "What luck that it happened at turning-in time!" As the
doctor stitched up the wounded
cheek he said: "So if the dog had
bitten you earlier in the afternoon
you would not have come back at
once?" The child looked up. "Who
would have tended my sheep?" she
asked.—*Children's Newspaper.*

Lamb's Book of Life.

Some time ago three children—
ten, seven, and four years old—arrived in St. Louis, having traveled
all the way from Germany, without
any escort or protection beyond a
New Testament and their own innocence and helplessness. Their
parents, who had emigrated from
the Fatherland and settled in Missouri, left them in charge of an
aunt, to whom they forwarded
money sufficient to pay the expenses
of the little ones to their new home
across the Atlantic. As the children could not speak any other
language than German, it is doubtful weather they would ever have
reached their destination had not
their aunt provided them with a
passport, addressed not so much to
an earthly authority as to Christian
mankind generally. She gave the
elder girl a New Testament, in-
structing her to show it to every
person who might accost her, and
especially to call their attention to
the first leaf of the book. Upon
that leaf were written the names
of the three children, their birth-
place and severel ages, and this
simple statement:—"Their father
and mother in America are
anxiously awaiting their arrival at
Sedalia, Missouri." This was followed by the irresistible appeal—
their guide, safeguard, and inter-
preter throughout a journey of more
than four thousand miles—"Verily
I say unto you, Inasmuch as ye
have done it unto one of the least
of these my brethren, ye have done
it unto me." Many were the acts
of kindness shown to the little travelers, many the hands held out to
smooth their journey, until they
reached their parents in perfect
safety.

Love—Voice of.

Workmen were blasting the
castle rock (Stirling), near where
it abuts upon a walk that lies open
to the street. The train was laid

and lit, and an explosion was momentarily expected. Suddenly trotting round the great wall of the cliff came a little child going straight to where the match burned. The men shouted, and by their very terror in shouting alarmed and bewildered the poor little thing. By this time the mother also had come round, in a moment saw the danger, opened wide her arms, and cried from her very heart, "Come to me, my darling!" and instantly, with eager pattering feet and little arms opened to her arms, the little thing ran back and away, and stopped not until she was clasped in her mother's bosom.—ALEXANDER B. GROSART.

Memory of Youth.

Many years ago I was told of a priest who was called to visit a dying man. He heard his confession and prepared him for death, but the dying man said to him: "The one thing which troubles me more now even than the great sins of my life, is a trick that I played when I was a boy. Not far from where I lived was a large common, in the middle of which two roads met and at these cross-roads a rickety signpost directed the traveler to his destination. The arms of the signpost were loose, and one day, for fun, I took them down and changed them, so that they pointed out the wrong road; and now that years have rolled by and I am dying, it worries me greatly to think how many a poor weary traveler across that common I sent on the wrong road. —A. G. MORTIMER.

Sanctification—Test of.

"If you at this minute are in the Holy Spirit as your environment and atmosphere, you can, for instance, go and have a romp with the children on the floor, with four or five children on your back, and still be a sanctified man. I always feel that a good test of a man's sanctification is to place him in a room with five children in one corner of the room and the man in the other; but if he is really a sanctified man the children will be grouped around him."—F. B. MEYER.

Seed—Planting.

Some of you may remember at the two hundred and fiftieth anniversary of our College, how the students marched in a great torchlight procession, with many original transparencies and banners, and how the Freshman Class, then only a month old as students, carried at their head this motto: "The University has been waiting two hundred and fifty years for us." That was very amusing; but to any one who could read the deeper facts of the University the motto conveyed a profound and solemn truth. All this great, historic, institutional life had been indeed slowly evolved for the sake of these newly-arrived light-hearted boys, and now on their conduct were resting the destinies of the future, and out of their wise uses of their student life were to come our later blessings.—F. G. PEABODY.

Son—A True Son.

Archbishop Tillotson's father, who was a plain Yorkshireman, approached the house where his son resided, and inquired whether John Tillotson was at home. The servant, indignant at what he thought his insolence, drove him from the door; but the Dean, who was within, hearing the voice of his father, instead of embracing the opportunity afforded him of going out and bringing in his father in a more private manner, came running out, exclaiming, in the presence of his astonished servants, "It is my beloved father!"

Will—A Surrendered.

A lady who had an only child said to Mrs. Pearsall Smith, "I do not dare to pray, 'Thy will be done,' because I am afraid God will take away my little boy or will send me some heavy trial." To which Mrs. Smith replied, "Suppose your child should come to you and say, 'I want to be and do just what you desire to-day,' would you say to yourself, 'Now is my opportunity to make this child do all the disagreeable duties I want done; I will take advantage of his willingness to please me by cutting his pleasures to-day, and will keep him at hard discipline'?" "No, no," said the mother, "I would give him the best day I could possibly plan." "And can you think that God is less just and loving than you?"—*The Quiver.*

Word in Season.

Sir Alexander Ball was one of those great men who adorned our navy at the end of the eighteenth century. The following anecdote is told of him by his friend the poet Coleridge. "In a large party at Malta I had observed a naval officer listening to Sir A. Ball with a mixed expression of awe and affection that gave a more than common interest to so manly a countenance. This officer afterwards told me that he considered himself indebted to Sir Alexander for that which was dearer to him than his life. 'When he was Lieutenant Ball,' said he, 'he was the officer I accompanied in my first boat expedition, being then a midshipman, and only in my fourteenth year. As we were rowing up to the vessel which we were to attack, amid a discharge of musketry, I was overpowered by fear, and seemed on the

point of fainting away. Lieutenant Ball, who saw the condition I was in, placed himself close beside me, and still keeping his countenance directed towards the enemy, pressed my hand in the most friendly manner, and said in a low voice, "Courage, my dear boy. You will recover in a minute or so. I was just the same when I first went out in this way." Sir,' added the officer to me, 'it was just as if an angel had put a new soul into me. With the feeling I was not yet dishonored, the whole burden of agony was removed; and from that moment I was as fearless and forward as the oldest of the boat's crew.'"—COLERIDGE.

Youth—Blessing of.

Pitt, who was Prime Minister of England when twenty-four, was once taunted by an old man with his extreme youth. "The atrocious crime of being a young man," he said, "I shall not attempt to palliate or deny, but content myself with wishing that I may be one of those whose follies may cease with their youth, and not of that number who are ignorant in spite of experience." Therefore, let all rejoice in their youth, who have their life before them; let them not rob youth of its chief charm by despising it, and hurrying out of it before their time.— E. GRIFFITH-JONES.

Youth—Promising.

Rossetti, the artist, told the story that one day an elderly man came into his studio. He had brought specimens of his paintings and drawings with him, and he begged Rossetti to give him a candid opinion about them. Rossetti looked at them, and at once saw that there was nothing of value in them whatever. He managed in a kindly way to let the man understand; and then the man drew out from under his coat another set of sketches and spread them out before Rossetti. The old man said that these were the work of a young student. Rossetti looked at them and saw at once that they displayed remarkable talent. He was delighted with them and declared that without a doubt the young student would distinguish himself. And then the old man said: "Sir, I was that student." And that is the moral tragedy of every life. The possibilities are one thing, the realities are another thing; the capabilities are one thing, the achievements are another thing.—ANDREW MUTCH.

Youth—Perpetual.

Never, my heart, wilt thou grow old!
My hair is white, my blood runs cold,
And one by one my powers depart,
But youth sits smiling in my heart.

Downhill the path of age! oh, no;
Up, up with patient steps I go;
I watch the skies fast brightening there,
I breathe a sweeter, purer air.

Beside my road small tasks spring up,
Though but to hand the cooling cup,
Speak the true word of hearty cheer,
Tell the lone soul that God is near.

Beat on, my heart, and grow not old!
And when thy pulses all are told,
Let me, though working, loving still,
Kneel as I meet my Father's will.

—LOUISA JANE HALL.

The Bridge Builder.

We are prone to forget the bridges that have been built for us by the generations that have gone on before us. We are prone to forget the "Appleseed Johnnies," the "Pioneers," the "Missionaries," the "Scouts" who have paced the way; those who have "cleared a free way for the feet of God." But a poem like the "Bridge Builder," by Will Allen Dromgoole, makes us remember to whom we owe our tribute of praise and affection; to our fathers and our mothers; to those others who have gone before us and made the hard ways easier for us.

An old man, going a lone highway,
Came at the evening cold and gray
To a chasm vast and deep and wide,
Through which was flowing a sullen tide.
The old man crossed in the twilight dim,
The sullen stream had no fears for him;
But he turned when safe on the other side
And built a bridge to span the tide.

"Old man," said a fellow pilgrim near,
"You are wasting your strength with building here;
Your journey will end with the ending day;
You never again will pass this way;
You have passed the chasm deep and wide;
Why build you the bridge at eventide?"

The builder lifted his old gray head—
"There followeth after me a youth,
Whose feet must pass this way forsooth;
This chasm that has been naught to me,
To that fairhaired youth may a pitfall be;
He, too, must cross in the twilight dim;
Good friend, I am building the bridge for him."

HOME

Home Influence.

A well-informed writer in the Kilmarnock Standard states that Thomas Carlyle, not long before his death, was in conversation with the late Dr. John Brown, and expressed himself to the following effect: "I am now an old man, and done with the world. Looking around me, before and behind, and weighing all as wisely as I can, it seems to me there is nothing solid to rest on but the faith which I learned in my old home, and from my mother's lips." —*The Treasury of Religious Thought.*

Home Makes the Man.

Home is the first and most important school of character. It is there that every human being receives his best moral training or his worst; for it is there that he imbibes those principles of conduct which endure through manhood, and cease only with life. It is a common saying that "Manners make the man"; and there is a second, "Mind makes the man"; but truer than either is a third, that "Home makes the man," for the home-training includes not only manners and mind, but character. It is mainly in the home that the heart is opened, the habits are formed, the intellect is awakened, and character molded for good or for evil.—S. SMILES.

Home—A Christian.

G. Campbell Morgan says: My father came into my house soon after I was married, and looked into every room, and then he said to me: "Yes, it is very nice, but nobody will know, walking through here, whether you belong to God or the devil." I went through and looked at the rooms again, and I thought: "He is quite right." So we made up our minds straightway that there should be no room in our house, henceforth, that had not some message, by picture or wall text, for every corner should tell that we serve the King.

Home—A Defective.

The most miserable homes I have ever known have often been those that ought to have been the happiest; I envied them before I got to know the whole story. The house was a palace; the head of the household had worked hard, had made money; he could command every luxury, and it was his one pride that everything that money could command was at the disposal of every member of his home-circle; art had done its best, culture had added its sweetest ministries; everything there —everything but the delicate courtesies, the ingenious devices of love, which are life's most perfect graces. —J. M. JONES.

Home—An Ideal.

Grove mentioned that at some period when Havana was under martial law, a man had been killed in a row in the street. Everybody ran away except an Englishman, who, having nothing to do with the murder, thought there was no occasion to do so, and was, of course, immediately arrested. Some one naturally was found to swear that he was the culprit, and he was sentenced to be shot next morning. The English Consul (Mr. Crawford), hearing what was going on, went in full uniform to the place of execution and claimed the man as a British subject. The officer in charge of the firing party showed his orders, and said he could not give him up. "Very well," said Mr. Crawford, "at least you will not object to my shaking hands with him before he is shot?" "By no means,"

277

was the answer. He then walked up, whipped the Union Jack out of his pocket and threw it round the man. "Now," he said to the officer, "shoot if you dare." The officer applied for instructions to the Governor, and the prisoner's innocence was soon made clear.—M. E. GRANT DUFF.

Home—Christ in the.

The Rev. Dr. Nettleton, while passing the residence of a gentleman in one of his walks, went up to the door and knocked. A young woman came to the door, of whom he inquired "If Jesus dwelt there." Quite astonished, she made no reply. Again he asked, "Does Jesus Christ dwell in this house?" "No, sir," said she, and invited him to come in. "Oh no," said he, very sadly; "if Christ is not here, I can't come in," and he turned and went away. The next time he preached in that city, a young woman met him as he was leaving the church, and with tears in her eyes, asked if he recollected inquiring at a house, if Christ dwelt there. "Yes," said he, "I do." "I am that person," said she, "of whom you inquired, and it has been blessed to my soul." —H. L. HASTINGS.

Memory—Grateful.

In the midst of his greatest prosperity George Moore never forgot "auld Cumberland." His mind was always turning back to the home of his birth and the scenes of his boyhood. The very name of Cumberland had a charm for him. When any Cumberland lad called upon him at his office, he welcomed him cheerfully, asked him to his house, and often got him a situation.—S. SMILES.

Home—Jesus in the.

A French painter made a sensation in Paris by the manner of his work. He fitted up a cab for a studio, and drove about the street, stopping here and there to make sketches of place and things he saw. People did not see him shut up in his cab, looking out upon them through his little window, and taking his pictures of the nooks and corners and byways of Parisian life. He thus caught all manner of scenes and incidents in the city's hidden ways. He then transferred his sketches to canvas, and put Christ everywhere among them. When the people saw his work, they were startled, for they saw themselves in their every day life, in all their follies and frivolities, and always Christ in the midst—every kind of actual life on the canvas, and in the heart of it all—the Christ. Suppose this painter were to visit our town this year, and photograph us in all the events of our home life, our church life, our civic life, what kind of pictures would he see? Whatever the kind, Jesus will surely be "in the midst" of every event of the day.— ONWARD.

Home—Love in.

A young woman who runs a power sewing-machine for fifty hours a week in a factory tells the following story of her married life: "My husband, left an orphan, never had a chance to go to school or learn a trade. He is a teamster, and makes me very little money, but he loves me enough to trust me with all he earns. We have nothing that rich people have, and we are boarding until we can furnish a little home for ourselves. My husband does not go to saloons or places of that sort, and he never goes out for pleasure without me. Do you think it hurts me that he can't give me fine clothes when every day he tells me I am the best thing God ever gave him? Every night he kisses my hands that have worked so hard all day. We have been married over a year, and never a cross word. I did not know any one could be so happy. Do you think I mind working to help a man like that? His love makes everything worth while." Here is a man, ignorant of books, with no business training, yet possessing the rare faculty that guides his home life in ways of happiness and peace.—*The Expositor.*

Home, Sight of.

In the history of the memorable retreat of the ten thousand Greeks under Xenophon it is said that when they reached the summit of Mount Theches, from whence they descried in the distance the tremulously bright blue of the waters that were to bear them home, in raptures of joy they instantly shouted out, "The sea! the sea!" There was one enthusiastic rush, one simultaneous cry; they embraced each other and wept, and in a moment the pang of discomfiture and the toilsome march of five or six hundred leagues were forgotten and repaid.

Modern Marriage.

Something new in marriage vows was heard recently when Mary J. Dildine of Geneva and Lester W. Wesner of Watsonville, Pa., were married by City Judge George F. Ditmars. At the request of the bride, the words, "As long as we love each other or until legally divorced," were substituted for the customary "Until death do us part." —*Evening Tribune Times.*

No Home.

The following story contains more truth than fiction, and may suggest a cause for the lack of devotional life to-day. A real estate salesman tried to sell a house to a newly-married couple. Said the wife: "Why buy a home? I was born in a hospital, reared in a boarding school, educated in a college, courted in an automobile, and married in a church; get my meals in a cafeteria; live in an apartment; spend my mornings playing golf, my afternoons playing bridge; in the evenings we dance or go to the movies; when I'm sick I go to a hospital, and when I die I shall be buried from an undertaker's. All we need is a garage with bedroom."—*The King's Business.*

Spiritual Orphans.

The *"Pathfinder"* points out the astounding fact that of all the children in our orphan asylums, only five per cent are actually orphans, while sixty-five per cent have both parents living! Let the advocates of loose marriage ties figure that out and tell us what condition we shall be in when people get away altogether from the Bible view of marriage.—*The King's Business.*

The House of Quiet.

Mr. A. C. Benson has described in *"The House of Quiet"* the life of a man who had attained, after a youth of unstable health, to an apparently sound constitution, and was now living out a full and happy and useful life in London. Suddenly his old delicacy of health reappeared. He consulted an eminent physician. He came out of the consulting-room with a virtual sentence of death. "To say farewell to the bustle and activity of life; to be laid aside on a shelf like a cracked vase, turning as far as possible my ornamental front to the world; to live the shadowed life, a creature of rules and hours—a degrading and humiliating role." But he accepted the will of God. He took up his cross. He passed into *"The House of Quiet,"* expecting only the peace of a difficult resignation. But in *"The House of Quiet,"* a new life began. An unexpected feeling of the possibilities of life dawned. His perceptions became more delicate. The gush of morning air, the liquid song of birds, the sprouting of the green buds, the babble of the stream gave a new delight. His intellectual life grew strong, eager, discerning. A quickened taste for pure and noble reading, and a fresh joy in beauty, filled him with rapture. Then there swelled within him a more deliberate intention of enjoying simple things and of expecting beauty in homely life. At last he awoke to his true service. He had hitherto looked on at life around him with a dimmed eye and dulled ear. Now all the cries of the sick and the pained, and all the eager and appealing voices of the young and wistful, and all the soft, low sobbing of the bereaved fell upon his ears. All the needs, daily and clamant, of his neighbors rose up in appeal. This broken man, walking on the edge of death's abyss, gave up his life and used his feeble strength to help and to comfort others. He found that he had entered a new world. He no longer lived in the isolation of the strong, the successful, the selfish. New felicities swelled within his heart. New and unhoped-for strength was given. His life became a life of faith and love; and that rest which is our deepest satisfaction is always their first-born child.—W. M. CLOW.

The Revival Needed.

The revival society most needs to-day is not the revival of trade. That will come in due time. It will not be the revival of good government. That is coming. But society needs more than civic reform. The revival society most needs to-day is not the revival of racial purity, of physical soundness, of eugenics. That, too, is important. The body is holy, but it still remains a fact that man merely has a body, while he is a soul. It is not the revival of philanthropy. Philanthropy is in a state of revival. The revival society most needs to-day is not a church revival. To be sure that kind of revival is desperately needed, and there can be no hope of any permanent improvement in society that does not take into account the potent influence which only the church can wield. The revival society most needs to-day is the revival of an institution which is older than all these, more important than any and all of them combined, and which, if permitted permanently to suffer eclipse and decline, will seal the doom of human progress. I refer to the home. The revival society most needs to-day is the revival of the Christian home.— JAMES I. VANCE.

HEAVEN

Heaven a Prepared Place.

A scoffing infidel, of considerable talents, being once in the company of a person of slender intellect, but a real Christian, and supposing, no doubt, that he should obtain an easy triumph in the display of his ungodly wit, put the following question to him: "I understand, sir, that you expect to go to heaven when you die; can you tell me what sort of a place heaven is?" "Yes, sir," replied the Christian, "heaven is a prepared place for a prepared people; and if your soul is not prepared for it, with all your boasted wisdom you will never enter there."

Heaven Always Light.

When a ragged school was first opened, a little boy with a few others had been brought up from the building used formerly, and given to understand that here he was to live now, and be cared for by those who loved him. But when he went that night to his clean couch, in that fine room, so neat and so spacious, he was very joyously excited. And the moon was at the full also, and through the windows came the broad silver beams, glinting up from the crusted snow, until the apartment was lit almost as in the day. Long after the hour of usual slumber, a lady passing found him wide awake, and asked him why he was not sleeping. "Oh, they don't have any night here!" he answered.

Heaven in the Heart.

You might put a blind man in the Louvre of Paris, and he might walk among the acres and prairies of pictures there, and not be conscious that he had seen the stroke of one artist-hand. You might bring a deaf man within the sound of all the bands of heaven and of earth, and there would be no music to his consciousness. And if a man is not prepared to enjoy the felicities of heaven, those felicities will be nothing to him. Heaven is not heaven except to those who have the initiation of it in themselves. They carry it in their own heart first.— H. W. Beecher.

Heaven—Homesick for.

It was said of a great writer that he had a nostalgia for the beautiful. Of Dr. Bonar it may be said that he had a nostalgia for heaven. All his life on earth he was homesick. He was of those who declare plainly that they seek a country. Looking over the first volume of his Hymns, I find such titles as "No more Sea," "The Change," "The Homesickness," "Dawn," "The Morning Star," "Hora Novissima," "Rest Yonder," "How Long?" "A Little While," "Not Very Far." These are but a few among many. In one early hymn he frankly names his pain. He speaks of his "dull weight of loneliness," of his "greedy cravings for the tomb," and says,

It is not that I fear
To breast the storm or wrestle
     with the wave,
To swim the torrent or the blast
     to brave,
To toil or suffer in this day of
     strife,
As He may will who gave this
     struggling life;
But I am homesick.

—T. W. Parsons.

Heaven—Hope of.

How desolate must old age be to the man who has no heaven beyond; who stands trembling with infirmities, declined in ear, and eye, and

281

tongue; his hand palsies, his memory gone—looking back across the dreary stretch of life that he has just passed over, and forward with fear to the life of which he thought so little! How glorious for an old man to stand, as Moses stood, upon the top of the mount, looking across the Jordan into the promised land, and viewing the fair possessions that awaited him! Moses died, and did not go over; but the old man shall die, and go over, and shall find it in that day a land rich, beautiful, and glorious.—H. W. BEECHER.

Heaven—Material.

There is a saying of Haxlitt's, bold, and at first seeming wondrous true;—"In the days of Jacob there was a ladder between heaven and earth; but now the heavens have gone farther off and have become astronomical."—GEORGE DAWSON.

Heaven—Road to.

A poor drunken man once reeled up to old Bishop Wilberforce in St. James's Square, and said, "Bishop, how am I to be sure of getting to heaven?" The bishop looked at him, and said, "Don't you know that? My mother taught me that as I knelt at her knee in my childhood. My poor friend"—the poor wretched creature under the power of strong drink was reeling at his side—"my poor friend," said the bishop with that calm, quiet face that we remember so well, "turn to the right and go straight on."—G. H. WILKINSON.

Heaven—Traveling.

Strive after union with God; but do not too readily or easily believe that you have attained to it. The traveler, after many fatigues and dangers, arrives at the top of a mountain. As he looks abroad from that high eminence, and in that clear atmosphere, he sees his native city: and it seems to him to be very near. Overjoyed at the sight, and perhaps deceived by his position, he proclaims himself as already at the end of his journey. But he soon finds that the distance was greater than he supposed. He is obliged to descend into valleys, and to climb over hills, and to surmount rugged rocks, and to wind his tired steps over many a mile of weary way, before he reaches that home and city, which he once thought so near. —MADAME GUYON.

Heaven—Waiting for.

Ruskin was in the world, but no longer of it. He was alive, yet only waiting for the end. In 1891 his friend, the Bishop of Carlisle, was staying at Brantwood. The Bishop was to leave Brantwood at an early hour. Mr. Ruskin expressed a strong wish to take leave of him and Mrs. Goodwin, if they would not mind coming to his bedroom. As the departing guests came into the room to say good-bye, a look came over Ruskin's face as though he had expected something more than the ordinary leavetaking. There was a moment's silence. Then the Bishop, quickly understanding what was passing in the other's mind, raised his hands over him, and said, "The Lord bless you and keep you. The Lord lift up the light of His countenance upon you, and give you peace both now and for evermore. Amen."—E. T. COOK.

Riches in Glory.

It is the custom for travelers abroad to take with them letters of credit, good in any large city in the world. Such letters are customarily drawn for a specific amount, and the banker who issues them is secured by the prepayment of the money or the deposit of ample securities. Sometimes, however, an unlimited letter of credit is issued, and is made good simply by the name of a responsible endorser. Such an unlimited letter of credit is freely offered to every needy pilgrim on earth on his journey heavenward. Here it is. "My God shall supply all your need, according to His riches in glory by Christ Jesus."—CYRUS C. FOSS.